PUBLIC WELFARE

Arthur Spindler

Social Welfare and Health Systems Consultant
Former D/HEW Program Planning and Evaluation Officer

HUMAN SCIENCES PRESS
72 Fifth Avenue   3 Henrietta Street
NEW YORK, NY 10011 ● LONDON, WC2E 8LU

Library of Congress Catalog Number 78-15480

ISBN: 0-87705-325-1

Copyright © 1979 by Human Sciences Press 72 Fifth Avenue, New York, New York
10011

Printed in the United States of America
89 987654321

Library of Congress Cataloging in Publication Data

Spindler, Arthur.
    Public welfare.

    Includes index.
    1. Public welfare—United States. I. Title.
HV91.S64   361.6'2'0973   78-15480
ISBN 0-87705-325-1

CONTENTS

List of Tables, Charts, Figures   5

Foreword   9

Preface   12

1. Introduction   17
2. The Public Welfare Populations   50
3. Public Welfare Programs Within the Federal/State System: Income Maintenance Programs   75
4. Public Welfare Programs Within the Federal/State System: Social Services, In-Kind, and Special Population Programs   128
5. Public Welfare Organization   199
6. Staffing and Personnel Administration in the Public Welfare System   236
7. Public Welfare Financing and Budgeting   279
8. Public Welfare Methods   335
9. Public Welfare Relationships   411

10. **The Public Welfare System in Perspective:**
    Looking Ahead   **437**
Appendix: **Supreme Court Decisions Affecting**
Public Welfare   **493**
Index   **506**

List of Tables, Charts, and Figures

Table 1.1 State Public Welfare Agencies   30–32

Table 1.2 Federal Laws Serving Public Welfare Individuals and Families   36–39

Table 2.1 The Potential Public Welfare Population, 1975   51

Table 2.2 Eligible Beneficiaries of Public Welfare Programs and Activities   52

Table 2.3 Number and Percent of Persons Below the Low-Income Level   56

Table 2.4 Poverty Index   57

Table 2.5 Summary of Annual Budgets for a Four-person Family at Three Levels of Living, Urban United States, Autumn 1976   58

Table 3.1 Benefits and Services Under Public Welfare Programs   78–79

Table 3.2 Aid to Families with Dependent Children: Recipients of Money Payments and Amount of Payments, by State, December 1975   84–85

Table 3.3 Aid to Families with Dependent Children, Unemployed Father Segment: Recipients of Money Payments and Amount of Payments, by State, December 1975   86–87

Table 3.4 The Trend in AFDC Recipients and Payments, 1950–1975   88

Table 3.5 AFDC Family with Four Recipients 1/: Monthly Amount for Basic Need Standard, Payment Standard, and Largest Amount Paid in July 1975, by State   98–99

Table 3.6 Persons Receiving Federally Administered SSI Payments January 1974–May 1977   109

Table 3.7 Supplemental Security Income for the Aged, Blind and Disabled: Number of Persons Receiving Federally Administered Payments and Total Amount, by Reason for Eligibility, May 1977   110

Table 3.8 Supplemental Security Income for the Aged, Blind, and Disabled: Amount of Total Payments, Federal SSI Payments, and State Supplementary Payments, 1974–1977   110

Table 3.9 Administration of Supplemental Security Income Program, 1977   112–113

Table 3.10 General Assistance: Recipients of Money Payments and Amount of Payments, by State, December 1975   120–121

Table 4.1 Social Services State by State   140–141

Table 4.2 Recipients With Medical Vendor Payments by Basis of Eligibility of Recipients and by HEW Region and State (December, 1975)   154–155

Table 4.3 Amounts of Medical Vendor Payments by Basis of Eligibility of Recipients
and by HEW Region and State (December 1975)   156–157
Table 4.4 Distribution of Participants and Dollars by Category of Assistance: Medical
Assistance Program   158
Table 4.5 Distribution of Amounts of Medical Vendor Payments by Type of Service,
January to March 1975   158
Table 4.6 Medical Services State by State, June 1, 1976   160
Table 4.7 Food Stamp Program   180
Table 4.8 Food Stamp Program Statistical Summary of Operations September 1975 181–182
Table 4.9 Win Employment and Training Activities, Fiscal Years 1974–75   185
Chart 5.1 Organization Chart Federal Government Organization for Public Welfare
Responsibilities   200
Chart 5.2 Food and Nutrition Service Organization Chart   202
Chart 5.3 Employment and Training Administration Organization Chart   204
Chart 5.4 Social Security Administration Organization Chart   205
Chart 5.5 Office of Human Development Services Organization Chart   206
Fig 5.1 Standard Federal Regions   207
Fig 5.2 The FNS Regions   208
Chart 5.6 Typical Organization Chart of State Welfare Agencies   214
Chart 5.7 Connecticut Welfare Department Organization Chart   221
Chart 5.8 District of Columbia Department of Human Resources Organization Chart 222
Chart 5.9 Iowa Department of Social Services Organization Chart   223
Chart 5.10 Hennepin County Welfare Department Organization Chart   227
Table 6.1 Staffing of Public Welfare Functions 1974–1975   238
Table 6.2 Basic Staffing Pattern of State Public Welfare Agencies   239–244
Figure 6.1 Outline of Job Development Process   248
Table 6.3 Public Assistance: Aggregate Number of Employees Attending Workshops,
Seminars, and Employees on Educational Leave, Fiscal Year 1975   259–260
Table 6.4 Public Assistance: Total Expenditures for Selected Staff Development
Activities, by State, Fiscal Year, 1975   261–262
Chart 7.1 Public Welfare Expenditures by Program, Fiscal Year, 1975   279
Table 7.1 Public Welfare Expenditures by Program, Fiscal Year, 1975   280–281
Table 7.2 Public Welfare Expenditures by Program, Fiscal Year, 1975   290–301
Figure 8.1 To Apply for Assistance   346
Table 10.1 Year 2000 Alternate Projections   439
Figure 10.1 Public Welfare Balance Sheet   484–489

FOREWORD

Help for the oppressed, the disadvantaged and the needy is a hallmark of the American philosophy. Our nation was founded to free people from the many forms of oppression, including lives locked into poverty and hopelessness. One of the purposes of the federal government, as described by the framers of our constitution was "to promote the general welfare." We are a caring and giving people. But while our philosophy of government is accepted as fact, changes in our socio-economic environment have seen the "land of opportunity" become a "land of technology and competition for limited opportunity."

At times of extreme national crisis, such as the great depression of the 1930's, programs have been enacted to aid the victims of economic disaster. But even these actions have been presumed to be temporary necessities. Among our great expectations, we assume that crises will pass and that almost all personal needs can and will be met by the normal market place actions of our economy. Experience should have taught us that our assumptions about poverty, its causes and its remedies, are frequently wrong—that as a nation we are basically uncomfortable and uncertain about poverty and dependency—and that the values which influence our thinking about today's problems are frequently rooted in an earlier and less complex time.

It is within this ambiguous and sometimes contradictory context that the public welfare system—representing our sometimes reluctant attempts to assuage the symptoms of dependency and of alienation from the American "mainstream"—has developed since the mid-1930's. It is a system that is too little understood. But in a democracy whose aim is to "promote the general welfare," government leaders must be able to understand the goals, strengths and weaknesses of the public welfare system. The people who are called upon to support the system and the people who are served by the system must be informed about it. All this requires an accurate, unbiased, complete and clear description of public welfare programs together with their administration and financing. Without such informed understanding, there is no way to assess the effectiveness of welfare nor to weigh intelligently the alternatives for change and improvement.

Recent controversy has attacked not only the inefficiencies of public welfare programs but questioned their very place in our economy. It has heightened public interest and generated an extensive literature. Whether or not the public's factual knowledge has been increased in the process is subject to debate. At the same time, proposals to reform the "welfare mess" have been given high priority by national administrations of both political parties. It is surprising, even startling, that there has been no single major work that fully describes and explains the public welfare system in the United States as it currently exists.

The publication of this volume, therefore, fills a critical information gap at a time of national debate on welfare issues. It is current, authoritative, and written in non-technical language. Merely to say that it is comprehensive does not adequately express the encyclopedic range and the depth of its coverage. Logically organized, with full indexing and references, *Public Welfare* should be so widely utilized as to become the essential text book and resource reference in its field. In addition to documenting the current system, identifying current policy issues and alternatives, Mr. Spindler reviews the historical context in which public welfare programs evolved. This book will be useful to students and teachers at all levels, in political science, public administration, social work and related fields; to program managers, planners, trainers and other staff, not only in public welfare agencies, but also in public health, medical care, rehabilitation, manpower, and other human service programs; and to the interested and concerned general public.

In one sense the term "public welfare" is defined by the programs that are established by law. While the general public, as well as those who are more directly involved in these programs, are acutely aware of their complexity and diversity, there is much more to it, for better or worse, than is generally understood.

The American Public Welfare Association believes that the highest purpose of a democracy should be to promote and safeguard the wellbeing of its people. The public welfare system—though little understood and frequently maligned—is the principal social institution for achieving these humane goals. The challenges to our democracy, the public welfare system, to governmental and voluntary policy makers, and to our individual and collective humanity have never been greater.

Because of our stated belief in both the broad purpose of public welfare and the imperative need for sound information that clarifies the American system, we are pleased this book is now available. Policy makers, administrators, public welfare employees, educators, and the general public will find it helpful in strengthening the public welfare system. For it will take strong and credible services to meet the challenges of human need in the last years of the 20th Century.

Edward T. Weaver
Executive Director
American Public Welfare
   Association
Washington, D.C.

PREFACE

Public welfare is of intense concern to the individual recipient for his* survival; to the nation as perhaps the most critical social problem of the day; to thoughtful people as the determinant of the future of the country. The past decade or two has produced uncounted volumes of materials and limitless unpublished discussions on the problem and its possible solution, and more can be expected. However, in all of this, public welfare lacks a precise definition, a universal acceptance of what it includes, what it covers, what public welfare programs and activities are, how they function, and how effective they are. Perhaps the complex nature of public welfare is partially at fault. Perhaps it is because public welfare is not recognized as a uniform concept but as a collection of a half-dozen or more discrete programs operated by over 1200 separate public welfare organizations. Whatever the reasons, there is a need to clarify what public welfare is, and is not, so that welfare recipients, welfare workers and administrators, government executives and legislators, the public media, and the public can achieve a meeting of the mind when they

*Unless specifically applicable to an individual, "he," "his," "him," or "man" includes "her," "she," or "woman."

13

discuss the subject. At the least, they should be assured they are discussing, or arguing, about the same areas of concern.

This book is written to attempt to fill this need. Public welfare is described and explained as it functions through the network of federal, state, and local welfare agencies to give a well-needed information basis. It is a roundup of available information organized to explain the public welfare system with a richness of material from many sources. It attempts to answer questions on the number and characteristics of the population groups served by public welfare; the public welfare programs; the public welfare organization in federal, state, and local governments; the staffing of public welfare agencies; public welfare financing and budgeting; public welfare methods; and public welfare relationships with other social organizations. Finally, the book provides a discussion of the policy options and policy issues we as a nation face in resolving the problems and the alternatives under consideration in welfare reform, comprehensive social services, and national health insurance. Throughout, an effort was made to provide insights to help the reader understand the subject more fully.

Public welfare means different things to different people. To the welfare recipient, it means assistance checks, the help of social workers of the welfare agency, the doctor's office or clinic which gives him free medical care, food stamps, and the public employment office to which he goes to be registered.

To the public welfare worker, it means his agency and its functions, the long lines of recipients waiting to be interviewed, the daily schedule of home visits, the voluminous case files, agency manuals of regulations, forms, procedures to be followed, the review of applications, the computation of recipient assistance payments, the investigation of family relationships, income and resources.

To the welfare administrator, it means organizing, managing, planning, and coordinating welfare programs; staffing welfare offices; preparing reports; estimating caseloads; preparing and justifying agency budgets; keeping abreast of the latest changes in federal regulations; working with other social agencies; dealing with the public media; answering public inquiries; recipient complaints; reporting to his superiors; the chief executive, and legislature on welfare caseloads and costs. To the governor, mayor, and county commissioner, it means studying and working to control the rise in welfare caseloads and budgets; working to balance his government's revenues and budgets for welfare and all other public programs and activities; seeking ways and means to maximize federal financial participation, formulating and defending his revenue and budget proposals before the legislature and the public; dealing with the public media, welfare rights and public interest groups on welfare issues and problems; the adequacy of assistance payments; tax rates; the effects of inflation; unemployment; jobs; urban deterioration; poor housing; rising medical care costs; social unrest; and crime and delinquency.

To members of Congress and state and local legislators, it means working to control rising welfare costs; considering proposals for welfare reform, national health insurance, the housing crisis, urban deterioration, inflation, unemployment, poverty, the environment; always being alert to the public attitude, the public media, his constituents posture on welfare and social problems.

To the public, it means concern with rising caseloads and budgets, rising taxes, "welfare cheaters," Medicaid fraud, inflation, unemployment, jobs, inadequate housing, urban deterioration, and the apparent inability of government leaders and their representatives in Congress and state and local government legislators to cope with them.

To the professions, public welfare means a socioeconomic phenomenon of the maldistribution of national income and resources, with political/historic roots; for economists, calling for an economic solution; for sociologists, for a national resocialization effort.

I have been a long time concerned participant and analyst in the public welfare system at both federal and local government levels. I was a senior official of the Social and Rehabilitation Service (SRS), U.S. Department of Health, Education, and Welfare (D/HEW) as Director of Program Planning before my retirement and Planning-Programming-Budgeting (PPB) Officer for the Office of Welfare Administration, D/HEW, the predecessor agency to SRS. Prior to that, I was Director, Planning and Research Division of the District of Columbia Department of Public Welfare, a senior member of the Office of Program Planning, D.C. Department of Public Health and Comptroller of D.C. General Hospital. My field is public administration and political science.

I have done a good deal of thinking and study in these fields, have written extensively on them, been a speaker at public welfare conferences and have lectured at various universities. I am currently a social welfare and health systems consultant for federal, state, and local governments and research organizations. I am a member of the American Public Welfare Association, the Operations Research Society of America and other social and health societies.

I conceived the book when I organized and taught a course in public welfare administration in the Graduate School of the U.S. Department of Agriculture and, later, as a contract instructor for SRS to train its employees in public welfare.

I wish to acknowledge the assistance and encouragement of many of my former colleagues at D/HEW for the sources and materials they provided so freely to make this book possible. Opinions expressed, inferences and conclusions drawn are my own. I wish to express deep appreciation to Ann Altman Preston who typed the manuscript and offered her steady support to its completion. The legal research for the appendix on Supreme Court decisions was conducted by my son, Kenneth J. Spindler, a third-year law student.

Arthur Spindler
Bethesda, Maryland

Chapter 1

INTRODUCTION

The American federal/state public welfare system is a major national enterprise with annual expenditures in 1975 of $38.5 billion, employing about 340,000 people in all 50 states and four federal jurisdictions (Guam, the Virgin Islands, Puerto Rico, and the District of Columbia), affecting directly one of every six Americans, over 37 million people, the poor and near-poor and other disadvantaged. The way the system performs affects our country materially, socially, ethically, and morally; in fact, it determines the viability of American institutions as well as the quality of American life. Economists have long pointed out the substantial financial implications of public welfare programs in stabilizing the American economy as public assistance expenditures are used to purchase daily necessities, and flow immediately back into the economy and produce new tax revenues.[1]

The American Public Welfare Association expressed the role of public welfare in American society in its *Statement of Principles: Essentials of Public Welfare.*[2]

> The highest purpose of a democracy should be to promote and safeguard the well-being of its people. Each individual should be assured a valid opportunity to fulfill his potentials and aspirations

17

and to contribute to the extent of his ability to the common good
. . .

Public welfare must be seen as one part of human services
which includes education, health care, housing, employment opportunity, manpower training programs and others which add up
to a better life for all the people. While public welfare continues
to focus on the needs of the most vulnerable people in society, it
has an additional obligation to contribute, along with other services, to the general level of living . . .

Another perspective of the role public welfare plays was
expressed by Tom Joe, former D/HEW official[3]:

Welfare has been the receptacle for the failures of all of our social
institutions and social insurance programs which are only now
starting to be held accountable for their deficiencies. If there can
be said to be a theory behind the present system, it is that welfare
should act as a safety net to catch the people who have slipped past
the programs and institutions that are the primary line of defense
against poverty and dependency; the education system which
should prepare people for participation in the mainstream of society, juvenile delinquency programs, and the legal system in general, which should serve to reintegrate people into society instead
of reinforcing their alienation from it; the health institutions,
workmen's compensation, vocational rehabilitation, and other
programs which should prevent individual incidents of illness or
injury from resulting in life-long dependency; and the manpower
development and unemployment insurance programs which
should deal with problems of joblessness before they lead to welfare dependency.

Each of these programs, and the many others which could be
added to the list, was designed in response to an identified need.
But the existence of the catch-all welfare net has, in effect, taken
the pressure off the other programs. So, while welfare rolls and
costs have "burgeoned" or "spiraled," the institutions which
should be keeping people off welfare have completely failed to
keep pace with normal increases in need and demand for services,
and they have not even begun to deal with the increased pressures
brought on by a deflated economy. In the thirty years since its
inception, the welfare program has multiplied twenty-fold through
a process of picking up the pieces—a process which has built a
program almost entirely devoid of internal rationale or consis-
tency of purpose. Welfare, if considered to be limited to public
assistance payments, is a program set apart from other social programs—but more stigmatized and despised.

There is a need to review the public welfare system as it is now organized and as it now performs, and to explain its complexities in a concise, understandable manner. The need to understand how the system works and its strengths and weaknesses, how it is funded and how the taxpayers money is spent and for what purposes, are critically important at a time when the nation is considering and deciding what further changes should be made to develop a better way to deal with poverty and its manifold problems.

Ever since the enactment of the Social Security Act in 1935 public welfare administration has been under public scrutiny in one way or another. In the beginning federal aid was concentrated primarily on public assistance for the aged and blind and dependent children deprived of parental support because of the death, incapacity, or continued absence of a parent, on child welfare services and on public work projects. Provisions were enacted later for the disabled and for medical assistance to the aged, subsequently broadened into Medicaid. Other programs and special provisions, such as food stamps, housing benefits, work and training projects and programs, unemployed father assistance, foster care, emergency assistance, help with home repairs, and broadened social services provisions were added at different times.

Although much has been and is being written about public welfare and social welfare generally, these discussions are concerned primarily with issues, theories, solutions and the impacts of poverty sociologically and economically. Little has been written describing the organization, administration, methods, and processes of the federal/state system itself. This book attempts to do so, not only for the serious academic student and the many public welfare practitioners but for the general public seeking to form an intelligent judgment amidst the intense public controversy and the torrent of words and thoughts it confronts in the public media. How can one decide change in public welfare in this critical area of American experience without fully understanding what today's public welfare system (or nonsystem as it has been called) actually is? Which features and programs of the present system are effective in achieving the public welfare goals of social and economic self-sufficiency? Which features and programs are not effective and should be replaced? Will proposed changes improve or worsen the way the present system works to support the poor and the near-poor? Will proposals for change cost more or less than the costs of the existing system?

These are some questions which a more complete knowledge of the present system will help to respond to more intelligently. Moreover, in the event of welfare reform, social services, or health care changes, this knowledge should prove to be of immeasurable value to decision-makers in selecting the one best way to effect change. Also, it will be invaluable to government administrators responsible for the major job of converting smoothly the massive governmental mechanisms to new organizational patterns, financial arrangements, processes, staffing, and the allocation of resources.

The contents of this book cover the demographic characteristics of the over 37 million Americans, mainly poor and near-poor, who are actual or potential beneficiaries of the public welfare system (See Chapter 2); a description of public welfare programs: their objectives, legal basis, historical background, organization responsibilities, eligibility factors, services, benefits, principal methods and procedures (See Chapters 3 and 4); the organization of public welfare agencies at federal, state, local, and neighborhood levels (See Chapter 5); staffing and personnel administration of public welfare agencies (See Chapter 6); the sources and methods of funding and budgeting of the public welfare system (See Chapter 7); public welfare methods and processes (See Chapter 8); the relationships between public welfare and other governmental and private programs and agencies (See Chapter 9); and a holistic review of public welfare, public policy options, issues, and alternatives for change and reform (See Chapter 10). Throughout, trends, dilemmas, and social and economic implications and considerations of the subject are explained.

CHARACTERISTICS AND CONSIDERATIONS

The more pervasive characteristics of public welfare need to be clearly understood in any assessment of public welfare and in planning for the future. Public welfare programs are the expres-

sion of national policy compromises between conflicting political and social ideologies. Those imbued with the American
ideals of economic independence and self-sufficiency and the
American dream of the self-made man generally have little pa-
tience for the man who fails to attain to this high expectancy of
achievement, irrespective of the reasons for his failure. This
outlook places high emphasis on work and the work ethic as the
means to achieve economic independence and pays scant attention to the impact of prevailing low wage levels on the ability to
achieve adequate self-support. Furthermore, this attitude
clashes with the Judeo-Christian postulates of charity and social
justice which firmly support aid to those who cannot provide
adequately for themselves by their own efforts without fault of
their own and who for one reason or another cannot be fully in
control of their own situation.

These conflicts and the resulting compromises are reflected
in the policies governing public welfare in specific ways. The
most outstanding example is the wide variation in the adequacy
of family assistance levels between the states as described in
Chapter 3. The differences result from social and economic
factors, the former the social, ethical and moral attitudes towards the poor, the latter the economic capacity of the state to
provide the local or state resources needed to fund the public
assistance program; and the practical necessity to keep assistance payments levels related to the low-income level prevailing
in the community.

Undoubtedly, policy formulation and interpretation in
practice are colored by the position and attitudes one holds in
relation to the above basic premises. Federal legislation enacted
to provide grants-in-aid to the states for money payments to or
on behalf of needy individuals and families left the states free to
determine their own need standards and payment levels.

The growth and proliferation of programs over the years
also has brought on greater competition among programs in the
process of allocating limited resources among them. The question of whether it is preferable to provide individuals and families with money with which to pay for goods or services or to
provide them with the goods and services through providers
who are in turn paid by the agency remains a moot question in

the continuing debate how to best provide for those in need of such help.

Policies covering different public welfare programs are not uniform, but may differ widely. For example, policies affecting eligibility for cash assistance and food stamps, emanating separately from two federal agencies, may differ substantially, creating confusion when the same welfare agency personnel at county or city level is given responsibility to administer both programs. The lack of correlation between the laws affecting these programs carries over into other levels of their administration and presents many problems to the agencies administering them. At the state level, different programs either are required to or may be located within the same state agency. At the local level they may then be handled by the same unit or staff. The agency representative who deals directly with the individual or family must be familiar with and be able to deal with different sets of policies in the same set of circumstances. To the beneficiary, these differences are perplexing and difficult to understand. However, since these differences stem largely from federal laws and administrations, the state or local agency is faced with a situation over which it has little control. It must accept this reality and work within it.

Public welfare operates in a complex structure involving federal, state and local government levels. In addition, at both the federal and state level, regional structures are interposed. Furthermore, administrative patterns vary within the states. In some the program is state administered where the state agency has full control over agency structure, development of policy and procedure, and staffing of all units. In others, the state merely exercises supervision of the program, sets general policy and then sees to it that it is carried out by local units that have substantial autonomy for administration and staffing.

There is great variation among the states as to the combination of programs within an administrative structure. There has been a trend to combine programs into one or more agencies. However, there appears to be no firm or uniform pattern. Thus income maintenance, social services, mental health, vocational rehabilitation services, employment services, institutional care programs may be separate or combined in one form or another.

In recent years there has been a movement toward so-called umbrella agencies bringing as many programs as feasible or consonant with specific state objectives together into one agency structure. Within such structures, there are different degrees of integration with respect to administration, policy development, and support services. (Chapters 5 and 9 will provide a fuller discussion of this subject.)

Another variation affecting administration is the dependence of the agency on state central support services outside the agency such as state purchasing departments, state budget and accounting agencies. Such dependence may present problems when essential program requirements are subordinated to priorities of other programs or considerations and the agency is hardpressed to meet its statutory responsibilities.

Political tradition, with its inherent emphasis on local government, has resulted in the maintenance of many small administrative units irrespective of considerations of efficiency of operation and cost effectiveness.

The creation of the Supplementary Security Income (SSI) program under federal administration effective January 1974, brings into being a new constellation of program structure and interrelationships. States retain responsibility for supplementing the federal payment where this is required to maintain the 1973 payment level. However, they have the option of having the supplement administered through the federal agency as their agent or under their own auspices. A similar option applies to the determination of eligibility for Medicaid under Title XIX of the Social Security Act, for those covered under the SSI program.

Meeting acceptable standards of accountability in public welfare programs has been a particularly irksome problem over the years. (Chapter 8 deals with this in greater detail.) One of the reasons has been the lack of adequate and precise definitions which would provide a firm basis for measuring results. Like other areas of human endeavor, the activity itself often can be defined and measured in terms of time but agreement on the measurable results of the activities is more difficult to achieve. In the face of complex policies and inadequate manpower resources, efforts at achieving accuracy and correctness of decisions on eligibility within defined tolerance limits have been difficult. With technological advances in information systems, these difficulties may be minimized as time goes on. In general, however, inadequate systems of accountability have resulted in the current crises of creditability, especially in social and medical services programs. Many individuals and families are eligible for benefits simultaneously under different programs, but adequate information is not available on the combined benefits they receive. This makes for difficulties in planning, program efficiency and establishing national goals for aid for the needy.

Valid differences exist between public welfare programs and other programs in the administrative complexities in the establishment of eligibility. Public welfare programs are designed to provide aid and services to individuals and families on the basis of need and other eligibility requirements, calling for a means test based on the absence of financial and other resources, a process requiring sensitive staff value judgments. In contrast, entitlement for other programs, such as employment training, unemployment compensation and rehabilitation is based on the existence of positive official records of earnings and employment. Public welfare practices must allow for wider latitude in eligibility determinations by individual workers than that of other programs.

THE PUBLIC WELFARE SYSTEM DEFINED

The public welfare system is defined as the composite of governmental organizations and their administration, authorized by the Social Security Act of 1935, as amended, and other legislation which provide services and assistance to needy and disadvantaged individuals and families towards the goal of maximum social and economic self-sufficiency and independence. This definition is neither the broadest usage taking in all possible human service programs nor its more limited use referring merely to public assistance and related social services.

The term "public welfare" has no precise, universally accepted definition. It is used generally with reference to a wide variety of governmental services at all governmental levels to individuals and families designed to help them meet financial and social needs. Financial and social needs covers a wide span of programs administered through different agencies; among them the public welfare agency has had the greatest prominence. However, many services are also provided through other agencies, such as institutions, health, labor, corrections, and education.

The term "public" refers to the tax-supported programs, activities, and agencies of government, constitutionally and legally authorized at federal, state and local levels. The term "welfare" encompasses the following programs and activities of public agencies and other organizations providing services under arrangements with such agencies:

INCOME MAINTENANCE. (also named assistance payments, public assistance, income security, security welfare payments).

This is the payment of money to or on behalf of eligible needy individuals and families to help them meet their basic needs for food, clothing, shelter, personal and household necessities. Three programs of income maintenance are provided: Aid to Families with Dependent Children (AFDC), Supplemental Security Income (SSI), and General Assistance (GA).

SOCIAL SERVICES.   These services are for individuals and families including public assistance recipients and applicants and other specified low-income persons. The provision of a wide variety of helping services to eligible individuals and families to attain or retain their capability of self-sufficiency, self-support, or to strengthen family life.

CHILD WELFARE SERVICES.   These services are for homeless, delinquent, neglected, abused or dependent children and their families. The provision of a wide variety of helping services for prevention, protection, remedying, and solution of problems of children, promoting their welfare, strengthening family life, providing for adequate care of children in foster homes, day care and other child care facilities.

MEDICAL ASSISTANCE FOR THE POOR (MEDICAID).   This is for the provision of medical services for public assistance recipients and medically indigent persons.

FOOD STAMPS.   These are provided to low-income households to help finance basic food needs for the family.

CUBAN REFUGEE ASSISTANCE.   The provision of financial assistance and a wide variety of helping services to Cuban refugees to achieve their resettlement, adjustment, self-support, and self-sufficiency in the United States. More recently, 1975–1978, it also covered Vietnamese and Cambodian refugees.

REPATRIATED U.S. NATIONALS ASSISTANCE.   The provision of travel, temporary financial assistance, and helping services to U.S. citizens and their dependents who are destitute or mentally ill in a foreign country.

WORK INCENTIVE PROGRAM (WIN).   The provision of supportive services, day care and employment training, development and employment services to registered youth and heads of households of AFDC families to help them become self-supporting.

We can observe three different categories of the above functions among state and local welfare agencies:

Core Functions

These functions are found in *all* state and local public welfare agencies:

> Income maintenance—eligibility determinations and payments administration
>
> Social services—eligibility determinations and the provision of services
>
> Medical assistance—eligibility determinations
>
> Food stamps—eligibility determinations, administration and distribution of food stamps
>
> Work incentives—referrals to the WIN agencies and the provision of supporting social services and day care.

Supplemental Functions

These functions are found in *most but not all* state and local public welfare agencies:

Child welfare services—Some state governments (e.g., Ohio, Pennsylvania) have assigned responsibility for this program to separate county agencies. Federal regulations under the Social Security Act state that federal policy is that the state agency responsible for the state plan approved under Title XX (social services for individuals and families) will also administer or supervise the administration of the child welfare services plan (under Title IVB), except that if on January 2, 1968, the two programs were administered by separate agencies, they may continue to be administered separately.[4]

Medical assistance program administration—Title XIX of the Social Security Act authorizing the medical assistance program gives to the states the option of selecting the agency to be made responsible for administering the program. However, the act requires that the eligibility determination function be conducted by the state or local agency administering income maintenance and social services for old age assistance recipients, i.e., the public welfare agency. Eleven states have separate agencies, usually the state public health agency, responsible for program administration.

Cuban refugee assistance—This program is administered by the city of Miami, Dade county, and the state of Florida in conjunction with the U.S. Department of Health, Education and Welfare. Resettlement of Cuban refugees throughout the country has placed upon many state and local public welfare agencies responsibilities for their financial assistance and social services. With the number of refugees diminishing and the program winding down, this program will gradually end within the next few years.

Repatriated U.S. nationals assistance—Services by state and local public welfare agencies are being provided to repatriated citizens under this program primarily at the points of entry for foreign travelers, namely, New York, Boston, San Francisco, New Orleans, Miami, Los Angeles, and Washington D. C. The agencies in these cities are called upon to provide emergency help for these persons.

Income maintenance for needy aged, blind, and disabled— With passage on January 1, 1974 of the Supplemental Security Income Program under the Social Security Amendments of 1972 to provide financial assistance to aged, blind, and disabled persons, responsibility of state and local public welfare agencies for this caseload changed. Payments are made by the Social Security Administration, and those states with a payments level in 1973 greater than the new uniform national standard are required to provide supplemental amounts to their former aged, blind, and disabled recipients. Other states are no longer required to make provision for state maintenance assistance for these groups of recipients, although most do. This marks an exception to the provision of core functions for income maintenance found in all state and local public welfare agencies.

Other Human Service Functions

The third category of public welfare functions or other human service programs and activities that are assigned to state and local public welfare agencies authorized in the given jurisdictions. Examples may be found in state, county, and city agencies including operation of institutions for the aged or mentally retarded, crippled children, mental health, and juvenile delinquency prevention programs, services for the blind, correctional rehabilitation, day care, employment development, vocational rehabilitation, and community programs.

The term "public welfare" does not appear in the names of federal government organizations responsible for the public welfare functions and activities described above, and is found in only nine states. A few states include the term "welfare" in their agency titles (Table 1.1). Various other terms for public welfare agencies in different states and counties include social and rehabilitation services, social services, family services, public aid, economic security, human resources, and institutions.

No single executive agency of the federal government is responsible for the public welfare system in its entirety. The federal agencies responsible for the different public welfare programs include the Department of Health, Education and Welfare, primarily the Health Care Financing Administration, Office of Human Development Services and the Social Security Administration*; the Food and Nutrition Service of the Department of Agriculture, and the Employment and Training Administration of the Department of Labor. These are described more fully in Chapter 5.

THE SOCIAL SECURITY ACT

The Social Security Act, enacted August 14, 1935, and amended frequently, provides the legal basis for the public welfare system; however, it covers much more. It is the single most important social welfare statute created to soften the hardships of the Great Depression in the early 1930s. Since then, it has grown in scope and importance in the social programs it authorizes affecting all Americans, the public social policies it expresses, and the influence it plays in national social and economic affairs. It has been the vehicle most relied upon in the intervening years from 1935 to the present to respond to' social crises, conditions, and problems unrecognized when the law was first enacted. In addition to the public welfare programs, it authorizes:

Title II. Federal Old-Age, Survivors, and Disability Insurance Benefits.

Title III. Grants to States For Unemployment Compensation Benefits Administration.†

---

*Prior to the spring of 1977, the principal welfare agency within D/HEW was the Social and Rehabilitation Service. At that time it was abolished and its welfare program responsibilities distributed among the three departmental agencies shown above.

†Text continues on page 32.

Table 1.1 State Public Welfare Agencies

JURISDICTION	AGENCY
Alabama	Alabama Department of Pensions and Security
Alaska	Alaska Department of Health and Social Services
Arizona	Arizona Department of Economic Security
Arkansas	Arkansas Department of Human Services
California	California Health and Welfare Agency
Colorado	Colorado Department of Social Services
Connecticut	Connecticut Department of Social Services
Delaware	Delaware Department of Health and Social Services
District of Columbia	District of Columbia Department of Human Resources
Florida	Florida Department of Health and Rehabilitative Services
Georgia	Georgia Department of Human Resources
Guam	Guam Department of Public Health and Social Services
Hawaii	Hawaii Department of Social Services and Housing
Idaho	Idaho Department of Health and Welfare
Illinois	Illinois Department of Public Aid
	Illinois Department of Children and Family Services
Indiana	Indiana Department of Public Welfare
Iowa	Iowa Department of Social Services
Kansas	Kansas Department of Social and Rehabilitation Services
Kentucky	Kentucky Department of Human Resources

Louisiana	Louisiana Health and Human Resources
Maine	Maine Department of Human Resources
Maryland	Maryland Department of Human Resources
Massachusetts	Massachusetts Executive Office Of Human Services, Department of Public Welfare
Michigan	Michigan Department of Social Services
Minnesota	Minnesota Department of Public Welfare
Mississippi	Mississippi Department of Public Welfare
Missouri	Missouri Department of Social Services
Montana	Montana Department of Social and Rehabilitation Services
Nebraska	Nebraska Department of Public Welfare
Nevada	Nevada Department of Human Resources
New Hampshire	New Hampshire Department of Health and Welfare
New Jersey	New Jersey Department of Human Services
New Mexico	New Mexico Health and Social Services Department
New York	New York State Department of Social Services
North Carolina	North Carolina Department of Human Resources
North Dakota	Social Services Board of North Dakota
Ohio	Ohio Department of Public Welfare
Oklahoma	Oklahoma Department of Institutions, Social and Rehabilitative Services
Oregon	Oregon Department of Human Resources
Pennsylvania	Pennsylvania Department of Public Welfare

Table 1.1   (Continued)

Puerto Rico	Puerto Rico Department of Social Services
Rhode Island	Rhode Island Department of Social and Rehabilitative Services
South Carolina	South Carolina Department of Social Services
South Dakota	South Dakota Department of Social Services
Tennessee	Tennessee Department of Human Services
Texas	Texas Department of Public Welfare
Utah	Utah Department of Social Services
Vermont	Vermont Agency of Human Services
Virginia	Virginia Department of Welfare
Virgin Islands	Virgin Islands Department of Social Welfare
Washington	Washington Department of Social and Health Services
West Virginia	West Virginia Department of Welfare
Wisconsin	Wisconsin Department of Health and Social Services
Wyoming	Wyoming Department of Health and Social Services

Title V. Maternal and Child Health and Crippled Children's Services.

Title XII. Advances to State Unemployment Funds.

Title XVII. Grants for Planning Action to Combat Mental Retardation.

Title XVIII. Health Insurance for the Aged and Disabled (Medicare).

A good beginning in understanding the intricacies of the public welfare system is to understand how public welfare programs are provided for in the general outline of the act.

Title I authorizes grants to Puerto Rico, Guam, and the Virgin Islands for old age assistance. These jurisdictions are excluded from coverage under the SSI program under Title XVI.

Title IV authorizes grants to states for income maintenance to needy families with children (AFDC), child welfare services, the WIN program, and the child support enforcement program.

Title VII vests the administration and responsibility for carrying out the provisions of the act in the Secretary of Health, Education and Welfare and authorizes training grants for public welfare personnel and grants for expansion of undergraduate and graduate programs of social work.

Title X authorizes grants to Puerto Rico, Guam, and the Virgin Islands for Aid to the Blind. These jurisdictions are excluded from coverage under the SSI program under Title XVI.

Title XI contains miscellaneous provisions affecting the public welfare system:

authority of the Secretary to issue rules and regulations

limitations on the disclosure of information

penalties for fraud

limitations on payments under the Act to Puerto Rico, the Virgin Islands and Guam

authorizations for cooperative research or demonstration projects

public assistance payments to legal representatives

issuance of medical care guides and reports for public assistance and medical assistance

program of assistance for destitute U.S. citizens returned from foreign countries

appointment of advisory councils

authorization for public welfare demonstration projects

administrative and judicial review of administrative determinations

alternative methods for federal payment with respect to public assistance expenditures

federal participation in payments for repairs to homes owned by public assistance recipients

prior approval by the Secretary of experimental, pilot, demonstration, or other projects under the Act

> payments to states to provide institutional services to adult recipients in intermediate care facilities
>
> authorization for Professional Standards Review Organizations

Title XIV authorizes grants to Puerto Rico, Guam, and the Virgin Islands for Aid to the Permanently and Totally Disabled. These jurisdictions are excluded from coverage under the SSI program under Title XVI.

Title XVI authorizes the federally-administered SSI program of income maintenance for the three so-called adult categories (the aged, blind, and disabled) in all fifty states and the District of Columbia. Titles I, X, and XIV continue income maintenance programs for the adult categories in Guam, the Virgin Islands, and Puerto Rico.

Title XIX authorizes the Medicaid program and the program of grants to states for medical assistance.

Title XX authorizes grants to states for social services to individuals and families.

OTHER LAWS RELATING TO THE PUBLIC WELFARE SYSTEM

In addition to the Social Security Act, two other federal laws are directly responsible for specific public welfare programs: The Food Stamp Act of 1964 as amended, and the Migration and Refugee Assistance Act of 1962 for refugee assistance. However, the effective functioning of the public welfare system depends upon, and affects, other federal and state laws which authorize human service programs for low-income individuals and families. The major federal laws are listed in Table 1.2. In the ensuing chapters, particularly Chapter 9, the interrelationships of these will be described. State laws on the public welfare system mirror the federal laws. They customarily contain the requirements to qualify the state for federal financial participation.

THE FEDERAL/STATE PUBLIC WELFARE CONCEPT

The public welfare system is a constitutional instrument for "promoting the general welfare," in this instance, the welfare of categories of poor and near-poor persons, disadvantaged or threatened children, Cuban Refugees, and destitute and mentally ill citizens returning from foreign lands. Specifically, the federal government involvement in public welfare programs under the Social Security Act and under the Food Stamp Act is justified under the commerce clause of the U.S. Constitution Article 1, Section 8 under which the federal government has authority to regulate interstate commerce, and the Migration and Refugee Assistance Act for Cuban Refugee Assistance under the same section applying to commerce with foreign nations.

What is quite important in characterizing the federal/state system are the constitutional restraints placed upon the federal government on the authority and prerogatives reserved to the states, legally placing the states in a position of supremacy. This is one of the most important controlling factors in shaping the public welfare system. For the state governments decide whether and to what extent they are to provide for a public welfare program, what groups of individuals are eligible, what state agencies should administer the program, how it should be organized, what funds should be provided and from what revenue sources, what methods and processes should be used, how large the agency and program should be, and what state officials are to set policies and be held accountable.

We must remember that state programs of income maintenance, social services, medical assistance, and other helping services predate enactment of the Social Security Act in 1935. Further, state governments continue to offer some social programs without benefit of federal aid, for example, the General Assistance Program of income maintenance to needy individuals and families not eligible for the AFDC categorical programs or the aged, blind and disabled under the SSI program. The states vary in the payment levels and eligibility limits for the GA Program, but they provide for such poor persons as older persons under aged 65, families without children, and temporarily and partially disabled individuals. A description of the GA Program is provided in Chapter 3.

Each state government also decides whether its welfare programs should be administered by a state agency throughout the state or whether its counties and cities should be given this

Table 1.2 Federal Laws Serving Public Welfare
Individuals and Families

PUBLIC WELFARE	Social Security Act of 1935, as amended
	Food Stamp Act of 1964, as amended
	Migration and Refugee Assistance Act

EDUCATION

Preschool	Community Services Act of 1974 (Head Start)
Elementary and secondary	Elementary and Secondary Education Act of 1965, as amended
	Head Start-Follow Through Act of 1974
Vocational	Vocational Education Act of 1963, as amended
Higher	Higher Education Act of 1965, as amended
	Educational Amendments of 1972
Adult	Adult Education Act of 1966, as amended
Minority group	Emergency School Aid of 1972, as amended
	Bilingual Education Act of 1936
Handicapped children	Education of the Handicapped Act of 1968, as amended
Indian	Indian Education Act
	Indian Adult Vocational Training Act of 1956

FOOD AND NUTRITION

Commodity Food Distribution	Agricultural Adjustment Act of 1938, as amended
	Agricultural Act of 1949, as amended
	Food and Agricultural Act of 1965
School Food Programs: School lunch, Break-	National School Lunch Act of 1946, as amended

fast, Milk, Women, Infants and Children Supplemental Food Program (WIC), Child Care Food Program, etc.	Child Nutrition Act of 1966, as amended
Nutrition Program For the Aged	Older Americans Act of 1965, as amended

HOUSING AND COMMUNITY DEVELOPMENT

Public housing	United States Housing Act of 1937, as amended
Housing for low-income families	National Housing Act of 1934, as amended Housing and Urban Development Act of 1965, as amended
Community planning and development	Housing and Community Development Act of 1974
Indian housing improvement	Snyder Act of 1921

EMPLOYMENT AND TRAINING

Comprehensive employment and training	Comprehensive Employment and Training Act of 1973
Apprenticeship training	National Apprenticeship Act of 1937
Employment Services	The Wagner-Peysner Act of 1933, as amended
Senior community service employment	Older Americans Act of 1965, as amended
Minimum wage and hours standards	Fair Labor Standards Act of 1938, as amended
Age discrimination in employment	Age Discrimination in Employment Act of 1967, as amended
Farm labor contractor registration	Farm Labor Contractor Registration Act of 1963
Job discrimination	Civil Rights Act of 1964, as amended

Table 1.2 (Continued)

HEALTH

Family planning	Public Health Service Act of 1912, as amended
Community mental health centers	Community Mental Health Centers Amendments of 1975
Alcohol and drug abuse education	Alcohol and Drug Abuse Education Act of 1970, as amended
Drug abuse prevention and treatment	Comprehensive Drug Abuse Prevention and Control Act of 1970
	Drug Abuse Office and Treatment Act of 1972
Alchohol abuse and Alcoholism prevention, treatment, and Rehabilitation	Comprehensive Alcohol Abuse and Alcoholism Prevention, Treatment and Rehabilitation Act of 1970, as amended
Health maintenance organization	Health Maintenance Organization Act of 1973
Childhood lead-based paint poisoning control	Lead-Based Paint Poisoning Prevention Act of 1971
Veterans health services	Veterans Health Care Expansion Act of 1973 and other Veterans legislation
Appalachian health programs	Appalachian Regional Development Act of 1965, as amended
Civilian health and medical program of the uniformed services (CHAMPUS)	Military Medical Benefits Amendments of 1966

VOCATIONAL REHABILITATION

Rehabilitation Act of 1973

AGING

Special programs for the aging	Older Americans Act of 1965, as amended
Foster grandparents and retired senior volunteers	Domestic Volunteer Service Act of 1973

ADMINISTRATION OF JUSTICE

Juvenile delinquency	Juvenile Justice and Delinquency Prevention Act of 1974, as amended
Law enforcement assistance	Omnibus Crime Control and Safe Streets Act of 1968, as amended
Narcotics and drug abuse	Comprehensive Drug Abuse Prevention and Control Act of 1970, as amended
Community relations service	Civil Rights Act of 1964, as amended

INCOME SECURITY AND BENEFIT PAYMENTS

Disabled coal miners benefits	Federal Coal Mine Health and Safety Act of 1969, as amended by the Black Lung Benefits Act of 1972
Veterans benefits	Veterans Benefits Act, as amended
Railroad retirement benefits	Railroad Retirement Act of 1971, as amended
Longshoremen's and harbor workers' compensation	Longshoremen's and Harbor Workers' Compensation Act of 1927, as amended
Indian assistance payments	Snyder Act of 1921

OTHER FEDERAL PROGRAMS

Community action	Community Services Act of 1974, as amended
VISTA volunteers	Domestic Volunteer Service Act of 1973
Federal youth and handicapped employment	Civil Service Act of 1883, as amended
Small business assistance	Small Business Act of 1953, as amended
Legal services corporation	Legal Services Corporation Act of 1974
Indian social services	Snyder Act of 1921
Federal income taxes	Federal Income Tax Legislation

authority, with a state agency exercising supervision and monitoring of local government bodies.

The conceptual role of the federal government in state public welfare programs is to help shape, guide, and influence these state decisions through its financial aid (i.e., the power of the purse) and provide technical, administrative, and professional assistance, knowledge, and oversight of the federal agencies. But the central fact of this relationship is that each state government, not the federal government, is vested with the authority to make the controlling decisions about its public welfare programs and administration. To illustrate this point, Nevada did not enact a law authorizing public assistance payments to permanently and totally disabled persons, thus, this program was inoperative in Nevada. Similarly, Arizona has not enacted a law authorizing a medical assistance program for its public assistance recipients and other medically needy persons. Arizona government leaders decided that the preponderance of low-income persons, who are mainly reservation Indians, already receive medical services from the U.S. Indian Health Service.

One must further qualify the federal/state relationship in underlining the fact that the federal government provides more than half of the funds for public welfare programs, as detailed in Chapter 7, so that federal requirements and policies have been and will continue to be de facto determinants of the public welfare system in this country.

Nevertheless, there are 54 variations of such systems: each of the fifty states, the three territories, and the District of Columbia. No two states or territories are alike in all its features: need standards, payment levels, social and medical services provided, organization pattern, number and type of its personnel, service providers, size of budget, location of offices, procedures, methods, and relationship with other human service agencies. Nor are they altogether different. The federal regulations prescribe the common features for all which will be described in later chapters.

The action by Congress in approving the Social Security Amendments of 1972 creating the SSI program for maintenance assistance for aged, blind, and disabled recipients as a federally centralized program dramatically and effectively moved the decision-making and administrative powers over this one program from the state governments, leaving them residual authority for supplemental payments to the aforementioned recipients. This, however, does not affect the states' responsibilities for social services or medical assistance for this group. As will be explained more fully in Chapter 3, however, there is a noted impact upon the state social services and medical assistance programs with the increased number of aged, blind, and disabled recipients gaining eligibility for services from their eligibility under the SSI program.

THE STATE PLAN CONCEPT

The state plan is the vehicle for carrying out the federal/state relationship. The state plan is a comprehensive statement submitted by the state agency describing the nature and scope of its program and giving assurance it will be administered in conformity with the specific requirements stipulated in the federal law and regulations. The state plan contains all information necessary for the federal agency to determine whether the plan can be approved, as a basis for federal financial participation in the state program.[5]

Each state is required under the Social Security Act regulations to prepare plans for income maintenance and social services for individuals and families, child welfare services, medical assistance, and social services for aged, blind, and disabled recipients. The state may submit the common material on more than one program as an integrated plan. However, it must identify the provisions pertinent to each title since a separate plan must be approved for each public assistance title.[6] Also, the public welfare agency must prepare a "State Plan of Operations" for its food stamp program.

Each of the state plans for income maintenance, social services, medical assistance, and child welfare services under the Social Security Act contains the following common requirements:

1. That the state provide the program be in effect in all political subdivisions of the state.
2. That the state participate financially in the program.
3. That the state establish or designate a single state agency to administer or supervise administration of the plan.
4. That the state grant an opportunity for a fair hearing to any individual claiming his application for assistance is denied or is not acted upon with reasonable promptness.
5. That the state provide such methods of administration necessary for the proper and efficient operation of the plan, including establishment and maintenance of personnel standards on a merit basis.
6. That the state provide for the training and effective use of paid subprofessional staff, with priority given for full or part time employment of recipients and other poor persons and use of nonpaid or partially paid volunteers.
7. That the state agency make reports prescribed by the U.S. Department of Health, Education and Welfare.

The state plans, in addition, reflect other program requirements which states are to meet appropriate to the legal requirements expressed in the Social Security Act for that particular program. The details of these requirements will be described in Chapters 3 and 4.

The Food Stamp program requirements for a state plan of operations contains many of the above common features of the plans for the Social Security Act programs, with different requirements reflecting the nature of the program and the operational requirements of the Food and Nutrition Service of the Department of Agriculture. These are also described in Chapter 4.

Review and Approval of State Plans

State plans under the Social Security Act are submitted first to the Governor or his designee for review and then to the Department of Health, Education and Welfare's office in the region in which the state is located. The state plan of operations for the Food Stamp program is submitted directly to the Administrator of the Food and Nutrition Service in Washington. Gubernatorial review is nominal for technical plan changes, but his reservations and objections to the more serious amendments, such as those affecting state budgets, or impact on his social, economic, or political philosophies, have created instances of public and political confrontation between state and federal governments. To minimize such frictions, state officials are encouraged to obtain consultation with federal officials when a plan is in process of preparation or revision.

Once agreement on a state plan or amendment is reached and a determination is made that federal legal and regulatory requirements are met, official notification of such decisions is sent to the Governor and the state agency. Federal payments (grants) are made under the approved plans each quarter for expenditures made by the states. The amount of the payments is based on fiscal estimates submitted by the state agency 45 days in advance of the quarterly period, and fiscal reports of actual expenditures 30 days after the period ends. The procedure for payments is spelled out in Chapter 7, but suffice it to say that these transactional accounting operations transferring billions of federal dollars annually to the states are one of the most crucial financial processes for keeping state and local governments solvent and able to meet the administrative costs of their public welfare programs, make income maintenance payments to 15 million poor, and provide them and other poor with social, medical, and other needed services.

On June 27, 1973, in order to facilitate the state plan mechanism, the Administrator of the Social and Rehabilitation Service, D/HEW authorized adoption of a uniform simplified preprinted format for state plans, requiring a minimum of descriptive narrative material. The move towards a simplified format derived from the administrative burden on both state and federal agencies of the previously elaborate, long and detailed contents of state plans, differing one state from another. These plans had caused controversy in interpretation, protracted negotiations between federal and state officials on the adherence of their provisions to federal regulations, state agency appeals and judicial review of adverse (to the states) decisions by federal officials and an undue amount of time and effort of both federal and state personnel devoted to the negotiating process. It became apparent that such resources could better be applied to efforts to manage and resolve the large substantive and administrative problems which confronted the public welfare programs.

The federal government exercises oversight of the administration of the state plans by periodic review of state and local administration by its regional office personnel, by a program of financial audit of expenditures under the plans by an audit staff of the responsible federal agency (Departments of Health, Education and Welfare; Labor; and Agriculture) and, independently, by the General Accounting Office. In addition, the Departments of Health, Education and Welfare and Agriculture's Food and Nutrition Service administer quality control programs to check on the correctness of determinations of eligibility by state and local agencies for public assistance, services, and food stamps, and the correctness of payments to recipient individuals and families. Finally, reports concerning public welfare administration, finances, and programs are required of state and local agencies. State governments maintain oversight activities of their own, paralleling those of the federal government. These are also reinforced by state and local budget processes, the exercise of budget controls, and reviews and approvals of each agency's budget by state and local chief executives and legislatures.

The findings of these oversight activities of noncompliance of a state program with its plan, that is, its failure to meet a federal requirement, represents a potential threat to withholding federal funds, for each of the federal statutes makes this a condition for federal financial participation in the program. A question of noncompliance may arise from an unapprovable change in the approved state plan, the failure of the state to change its approved plan to conform to a new federal requirement, or the failure of the state in practice to comply with a federal requirement whether or not its state plan has been amended.[7] In practice, individual findings of noncompliance are reported to the state agency, and changes are negotiated between federal and state officials. Formal appeals by state officials to federal administrators are provided for, when agreement cannot be reached by lower echelon officials. If agreement cannot be reached between state and federal administrators, the state may request review of the Secretary of the agency before a final determination is made. Further appellate processes to the U.S. Court of Appeals are available if a state is dissatisfied with the Secretary's decision. The court has jurisdiction to affirm the Secretary's decision, or set it aside in whole or in part, or, for good cause, to remand the case for additional evidence. The judgment of the court is subject to review by the U.S. Supreme Court.[8]

All parties realize the counterproductive effect of the action to withhold federal funds: to the individual beneficiary of the program, to state and local agencies' ability to provide welfare benefits and services to the people in need, to the federal government's moral and ethical concern for the social and economic goals of its public welfare legislation. No stone is left unturned, every administrative accommodation is sought to reach compromise and agreement to avoid this drastic step.

THE INDIVIDUAL AND THE FEDERAL/STATE PUBLIC WELFARE SYSTEM

There are inherent rights and responsibilities of the individual applying for or receiving maintenance payments or services of a state and local public welfare agency. Equally, the agency has inherent obligations and responsibilities to respond to the individual in discharging its purpose. Given the sensitivity of public welfare programs—on the one hand, requiring personal, quite frequently, intimate information about the individual, his family relations, his household, his physical and mental health, employment, education and training, sources and amount of income, ownership of resources; while on the other hand, necessitating a continuing review and open communication between the individual and the agency—the interrelationship between agency and individual is indeed a signal characteristic of the public welfare system.

Any individual citizen or alien lawfully in this country may request that another person apply in his behalf to a state or local agency and receive a prompt decision upon his request for assistance or services with no discrimination by reason of race, sex, religion, national origin, political belief, citizenship, or durational residency requirement. The only exception is the Social Security Act provision under the SSI program which permits a state to exclude an individual who has been absent from its borders for a period in excess of 90 consecutive days until he has been present in the state for 30 consecutive days.

No individual is required to apply for assistance or services or is required to accept them if offered. This needs to be qualified in a number of instances, however. In the case of a dependent child removed from his home or the home of a relative by a judicial determination and placed in a foster home or child care institution, foster care or institutional services must be provided under the state law as prescribed by the court. This same concept also applies to delinquent, abused, and neglected children placed under court supervision and receiving child welfare services, in which the state or local agency serves as agent for the court. For another group of persons, including heads of households and youth from families receiving AFDC required to register for the WIN program, failure to register or undergo training, employment or other required social services, unless for good cause, will result in the state or local agency discontinuing income payments for themselves, but not the children in their families.

Recipients receiving payments are free to spend them as they wish without government intervention. Although payments are made to help cover their basic needs for food, clothing, shelter, and other necessities, they may be used for purchases of other items, or be used for necessities in different proportions or amounts than those which the payments are based.

Any individual has the right to appeal the action of the state or local agency to deny assistance payments or services in the amount or type he deems he is entitled to, and must be provided with a fair hearing and legal assistance for such hearing.

In fiscal year 1975, 133,058 requests for fair hearings were received by 48 state agencies. Three-fourths of these were filed under the AFDC program, with another one-fourth under the

Medicaid program. About three-fourths of the requests were disposed of by a formal hearing. More than a quarter of the requests resulted in a change in favor of the claimant.[9]

Any individual is entitled to examine state and local agency program manuals, rules, and regulations concerning eligibility, need standards, and amounts of assistance payments, recipient rights, and responsibilities and services offered by the agency. He is also entitled to a copy of such materials without cost, or at a reasonable charge to cover the cost of reproducing the material.

Agency procedures and methods must be designed and executed to give full respect for the rights and dignity of applicants and recipients of the agency's programs. Moreover, the confidentiality of records and information about individual applicants and recipients and agency actions in specific cases is assured and the disclosure of such information is proscribed, usually through an order issued by a court having jurisdiction to issue such orders in a legal matter in which the information is indispensable to its resolution.

All individual applicants and recipients have an implicit obligation to provide the agency complete, honest, and current information which the agency requires to make an initial determination of eligibility for assistance payments, services, or food stamps or to confirm continued eligibility. Individuals are also obligated to cooperate with the agency in its activities to corroborate the information they supply. On its part, the agency has an obligation to limit its requests for applicant or recipient information to essentials in order to make agency determinations of eligibility and entitlement for payments or services.

Misrepresentation of information by an individual with the intent to defraud a government in receiving assistance payments or services is punishable under federal and state law by a fine not exceeding $1,000, or by imprisonment not exceeding one year, or both.

In fiscal year 1975, state agencies reported there were over 144,000 AFDC cases which involved questions of recipient fraud disposed of by administrative action. Of these, 81,000 cases were determined to be sufficient to support a question of fraud. Another 40,000 cases, or 49 percent, were referred to law enforcement officials for action. During the year, 38,000 cases were disposed of by legal action. An additional 18,000 prosecutions were initiated and, in 5,570 cases, reimbursement of amounts falsely paid was arranged.

Over 27,000 recipient fraud cases were disposed of without referral to law enforcement officials. In more than half of these (58 percent), reimbursement by the recipient was made.[10] The trend in fraud cases has risen as state public welfare agencies continue improvement in detecting and reporting suspected fraud, initiate procedures to assist in correcting agency practices in eligibility determination processes leading to overpayments, and stressing to clients their legal responsibilities as recipients of assistance payments and services.

NOTES

1. Background for Action. The Report of the New York State Temporary Commission to Review the Social Services Law, State of New York. Legislative Document (1974) No. 26, p. 93.

2. American Public Welfare Association. Essentials of public welfare: a statement of principles. American Public Welfare Association, 1616 L Street, N.W., Washington, D.C. Approved by the Board of Directors, December 8, 1970.

3. *Public Welfare,* Winter 1975, **33,** (1), 51.

4. Social Services Program for Individuals and Families. 45 CFR 228 effective October, 1975, and Social Security Act as amended Public Law 93-647.

5. Part 201.2 Grants to States for Public Assistance Programs. 45 CFR 202.

6. Ibid., Part 201.3.

7. Ibid., Part 201.6.

8. Ibid., Part 201.7.

9. Fair Hearings in Public Assistance July–December 1974 and January–June 1975. DHEW Publication No. SRS 76-03257 NCSS Report E-8, U.S. DHEW, SRS, Office of Information Sciences NCSS, Washington, D.C., July 1975 and January 1965 respectively.

10. Disposition of Public Assistance Cases Involving Questions of Fraud. Fiscal Year 1975, DHEW Publication No. SRS 76-03256 NCSS Report E-7 (FY 1975) U.S. DHEW, SRS, Office of Information Sciences NCSS, Washington, D.C., March 1976.

Chapter 2

THE PUBLIC WELFARE POPULATIONS

Over 37 million people—one of every six Americans—comprise the potential population for whom the public welfare system functions (Table 2.1). They are primarily, but not all, poor and near-poor. There are others from middle and upper economic classes among them, an estimated 400,000 children and their families neither poor or near-poor who receive child welfare services annually* and a small number, approximately 100 mentally ill citizens returning from abroad to become a temporary responsibility of the system.

From these potential groups (for we cannot classify this large segment of the American people a single homogenous group) are drawn two kinds of welfare beneficiaries: those who receive cash payments and those who do not. The first group are the 16.8 million recipients of AFDC, SSI and GA programs who also receive social services, medical care, food stamps, and employment training and employment services (Table 2.2). The second group are the noncash recipients of social services, medical care, food stamps, and other nonmonetary welfare assis-

---

*Potentially all 83 million children in the United States are beneficiaries of the child welfare services program.

tance. The aggregate number of persons of the second group is not known, because individuals in the group receive multiple benefits and an unduplicated count or estimate has not been made. Medically indigent persons also may receive food stamps, so do noncash recipients of social services. Food stamp beneficiaries also may receive medical or social services of public welfare agencies. All of them comprise the public welfare caseload.

Table 2.1   The Potential Public Welfare Population, 1975[a]
(in millions)

Poor	25.9
Near-poor	11.3
Nonpoor (children under child welfare supervision, repatriated U.S. nationals)	.4
Total	37.6

[a]*Characteristics of the population below the poverty level: 1975.* Bureau of the Census, Department of Commerce, Washington, D.C. Series P-60 No. 106, June 1977 Table 1. Persons Below the Poverty Level by Family Status, Sex of Head and Race and Spanish Origin 1959 to 1975, p. 15.

In 1975, official reports indicate there were 2.2 million noncash, medically-indigent recipients; 10 million noncash, food stamp beneficiaries; about 400,000 nonpoor children under child welfare supervision; an unknown number of noncash, social service beneficiaries; and a small number of Cuban refugees and repatriated U.S. nationals. If these were different persons, they would number 11.5 million. If the 2.2 million medically indigent persons also received food stamps, their number would be included in the 10 million noncash recipient food stamp beneficiaries and the aggregate number of other welfare recipients would be 9.3 million (11.5 million less 2.2 million). To further confuse the number of persons benefitting directly from public welfare is the probability that the 16.8 million cash payment recipients reported (itself an average) may include recipients who are counted more than once during the year because they may have discontinued payments one month and reapplied and became eligible for cash payments another month.

This phenomenon is not unique to the public welfare system. It was the subject of a special study by the Subcommittee on Fiscal Policy of the Joint Economic Committee in 1972.[1]

Table 2.2 Eligible Beneficiaries of Public Welfare Programs and Activities

	AFDC	SSI	GA	Title XX	Child Welfare	Medicaid	Food Stamps	WIN	Refugee Assistance	U.S. Repatriates
Poor:										
Children	x		x	x	x	x	x	x	x	x
Families with children	x		x	x	x	x	x	x	x	x
Childless families		x	x	x		x	x		x	x
Unrelated individuals		x	x	x		x	x		x	x
Near poor:										
Children				x	x	x	x		x	x
Families with children				x	x		x		x	x
Childless families				x			x		x	x
Unrelated individuals				x			x		x	x
Non-poor:										
Children					x					x
Families with children					x					x
Childless families										x
Unrelated individuals										x

Many persons receiving benefits from public income transfer programs are aided by more than one such program in the form of
cash, medical care, subsidized housing, and free or reduced-price
food. In fact, it is estimated that 26 of the largest federally-funded
income transfer programs and the major non-Federal programs,
which are expected to have a gross total of 119 million beneficiaries in fiscal year 1972, will actually be aiding no more than 60
million different individuals. The gross number of 64 million recipients in the 10 Federal programs and the non-Federal programs
basing assistance on need criteria is probably about 25 to 30 million different individuals . . ."

Applying this same rule of thumb, we can estimate that (1)
about 25 million persons actually received public welfare benefits in 1975, (2) not all beneficiaries received all welfare assistance and services available and (3) about 17.6 million
potentially eligible poor and near-poor were not part of the
welfare population.

Neither the estimated 25 million *actual* recipients of public
welfare programs nor the potentially eligible groups are static,
unchanging, or readily identifiable. Rather, they are a fluid,
dynamic, changing stream of individuals and families whose
personal, social, or economic circumstances, problems and
needs cause them to become applicants and beneficiaries of
public welfare agencies. Their welfare status may be only a day
or a week to help them through a family crisis, or it may be for
a lifetime as an institutional resident suffering an irreversible
physical or mental illness. They may be in and out of the system
repeatedly. They may receive maintenance payments for a six-
month period, become self-supporting for three months, go off
welfare rolls, then require maintenance payments again. They
may require only one service or all services simultaneously, as
for example a middle-income family man, socially and economically independent, suffers a serious illness and finds himself
unable to pay his medical bills and support his family, and so
applies for medical assistance. A Cuban refugee dentist, formerly independent, is offered resettlement aid to start practicing anew in a midwestern city.

A statistical projection from a five-year survey conducted by
the University of Michigan Institute for Social Research shows
that twice the number of poor persons in the survey were in

poverty during one of the five years. Thus, the researchers concluded that about 50 million Americans, or one-fourth of the population, are likely to fall below the poverty line at some time over a period of a few years.[2]

The reasons for terminating assistance payments also reveal the changing character and number of the recipient population. An increase in earnings or resources is the principal reason for terminating many cases, many resulting from an increase in social security benefits. Death of recipients is another prominent reason, particularly among the aged, blind, and disabled. Changes in family relationships or a recipient's living arrangements making them ineligible for continued assistance payments also occurs, as does employment of an AFDC family head.

In the course of an average day, most applicants who apply to public welfare agencies become eligible, receive payments, services, food stamps, become rehabilitated, and have their cases closed. The numbers in each of these statuses fluctuate and the aggregates are the statistics which are quoted by public officials. For example, during a three-month period, April through June, 1975, state public assistance agencies* reported receiving 1.6 million applications for maintenance payments and medical assistance; an average of 24,000 daily. During this same period, 404,000 applications for money payments were approved (or 75 percent of those processed) and 381,000 requests for money payments were discontinued. Applications for medical assistance were also approved at a rate of 64.8 percent.[3]

The poor and near-poor who do not apply for public assistance or services experience the same pattern of change in their personal, social, and economic circumstances. The poor family able to meet its basic needs without income maintenance payments may succeed through its own efforts to move upwards from mere survival to long-term independence. Or, meeting misfortune, the family's ability to earn enough may end when the head of household loses his job and becomes dependent upon public welfare. We can describe the movement, if any, of the potential groups in one of two directions: upward to social

---

*Reports were not available from Connecticut, District of Columbia, Guam, and Wyoming.

and economic independence or downward to public welfare dependency. As noted earlier, these changes may occur frequently or may be a once-in-a-lifetime occurrence. They may be for short duration, with the family requiring some kind of help for several months, possibly during a period of unemployment, or for longer spells, possibly the life span of the family unit.

THE MEANING AND MEASUREMENT OF POVERTY

The concept and definition of poverty are necessarily subject to personal, social, cultural, economic, and political interpretation and probably will always remain so. In the absence of finite agreement and the overriding national need for an index of poverty, the Social Security Administration in 1964 developed, and a Federal Interagency Committee updated, refined, and established in 1969 a poverty index based on the U.S. Department of Agriculture's 1961 Economy Food Plan designed for "emergency or temporary use when funds are low." This provided for total food expenditures of only 75 cents a day per person in 1966 in an average four-person family and twice this amount to cover all family living items other than food. This poverty index reflects the different consumption requirements of families based on their size and composition, sex and age of the family head and farm and nonfarm residence. To keep the index constant over time, the numbers are updated annually based on changes in the Consumer Price Index developed by the Bureau of Labor Statistics, Department of Labor.

Since 1959, the number of poor persons has declined with the most significant drop in the number of family members (Table 2.3).

The popular, common figure of the poverty index often referred to is the annual figure for a nonfarm (urban) family of four. In 1977, the index figure was $5,850; in 1976, $5,500, in 1975, $5,050. This means that an average family of four persons living in a city in 1977 would require an annual income of $5,850 to meet its basic needs for food, clothing, housing, and other necessities. Of 215 million persons in the United States in 1975, 25.9 million were classified "poor" on this basis (Table 2.4).

Table 2.3   Number and Percent of Persons
Below the Low-Income Level
(numbers in millions)

Year	Poor	% of Total U.S. Population	No. In Families	No. of Unrelated Individuals
1959	39.5	22.4%	34.6	4.9
1960	39.9	22.2	34.9	4.9
1961	39.6	21.9	34.5	5.1
1962	38.6	21.0	33.6	5.0
1963	36.4	19.5	31.5	4.9
1964	36.1	19.0	30.9	5.1
1965	33.2	17.3	28.4	4.8
1966	28.5	14.7	23.8	4.7
1967	27.8	14.2	22.8	5.0
1968	25.4	12.8	20.7	4.7
1969	24.3	12.1	19.4	4.9
1970	25.4	12.6	20.3	5.1
1971	25.6	12.5	20.4	5.2
1972	24.5	11.9	19.6	4.9
1973	23.0	11.1	18.3	4.7
1974	24.3	11.6	19.4	4.8
1975	25.9	12.3	20.8	5.1

Source: Current Population Reports, Consumer Income, Series P-60, No. 106, Table 1. Persons Below The Poverty Level By Family Status, Sex Of Head And Race And Spanish Origin: 1959 to 1975 (p. 15). U.S. Department of Commerce, Bureau of the Census, Washington, D.C., June 1977.

The size of the "income deficit," that is, the difference of income of poor families and the poverty index amounted to $10.6 billion in 1975, compared with $18.1 billion in 1959, about a 40 percent reduction. For the average (median) poor family, it was $1,500 in 1975, approximately a 14 percent reduction from the average of $1,765 in 1959. For the 5.1 billion unrelated individuals, the income deficit in 1975 was $5.5 billion compared to $7.1 billion in 1959, more than a one-fifth reduction. For the average (median) poor individual, it was $839 in 1975, a more than one-third reduction from the average of $1,348 in 1959.[4]

To provide a fuller understanding of poverty in the United States, the federal government provided another measure, that of the number of persons whose income is 125 percent above the poverty index. This is the *near-poor* index. In 1975, 37.2 million persons had an income above 125 percent of the poverty level (for a nonfarm family of four, $6,875 [$5,500 X 125 percent], or 11.3 million persons in addition to the 25.9 million poor. The persons with an income at or below the near-poor income index and above the low income index are presumed to live independently and marginally to meet their basic living expenses. Their income is assumed not to be able to cover in full such other added expenses as costly medical care or the purchase of expensive luxuries. This near-poor group is part of the target group of potential beneficiaries of the public welfare system.

Table 2.4   Poverty Index

| Family Size | April 1, 1977 | | | | | | April 1976 | |
| | Continental U.S. | | Hawaii | | Alaska | | Continental U.S. | |
	Non-farm	Farm	Non-farm	Farm	Non-farm	Farm	Non-farm	Farm
1	$2,970	$2,550	$3,430	$2,940	$3,720	$3,200	$2,800	$2,400
2	3,930	3,360	4,530	3,870	4,920	4,210	3,700	3,160
3	4,890	4,170	5,630	4,800	6,120	5,220	4,600	3,920
4	5,850	4,980	6,730	5,730	7,320	6,230	5,500	4,680
5	6,810	5,790	7,830	6,660	8,520	7,240	6,400	5,440
6	7,770	6,600	8,930	7,590	9,720	8,250	7,300	6,200

Income levels for families of one through six persons for the continental U.S., Hawaii, and Alaska, and the comparison table for 1976–77.
Source: Department of Labor, Labor Press Service, Press release April 25, 1977.

The contrasts between the income levels of the poor and near-poor are sharpened when they are studied in relation to another set of data developed by the Bureau of Labor Statistics. This data represents adequate but modest levels of living for three categories of urban families. The Bureau of Labor Statistics developed three hypothetical budgets for a family living based on estimates of costs for goods and services: lower, intermediate, and higher for a family of four: a 38-year-old husband employed fulltime, his nonworking wife, a boy of 13, and a girl of 8. In 1976, the lower budget level was $10,041; intermediate level, $16,236; and higher level, $23,759 (Table 2.5).

Table 2.5   Summary of Annual Budgets for a Four-person
Family at Three Levels of Living, Urban United States,
Autumn 1976

	Lower budget	Intermediate budget	Higher budget
Total budget	$10,041	$16,236	$23,759
Total family consumption	8,162	12,370	17,048
Food	3,003	3,859	4,856
Housing	1,964	3,843	5,821
Transportation	767	1,403	1,824
Clothing	799	1,141	1,670
Personal care	265	355	503
Medical care	896	900	939
Other family consumption	468	869	1,434
Other items	451	731	1,234
Taxes and deductions	1,429	3,134	5,476
Social security and disability	604	898	911
Personal income taxes	825	2,236	4,565

Note: Because of rounding, sums of individual items may not equal totals.
Source: Department of Labor, Bureau of Labor Statistics Release, Week of May 2, 1977.

The federal government has undertaken a study to update and improve the validity of the poverty guidelines. The study is reviewing a number of perceived limitations and criticisms. One of these is the belief that the guidelines overstate poverty because they do not include "noncash" benefits to the poor, such as food stamps, public housing, Medicare and Medicaid benefits when estimating personal income. Another is the belief that the guidelines underestimate poverty because they are based on inflation figures of the cost of living of the general population and not the specific cost of living of the poor, which are significantly different. It is believed that the poor have been affected more by inflation than the nonpoor.[5]

CHARACTERISTICS OF LOW-INCOME POPULATIONS[6]

Families with a female head comprise a larger proportion of low-income families than of nonpoor families (43 percent compared to 9 percent). This difference prevails for both white and black families. However, regardless of poverty status, families headed by a woman account for a greater proportion of the black population than of the white population. One-third of low-income white families are headed by a female compared to 8 percent of those above the low-income level (64 percent) and about 23 percent of black families above the low-income level.

Persons of Spanish origin* and blacks are also overrepresented in the poverty ranks. About 10 percent of the low-income population is comprised of Spanish persons compared to about 4 percent of the population above the low-income level. For blacks, the difference is more pronounced: about 32 percent of the population below the low-income level was black compared to 9 percent of those above that level.

In addition, the aged and the young (related children under 18 years old) account for a larger proportion of poor persons than of the nonpoor. This relation held for both whites and blacks. However, the aged comprise a larger proportion of the white population than of the black population whereas the reverse relationship is true for children.

Geographic Distribution and Residence in Low-Income Areas

About 59 percent of low-income persons compared to 70 percent of nonpoor reside in metropolitan areas. Residents of non-metropolitan areas are more likely to live in poverty areas than residents of metropolitan areas regardless of poverty status.

Within metropolitan areas, regardless of poverty status, blacks are more likely to live in low-income areas than whites. About 47 percent of blacks above the poverty level compared to 6 percent of whites above the poverty level lived in these areas.

In metropolitan areas, about half of the low-income residents of poverty areas are children compared to 38 percent for low-income residents outside of poverty areas. In contrast, the proportion of children among the nonpoor population are about one-third in both poverty and nonpoverty areas.

*Includes all persons in families with head of Spanish origin and Spanish unrelated individuals.

Type of Income

Families below the low-income level are less likely to have some income from earnings than those above the low-income level (63 percent compared to 93 percent). Income from earnings account for 47 percent of the aggregate income of the poor compared to 88 percent for the nonpoor.

While the majority of families both above and below the low-income level receive some income from sources other than earnings, there are significant differences in the type of other income received. For families below the low-income level, public assistance and Social Security payments are the largest categories of unearned income, while for families above the low-income level income from sources other than government programs (e.g., dividends, interest, rent, and private pensions) are the largest category. About one-half of the nonpoor received income from sources other than government programs, compared to one-fifth for those below the low-income level. About 36 percent of the low-income families receive income from public assistance. For about two-fifths of these families, it was their only source of income. One-fourth of all low-income families receive income from Social Security, and for about one-fourth of them, it accounts for their total income. For each type of income, families below the low-income level have a higher percent with that type of income only than do families above the low-income level.

Work Status

The low-income population, as well as the total population, can be subdivided into several groups with regard to the work force. Children under 14 years old depend primarily on the earning capacity of their parents or other adults; and the great majority of the aged depend on the income set aside when they were working. These two groups account for 48 percent of the low-income population as compared to 33 percent of the population above the low-income level. The remaining portion of the population are of working age (14 to 64 years old). There are 12.7 million low-income persons in this age group.

About 47 percent of low-income persons 14 to 64 years old compared to 73 percent of those above the low-income level work at some time during the year. Of those who work, about one-fourth of the poor and three-fifths of the nonpoor work year-round and fulltime. The figures for the poor do not vary by race; however, among the nonpoor, there is some evidence that blacks are more likely to work year-round full time than whites. A greater proportion of nonpoor mothers (wives and female heads of families and subfamilies with own children) than of poor mothers work at some time during the year. Of these mothers who work, 16 percent of the poor and 39 percent of the nonpoor work year-round and full time. These proportions are higher for blacks than for whites regardless of poverty status.

Reasons for not working also vary by poverty status. Low-income persons who do not work are more likely to be ill or disabled than those above the low-income level. Persons above the low-income level are more likely not to work because of family responsibilities than their counterparts below the low-income level.

Educational Attainment

The low-income status of family heads 25 years old and over tends to vary inversely with years of school completed. For example, about 22 percent of family heads who had completed less than 8 years of school below the low-income level, while only about 3 percent of those with at least one year of college are poor. Although this relation holds for both races, black family heads are more likely to be below the low-income level regardless of their educational attainment. About 37 percent of black family heads who had completed less than 8 years of school are below the low-income level compared to 19 percent for white family heads. About 12 percent of black family heads with some college education are poor compared to 2 percent for whites.

About 46 percent of low-income family heads had completed less than one year of high school compared to 22 percent for family heads above the low-income level. The proportion of low-income family heads who did not finish high school compare to 67 percent of low-income whites. The figures for family heads above the low-income level are 56 percent and 36 percent, respectively. Family heads with one year or more of college represent about 9 percent of those below the low-income level, but about 28 percent of those above the low-income level.

Families Headed by Females

Families with a female head are more than five times as likely to have incomes below the low-income level as those headed by a male; the poverty rates are 33 percent and 6 percent, respectively. Female heads of both white and black families are more likely to be poor than their male counterparts; however black family heads of both sexes have higher poverty rates than whites. Among female headed families, the poverty rate for blacks is 53 percent compared to 24 percent for whites. In contrast, among male-headed families, the poverty rates are 16 percent and 5 percent, respectively.

The presence of children appears to be an important factor in determining the poverty status of families headed by a woman, while it hardly affects the poverty status of those headed by a man. The poverty rate for families with a female head without children present is 10 percent, as compared to 45 percent for similar families with children. This sizeable difference in poverty rates is observed for both blacks and whites. For families with a male head, the comparable rates, regardless of the presence of children, are about 6 percent. Low-income families headed by females are more likely to have children than those with a male head. About 89 percent of low-income families with a woman as a head have children under 18 years present compared to 58 percent of low-income families headed by a man.

The different roles children play in the poverty status of male- and female-headed families can be explained by the fact that presence of children does not affect a man's work status. About 45 percent of all low-income female heads 14 to 64 years old do not work because of family responsibilities. The number of men who do not work because of family responsibilities is insignificant. This is not to say that low-income female heads of families with children do not work. Of all low-income female heads of families and subfamilies with own children, about 42 percent work at some time during the year; the proportion is higher for whites than for blacks.

The poverty rate for working mothers who are heads of families and subfamilies is considerably lower than that for those who do not work (28 percent compared to 66 percent). Black mothers are more likely to have incomes below the low-income level than white mothers regardless of whether they work. Obtaining work does not necessarily eliminate the high poverty rate of black female heads since these persons frequently obtain low-paying jobs. Even in such families in which the head works year-round full time, the poverty rate is 17 percent compared to 7 percent for comparable white families.

In general, low-income female heads of families (regardless of presence of children) between 14 and 64 years old are less likely to work than low-income male heads of the same age group. Of the women who headed low-income families, about 41 percent work at some time during the year. Although there is some evidence that the proportion of low-income white female heads who work is higher than that for similar blacks, a greater proportion of blacks than whites work year-round and full time (22 percent compared to 14 percent). In contrast, about 78 percent of poor male family heads, regardless of race, work at some time during the year and 47 percent of these work all year at a full-time job.

Female heads also differ from male heads in the type of income received. About 72 percent of low-income families headed by a male have some income from earnings compared to 51 percent of low-income families headed by a female. Social Security is the largest category of income other than earnings for low-income families headed by a man, while public assistance is the largest category for low-income families headed by a woman. This relation does not hold for low-income families headed by black males. The proportion of such families receiving Social Security is not significantly different statistically from that receiving public assistance (28 percent compared to 25 percent). The receipt of public assistance for low-income families headed by a female varies by race; the proportion is 50 percent for whites and 71 percent for blacks.

Low-income female heads of families tend to be younger on the average than low-income male heads. Female heads under 35 years account for about 50 percent of all low-income female heads compared to 28 percent for low-income male heads. Conversely, 23 percent of all male heads and 9 percent of all female heads below the low-income level are 65 years old and over. Among male family heads the poverty rate is highest for the aged (11 percent), while among female family heads the poverty rate is highest for the young (54 percent).

The Aged

The poverty rate for persons 65 years and over is 19 percent compared to 11 percent for those under 65 years. Aged persons living in families are less likely to be poor than those who live alone or with nonrelatives (i.e., unrelated individuals) and depend on their own incomes. About 10 percent of the aged persons living in families are below the low-income level compared to 37 percent of the aged unrelated individuals. Aged female unrelated individuals are more likely to be poor than comparable aged males (40 percent compared to 26 percent). However, the poverty rate for elderly persons living in families is about the same (one-tenth) regardless of their sex.

Unrelated individuals comprise about three-fifths of all low-income aged persons compared to only one-eighth of those under 65 years. The family status of low-income aged persons varies by sex. Aged females below the low-income level are more likely to be living alone or with nonrelatives than aged males. About 73 percent of aged females below the low-income level are unrelated individuals compared to 34 percent for aged males.

About 17 percent of aged men below the low-income level work at some time during the year compared to 36 percent of the elderly males above the low-income level. For women, the comparable figures are 7 percent and 15 percent, respectively. A greater proportion of the aged poor than the nonpoor, regardless of sex, report illness or disability as their main reason for not working.

CHARACTERISTICS OF ASSISTANCE PAYMENTS RECIPIENTS

The characteristics of recipients of assistance payments are essentially those described above for the poor with respect to their geographic distribution, residence, and educational attainment. They differ, however, in matter of degree in other respects, such as racial composition, work status, families headed by females, and age composition, primarily because of the restrictive provisions of eligibility requirements of state and local assistance payments programs described more fully in Chapters 3 and 4. The AFDC program limits eligibility to families with children, with a preponderance of single-headed, largely female families. It omits childless couples and two-parent families with children where one of the parents is employed. The SSI program limits eligibility to aged, blind, and disabled, omitting nondisabled, or partially or temporarily disabled poor individuals under age 65. Moreover, the AFDC program, as well as most state GA programs, places income and resources limits below the poverty index level, except in a few state programs, thus excluding other low-income individuals and families with income or resources above the federal or state standards but at or below the poverty index.

Of the more than 16.8 million persons receiving money payments in 1975, two-thirds or 11.4 million were recipients of AFDC; 976,000 million received GA, and 4.4 million received SSI payments. Immediately prior to the start of the SSI program on January 1, 1974, 1.8 million persons received Old Age Assistance (OAA), 77,900 received Aid to the Blind (AB), and 1.2 million received Aid to the Permanently and Totally Disabled (APTD) assistance; thus, the SSI caseload initially amounted to over three million persons.

AFDC Families

Of the 11.4 million AFDC recipients in 1975, eight million were children in 3,555,000 families. The *Findings of the 1973 AFDC Study* conducted by the National Center For Social Statistics of the Social and Rehabilitation Service, of the D/HEW[7] revealed the average AFDC family to be a mother and two children, a median of 3.6 persons. One-third of the families had only one child recipient; three-fourths of AFDC families lived in a metropolitan area and about 20 percent lived in a city of one million or more. Over 13 percent of families lived in public housing; three-fourths in rented or private housing.

Whites and blacks were represented evenly on AFDC rolls. Spanish-speaking recipients were over 13 percent. American Indians and other minorities constituted the small remainder of AFDC families.

Families with a father at home were in the minority: 17 percent of all AFDC families. Three-fourths of the families were headed by natural or adoptive mothers of the children. The remaining households were headed by a stepfather and other unrelated males and females. Absence of the father because of marital breakup was the major reason that children received AFDC payments. Close to half the families had one or more illegitimate children. A majority of families had young children. The youngest child in six of ten families was under six years of age. Some children worked to augment family income. Most children ages 14 to 20 were enrolled in school. Children ages 18 to 20 who received AFDC were required to be students or take vocational or technical training.

Half of the mothers were under 30 years of age; only 11.7 percent were age 45 and over. Over one in four mothers graduated from high school; 12.6 percent of mothers had not completed the eighth grade; and few attended college. One in six mothers worked full or part time. Close to half of the women were needed as full-time homemakers to care for their children. Less than 10 percent were incapacitated. The usual occupation of women was service work as waitress or beautician. Twenty-two percent had never been employed.

About half the fathers in the AFDC household were middle-aged or older; their median age was 41 years; and close to one-fourth were between the ages of 30 and 40. About two-thirds had not graduated from high school and, of these, almost half had not completed the eighth grade. Only 17 percent were high school graduates while few attended college. About four in ten fathers were in the labor force; three in ten were looking for work. One-half of the fathers were incapacitated. Their usual occupation was blue collar work, such as craftsman, operative, or laborer. Over half were in this latter category of laborer.

Forty percent of AFDC families were receiving assistance for 18 months or less. However, ten percent were on assistance for four years and upwards. Their income other than assistance payments was principally earnings, contributions from absent fathers, and social security benefits. One-third of the families had one or more members registered for the WIN program. Most families received social services, medical care, and food stamps for which they were eligible automatically.

Aged, Blind, and Disabled

The characteristics of the aged, blind, and permanently and totally disabled receiving assistance payments are, by and large, static and stable. They do not vary year by year, are not subject to abrupt change in their personal, social, and economic condition. The SSI program assumed the payments for state aged, blind, and disabled caseloads and the new national standards for eligibility became applicable to new applicants. It is reasonable to assume that the demographic characteristics of the new would differ only slightly from the old. The following is a description of their characteristics in 1970–1971, developed by the National Center for Social Statistics.[8]

AGED.   The median age of the 1.8 million aged recipients is 75.5 years, two-thirds of whom are white females. More than half of the recipients are widowed; 70 percent have one or more living children. Most recipients live with their spouses, children, or other relatives; a minority live alone. Ten percent of the aged are in institutions. Their educational level is low, averaging completion of only six grades. Two-thirds were previously employed, those in cities doing service or unskilled blue collar work, those in rural areas as farmers or farm laborers. The average aged recipient received maintenance payments for five and one-half years, one-fourth received payments for ten years or longer. Two-thirds of the recipients received income from other sources, largely from social security benefits and other pensions. All are enrolled in the medical assistance program. Their participation in the food stamp program for which they are automatically eligible is low: only two of every ten recipients.

DISABLED.   The 1.2 million disabled recipients average 55 years of age, over half of them are female, two-thirds are white. Three of every ten recipients are married or widowed. They all suffer from such severe, permanent disabilities as heart conditions, circulatory ailments, mental illness, and developmental disabilities. Nine of every ten recipients, however, are not confined to bed. More than three-fourths live with their spouses, children, or other relatives; the others are institutionalized. Their average level of education is also low, completing only seven grades of schooling. Two-thirds were previously employed in blue collar or service work. One of every ten recipients has received maintenance payments for ten years or longer. On the average, they received payments for two and one-half years. One of every three recipients receives income other than from their maintenance payments, largely from social security benefits. Only 25 percent participate in food stamp programs; all are covered by the medical assistance program.

BLIND.   The 77,900 blind recipients average 60 years of age, a majority are white females. Eighteen percent were blind at birth; 15 percent are totally blind. Fourteen percent are confined in their own homes or are institutionalized. One-half are married or widowed, with one or more living children. One of every five recipients live alone, except for those in institutions; the remainder live with their spouses, children, or relatives. They average seven grades of schooling. More than half were previously employed in blue collar or service work. They receive maintenance payments for an average of six years or longer. Half of them have other income than maintenance payments, largely from social security benefits and other earnings. Under 20 percent participate in the food stamp program; as with the other adult categories, all are eligible for the medical assistance program.

General Assistance Recipients

The close to one million GA recipients are a diverse group of poor. Their common bond is that they are in need of financial assistance but do not qualify for maintenance payments under the AFDC or SSI programs. They all require emergency aid. They receive cash, or vendor payments are made in their behalf to suppliers of goods and services. The GA program is supported by states, counties, and cities, not the federal government. Since their eligibility for aid varies by state and within some states by county or city, it is difficult to provide a meaningful characterization beyond this point. In some jurisdictions, recipients are families with children whose parents are employed or employable, needing emergency assistance. In others the parents must be unemployable to receive aid. Childless couples, poor and unemployable, facing an emergency, are covered. Individuals temporarily unemployed are included in some jurisdictions. Persons with a permanent but partial disability are not included. However, persons with a temporary illness or in an accident are covered in some states. Children ineligible for the AFDC program are covered if they have a special medical or dietary need which their parents cannot afford to provide. Children who require foster care not covered under another program are eligible.

The turnover of cases is rapid and the numbers and types of recipients for general assistance fluctuate with the unforeseen emergency conditions which they face. State and local agencies move to transfer recipients to federally funded assistance programs whenever and wherever possible to reduce the financial load which the states and localities bear.

CHARACTERISTICS OF NONRECIPIENT CHILDREN UNDER CHILD WELFARE SUPERVISION

Of the estimated three million children under child welfare supervision, about 400,000 were children from middle and upper income classes. They are delinquents, abused, neglected, abandoned children, unmarried mothers, and pregnant girls, or children who have lost their parents who have become known to state and local agencies and/or are placed under the supervision of such agencies by courts for protection and adequate care. One of every ten children live in their own homes with parents or with other relations, the others are placed in foster or adoptive homes, in child care institutions, group homes, or in other independent arrangements.

CHARACTERISTICS OF CUBAN REFUGEES

Cuban political policies determined the socioeconomic character of the 600,000 Cuban refugees in this country. The Castro government only permitted individuals and families to leave who were deemed undesirable, unproductive, nonresponsive, unsympathetic, or dangerous to the Cuban regime. They also included Cubans who escaped illegally. Poor, aged, and ill persons and their dependents as well as middle- and upper-class professionals, for example, doctors, lawyers, teachers, dentists, and nurses arrived in Miami from Cuba, all with no resources, having been required to leave all their worldly possessions in Cuba. They were a mixed group with common problems of language barriers, no funds, a need to be acclimatized to a new land and new culture, many with few marketable skills, lacking in education, and in poor physical and mental health. Children and aged persons predominated; however, with the assistance provided, eight out of ten refugees in a period of a few years have become fully self-supporting, taxpaying, contributing members of the communities in which they live.

CHARACTERISTICS OF THE MEDICALLY INDIGENT (NONRECIPIENTS)

Most state medical assistance programs include individuals and families who are eligible for but do not receive payments, or whose income and resources exceed the state's standards for eligibility for such payments but insufficient to meet the costs of medical care. Over 2.2 million persons are in the former group, that is, those eligible but do not receive maintenance payments, and over 7.2 million are in the latter group.

CHARACTERISTICS OF NONRECIPIENT FOOD STAMP RECIPIENTS

Over ten million persons who do not receive maintenance payments are recipients of the food stamp program. Most are poor or near-poor, a large proportion of whom are unemployed, or working but with an income below the national food stamp monthly income standard of $540 for a family of four. Their level of economic independence is generally higher than public assistance recipients; they are better able to meet other household needs through their own income and resources but are not able to meet their food expenditures. They include aged persons living in their own households, with relatives or in nursing homes, families without children, those with children and working parents or employable parents, and single adults who are unemployed or unemployable.

CHARACTERISTICS OF NEEDY AND DISADVANTAGED BUT NONRECIPIENTS OF THE PUBLIC WELFARE SYSTEM

Who are the 12 million persons who fall into the gap between the 37 million *potential* low-income and other persons who theoretically can benefit from the public welfare system and do not, and the 25 million recipients who do receive money, services, and food from the system? The varied and complex answers to this question reveal the varied and complex characteristics of the individuals and families as well as the complexities of the public welfare system itself and the issues surrounding it.

The statistical basis for the poverty index has already been described. Included in the 12 million nonbeneficiaries are low-income persons who do not regard themselves as poor, are able to live independently, *do not need or want* public welfare assistance or services.

Needy, disabled, and aged persons able to benefit from public welfare assistance or services are *not aware* of them or their legal entitlement for them, despite the widespread out-reach and information programs of public and voluntary agencies and the public media.

Needy, disabled, and aged persons are *ineligible* to benefit from public welfare assistance or services because of narrow, categorical rules, regulations, and administrative limitations and barriers imposed by federal and state laws. Some examples: low-income childless couples, two-parent families with children with an employed father, and partially disabled poor individuals are all ineligible for federally supported maintenance assistance; employable parents must first register for work training and employment under the Food Stamp Act to receive food stamps, or to receive AFDC assistance under the Social Security Act; in some states, emergency aid under the GA program is unavailable to persons who can work.

Not all public welfare programs and services are available universally or adequately in all political jurisdictions, although the Social Security Act and other laws make this a condition for federal financial participation. An example, day care services in some localities are not provided because state social services budgets are insufficient. Another example is the prevailing inability of state and local public welfare agencies to employ enough social work staff to serve all potentially eligible clients, as will be discussed in Chapter 6, makes it impossible to meet their needs for counseling. A third example: the small monthly assistance payments for AFDC families in some states is grossly inadequate to meet their basic needs and discourages potentially eligible families from applying to state public welfare agencies. A fourth example: in some states needed dental services are unavailable to medical assistance eligibles because it is not one of the prescribed medical services under the state plan.

Finally, ethical and moral issues central to political decisions about the public welfare system question whether and to what extent the government should or could meet *all* the needs of this group or whether American society would not be better served by having all its people meet their own needs through their own resources, independent of government intervention. There are sharply divergent attitudes: some argue for a universal public social welfare system with entitlement of all 215 million Americans, others argue to dismantle the present public welfare system. The American character for compromise would indicate a changed system somewhere between these two extremes. On the one hand, extending the public welfare system to reach a high proportion of the 12 million potentials not now being served—and improving the system for the 25 million now being served—but imposing ethical mechanisms first, to assure that all 37 million disadvantaged persons utilize their own resources to meet their individual needs to live independent and productive lives as a precondition for entry into the system and, second, that the objectives of the system will be to recondition, rehabilitate, and prepare individuals to return to independent living to their maximum ability with minimum dependence upon others. This is a quandary for the future and bears further discussion that can be found in Chapter 10.

NOTES

1. Studies in Public Welfare Paper No. 1. Public Income Transfers Programs: the Incidence of Multiple Benefits and the Issues Raised by their Receipt, James Storey, A Study of the Subcommittee on Fiscal Policy of the Joint Economic Committee, U.S. Congress. U.S. Government Printing Office, Washington, D.C., April 10, 1972.

2. *The Washington Post.* May 8, 1974, p. 1.

3. Applications and Case Dispositions for Public Assistance. April–June 1975. DHEW Publication No. (SRS) 76-03109 NCSS Report A-12. Office of Information Sciences, NCSS, SRS, DHEW, Washington, D.C., October 1975.

4. Characteristics of the Population Below the Poverty Level: 1975, Bureau of the Census, Department of Commerce, Washington, D.C., Ibid., Table 2. Persons below 125% of the Poverty Level by Family Status, Sex of Head and Race and Spanish Origin: 1959 to 1975, p. 18.

5. *The Washington Post.* July 10, 1976.

6. This material is abstracted from Current Population Reports, Characteristics of the Low Income Population 1972 Bureau of the Census, Department of Commerce Series P-60, No. 91, Washington, D.C., December 1973.

7. DHEW Publication No. (SRS) 74-03764 NCSS Report AFDC-1 (73) Washington, D.C., June 1974.

8. Burnside, B. *Who are the recipients of public assistance.* Washington, D.C.: National Center for Social Statistics, SRS, DHEW, Reprinted from Rehabilitation Record, May–June 1971, July 20, 1971.

PUBLIC WELFARE PROGRAMS WITHIN THE FEDERAL/STATE SYSTEM: INCOME MAINTENANCE PROGRAMS

This and the next chapter describe the ten core programs which comprise the public welfare system: their objectives, legal basis, historical background, organizational responsibilities, case-loads, and costs, eligibility factors, services and benefits, and principal methods and procedures:

    I. *Income Maintenance Programs*
        Aid To Families With Dependent Children (AFDC)
        Supplemental Security Income (SSI)
        General Assistance (GA)
    II. *Social Services Programs*
        Social Services to Individuals and Families—Title XX
        Child Welfare Services
  III. *In Kind Programs*
        Health: Medical Assistance (Medicaid)
        Food: (Food Stamp)
        Manpower Training and Employment: Work Incentive (WIN)
  IV. *Special Population Group Programs*
        Cuban Refugee Assistance
        Repatriated U.S. Nationals Assistance

The four-part classification of programs is indicative of the common objectives which programs share: the three income maintenance programs have the objective of maintaining eligible poor individuals and families to cope with their daily financial needs for the essentials of food, clothing, housing, and other necessities. The social services programs have the objective to meet the nonfinancial needs of children, families, and adults to help move themselves to a better level of personal and social independence to the maximum of their capabilities; if possible, to achieve self-support and economic independence. For children, the objectives are to insure their normal growth and development and provide them with protection and preventive services to give them an environment of security and opportunity for their immediate and future benefit. The in-kind programs have the objectives of meeting special needs to supplement the other basic programs of support and, through these means, provide beneficiaries with opportunities for self-care, self-support, and independent functioning, socially, psychologically, and economically. The special population group programs provide Cuban refugees and, in 1975 Vietnamese and Cambodian refugees, and repatriated U.S. nationals, support during a traumatic period in their lives to help them overcome obstacles towards their return to normal (middle-class?) functioning under American standards.

The analysis of the benefits and services available under the ten programs (Table 3.1) show them not to be mutually exclusive, that is, benefits and services under one program may be available under other programs in the system. In some cases, the benefits may be available to the same groups of children, families, or adults, as, for example, social services provided AFDC children under the Title XX social services program, the child welfare services program, as well as the medical assistance program. The point of entry of a child into the public welfare network may be one determinant of the primary program under which services are provided. The funding source, whether federal, state, or local government may be another determinant. As will be discussed in chapter 7 on financing, state and local agencies seek to shift caseloads to those which have the most favorable federal matching. Referrals between and among welfare programs are common, and different programs participate in efforts to resolve the recipient's problems. Moreover, referrals from/to programs outside the public welfare network help to create a patchwork of interrelationships on behalf of, if not sometimes in conflict with or duplication of, the steps taken to reach the publicly desired objectives sought. These will be discussed more in detail later in Chapter 9 public welfare relationships.

INCOME MAINTENANCE PROGRAMS

There are three major programs of cash payments to low-income individuals and families administered by federal, state, and local governments and the territories as part of the public welfare network: Aid to Families with Dependent Children Program (AFDC), Supplemental Security Income Program (SSI), and the General Assistance Program (GA). Cash payments are also made to Cuban Refugees and to some repatriated U.S. citizens. These will be referred to separately under the description of these two special assistance programs.

There are, in addition, other governmental cash payment programs to special groups of low-income persons not part of the public welfare system which relate to the subject.[1] These are primarily of two types: (1) those programs which are "income tested," that is, are available to persons who meet financial eligibility requirements of specified income and resources limits; and (2) those programs which are not income tested but have other nonfinancial eligibility requirements which all persons, poor and nonpoor alike must meet. In the first group are veterans pensions programs administered by the Veterans Administration and the program of General Assistance to Indians administered by the Bureau of Indian Affairs, U.S. Department of the Interior. The second group includes (1) the Old-Age, Survivors, and Disability Insurance Program (OASDI) administered by the Social Security Administration (2) the Railroad Retirement Benefits and the Railroad Unemployment Insurance programs administered by the Railroad Retirement Board, (3) the Federal/State Unemployment Compensation program ad-

Table 3.1 Benefits and Services Under Public Welfare Programs

	AFDC	SSI	GA	Title XX	Child Welfare	Medicaid	Food Stamps	WIN	Refugee Assistance	U.S. Repatriates
Adoption services				x	x					
Cash payments to meet basic needs	x	x	x						x	
Chore services				x						
Community development				x					x	
Day care for adults				x					x	
Day care for children				x	x				x	
Education-related services				x	x			x	x	
Emergency assistance: cash	x	x	x						x	x
services				x	x				x	
Emergency shelter for children				x	x				x	
Family planning services				x	x	x		x	x	
Food coupons							x		x	
Home management				x	x			x	x	
Homemaker services				x	x			x	x	
Housing improvement services				x	x			x	x	
Information and referral	x	x	x	x	x	x	x	x	x	x
Institutional services				x	x	x	x	x	x	x
Legal services				x	x			x	x	x
Manpower training and employment services				x				x	x	

Table 3.1 (Continued)

	AFDC	SSI	GA	Title XX	Child Welfare	Medicaid	Food Stamps	WIN	Refugee Assistance	U.S. Repatriates
Medical services			x	x	x	x		x	x	
Nutrition services				x	x	x		x	x	
Payments for foster care for children	x		x	x						
Payments for foster care for adults				x						
Payments for housing repairs	x									
Payments for transportation and relocation								x	x	x
Protective services for adults				x					x	
Protective services for children				x	x				x	
Psychological services				x	x	x		x	x	x
Referrals for VR services	x	x	x	x	x	x	x	x	x	
Social services counseling				x	x			x	x	
Special services for the blind				x	x				x	x

ministered by the U.S. Department of Labor and state employment security agencies, (4) the Trade Readjustment Allowances program administered by the U.S. International Trade Commission, (5) the Veterans Compensation, Dependency and Idemnity program of the Veterans Administration, and (6) the program of Special Benefits for Disabled Coal Miners of the Department of Labor.

Finally, reference must be made to the indirect, but very real, impact of the federal and state income tax systems upon the financial needs of low-income persons receiving public welfare cash payments. Tax rates to exclude the poor, allowances for special groups, such as the aged and blind, personal exemptions allowed and other exemptions and exclusions are of material benefit, although not direct cash payments per se, to those poor with earnings and income other than from public assistance. This is discussed more fully in Chapter 9.

AID TO FAMILIES WITH DEPENDENT CHILDREN PROGRAM

The objective of this program is to encourage the care of dependent children in their own homes or in the homes of relatives by enabling each state to furnish financial assistance to needy dependent children and to the parents or relatives with whom they are living to help maintain and strengthen family life and to help such parents or relatives to attain or retain capability for self-support.

Background

This program was enacted in 1935 to provide financial assistance to needy children under age 16 who were deprived of parental support because of the death, incapacity, or absence from the home of a parent. Amendments in 1939 extended the age to under 18 if the child of ages 16 or 17 was regularly attending school. The federal requirement for such school attendance was dropped by an amendment effective July 1, 1957. Amendments extended coverage to a needy parent or other relative with whom a dependent child is living (1950), to a second parent (incapacitated or spouse of an unemployed parent, if the state elects to include the unemployed father) when both are in the home (1962), and to children age 18 and under age 21 when attending school, or college, or a vocational or technical training course (1964–65). Amendments in 1961 permitted states to assist families in which the father was in the home and unemployed if the state so elected, and extended coverage to children placed in foster homes following removal from AFDC homes through court action (at first permissive, made mandatory in 1969). A 1967 amendment provided federal participation in emergency assistance to families with children.

In 1962 amendments required states to take into account work-related expenses in determining eligibility and amount of payment and permitted states to disregard certain income and earnings to be conserved for future identifiable needs of children. From July 1, 1965, to June 30, 1969, a state could disregard $50 a month of income earned by a child under age 18 but no more than $150 a month per family. Effective July 1, 1969, states were required to disregard all earnings of a dependent child who was a full-time student or a part-time student not fully employed plus the first $30 and one-third of the remainder of monthly earnings of other individuals included in a recipient family in determining amount of payment. This disregard did not apply to determining eligibility of an applicant who had not received AFDC within four months preceding the application.

A 1950 amendment required states to notify appropriate law enforcement officials when assistance is provided for children deserted or abandoned by a parent.

The programs were initiated in 40 states in 1936 and 1937; in 10 states between 1938 and 1945 and in one state, Guam, Puerto Rico, and the Virgin Islands between 1950 and 1959. In January 1976, 26 states, the District of Columbia, and Guam included assistance to families with unemployed fathers in their AFDC programs, and 23 states, the District of Columbia, Puerto Rico, and the Virgin Islands had programs of emergency assistance (under title IV-A) to needy families with children.

Administering Agencies

The Office of Family Assistance, Social Security Administration of the Department of Health, Education and Welfare administers federal grants to states. The AFDC program is administered by a state agency through district or county offices in 30 states, the District of Columbia, and the three territories and administered by local agencies with state supervision in 20 states. The program is statewide in all states.

Caseloads

In December, 1975, the average caseload was 3,485,000 families with 8,078,000 children and total of 11,328,000 recipients. Table 3.2 shows the distribution of the AFDC caseload for that month by state, the District of Columbia and the territories.[2] It is significant to an understanding of the program that one-half of the caseload and over 60 percent of payments to recipients are in nine states: California, Georgia, Illinois, Massachusetts, New Jersey, New York, Ohio, Pennsylvania, and Texas. The average monthly payment per family was $231.94. Five states made the highest average payment:

Massachusetts	$381.94
New York	356.55
Hawaii	338.53
Wisconsin	298.07
Michigan	287.04

The five states with the lowest average payments were:

Mississippi	$48.61
South Carolina	89.77
Alabama	94.58
Georgia	100.48
Tennessee	104.72

The five states which made the highest total payments aggregating over 52 percent of total payments were:

New York	$131.5 million
California	122.9
Illinois	64.3
Michigan	59.7
Pennsylvania	55.6

The five states which made the lowest total payments were:

Wyoming	$401 million
Nevada	815
Montana	1.068
Alaska	1.094
North Dakota	1.114

The Unemployed-Father (UF) segment of AFDC in December, 1975 averaged 120,000 families with 307,000 children and a total of 527,000 recipients. Table 3.3 shows the distribution

Table 3.2 Aid to Families With Dependent Children: Recipients of Money Payments and Amount of Payments, by State, December 1975

(Includes Nonmedical Vendor Payments, Unemployed Father Segment, and AFDC-Foster Care Data)

STATE	NUMBER OF FAMILIES	NUMBER OF RECIPIENTS		PAYMENTS TO RECIPIENTS TOTAL AMOUNT	AVERAGE PER		PERCENTAGE NOV 1975 IN--		PERCENTAGE CHANGE FROM DEC 1974 IN--	
		TOTAL (6)	CHILDREN	TOTAL AMOUNT	FAMILY	RECIPIENT	NO. OF RECIP.	AMOUNT	NO. OF RECIP.	AMOUNT
TOTAL #	3,555,007	11,386,681	8,088,539	$824,559,006	$231.94	$72.41	0.4	2.4	3.5	14.3
ALABAMA	52,132	166,498	123,580	4,930,593	94.58	29.61	*	-0.1	5.3	5.7
ALASKA	3,864	10,621	7,882	1,493,849	283.09	102.99	1.8	1.5	-8.4	0.3
ARIZONA	20,636	68,328	51,295	2,773,770	134.41	40.60	0.3	0.1	-3.1	8.6
ARKANSAS	34,472	108,557	80,485	4,252,838	123.37	39.18	-0.1	-0.1	-9.3	10.4
CALIFORNIA (ANNOTATIONS)	405,104	1,428,848	983,957	122,656,777	264.15	85.98	-0.7	-0.2	-0.1	20.3
COLORADO	31,762	94,984	66,857	6,590,500	207.37	69.39	-3.9	-4.0	-1.7	0.6
CONNECTICUT	42,057	134,673	97,177	11,076,141	263.36	82.24	-0.3	-0.3	0.5	10.3
DELAWARE	10,302	31,695	22,938	2,001,415	194.27	63.15	0.4	1.0	-0.5	20.9
DIST OF COLUMBIA	32,359	103,628	74,651	7,566,729	233.84	73.02	-0.6	-1.1	0.7	5.3
FLORIDA	80,990	251,571	187,591	10,077,824	124.43	40.06	0.7	-1.1	-3.4	20.0
GEORGIA	102,034	309,470	229,359	10,332,711	100.48	33.39	-1.7	-0.1	-11.3	-7.7
GUAM	821	3,341	2,620	165,612	201.72	49.57	-0.1	1.8	0.6	17.4
HAWAII	16,552	54,120	37,288	5,603,349	338.53	103.54	1.5	1.2	13.5	26.5
IDAHO	6,588	19,657	13,846	1,643,779	249.51	83.62	1.1	3.5	3.0	20.9
ILLINOIS (ANNOTATIONS)	230,486	803,269	577,959	64,202,231	278.90	80.03	0.4	1.9	5.9	11.9
INDIANA	57,352	176,291	126,767	9,613,694	167.63	54.53	0.4	0.3	10.8	27.4
IOWA	29,867	94,488	64,628	8,245,857	276.09	87.27	-0.3	1.2	13.8	15.2
KANSAS	25,022	74,060	54,496	5,551,003	221.85	74.95	-2.9	-8.1	13.0	27.0
KENTUCKY	62,745	197,914	136,704	11,210,893	176.67	56.60	2.0	1.6	25.4	26.7
LOUISIANA	67,737	232,557	174,763	8,282,170	122.27	35.61	-0.3	0.4	-0.7	22.8
MAINE	# 21,075	68,205	49,006	3,623,105	171.91	53.12	-1.4	-0.7	-14.8	-9.1
MARYLAND	70,080	218,212	156,419	12,862,553	183.83	59.04	1.1	1.5	1.8	13.5
MASSACHUSETTS (ANNOTATIONS)	113,673	350,881	249,320	43,416,342	381.94	120.98	0.3	32.5	2.5	11.3
MICHIGAN	208,143	675,629	471,768	59,744,697	287.04	88.43	1.3	-0.8	5.2	16.1
MINNESOTA	44,610	130,008	91,541	11,859,566	265.85	91.22	1.1	1.7	5.1	17.8
MISSISSIPPI	55,081	186,196	143,525	2,677,422	48.61	14.38	0.1	*	0.9	1.5
MISSOURI	87,619	273,126	197,524	12,270,060	140.04	44.92	-0.6	0.3	6.1	23.3
MONTANA	6,481	19,694	14,388	1,068,010	164.79	54.23	-0.8	0.5	-12.7	-13.6
NEBRASKA	11,879	37,037	26,552	2,452,433	206.45	66.22	0.6	0.6	-3.1	15.1
NEVADA	5,424	15,810	11,492	814,963	150.25	51.55	5.7	1.7	9.9	19.0

NEW HAMPSHIRE	8,810	27,176	18,883	2,029,347	230.35	74.67	0.1	-0.7	5.4	5.2
NEW JERSEY	135,708	451,873	323,018	37,373,276	275.39	82.71	-0.3	0.5	2.4	5.9
NEW MEXICO	18,792	60,025	43,933	2,608,039	138.78	43.45	0.2	0.9	-1.9	1.6
NEW YORK	360,696	1,230,410	861,319	131,457,327	356.55	106.84	0.6	2.6	3.0	9.9
NORTH CAROLINA	67,742	191,983	139,498	10,530,159	155.45	54.85	0.8	0.8	16.3	19.7
NORTH DAKOTA	4,508	13,589	9,872	1,114,403	247.21	82.01	-0.8	-1.6	0.1	26.5
OHIO	185,346	577,721	397,190	37,857,365	204.25	65.53	1.1	1.4	9.6	32.6
OKLAHOMA	27,670	88,350	66,964	5,241,696	189.44	59.33	-1.9	-2.0	-8.8	-3.1
OREGON	37,875	110,176	73,936	9,373,133	247.48	85.07	3.4	4.6	9.5	37.1
PENNSYLVANIA	194,592	637,567	437,042	55,602,098	205.74	87.21	0.5	2.7	0.6	16.9
PUERTO RICO	# 44,487	# 208,064	# 151,881	# 2,004,673	45.06	9.63	-1.4	-1.3	-11.6	-9.1
RHODE ISLAND	16,023	53,829	37,602	4,152,883	246.86	77.15	0.2	1.1	5.2	10.2
SOUTH CAROLINA	44,577	138,591	102,442	4,001,687	89.77	28.87	-0.2	0.6	3.7	11.5
SOUTH DAKOTA	8,216	25,046	18,403	1,686,316	205.25	67.33	0.1	0.5	2.6	7.2
TENNESSEE	69,728	212,003	155,659	7,301,812	104.72	34.44	0.3	0.4	6.4	11.9
TEXAS	108,481	360,951	267,797	11,800,914	108.78	32.69	-0.6	-0.5	-7.2	-2.4
UTAH	13,133	37,389	25,843	3,145,236	239.49	84.12	1.3	6.4	12.2	27.9
VERMONT	7,139	23,988	15,734	1,949,520	273.08	81.27	1.1	1.7	17.3	25.1
VIRGIN ISLANDS	# 1,121	# 3,874	# 3,176	# 145,364	129.67	37.52	-1.2	-1.2	-6.4	-4.2
VIRGINIA	59,976	180,201	129,096	11,549,782	192.57	64.09	0.3	0.5	4.3	10.0
WASHINGTON	48,295	144,175	94,815	12,416,478	257.10	86.12	1.3	2.6	-0.3	13.3
WEST VIRGINIA (E)	22,615	74,252	50,769	3,784,604	167.35	50.97	0.5	0.7	9.3	7.1
WISCONSIN	60,626	181,728	128,639	18,070,950	298.07	99.44	1.9	1.9	15.6	19.2
WYOMING	2,284	6,412	4,668	400,974	175.56	62.53	-1.8	-0.4	-7.0	14.2

* INCREASE OR DECREASE OF LESS THAN 0.05 PERCENT

(E) ESTIMATED DATA

& INCLUDES AS RECIPIENTS THE CHILDREN AND ONE OR BOTH PARENTS OR ONE CARETAKER RELATIVE OTHER THAN A PARENT IN FAMILIES IN WHICH THE REQUIREMENTS OF SUCH ADULTS WERE CONSIDERED IN DETERMINING THE AMOUNT OF ASSISTANCE.

INCOMPLETE. DATA FOR FOSTER CARE NOT REPORTED BY PUERTO RICO AND THE VIRGIN ISLANDS; CASE DATA FOR FOSTER CARE NOT REPORTED BY MAINE.

Source: Public Assistance Statistics. December, 1975. DHEW Publication No. (SRS) 76-03100 NCSS Report A-2

Table 3.3 Aid to Families with Dependent Children, Unemployed Father Segment: Recipients of Money Payments and Amount of Payments, by State, December 1975 (includes nonmedical vendor payments)

STATE	NUMBER OF FAMILIES	NUMBER OF RECIPIENTS ---	
		TOTAL (&)	CHILDREN
TOTAL	131,546	577,294	332,691
CALIFORNIA (ANNOTATIONS)	38,551	161,790	98,646
COLORADO	1,692	6,979	3,693
CONNECTICUT	774	3,392	1,921
DELAWARE	136	566	298
DIST OF COLUMBIA	217	1,002	622
GUAM	9	46	30
HAWAII	382	1,719	974
ILLINOIS (ANNOTATIONS)	13,708	66,479	39,610
IOWA	649	2,712	1,436
KANSAS	263	1,188	662
KENTUCKY	4,297	19,657	11,339
MARYLAND	1,680	7,233	4,007
MASSACHUSETTS (ANNOTATIONS)	4,296	18,710	10,820
MICHIGAN	16,225	75,330	43,069
MINNESOTA	1,282	5,662	3,162
MISSOURI	44	214	126
MONTANA	87	387	213
NEBRASKA	40	203	124
NEW YORK	6,358	29,044	16,414
OHIO	18,529	77,823	41,886
OREGON	4,207	17,439	9,141
PENNSYLVANIA	5,953	25,406	13,598
RHODE ISLAND	597	2,686	1,518
UTAH	937	4,533	2,660
VERMONT	1,352	6,042	3,413
WASHINGTON	4,085	16,890	9,003
WEST VIRGINIA	1,745	7,767	4,951
WISCONSIN (E)	3,451	16,395	9,355

\# Data not available

X Average payment not computed on base of fewer than 50 families or recipients; percentage change on fewer than 100 recipients.

(E)Estimated data

& Includes as recipients the children and one or both parents or one caretaker relative other than a parent in families in which the requirements of such adults were considered in determining the amount of assistance.

Source: Public Assistance Statistics. December, 1975. DHEW Publication No. (SRS) 76–03100 NCSS Report A-2.

| ---- PAYMENTS TO RECIPIENTS -------- | | | --- PERCENTAGE CHANGE FROM --- | | | |
| TOTAL AMOUNT | ---- AVERAGE PER ---- | | NOV 1975 IN-- | | DEC 1974 IN-- | |
	FAMILY	RECIPIENT	NO. OF RECIP.	AMOUNT	NO. OF RECIP.	AMOUNT
$43,470,312	$330.46	$75.30	5.8	8.2	37.2	51.3
11,501,609	298.35	71.09	5.4	5.4	18.2	29.9
488,147	288.50	69.95	-7.0	-8.3	10.0	21.4
273,750	353.68	80.70	11.8	8.4	#	#
34,427	253.14	60.83	7.0	3.2	52.2	71.8
69,520	320.37	69.38	4.8	6.6	6.0	15.2
2,577	X	X	X	X	X	X
163,230	427.30	94.96	3.3	1.5	-25.3	-16.2
4,826,072	352.06	72.60	0.3	3.3	20.1	20.7
243,400	375.04	89.75	19.3	15.6	297.1	310.9
73,564	279.71	61.92	-4.0	-12.5	70.2	80.0
1,168,299	271.89	59.43	15.0	16.8	#	#
411,913	245.19	56.95	19.5	20.5	98.8	123.7
2,022,698	470.83	108.11	5.6	37.3	36.9	49.0
6,654,413	410.13	88.34	8.4	8.9	42.5	59.9
453,320	353.60	80.06	17.1	15.6	37.7	56.8
8,821	X	41.22	92.8	101.1	X	X
23,207	266.75	59.97	156.3	124.3	#	#
10,558	X	52.01	3.0	1.5	X	X
2,671,905	420.24	92.00	7.8	9.2	49.9	59.0
4,750,909	256.40	61.05	3.1	3.9	36.9	71.9
1,299,309	308.84	74.51	12.3	13.6	2.1	19.7
2,053,601	344.97	80.83	4.6	7.7	143.0	175.5
190,445	319.00	70.90	8.2	10.3	28.3	37.1
332,275	354.62	73.30	2.0	6.5	15.8	28.9
458,582	339.19	75.90	3.5	2.9	82.5	99.3
1,463,824	358.34	86.67	15.5	26.5	-6.5	10.7
425,434	243.80	54.77	5.5	5.1	152.8	76.7
1,394,503	404.09	85.06	2.1	2.5	101.2	122.7

of the AFDC-UF caseload that month. California, Illinois, Michigan, and Ohio aggregated more than two thirds of the total number of AFDC-UF caseload and total payments.

Trends

The general upward trend in the AFDC caseload was interrupted by decreases during the war years, 1942 to 1945, and the Korean conflict, 1950 to 1953, and has been marked by a rapid rate of increase in recent years. The number of recipient families decreased to 547,000 in 1953 from 651,000 in 1950, then increased to 803,000 in 1960, 2,552,000 in 1970 and 3,555,000 in 1975 (December of each year). The total number of recipients, including children and parents or other adult relatives increased from 2,233,000 in 1950 to 9,657,000 in December 1970 and to 11,386,681 in December 1975 (Table 3.4). The number of families receiving AFDC because of the unemployment of the father increased from 48,200 in December 1961 to 131,546 in December 1975. The number of states with unemployed father programs increased from 15 in December 1961 to 26, including the District of Columbia and Guam in December 1975.

Table 3.4   The Trend in AFDC Recipients and
Payments, 1950–1975

	Number of Families (in thousands)	Payments (in millions)
1950	651	$ 556
1955	602	633
1960	803	1,055
1965	1,054	1,809
1969	1,875	3,565
1970	2,552	4,857
1971	2,918	5,653
1972	3,123	7,020
1973	3,156	7,292
1974	3,312	7,991
1975*	3,485	9,214

*1975 data from Public Assistance Statistics, January, 1976.

Source: Table 486 Public Assistance-Payments and Recipients, the
1976 Statistical Abstract of the United States. 96th Edition,
Bureau of the Census, Department of Commerce, U.S. Government Printing Office, Washington, D.C. 20402, p. 304.

The number of children under 18 years of age in the general population increased from 48 million in 1950 to 83 million in 1974. During this time the number of children receiving AFDC per 1,000 under age 18 in the population increased from 34 to 116.

Eligibility Requirements

FEDERAL REQUIREMENTS.   Children must be under age 18 (or, if regularly attending school, college, or vocational or technical training course, under 21), must be lacking parental support or care because of a parent's death, continued absence, or physical or mental incapacity (or, at state option, because the father is unemployed), and must be needy (as defined by the states). In addition, the child must be living with a parent or other relative within specified degrees of relationship by blood or marriage; except that a child is eligible for foster care payments to foster parents or to a child care institution if the child was removed from the home of parents or relatives receiving or eligible for AFDC payments following a judicial determination that continued living in the home would be contrary to the welfare of the child.

In 23 states, the District of Columbia, Puerto Rico, and the Virgin Islands a family consisting of one or more children and a parent (or both parents) or specified relative may receive emergency assistance to needy families with children (money payment, in-kind, or voucher payment) not in excess of 30 days in a 12-month period in order to avoid destitution or to provide living arrangements, if the family is without available resources for reasons other than refusal of the child or relative of employment of training for employment. In 17 of these states, the program specifically covers migrant families.

UNEMPLOYED FATHER.   Benefits may be made available to a needy child whose father is unemployed only in a state which has elected to cover such fathers and *only* when the father (1) has been unemployed for at least 30 days prior to the receipt of such benefits, (2) has not without good cause refused a bona fide offer of employment or training for employment, (3) has six or more quarters of work in any 13-calendar-quarter period ending within one year prior to the application for such benefits (or the father received, or was qualified to receive, unemployment compensation within one year prior to the application for such benefits), (4) is registered with the state employment offices, and (5) is not receiving unemployment compensation for the week in which he receives AFDC assistance.

A state's definition of an unemployed father must include any father who is employed less than 100 hours a month, or whose employment exceeds that standard for a particular month only if his work is intermittent and the excess is of a temporary nature as evidenced by the fact that he was under the 100-hour standard for the two prior months and is expected to be under the standard during the next month.

State Options in Application of Eligibility Conditions[3]

AGE OF CHILDREN.   Children under age 18 only are included in AFDC payments in twelve states and under age 21 in fifty states, the District of Columbia, and the territories. Thirty-two states include an unborn child as eligible for the AFDC payment when there are no other eligible children.

SCHOOL ATTENDANCE.   Ten states have no school attendance requirement for children under age 18.

DEPRIVATION OF PARENTAL SUPPORT.   Twenty-six states provide that unemployment of a father is an acceptable reason for deprivation of parental support.

Most states do not consider that a parent's absence from the home for employment purposes meets the condition of "continued absence" and such families are not eligible for AFDC. A large number of states accept absence because of military service as "continued absence" and families of servicemen are eligible if other eligibility conditions are met.

PERSONS INCLUDED.   Eligible children and the parents or other needy relatives caring for eligible children are included in the program. Four states (Alaska, Minnesota, Nevada, Mississippi) do not claim federal matching for the spouse when both parents are in the home (one parent must be incapacitated or, in those states so electing, unemployed). Mississippi does not provide payments for either parent, only eligible children.

Income Test

INCOME LIMIT.   Countable income may not exceed the standard of assistance defined by the states. Assistance standards vary, by size of family, living arrangements, amount of rent paid, and other family circumstances. Income limits, as reported by the states, generally represent the highest amount of countable income a family of the specified size would have at the point they become ineligible for any AFDC benefit.

The six states with the highest income limits in July, 1975 were:

	Two-person family	Three-person family	Four-person family
Hawaii	$359	$428	$497
Oregon	261	337	413
Wisconsin	292	342	403
Connecticut	278	346	403
Alaska	300	350	400
New York	272	332	400

The six jurisdictions with the lowest income limits in July, 1975 were:

	Two-person family	Three-person family	Four-person family
Puerto Rico	$ 78	$108	$132
Alabama	80	108	135
Texas	86	116	140
Louisiana	92	128	158
Florida	111	144	170
Virgin Islands	92	131	166

TREATMENT OF EARNED INCOME.   All earned income is counted in determining need except the following:

1.   Up to $5.00 of monthly income from any sources (earned or unearned). Thirteen states disregard $5.00 per month per family from income from any source; Arizona disregards $5.00 per month of income of any child with income. Forty-three states allow no disregard under this option.

2.   All earned income of children receiving AFDC who are full-time students or part-time students who are not full-time employees.

3.   Income set aside for future identifiable needs, as allowed by the state (earned or unearned). Eighteen states have provisions for conservation of a child's earnings for future identifiable needs usually with qualifying conditions in respect to the child's age, grade in school, and demonstrated capacity to benefit from higher education. Thirty-six states make no provision under this option.

4.   WIN Incentive payments.

5.   The first $30 of a household's monthly earned income and one-third of the monthly income over $30.

6.   Work expenses (as allowed by the states). In determining initial eligibility for AFDC, the earnings disregard (item 5) is not allowed unless the family has received AFDC during one of the four months preceding the application for AFDC. If the family is eligible on this basis, the earnings disregard is allowed in determining the amount of the benefit. All states are required to disregard reasonable work expenses such as mandatory payroll deductions, transportation, uniforms, and cost of child care. However, the states vary in definitions of work expenses and amounts allowed.

TREATMENT OF UNEARNED INCOME.   All unearned income other than amounts excluded above is counted in determining need except the following: (1) the value of food stamp coupons and commodity distributions, (2) relocation assistance, and (3) undergraduate grants and loans.

ACCOUNTING PERIOD.   The accounting period is monthly. Only such net income and resources as are actually expected to be available in the next month(s) are considered, except that income received at one time for services rendered over a period of time, such as income from sale of produce, may be considered available during the period in which it is earned.

Assets Test

In addition to the home, personal effects, automobile needed for transportation, and income-producing property allowed by the state, the amount of real and personal property that can be reserved for each AFDC recipient may not exceed $2,000. There is considerable variation among the states in the extent to which and conditions under which the home, income-producing property, life insurance, automobiles, and other real and personal property may be held in applying asset limits as defined by the states. The value of nonexcluded assets which may be held by an eligible recipient family varies generally from $150 to $3,000 with a median limit of $1,000.

Other Conditions

WORK REQUIREMENTS. *Participation in WIN Program.*   The needs of any recipient certified to the Department of Labor for participation in WIN who refuses without good cause (not defined except that a mother may not refuse available child care services) to accept training, or employment offered by the state employment agency or other bona fide offer of employment, will not be considered in determining the family's need for assistance.

UNEMPLOYED FATHERS.   A family is not eligible for AFDC if the father is not registered with the state employment service or has refused, without good cause, a bona fide offer of employment or training within 30 days prior to receipt of AFDC.
Twenty-five states have work requirements beyond those which are mandatory for work incentive program participants, that is, work requirements which refer to acceptance of employment regardless of whether it is offered through a WIN project or whether a WIN project is available to the recipient. In these states, a family is not eligible for AFDC if an employable parent

(one state specifies the mother) refuses suitable or available employment, usually with the condition that adequate care is available for the children. Nine states also require that a child included in the payment, usually age 16 or over and not in school, accept suitable or available employment.

ACCEPTANCE OF TRAINING OR REHABILITATION.   In addition to the mandatory federal requirements for acceptance of training offered through the WIN program, 15 states require that an incapacitated parent accept recommended medical or correctional treatment and/or rehabilitative training as an eligibility condition for receipt of AFDC by the family. Two states require that the parent accept treatment of controllable disease, or recommended hospitalization for treatment of tuberculosis or mental illness. In the latter instance, the parent's refusal does not make the children ineligible.

CITIZENSHIP.   There is no federal requirement. A noncitizen or alien is eligible if he is legally admitted for permanent residence in the United States. The Supreme Court ruled in 1971 that citizenship requirements were unconstitutional.

LIEN, RECOVERY, OR ASSIGNMENT.   There is no federal requirement. Four states have provisions for liens on property and seven file claims against the estate of recipients for recovery of all or part of assistance received by the family. Two states provide for recovery from proceeds of personal injury or damage suits. Three states require assignment to the agency of bank accounts, life insurance, or other property as a condition of eligibility.

TRANSFER OF PROPERTY.   There is no federal requirement. Twenty-eight states have requirements that the applicant has not disposed of property prior to application without fair consideration or to make himself eligible for AFDC. In seven states, the applicant is ineligible if he has disposed of property in order to qualify for assistance within one to three years prior to application; in eight states the period of time considered is five years; in twelve states no time limit is specified. Twenty-three states have no requirements in respect to prior transfers of property.

RELATIVE RESPONSIBILITY.   Each state must have a program for establishing paternity of children born out of wedlock and for securing financial support for them and for other children receiving AFDC who have been deserted by their parents or other legally liable persons. States must give prompt notice to appropriate law enforcement officials of the furnishing of AFDC to children who have been deserted or abandoned by a parent. States must cooperate with each other in locating parents against whom support actions have been filed and in securing compliance with support orders.

Twenty states require as a condition of family eligibility that the parent or, in some instances, the other relative with whom the child is living take legal action or cooperate in legal action to obtain support from the absent parent.

INSTITUTIONAL STATUS.   Federal regulations require that children must live with parents or specified relatives except that assistance must be available to otherwise eligible children receiving foster care (in foster family homes or child-care institutions) who have been removed from a relative's home as a result of a judicial determination that continuation in such home would be contrary to the child's welfare and whose placement and care are the responsibility of a public agency. Certain kinds of temporary absence, such as boarding school or hospitalization, do not violate the "living with" requirement.

RESIDENCE REQUIREMENT.   A state may not impose a residence requirement which excludes any resident of the state. This is usually defined as a person who is living in the state voluntarily with the intention of making his home there.

SUITABLE HOME PROVISIONS.   A state may not deny assistance to a child because of the conditions of the home in which he is living unless other provisions are made for adequate care of the child. Nineteen states require that the child be living in a suitable home usually defined as a home which meets agency or legal standards of health and care, or in terms of the applicant being a fit or proper person to care for children. In these states assistance is supposed to be continued until other arrangements are made for the children.

Treatment of Assets in Determining Eligibility for AFDC

ASSETS EXCLUDED IN DETERMINING ELIGIBILITY.

The Home Property Owned and Occupied by the Applicant or Beneficiary.
Thirty-four states exclude the home property in determining
eligibility without requiring a determination of value. Thirteen
states set limits on the value of the home which may be owned
by the beneficiary. The limiting values in these 13 states are
from $2,500 equity to $25,000 assessed value (in a state which
assesses at 70 percent of market value). The median value limit
in these 13 states is $7,500. In three other states no specific
value limit is set but a judgment is made as to whether the value
is reasonable, of moderate value, or whether it exceeds that of
other modest homes in the community. In the remaining state
no maximum value is placed on the home but if the value exceeds $20,000 (based on a 100 percent assessment) an evalu-
ation and recommendation is made regarding disposal.

Other Real Property. Nine states exclude all income-producing
property; two states exclude income-producing property with
values from $1,000 to $5,000; three consider all real property
within the value set for the home—from $1,500 to $10,500; five
exclude real property other than the home with values from
$225 to $1,000; 26 include the value of other real property in
the allowable reserve; and six states require that all real property
other than the home be put up for sale.

Automobile. Twenty-eight states exclude one automobile, with
varying qualifying conditions such as age or value of the car or
a judgment as to whether it is essential for transportation, and
three states exclude more than one car from consideration.

Life Insurance. Twenty-nine states exclude from $500 to $5,000
cash or face value of life insurance per eligible person in determining eligibility. One state requires that cash or loan value of
life insurance be liquidated and utilized. Ten states specifically
include the cash or loan value of life insurance in the allowable
reserve. The remaining 11 states made no reference regarding
allowance insurance.

Allowable Nonexcluded Reserve. Forty-eight states allow reserves
valued from $150 to $3,000 per family. Four of these allow
reserves of $300 to $1,550 for a family of four with $25 to $200

additional for each family member; four more of these 48 states allow additional amounts up to a family maximum.

Cash Benefits

PRIMARY DETERMINANTS OF AMOUNT OF BENEFIT.   All states are required to establish cost standards for total maintenance needs. These include in all states the basic needs, that is, the amounts needed, as determined by the states, to purchase basic maintenance items such as food, clothing, household supplies, shelter, and utilities. Cost standards, as applied to individual families, vary by family size and may vary by living arrangements, amount of rent paid, ages and sex of children, and, in most states, by inclusion of amounts for common special needs such as school supplies, telephone, and transportation. Special items, such as special diets, are included under certain conditions in some states.

Because of these variables, comparisons between states are usually made in terms of the state cost standards for basic needs. Cost standards for basic needs for a family of four recipients as reported by the states represent the highest amount that would be considered necessary for these basic elements for a family living in rented housing, with no other persons in the household, and paying the maximum amount allowed for rent.

The established cost standards for such family of 4 persons in July 1975 varied from (Hawaii) $497 to (Puerto Rico) $132 per month (Table 3.5).

In 22 states the amount of the benefit is the difference between the beneficiary family's countable income and the family's needs as determined by the full cost standard.

In 13 states, the amount of the benefit is the difference between countable income and a payment standard which is from $20 to $271 less than the states' cost standards for basic needs.

In ten states the amount of the benefit is the difference between countable income and the state's cost standard or payment standard, or the state's maximum allowable payment to a family of four, whichever is less. Four states pay a specified percentage of the difference between the cost standard and

Table 3.5   AFDC Family With Four Recipients 1/: Monthly Amount for Basic Need Standard, Payment Standard, and Largest Amount Paid in July 1975, by State

State	Need standard 1/ — Amount of basic needs			Payment standard (Amount against which income is applied)	Largest amount paid for basic needs	
	Total	Other than rent	Rent		Amount	Percent of need standard
Alabama.............	$225	$185	$40	$135	$135	60
Alaska..............	400	(2/)	(2/)	400	400	100
Arizona.............	282	201	81	282	197	70
Arkansas............	290	250	40	255	140	48
California..........	389	(2/)	(2/)	349	349	90
Colorado 3/.........	264	183	4/ 81	264	264	100
Connecticut.........	403	234	5/ 169	403	403	100
Delaware............	287	226	6/ 61	287	258	90
District of Columbia...	349	(2/)	(2/)	297	297	85
Florida.............	230	(2/)	(2/)	170	170	74
Georgia.............	227	181	46	227	153	67
Guam................	(2/)	(2/)	(2/)	(2/)	(2/)	(2/)
Hawaii..............	497	232	265	497	497	100
Idaho...............	395	309	86	344	344	87
Illinois............	5/ 317	(2/)	(2/)	317	317	100
Indiana.............	363	263	100	318	250	69
Iowa................	376	288	88	356	356	95
Kansas..............	353	228	5/ 125	353	353	100
Kentucky............	235	(2/)	(2/)	235	235	100
Louisiana...........	5/ 203	(2/)	(2/)	158	158	78
Maine...............	349	234	115	349	219	63
Maryland............	314	(2/)	(2/)	242	242	77
Massachusetts 7/....	304	220	84	304	304	100
Michigan............	399	298	5/ 6/ 101	399	399	100
Minnesota...........	385	(2/)	(2/)	385	385	100
Mississippi.........	277	227	50	277	60	22
Missouri............	370	295	4/ 75	370	150	41
Montana 3/..........	227	159	68	227	227	100
Nebraska............	328	(2/)	(2/)	328	245	75
Nevada..............	329	(2/)	(2/)	230	230	70

State					
New Hampshire	346	221	125	346	346	100
New Jersey	356	(2/)	(2/)	356	356	100
New Mexico	239	178	61	239	206	86
New York	400	258	5/ 6/ 142	400	400	100
North Carolina	200	(2/)	(2/)	200	200	100
North Dakota	347	(2/)	(2/)	347	347	100
Ohio	431	(2/)	(2/)	254	254	59
Oklahoma	264	(2/)	(2/)	264	264	100
Oregon	452	310	4/ 142	413	413	91
Pennsylvania	349	256	5/ 93	349	349	100
Puerto Rico	132	112	20	132	53	40
Rhode Island	319	233	6/ 86	319	319	100
South Carolina	217	173	44	217	117	54
South Dakota	329	226	103	329	329	100
Tennessee	217	184	33	217	132	61
Texas	187	(2/)	(2/)	140	140	75
Utah	397	289	108	306	306	77
Vermont	458	337	5/ 121	367	367	80
Virgin Islands	166	(2/)	(2/)	166	166	100
Virginia	5/ 346	(2/)	(2/)	311	311	90
Washington	5/ 370	(2/)	(2/)	370	370	100
West Virginia	332	(2/)	(2/)	249	249	75
Wisconsin	456	326	5/ 130	403	403	88
Wyoming	270	(2/)	(2/)	270	250	93

1/ Four recipients may be represented by an adult and three children, two adults and two children, or three children with no allowance for the adult caretaker. In general, standards represent one adult and three children.

2/ Data not identifiable in the consolidated standard. Guam did not report.

3/ Allowance for summer months; winter allowance higher.

4/ Utilities included in rent.

5/ Represents highest of several shelter cost areas in State. Other shelter cost areas as follows: Connecticut: $169, $113, $98; Illinois: $317, $300, $267; Kansas: $125, $76, $67, $56; Louisiana: $203, $187; Vermont: $121, $102; Virginia: $346, $293, $272; Washington: $370, $348; Wisconsin: $130, $110, $85, $80. Michigan, New York, and Pennsylvania have differentiated local shelter cost areas or pay rent as budgeted.

6/ Average rent paid up to locally established maximums.

7/ Does not include rental exceptions and quarterly grant prorated monthly.

Source: Aid to Families with Dependent Children; Standards for Basic Needs, State Maximums and other Methods of Limiting Money Payments, July 1975. DHEW Publication No. (SRS) 76–03200 NCSS Report D-2 7/75. National Center for Social Statistics, SRS, HEW. April 1976.

99

countable income, and three states pay a specified percentage of the difference between the cost standard and countable income or the state's maximum allowable payment, whichever is less.

RELATIONSHIP OF BENEFIT AMOUNT TO FAMILY SIZE.
Amounts of benefit vary by family size as cost standards include specified amounts for individual needs of each person included in the assistance unit. In some states, the maximum amount allowed for rent also varies by family size. In most states with a maximum on the money payments, the maximum is adjusted per child up to a limit on the number of children (for example, "six or more") or up to a set amount of money. Nineteen states have family maximums of from $108 to $520 for families.

RELATIONSHIP OF BENEFIT AMOUNT TO PLACE OF RESIDENCE.
Cost standards for individual needs such as food and clothing are usually applied statewide but benefit amounts for the same family size may vary between urban and nonurban areas in a state as families living in urban areas are more likely to be budgeted for the maximum rental allowance than are families in other areas of the state where rental costs are lower. Twelve states have different cost standards for rent within the state, that is, the maximum allowable amount for rent varies by urban or rural areas in some states and in a few states, each county sets its own maximum for rent. In general, the highest payable benefits to a family of four are found in the New England and Middle Atlantic states and the lowest in South Central states.

RELATIONSHIP OF BENEFIT AMOUNT TO COST OF LIVING.
Prior to 1969 there was no requirement that cost standards or benefit amounts be related to the cost of living and most states adjusted cost standards on an ad hoc basis as funds were available. Between 1961 and 1967, the median cost standard for a family of four persons increased by 12.5 percent, from $191 to $215 per month.

The 1967 amendments to the Social Security Act required states to adjust to their cost standard by July 1969 to reflect changes in living costs since the standard figures were established, and required that any maximums or amounts paid were also to be proportionately adjusted. However, a state that was not able to meet full need could apply a reduction to the cost standards for payment purposes.

Between July 1974 and July 1975, the consumer price index rose from 148.3 to 163.3; the fiscal year averages were 139.8 for 1974 and 155.2 for 1975. The unemployment rate during this time also rose from 4.9 in 1973, to 5.6 in 1974, to 8.4 in July 1975. These economic indicators affected the AFDC program directly. With fewer resources available due to lack of employment opportunities, a larger unmet need occurred; with rises in the costs for consumption items, more families were in need of assistance.

For an illustrative family of four recipients—generally a mother with three children—increases in need standards were made in 25 states between July 1974 and July 1975; 26 states, however, made little or no change in their budgeted need standards. Two states showed small decreases. In the maximum or largest amount paid between July 1974 and July 1975 for a family of four recipients, 19 states granted significant increases of $20 to over $50; 12 states had increases up to $20; and in 22 states there was little or no change in the largest amount that could be paid.

In the percent of need met (the largest amount paid as a percent of the need standard) increases for 15 states ranged from three to over 25 percent in Kentucky. However, in seven states (Georgia, Idaho, Missouri, Nebraska, Oregon, Vermont, and West Virginia) there were declines of up to 10 percent in the extent of need met. In 1975, 23 states met 100 percent of need, an increase of three states (Alaska, Kansas, and Kentucky) from 1974.

PAYMENTS FOR HOME REPAIRS.   Vendor payments may be made by state or local public welfare agencies for repairing the homes owned and occupied by AFDC recipients when the homes (1) are so defective that continued occupancy is unwarranted, (2) unless repairs are made rental quarters will be necessary, and, (3) the cost of alternate rental quarters would exceed over a two-year period the repair costs needed to make the home habitable.

Procedures

Applications for AFDC assistance may be made at any state or local welfare office by mail, in person, or by telephone. Each agency accepts applications from the applicant himself, his designated representative, or someone acting responsibly for him. A decision on his application is made not in excess of 45 days and he is notified in writing of approval or denial for assistance payments and the reasons therefor. A decision is based on the facts supplied by or on behalf of the applicant. Such facts cover the applicant's need for assistance, his entitlement in meeting the state's eligibility requirements, such as age, sex, family composition and responsibilities, residence, nature and sources of income, resources, employment status, school attendance of youth between 16 and 21 years of age, health status, and other personal and household information required by the agency to make a determination. The agency verifies this information by questioning the applicant, examining the records and receipts supplied by the applicant, and by searching the agency's own records, other public records, or with the individual's knowledge and consent, obtaining information from other sources, such as home visits by agency workers, telephone inquiries or visits to landlords, neighborhood stores, banks, former employers, and relatives.

Regular monthly payments are made by check mailed to the family, or bimonthly in some states for larger families or special needs. In New York City and in several other cities, as an experiment, family heads are required to visit their local welfare office to receive their checks and simultaneously be cleared for availability for jobs listed with the local employment service office. Refusal to accept a bona fide job offer makes AFDC heads of households and youth not attending school ineligible to receive payments covering their own, but not their children's financial needs.

Although financial needs and available income are considered in determining the amount of assistance payments, and such payments are intended to meet the basic needs for food, clothing, housing, personal and household necessities, the monthly or semi-monthly checks recipients receive may be spent for any purpose, at any time—or not spent—at the recipients' discretion. Neither the local, state or federal government legally may interfere in this freedom, nor deny continued assistance or modify the amount of payments because of any disagreement on the use of the funds. However, as an exception to this, protective payments on behalf of a child or family must be utilized for the child or family for which they were made.

States use different methods for determining the amount of AFDC payments. The following are illustrations for AFDC payments in 1975 to a family of four in different states with requirements equal to the state's cost standard and countable income of $100 per month:

1. Countable income is deducted from the cost standard.
    Pennsylvania:

Cost standard (paid to a family with no income)	$349
Income	−100
AFDC payment	249

2. Countable income is deducted from the payment standard.
    Maryland:

Cost standard	$314
Payment standard (paid to a family with no income)	242
Income	−100
AFDC payment	142

3. Countable income is deducted from the cost standard but payment is no more than the specified maximum.
    Missouri:

Cost standard	$370
Income	−100
Deficit	270
AFDC payment (maximum allowable payable to a family of four; also paid to a family with no income)	150

4. Countable income is deducted from the cost standard and the payment is a specified percentage of the deficit. Delaware:

Cost standard	$287
Income	−100
Deficit	187
AFDC payment (90 percent of deficit)	168

A family with no income receives 90 percent of the cost standard or $258.

5. Countable income is deducted from the cost standard and the payment is a specified percentage of the resulting deficit or a maximum allowable amount, whichever is less. Mississippi:

Cost Standard	277
Income	−100
Deficit	177
40 percent of deficit	71
AFDC payment (maximum payment to a family of four persons)	60

A family of four persons with no income receives the maximum allowable payment of $60.

Continued eligibility for payments is reconsidered or redetermined within 30 days of the agency receiving information about changes in the family situation which may affect the amount of payment or the eligibility status of the family, or any of its members. Also, state and local agencies require that AFDC cases be reviewed routinely not less frequently than every six months.

To obtain the repair of their homes, AFDC heads of household or caretakers request financial assistance of the state or local public welfare agency. Prior to authorizing the repairs, the agency determines that the AFDC family is legal owner of the property, the property is so defective that continued occupancy is dangerous and unfit for the family, unless the repairs are made, the family must move to rented quarters, and the cost of rented quarters for two years exceed the cost of repairs. Once these facts are established, repairs are made and paid for by the agency.

SUPPLEMENTAL SECURITY INCOME (SSI) PROGRAM

The objective of SSI is to furnish financial assistance to needy aged, blind and disabled individuals to help them attain or retain capability for self-care, and, for blind and disabled persons, self-support.

Background

The program was enacted by the Social Security Amendments of 1972 (P.L. 92–603) and made effective January 1, 1974 for the 50 states and the District of Columbia.[4] It was the only major survivor of the welfare reform proposals for a national income maintenance program recommended by the President that year. Although welfare reform measures were passed by both houses of Congress setting up a federal program with uniform national standards and administration, agreement could not be reached on a compromise version covering families with dependent children. The SSI program for the aged, blind, and disabled was approved as a cash assistance program administered as a single category with uniform national payment and eligibility requirements, except for differences related to the conditions of age, blindness, and disability. The program replaces the federal/-state income maintenance programs for the adult categories authorized by the Social Security Act of 1935: Title I (OAA), Title X (AB), and Title XIV (APTD). Also replaced were the combined aged, blind, and disabled programs (AABD) in 18 states authorized under Title XVI in the Social Security Act of 1962.[5]

Even before the program's January 1, 1974 effective date, two further amendments to the Social Security Act modified key SSI program provisions:

(1) The Social Security Amendments of 1972 (P.L. 92-603):

—increased the basic federal SSI benefit from the monthly rate of $130 for an individual and $195 for a couple to be effective January 1, 1974, to $140 and $210 respectively, effective July 1, 1974;

—established a requirement that states supplement the SSI payment if necessary to assure that no one who was a recipient of OAA, AB, APTD state programs in December, 1973, will receive less beginning January 1, 1974. This affected 35 states, although most state officials indicated then they would provide supplements in any event;

—provided for continuing coverage of "essential persons" (a spouse under age 65) under SSI who were receiving assistance under a state plan in December, 1973.

(2) The Social Security Amendments of 1973:

—changed the effective date of the increase in rates ($140 for an individual and $210 for a couple) from July 1, 1974 back to January 1, 1974, and authorized increased rates by July, 1974 to $146 per individual and $219 per couple;

—postponed food stamp and surplus commodities program eligibility for SSI recipients through June 30, 1974. The 1972 Social Security Amendments prohibited such eligibility but passage of the Agriculture Act Amendments of 1973 (P.L. 93-86) lifted that prohibition for those SSI recipients who received increases in payments not equal to their former payments plus the cash value of food stamps or commodities.

SSI recipients continue to retain their food stamp eligibility.[6]

Public Law 93-368, enacted August 7, 1974 required that when social security benefits are automatically based on a cost of living computation, SSI benefits will be increased by the same percentage. Effective July 1, 1977, the SSI benefit floor was raised to $177.80 for individuals and $266.70 for couples.

Administering Agencies

The Social Security Administration of D/HEW through its more than 1200 local offices is responsible for administering the program. It also administers the mandatory supplements of 32 states, and the optional supplements for 17 of these. (Table 3.9) state and local public assistance agencies are responsible for administering the state supplementary payments in the 16 States which elected separate administration. All states except Arizona and Texas are providing for the mandatory supplementary payments.

Caseloads

An estimated 5.1 million aged, blind, disabled persons are eligible for the SSI program. Of these, 3.8 million are aged, 1.3 million are blind or disabled. In December, 1973, 3.1 million aged, blind, and disabled public assistance recipients under state programs were automatically transferred to SSI rolls, 1.8 million were aged and 1.3 million, blind and disabled. In May 1977, over 4.2 million persons received financial aid. (Table 3.7.)

Eligibility Requirements and Budgets

Individuals or couples may be eligible for federal benefit payments if their monthly income is less than the full monthly payment ($177.80 for an individual and $266.70 for a couple). People who are in hospitals or nursing homes getting Medicaid funds on their behalf are eligible for benefits of up to $25 a month in lieu of their regular benefits. People who fail to apply for annuities, pensions, workers compensation, and other such payments to which they may be entitled will not be eligible.

INCOME AS DEFINED BY THE PROGRAM.   In determining an individual's eligibility and the amount of his benefits, both his earned and unearned income are taken into consideration. The definition of earned income follows generally the definition of earnings used in applying the retirement test under the social security program. Unearned income means all other forms of income, including benefits from other public and private programs, prizes and awards, proceeds of life insurance not needed for expenses of last illness and burial (with a maximum of $1,500), gifts, inheritances, rents, dividends, interest, and so

**Table 3.6 Persons Receiving Federally Administered SSI Payments
January 1974–May 1977**

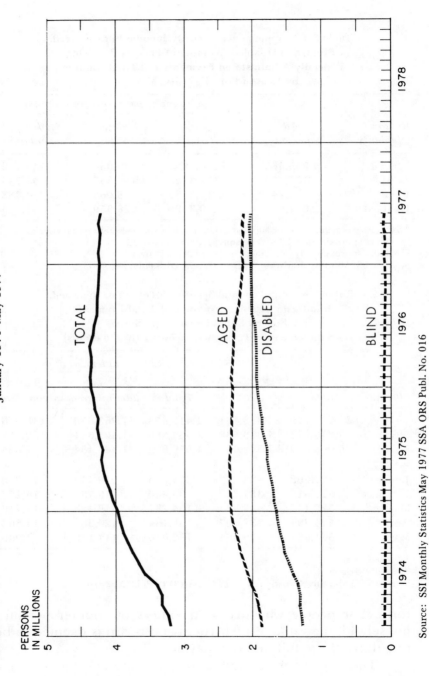

PERSONS
IN MILLIONS

TOTAL

AGED

DISABLED

BLIND

Source: SSI Monthly Statistics May 1977 SSA ORS Publ. No. 016

Table 3.7 Supplemental Security Income For the Aged,
Blind, and Disabled: Number of Persons Receiving
Federally Administered Payments and Total Amount,
by Reason For Eligibility, May 1977

Reason for eligibility	All persons	Amount of payments (in thousands)		
		Total	Federal SSI	State supplementation[a]
Total	4,235,466	$496,180	$379,064	$117,116
Aged	2,107,092	194,382	142,637	51,745
Blind	76,444[b]	11,456	8,069	3,388
Disabled	2,051,930[c]	290,342	228,359	61,983

[a]Excludes payments for state supplementation under state-administered programs.
[b]Includes approximately 22,000 persons aged 65 and over.
[c]Includes approximately 245,000 persons aged 65 and over.
Source: SSI Monthly Statistics. May, 1977, SSA ORS Publ. No. 016.

Table 3.8 Supplemental Security Income For the Aged,
Blind, and Disabled: Amount of Total Payments,
Federal SSI Payments, and State
Supplementary Payments, 1974–77 (in thousands)

Period	Total	Federal SSI	State supplementation		
			Total	Federally administered	State administered
1974	$5,245,719	$3,833,161	$1,412,558	$1,263,652	$148,906
1975	5,878,224	4,313,538	1,564,686	1,402,534	162,152
1976	6,068,079	4,512,061	1,556,018	1,388,154	167,864
1977					
January[a]	522,208	388,265	133,943	119,713	14,230
February	521,613	387,753	133,860	119,733	14,127
March[a]	522,162	387,925	134,237	119,488	14,749
April	524,791	389,627	135,164	120,364	14,800[b]
May	511,084	379,064	132,016	117,116	14,900[b]

[a]Revised data.
[b]Partially estimated.
Source: SSI Monthly Statistics. May, 1977, SSA ORS Publ. No. 016.

forth. For people who live as members of another person's
household, the value of their room and board is deemed to be
one-third of the full monthly payment.

These items are excluded from income:

1. $20 of any income (earned or unearned) other than income paid on the basis of need;
2. $65 of earnings a month and one-half above that (plus income necessary for fulfilling plans for self-support for the blind and disabled and work expenses for the blind);
3. within reasonable limits, earnings of a student regularly attending school;
4. an individual's irregular and infrequent earned income of $30 or less in a quarter and irregular and infrequent unearned income of $60 or less in a quarter;
5. any amount received from a public agency as a refund of taxes paid on real property or on food purchased;
6. the tuition and fees part of scholarships and fellowships;
7. home produce;
8. one-third of child-support payments from an absent parent;
9. foster care payments for a child placed in the household by a child-placement agency; and
10. supplementary benefits based on need and provided by a state or political subdivision.

EXCLUSIONS FROM RESOURCES.   Generally, individuals are not eligible for payments if they have resources in excess of $1,500, and couples will not be eligible if their resources are above $2,250. Those who were receiving aid to the aged, blind, and disabled in December 1973 under an approved state plan, but whose resources were greater than those permitted under the federal program, are considered not to have exceeded the maximum amount permitted under the state plan in effect for October 1972. The following are excluded from resources:

1. The home and appurtenant land to the extent that their value does not exceed a reasonable amount;*

*Text continued on page 113.

Table 3.9 Administration of Supplemental Security Income Program, 1977

State	Federal Administration No State Supplementation	Federal Administration State Supplementation	Federal Administration State Supplementation
Alabama			x
Alaska.			x
Arizona.			x
Arkansas		x	
California.		x	
Colorado			x
Connecticut			x
Delaware		x	
District of Columbia .		x	
Florida		x	
Georgia		x	
Hawaii.		x	
Idaho			x
Illinois.			x
Indiana			x
Iowa.		x	
Kansas.		x	
Kentucky.			x
Louisiana.		x	
Maine		x	
Maryland		x	
Massachusetts		x	
Michigan		x	
Minnesota			x
Mississippi		x	
Missouri.			x
Montana		x	
Nebraska			x
Nevada		x	
New Hampshire.			x
New Jersey.		x	
New Mexico			x
New York		x	
North Carolina			x
North Dakota.			x
Ohio.		x	
Oklahoma			x
Oregon			x

Table 3.9   (Continued)

State	Federal Administration No State Supplementation	Federal Administration State Supplementation	Federal Administration State Supplementation
Pennsylvania.		x	
Rhode Island		x	
South Carolina			x
South Dakota.		x	
Tennessee		x	
Texas	x		
Utah.			x
Vermont		x	
Virginia.			x
Washington		x	
West Virginia			x
Wisconsin.		x	
Wyoming.			x

Source: SSI Monthly Statistics May, 1977, SSA ORS Pub. No. 016

2. household goods, personal effects, and an automobile, not in excess of a reasonable amount;
3. other property essential to the individual's support (within reasonable value limitations);
4. life insurance policies, if their total face value is $1,500 or less—otherwise, insurance policies would be counted only to the extent of their cash surrender value;
5. resources of a blind or disabled individual necessary for fulfilling an approved plan of self-support; and
6. shares of certain nonnegotiable stock held in a Regional or Village Corporation by Alaskan natives.

The Secretary prescribes time limits and ways of disposing of excess property so that it will not be included as resources.

Definitions

AN ELIGIBLE INDIVIDUAL.   A resident of the United States and a citizen or an alien admitted for permanent residence or otherwise permanently residing in the United States under color of law, and aged, blind, or disabled.

AGED INDIVIDUAL.   One aged 65 or older is considered aged.

BLIND INDIVIDUAL.   An individual who has central visual of 20/200 or less in the better eye with the use of a correcting lens, or equivalent impairment in the fields of vision is considered blind.

DISABLED INDIVIDUAL.   A disabled individual who is unable to engage in substantial gainful activity by reason of a medically determinable physical or mental impairment that is expected to last or has lasted for 12 months or can be expected to result in death. (This definition is the same as that used for social security disability benefits.) A child under age 18 who is not engaging in substantial gainful activity will be considered disabled if he suffers from any medically determinable physical or mental impairment of comparable severity. A disabled individual will be entitled to a 9-month trial work period unless he has had a prior trial work period during a period of eligibility based on the same disability. A disabled individual who is medically determined to be an alcoholic or drug addict will not be entitled to benefits under this program unless he undergoes appropriate available treatment in an approved facility.

(Those blind or disabled individuals who were on the benefit rolls in December 1973 under existing state programs will be considered blind or disabled for purposes of this program if they met the definition of disability or blindness which was in effect as of October 1972.)

ELIGIBLE SPOUSE.   An eligible spouse is an aged, blind, or disabled individual who is the husband or wife of an individual who is aged, blind, or disabled and who has not been living apart from such other spouse for more than 6 months.

CHILD.   A child is an unmarried person who is not the head of a household and who is either under the age of 18 or under the age of 22 and attending school regularly.

DETERMINATION OF MARITAL RELATIONSHIP.   Appropriate state law applies in determining a marital relationship except that when two persons, for purposes of receiving social security benefits, are considered married and when two persons hold themselves out as married in the community in which they live, they will be considered married for purposes of this program.

The income and resources of a spouse living with an eligible individual are taken into account in determining the benefit amount of the individual, whether or not the income and resources are available to him. Income and resources of a parent may count as income of a disabled or blind child.

REHABILITATION SERVICES.   Disabled and blind beneficiaries are referred to state agencies for vocational rehabilitation services. A beneficiary who refuses without good cause any vocational rehabilitation services offered will not be eligible for benefits.

Procedures

Applications for SSI financial assistance may be made at the branch or district Social Security offices by mail, in person or by telephone. Applications are also made to the state or local public assistance office in those states which provide a supplemental payment and administer such payments separately from the federal payment. Applications are referred by the Social Security office to the state or local public assistance office when there is possible entitlement for a supplemental payment and such payments are administered separately from the federal payment. If the Social Security Administration administers both the federal and state supplemental payments under agreement with the state, separate applications to the state or local office are not necessary. Initially, when the program became operative on January 1, 1974, OAA, AB, APTD, or AABD recipients under their respective state programs were "grandfathered" into the SSI program by a mass transfer of state rolls to the respective district or branch offices.

Applications may be made by the applicant himself, his designated representative or someone acting responsibly for him. Information must be supplied on Social Security Administration forms covering for the applicant, his spouse, and other persons living in his household, personal information of age, residence, family and household relationships, place of birth, source and amount of earnings, and nature and value of resources. If the applicant applies as a blind or disabled person, he is required to submit a medical history and disability report and authorize the Social Security Administration to request any physician, hospital, agency, or other organization to disclose information about the applicant's condition. Personal interviews are held and full verification of applicant information is made by a claims representative of the branch or district office. Such documentation as birth certificates, rent receipts, bank statements, and tax receipts are requested and agency contacts may be made of relatives, employers, or others to furnish corroboration of the information on applications filed.

Applications for the SSI program are also considered applications for other federal benefit programs, including Medicaid and Medicare, state supplemental payments, and social security retirement and disability benefits. Applicants are referred to other agencies, unions, businesses, to file applications for benefits to which they may be entitled, including civil service pensions, veterans benefits, annuities, and pensions.

The medical records of applicants filing as blind or disabled are referred by the branch or district Social Security office to the state disability determinations unit of the state vocational rehabilitation agency. This unit determines blindness or disability eligibility for SSI benefits and whether the applicant may also benefit from vocational rehabilitation services. If so, such services are provided by the state agency. Blind or disabled applicants are required under the SSI program to accept vocational services if such services are believed to lead to employment and self-support.

Advance payments to SSI applicants may be made to presumptively eligible persons faced with a financial emergency. The amounts they receive may not exceed $100 for a single individual and $195 for a couple. Recovery of these amounts are made if the applicant is declared ineligible for SSI benefits.

Regular monthly payments are made to eligible SSI beneficiaries by check issued by the Treasury Department. Eligibility is determined by the claims representative in the branch or district Social Security office and authorization for payments is forwarded to the Social Security Administration Bureau of Data Processing computer headquarters in Baltimore, and forwarded to one of the four program centers in the area in which the beneficiary lives: Birmingham, Philadelphia, Chicago, and Richmond, California. Recipient records are maintained at these centers and mailing tapes for check disbursements are processed there. The amount of the checks cover SSI benefits and state mandatory supplemental benefits in those areas (32 states) where the Social Security Administration administers both federal and state supplemental payments. Otherwise, the checks cover only SSI benefits and a separate check is issued by the state for the state supplemental benefit, if any. Sixteen states provide this latter arrangement.

Redeterminations and review of continued SSI eligibility are made by the Social Security Administration through a highly automated process to detect errors and provide assurance of legal eligibility and the correctness of payments made.

GENERAL ASSISTANCE (GA) PROGRAM

The objective of GA is to provide emergency or short-term assistance to persons not eligible for other federally assisted cash payments and assistance programs to help them meet their basic needs for food, clothing, other necessities, or special needs not elsewhere obtainable.

Background

General assistance programs (also referred to as general relief, home relief, outdoor relief, emergency or direct relief) are administered and financed with various combinations of state and local government responsibility. There is no federal legislation and no federal financial participation in respect to these programs. Coverage, benefits, eligibility conditions, policies, and administrative methods vary considerably among the states, between counties in many states, and within counties in some states.[8]

All states except one have enabling authority for state or locally administered or financed general assistance programs. One state enacts separate legislation for each county or city which request authority to establish a local assistance program. State legislation has developed from historical concepts of local responsibility for poor or destitute persons. With the enactment and expansion of social security and federal/state categorical assistance programs, the general assistance programs are primarily directed toward persons with emergency needs and those who are not eligible for any of the federally assisted programs.

In 16 states, GA is limited to emergency or short-term assistance; most other states also provide continuing assistance to families or individuals under specified conditions; that is, assistance may be limited to unemployable individuals or to families with no employable members, or assistance may be provided when the wage earner is unemployed; in a few states, earnings of low-income workers may be supplemented.

State statutes generally have a historical basis dating back to early statehood (and colonial and territorial) legal provisions for care of paupers and indigents. Most state statutes have been revised following the enactment of social security programs and federally aided public assistance programs. A few states cite legal authority for general assistance in "poor laws" enacted in the 19th century.

Administering Agency

General assistance is administered by the state public assistance agency through local offices (the same offices which administer federally aided programs) in 18 states. In nine states the general assistance program is administered by local political jurisdictions under supervision of the state public assistance agency. In 20 states, general assistance is locally administered with no supervisory responsibility exercised by a state agency. In the remaining four states, only those local jurisdictions which receive some state funds for general assistance program operations are supervised by a state agency.

The county or an area unit of the state public assistance agency is the most common unit for administration in 40 states. In eight states, general assistance is administered by townships, towns, or municipalities and three states have combinations of county or township administration units.

Caseloads and Costs

Expenditures for general assistance benefits in 1975 amounted to $1.2 billion of which $1.1 billion was in the form of cash payments and the balance for medical vendor payments. The average number of cases amounted to 667,000 representing 964,000 recipients. In December 1975, the following eight states in the aggregate represented 78.9 percent of the cases and 83.2 percent of payments to recipients: (Table 3.10):

Table 3.10 General Assistance: Recipients of Money Payments and Amount
of Payments, by State, December 1975
(includes nonmedical vendor payments)

| STATE | NUMBER OF | | PAYMENTS TO RECIPIENTS TOTAL AMOUNT | AVERAGE PER | | PERCENTAGE CHANGE FROM NOV 1975 IN— | | PERCENTAGE CHANGE FROM DEC 1974 IN— | |
	CASES	RECIPIENTS		CASE	RECIPIENT	NUMBER OF RECIPIENTS	AMOUNT	NUMBER OF RECIPIENTS	AMOUNT
TOTAL 44 STATES	691,960	976,217	$99,581,215	$143.91	$102.01	2.2	0.3	14.6	21.4
ALABAMA	39	39	488	X	X	X	X	X	X
ALASKA	37	92	5,248	X	57.04	-13.2	-3.0	-73.9	-65.8
ARIZONA	3,595	3,595	289,871	80.63	80.63	4.1	3.8	-3.4	4.1
CALIFORNIA	49,014	51,901	5,329,846	108.74	102.69	0.4	2.9	-6.1	6.6
COLORADO	2,738	3,649	269,517	98.44	73.86	-8.3	-2.5	-18.6	-8.2
CONNECTICUT	13,752	24,372	1,774,920	129.07	72.83	-2.4	0.2	5.8	20.4
DELAWARE	1,879	3,459	115,398	61.41	33.36	2.8	1.3	-11.9	-8.8
DIST OF COLUMBIA	6,385	6,770	976,903	153.00	144.30	-0.4	0.5	16.3	25.5
GEORGIA	2,215	4,272	126,388	57.06	29.59	52.6	44.3	-13.1	117.9
GUAM	40	40	3,297	X	X	X	X	X	X
HAWAII	6,616	12,628	1,516,367	229.20	120.08	2.0	4.5	4.5	23.0
ILLINOIS	73,454	88,760	8,636,543	117.58	97.30	3.9	-15.1	9.2	1.4
IOWA (E)	4,220	10,736	363,767	86.20	33.88	0.0	0.0	#	#
KANSAS	6,315	9,776	887,860	140.60	90.82	-17.2	-17.0	33.1	52.0
LOUISIANA	4,465	4,676	249,960	55.98	53.46	-4.5	-4.3	-34.5	-33.5
MAINE	5,106	15,232	326,630	63.97	21.44	10.9	20.3	-8.9	-21.1
MARYLAND	17,982	19,426	1,981,418	110.19	102.00	3.6	4.5	36.6	33.8
MASSACHUSETTS	27,528	31,006	3,682,808	133.78	116.52	-2.7	0.2	-34.5	-31.1
MICHIGAN	63,241	75,625	9,881,331	156.25	130.66	2.4	-5.5	12.7	20.7
MINNESOTA	13,866	18,657	1,924,983	138.83	103.18	7.6	10.9	26.6	45.2

State									
MISSISSIPPI	914	1,151	15,011	16.42	13.04	4.3	10.4	-2.8	9.6
MISSOURI	8,641	9,357	583,195	67.49	62.33	0.1	-0.6	-18.3	-17.8
MONTANA	681	1,243	38,954	57.20	31.34	13.0	8.9	-27.3	-27.0
NEW HAMPSHIRE	1,591	3,798	134,789	84.72	35.49	7.8	13.3	-21.5	-28.3
NEW JERSEY	27,909	55,923	4,680,802	167.72	83.70	2.2	1.9	9.0	13.0
NEW MEXICO	373	398	29,452	78.96	74.00	4.5	8.0	20.6	27.2
NEW YORK	141,600	237,090	27,813,286	196.42	117.31	2.1	2.5	29.6	32.7
NORTH CAROLINA	2,462	5,262	101,433	41.20	19.28	9.9	1.0	-22.8	-15.8
NORTH DAKOTA	96	220	6,420	66.88	29.18	12.8	16.3	3.3	-8.5
OHIO	51,768	64,915	4,898,650	94.63	75.46	2.2	5.5	21.9	41.6
OKLAHOMA	97	175	1,870	19.28	10.69	5.4	13.3	-79.5	-71.5
OREGON	3,695	6,250	417,664	113.03	66.83	41.0	12.9	66.2	17.1
PENNSYLVANIA	111,501	144,350	17,896,015	160.50	123.98	3.2	4.2	41.8	43.4
PUERTO RICO	212	212	2,832	13.36	13.36	-3.6	-1.4	-17.2	-12.9
RHODE ISLAND	8,277	13,299	1,023,651	123.67	76.97	-10.3	0.3	4.4	19.2
SOUTH CAROLINA (E)	499	565	27,977	56.07	49.52	2.0	0.7	-35.5	-36.7
SOUTH DAKOTA	442	1,188	19,059	43.12	16.04	33.2	17.2	0.9	1.4
UTAH	2,208	2,424	251,538	113.92	103.77	17.0	22.2	28.8	36.3
VIRGIN ISLANDS	327	350	18,007	57.51	53.73	-4.4	-3.4	-0.3	2.0
VIRGINIA	8,119	10,981	888,175	109.39	80.88	3.8	2.8	9.4	12.8
WASHINGTON	9,062	13,674	1,577,211	174.05	115.34	-0.7	11.4	0.2	16.5
WEST VIRGINIA	2,964	9,293	154,695	52.19	16.65	10.7	-2.9	20.9	28.1
WISCONSIN (E)	5,821	8,314	639,352	109.84	76.90	-6.6	-4.5	-18.1	-11.1
WYOMING	214	474	16,834	78.66	35.51	42.3	17.0	0.0	8.9

\# DATA NOT AVAILABLE FOR COMPARABLE PERIOD.

X AVERAGE PAYMENT NOT COMPUTED ON BASE OF FEWER THAN 50 CASES OR RECIPIENTS; PERCENTAGE CHANGE ON FEWER THAN 100 RECIPIENTS.

(E) ESTIMATED DATA.

Source: Public Assistance Statistics, December 1975. DHEW Publication No. (SRS) 76-03100 NCSS Report A-2 (12-75). National Center for Social Statistics, SRS, DHEW. April 1976.

	Cases	Payments
New York	141,600	$27,813
Pennsylvania	111,501	17,896
Michigan	63,241	9,881
Illinois	73,454	8,636
California	49,014	5,330
Ohio	51,768	4,899
New Jersey	27,909	4,681
Massachusetts	27,528	3,682
Total	546,015	$82,818
Total All States	691,960	$99,581
Percent	78.9%	83.2%

Average payments per case in December, 1975 amounted to $143.91, with the five highest states averaging:

Hawaii	$229.20
New York	196.42
Washington	174.05
New Jersey	167.72
Pennsylvania	160.50.

At the other extreme, the five states with the lowest average payments were:

Puerto Rico	$13.36
Mississippi	16.42
Oklahoma	19.28
North Carolina	41.20
South Dakota	43.12.

Eligibility Requirements

The basic eligibility condition is need, but definitions of need vary considerably among states and often within states. Program policies vary by local jurisdictions in 28 states. Determination of need for emergency assistance may be based on the type and extent of need related to available income rather than on a uniform income criteria. States which provide continued assistance for maintenance needs generally apply income standards similar to (but often lower) than those applicable to the federal categorical programs.

Nineteen states grant assistance only to individuals who are unemployable and to families with no employable members. Nine states provide emergency assistance without regard to employability but grant continued assistance only to unemployable applicants. Other states extend assistance to unemployed persons. In five states and in some counties of four other states, general assistance may be used to supplement earnings of fully employed low-income workers, with or without dependents. In two other states, such assistance is limited to families with dependent children. (One state specifies that such assistance is extended only when need is critical.)

PERSONS INCLUDED.   In most states some type of assistance may be extended to families with minor children and couples or individuals with no children. However, in some states, families with children may receive assistance if the head is unemployed but couples or individuals are eligible only if they are unemployable.

INCOME TEST.   Nineteen states report that standards of assistance are the same as in one or more of the federally aided programs; 12 states used standards that are similar to a federal category but are generally less comprehensive. Five states use standards that are not comparable to the federal categories and 15 states have no generally accepted standards.

Most states consider all income available to meet need with no disregard of earnings (in states which supplement earnings) or exclusions for other purposes.

ACCOUNTING PERIOD.   For emergency assistance, current income (or ability to obtain credit in some states) is considered. For continuing assistance monthly income is considered.

ASSETS.   Property limitations are generally the same as in one or more of the federally aided programs in 23 states; more restrictive in 15 states; and no provisions are specified in 13 states. In most of the latter states, provisions vary at local discretion. Two states specify that the recipient must be "indigent" or "adjudged a pauper."

Other Requirements

WORK REQUIREMENTS.   Thirty-two states provide some type of assistance to employable but unemployed persons. Twenty-two of these require registration with the employment service, acceptance of assignment to a work project (eight states) or acceptance of available employment. Ten states reported no requirement. Four of these meet emergency needs only and in most of these requirements are determined at local discretion.

CITIZENSHIP.   One state requires U.S. citizenship, two states require that an applicant be a citizen or an alien meeting specified conditions. (One requires 15 years residence in the United States.)

LIENS, RECOVERY, OR ASSIGNMENT.   Twenty-nine states have no provisions for liens against property, assignment of resources, or recovery of assistance paid. Nine states have claims against property secured by liens or other legal security. Thirteen states may file claims against the estate of recipients.

RELATIVE RESPONSIBILITY.   Thirty-one states reported requirements for support by specified relatives, usually including spouses for each other and parents for minor children. Eleven consider adult children to be responsible for their parents and four extend responsibility to siblings and/or grandparents and grandchildren. Two states reported that general assistance is available only to persons with no relatives able to support and one specifies no relatives within the county able to support.

INSTITUTIONAL STATUS.   Four states reported that they provide general assistance to persons living in specified types of institutions.

RESIDENCE.   Sixteen states have no residence requirements, that is, they assist eligible persons in the state, including tran-

sients and migrants. Sixteen states reported durational residence requirements, that is, the applicant must have lived for a
specified period of time within the state, within the local jurisdiction or both. Typical periods of time were one year for the state
and six months for a local jurisdiction. Nineteen states required
that the applicant be residing in the state. Eleven states make
exceptions for emergency assistance and 16 make exceptions for
short-time assistance to nonresidents, usually pending return to
their place of residence. Eight states reported no exceptions for
nonresidents, transients, or migrants.

Cash Benefits

Money payments for maintenance needs are generally used in
24 states. In ten states vendor payments for rent, food, and so
forth, are generally made and in other states either method or
a combination may be used on an individual case basis or at the
discretion of local officials.

Other Benefits

Medical care costs may be paid from general assistance funds
under certain conditions in 36 states.

Some states use general assistance funds to pay transportation costs to return nonresidents to their place of residence.

Most states provide for indigent burials from state or local
funds.

Eligibility for commodities or food stamps generally is determined on the basis as for other assistance recipients. Commodities may be used to meet emergency needs in some
localities and general assistance recipients are required to purchase food stamps in a few states and localities.

NOTES

1. Studies in Public Welfare Paper No. 2, Handbook of Public Income Transfer Programs, Subcommittee on Fiscal Policy, Joint Economic Committee, U.S. Congress, October 16, 1972. U.S. Government Printing Office, Washington, D.C. Much of the text of the AFDC, GA, Medicaid, WIN, Food Stamp programs in this and the next chapter is drawn from this handbook and updated to reflect program regulatory changes and more recent case load experience, standards of need and payments, and other program characteristics.

2. Public Assistance Statistics. December 1975. DHEW Publication No. (SRS) 76–03100 NCSS Report A-2 72/75, issued by the National Center for Social Statistics, SRS, DHEW, April 1976. Washington, D.C.

3. Characteristics of State Plans for AFDC 1974 Edition Assistance Payments Administration, SRS, DHEW. Washington, D.C. 1974.

4. The territories of Guam, Virgin Islands, and Puerto Rico were excepted from the program and retain their individual income maintenance program for the aged, blind, and disabled under Titles I, X, and XIV of the Social Security Act.

5. Public Law 87–543 42 USC 1381–1385.

6. How the Food Stamp Program Works: A Resource Paper by Joe Richardson, Congressional Research Service, U.S. Library of Congress SUSFI 75–313 ED September 25, 1975. p. CRS-13.

7. Excerpted from Social Security Bulletin, March 1973. Social Security Administration, DHEW. Washington, D.C. p. 24–25.

8. The description of the State General Assistance Programs was derived from *Characteristics of General Assistance in the United States* Public Assistance Report No. 39 1970 Edition, DHEW, SRS.

Chapter 4

PUBLIC WELFARE PROGRAMS WITHIN THE FEDERAL/STATE SYSTEM: SOCIAL SERVICES, IN-KIND, AND SPECIAL POPULATION PROGRAMS

SOCIAL SERVICES PROGRAMS

There are two nationwide programs for the provision of social services by state and local public welfare agencies: social services to individuals and families (Title XX) and child welfare services. The services provided to Cuban Refugees, repatriated U.S. nationals, work and training registrants under the WIN program and services provided under the in-kind programs are discussed separately in this chapter.

There is no unanimity among social work professionals and public welfare administrators on the definition of *social services.* One general definition, oriented to and consistent with the Social Security Act, is: *nonfinancial supportive aid rendered to individuals and families to help them meet their personal, social, psychological, medical, economic, or other problems which interfere or otherwise prevent them from moving towards self-care, self-support, independent living, and strengthened family life.*

Federal and state laws and regulations—and the social work profession—have failed to establish a standard definition for the help, aid or assistance provided to people under the term "social services." Differences are philosophical as well as pragmatic.

They encompass the types, kinds, styles of services which are "social" and those which are not. For example: Is sentencing a delinquent to a jail term a "social service?" Is family planning a "social" rather than a "medical" service? (It is probably both when it includes counseling as well as medical and psychological examination.) Disagreement also is evident on the goals and objectives of social services (although those of the Title XX services program now govern), social work methods, the minimum qualifications of social service providers (particularly in the controversy over use of paraprofessionals), uniform qualitative standards for services, and the respective roles of government and private service agencies.

The literature of these and related subjects abound, but fail to reflect widespread agreement on much of the subject to provide professionals, clients, lawmakers, and the general public a basis for understanding and agreement. Perhaps this condition, however unsettling, reflects the society in which social services function: complex, imprecise, traumatic, uncertain. Nevertheless, public social services *are* provided for in the federal/state public welfare system where expedient day-to-day decisions, actions, and commitments are made and relationships are carried on to respond to the problems which clients bring to service workers in public welfare agencies or where social workers perceive problems of clients and communities. The successes in solving clients' problems are dependent in good measure upon the good sense and good faith of social workers, their training, dedication, knowledge, sympathetic understanding, and energies. Their successes are also dependent upon the community resources they rely upon as well as the public's understanding and support for their endeavors. Not the least, of course, is the clients' own efforts and determinations to help themselves.

SOCIAL SERVICES PROGRAM TO INDIVIDUALS AND FAMILIES— TITLE XX

The objectives of this social services program are:

1. achieving or maintaining economic self-support to prevent, reduce, or eliminate dependency;
2. achieving or maintaining self-sufficiency, including reduction or prevention of dependency;
3. preventing or remedying neglect, abuse, or exploitation of children and adults unable to protect their own interests, or preserving, rehabilitating, or reuniting families;
4. preventing or reducing inappropriate institutional care by providing for community-based care, home-based care, or other forms of less intensive care; or
5. securing referral or admission for institutional care when other forms of care are not appropriate, or providing services to individuals in institutions.

Background

Public social services for disadvantaged and dependent individuals and families predate the Social Security Act of 1935, but that act provided federal matching funds for the administrative expenses of state and local public welfare agencies. Part of these expenses covered the payrolls and related costs of social work to help public assistance applicants and recipients with their financial and social problems. With passage of the Social Security Amendments of 1956 (P.L. 84-880 approved August 1, 1956), explicit recognition was afforded social services to "place greater emphasis on helping to strengthen family life and helping needy families and individuals attain the maximum economic and personal independence of which they may be capable." Open-ended federal funds (with no ceiling on federal expenditures) at a 50 percent–50 percent ratio was authorized.

In the years following, with caseloads rising and state and local social services not demonstrably achieving that objective, greater federal financial incentives for social services were authorized. The Social Security Amendments of 1962 (P.L. 87-878, approved October 24, 1962) increased federal reimbursements for social services to 75 percent of state and local expenditures and authorized such reimbursements for the purchase of services from other public and voluntary service agencies. This change opened the floodgates to a manifold increase in claims for federal social services reimbursements as state and local governments sought to meet their budget crises through interagency service agreements for education, health, recreation, and other general government programs claiming them to be social services under the provisions of the Social Security Act. This aroused Congressional reaction to the perceived abuse of the open-ended funding arrangement and the 92nd Congress passed and the President approved the Social Service Amendments of 1974 (P.L. 93-647 approved January 4, 1975).

The new law was made effective October 1, 1975. A ceiling of $2.5 billion for matching funds for social services was fixed, with the funds allocated on the basis of population. Ninety percent of the funds were to be used for actual recipients, but some services were exempt from this limitation: work-related child care services, certain foster care services, family planning, services to the mentally retarded, and services to addicts and alcoholics who are receiving treatment. Services are directed toward each of the five goals specified in the act. An amount equal to at least 50 percent of the total federal expenditures in each state must be for persons receiving or eligible to receive AFDC, SSI, or Medicaid. Federal financial participation (FFP) is available for service costs, less fees collected, for all social services provided under the state's comprehensive annual service program operating in accordance with the federal social services regulations. The FFP rate of 75 percent is for the cost of all social services except family planning services which is covered by a higher rate of 90 percent. The ceiling of $2.5 billion allotted to the 50 states and the District of Columbia establishes the maximum federal amount for social services covered by the state's social services plan. If any state certifies its allotment is in excess of its needs, the excess becomes available to Puerto Rico (up to $15 million), Guam (up to $500,000), and the Virgin Islands (up to $500,000).

The law spells out two categories of social service beneficiaries: public assistance recipients and other low-income persons with a gross monthly income which does not exceed 115
percent of the state's median income, adjusted by size of family.
A state must charge reasonable fees for services to people whose
gross family income is above 80 percent of the state's median
income as adjusted for family size, and may charge fees for
persons with gross family income which do not exceed 80 percent of the state's median income, adjusted for family size.

Two years after the basic Title XX program was established,
on September 7, 1976, Public Law 94-401, the Child Day Care
Social Services Act amended Title XX in several important respects:

1.   States could extend eligibility for social services to
groups which have substantially all of their members with income below 90 percent of state medium income. Previously,
eligibility for services was determined on an individual basis
alone, except for children of migrant workers.

2.   Federal staffing standards for child day care serving
children aged six weeks to six years were suspended to October
1, 1977, although state staffing standards would have to be met
and standards could not be lowered from September 1975 levels.

3.   The $2.5 billion limit on social services was increased
by $200 million for fiscal year 1977 for child care, the addition
allocated among the states on a population basis (as the $2.5
billion available in the original law). The additional amounts are
to be applied to increase employment of welfare recipients and
other low-income persons in child care jobs. Their employment
by for-profit day care providers would be limited to $4,000 per
year per employee. Their employment by nonprofit and government day care providers would be limited to $5,000 per year per
employee. Since the for-profit providers would be entitled to a
tax credit of 20 percent for the added wages, or $1,000 per
employee, the limit on grants for profit, nonprofit, and government day care would effectively be the same: $5000 per year per
employee. The Internal Revenue Code granting the tax credit
equal to 20 percent of wages to employers hiring AFDC recipi-

ents, scheduled to expire June 30, 1976, was extended through September 30, 1977 to make this provision possible.

4. State welfare agencies were permitted through September 30, 1977 to waive federal staffing standards for child care centers and group day care homes which meet state standards if the children receiving federally funded day care represent no more than 20 percent of the total number of children served, provided the children cannot be placed in a facility which meets federal standards.

5. The federal standards were modified for family day care homes. The limitation on the number of children cared for in a family day care home could exclude in the count of the number of children served the mothers own children six years of age and older.

6. Full federal payment for child care expenditures under Title XX for fiscal year 1977 would be provided, in contrast to the 75 percent matching rate for such expenditures previously authorized.

7. Federal funding for social services to addicts and alcoholics was extended to fiscal year 1977 provided that full confidentiality requirements are met and the services are part of a comprehensive rehabilitation process. Funding for a seven-day detoxification period was authorized as a social service, even though social services funding is not available to persons in institutions.

Administering Agencies

The Public Services Administration, D/HEW Office of Human Development Services administers federal grants to states. The program is administered by a state agency through district or county offices in 30 states and by local agencies with state supervision in 20 states. The program is statewide in all states.

Caseloads

In 1975, an estimated 5.4 million individuals in families and 2.9 million aged, blind, and disabled persons received social services.

Eligibility Requirements

INCOME MAINTENANCE STATUS.   The following individuals are eligible on the basis of income maintenance status:

1. Recipients of AFDC;
2. those persons whose needs were taken into account in determining the needs of AFDC recipients; and
3. recipients of SSI benefits or state supplementary payments.

INCOME STATUS.   Individuals other than those described above are eligible if the family's monthly gross income is less than 115 percent (or, at state option, a lower percentage) of the median income of a family of four in the state adjusted for size of family.

MEDIAN INCOME.   The guidelines for median income are as follows:

1. On or before December 1 of each year, beginning with calendar year 1975, the Secretary promulgates the median income for a family of four to be used by the states for the purpose of establishing income levels for determining eligibility and establishing fee schedules under the services plan in the following fiscal year.
2. A state may establish an income level:
   a. at a lower level than 115 percent of the median income;
   b. at different levels for specific services under the services plan;
   c. at different levels for different categories of individuals;
   d. at different levels for different sizes of families within the limits for eligibility and fees set forth below in subparagraph 4.
3. A state shall not establish an income level which is in excess of 115 percent of the median income.
4. All median income figures used for eligibility at the 115 percent level and the imposition of fees above the 80

percent level are adjusted by family size according to the following percentages of the state median income for a family of four:

a. one person—52 percent
b. two-person family—68 percent
c. three-person family—84 percent
d. four-person family—100 percent
e. five-person family—116 percent
f. six-person family—132 percent
g. for each additional family member above six persons, add three percentage points to the percentage for a family of six.

SERVICES WITHOUT REGARD TO INCOME.   Information or referral services or services directed at the goal of preventing or remedying neglect, abuse, or exploitation of children or adults may, if provided under the services plan, be provided to all individuals who need them.

MONTHLY GROSS INCOME.   The guidelines for monthly gross income are as follows:

1. Monthly gross income means the monthly sum of income received by an individual from the following sources that are identified by the U.S. Census Bureau in computing the median income:
    a. Money wages or salary, i.e., total money earnings received for work performed as an employee, including wages, salary, Armed Forces pay, commissions, tips, piece-rate payments, and cash bonuses earned, before deductions are made for taxes, bonds, pensions, union dues, and similar purposes.
    b. Net income from nonfarm self-employment, i.e., gross receipts minus expenses from one's own business, professional enterprise, or partnership. Gross receipts include the value of all goods sold and services rendered. Expenses include costs of goods purchased, rent, heat, light, power, depreciation charges, wages and salaries paid, business taxes (not

personal income taxes), and similar costs. The value of salable merchandise consumed by the proprietors of retail stores is not included as part of net income.

c. Net income from farm self-employment, i.e., gross receipts minus operating expenses from the operation of a farm by a person on his own account, as an owner, renter, or sharecropper. Gross receipts include the value of all products sold, government crop loans, money received from the rental of farm equipment to others, and incidental receipts from the sale of wood, sand, gravel, and similar items. Operating expenses include cost of feed, fertilizer, seed, and other farming supplies, cash wages paid to farmhands, depreciation charges, cash rent, interest on farm mortgages, farm building repairs, farm taxes (not state and federal income taxes), and similar expenses. The value of fuel, food, or other farm products used for family living is not included as part of net income.

d. Social Security includes Social Security pensions and survivors' benefits, and permanent disability insurance payments made by the Social Security Administration prior to deductions for medical insurance and railroad retirement insurance checks from the U.S. government.

e. Dividends; interest (on savings or bonds); income from estates or trusts; net rental income or royalties include dividends from stockholdings or membership in associations; interest on savings or bonds; periodic receipts from estates or trust funds; net income from rental of a house, store, or other property to others; receipts from boarders or lodgers; and net royalties.

f. Public assistance or welfare payments include public assistance payments such as AFDC, SSI, state supplemental payments, and general assistance.

g. Pensions and annuities include pensions or retirement benefits paid to a retired person or his survivors by a former employer or by a union, either directly or through an insurance company; periodic receipts from annuities or insurance.

h. Unemployment compensation means compensation received from government unemployment insurance agencies or private companies during periods of unemployment and any strike benefits received from union funds.

i. Workers' compensation means compensation received periodically from private or public insurance companies for injuries incurred at work. The cost of this insurance must have been paid by the employer and not by the person.

j. Alimony.

k. Child support.

l. Veterans' pensions means money paid periodically by the Veterans' Administration to disabled members of the Armed Forces or to survivors of deceased veterans, subsistence allowances paid to veterans for education and on-the-job training, as well as so-called refunds paid to ex-servicemen as GI insurance premiums.

EXCLUSION FROM MONTHLY GROSS INCOME.   Excluded from computation of monthly gross income are the following:

1. Per capita payments to or funds held in trust for any individual in satisfaction of a judgment of the Indian Claims Commission or the Court of Claims;

2. payments made pursuant to the Alaska Native Claims Settlement Act to the extent such payments are exempt from taxation under section 21(a) of the Act;

3. money received from sale of property, such as stocks, bonds, a house, or a car (unless the person was engaged in the business of selling such property in which case the net proceeds would be counted as income from self-employment);

4. withdrawals of bank deposits;

5. money borrowed;

6. tax refunds;

7. gifts;
8. lump sum inheritances or insurance payments;
9. capital gains;
10. the value of the coupon allotment under the Food Stamp Act of 1964, as amended, in excess of the amount paid for the coupons;
11. the value of USDA donated foods;
12. the value of supplemental food assistance under the Child Nutrition Act of 1966 and the special food service program for children under the National School Lunch Act, as amended;
13. any payment received under the Uniform Relocation Assistance and Real Property Acquisition Policies Act of 1970;
14. earnings of a child under 14 years of age (no inquiry shall be made).

Services

Under federal regulations, states may divide their territory into geographic areas and provide different services in different areas. States establish a Comprehensive Annual Services Program Plan for services directed to the five goals. States determine the services they will provide (Table 4.1), but must include and identify (1) at least three services for SSI recipients who need such services, (2) at least one service for each of the five service goals, (3) family planning services, and (4) foster care services.

Social services are provided variously in the home, social service office setting, foster home, hospital, skilled nursing home, neighborhood community center, school, detention center, half-way house, prison, intermediate care facility, or other type of institution subject to the limitations of the federal regulation below. The services provided may include one or more of the following: information and referral, problem identification, problem diagnosis, education, personal and family counseling, treatment of the problem, rehabilitation and post-rehabilitation followup. They may be provided by a staff social worker of the state, city, or county welfare department or of an American

Indian Tribal organization, a social worker of a community agency under contract to the public agency, or a professional in solo practice, group practice or staff of an institution or agency, for skilled services running the gamut of human, social and economic problems faced by the social service client. Services may be offered singly or in combination, individually to persons and families, to groups, in the neighborhood or community or aimed at the target population of poor and disadvantaged.[1]

Not all persons and families need all services all the time or at any one time. For persons and families with a temporary condition of dependency or disability, diagnostic, treatment, and rehabilitation services of a relatively short duration may suffice to restore them to self-sufficiency. Persons and families with a long-term condition of greater severity will require extended services and have a prognosis of partial rehabilitation rather than of self-sufficiency. Such services—as to an aged woman with a heart condition—may help her financially or provide food and clothing; build up her morale through counseling; help with home care through homemaker services; and overcome her feeling of loneliness and alienation through volunteer visitors—and these can be made available through her remaining life. Services may be sequentially needed, as an adult who becomes blind at an early age, requiring first, intensive counseling to help him face up to his blindness; second, education to learn the Braille system; third, vocational training; and, fourth, job placement and orientation.

Limitations upon the following services have been established by federal regulation to receive FFP:

Minor medical and remedial care: Only when it is an integral but subordinate part of another social service and is not available to the individual under Medicaid or Medicare.

Room or board: Only when it is an integral but subordinate part of another social service and then only for six months or less in any 12-month period and for not more than one episode or placement.

Child care: Only when in-home care meets child care standards established by the state or by an Indian Tribal

Table 4.1 Social Services State by State

This chart shows which social services were being provided between October, '75 and March '76 by the 50
States and the District of Columbia. Indicated services
are not necessarily offered in all parts of a State. Chart

SERVICES	ALABAMA	ALASKA	ARIZONA	ARKANSAS	CALIFORNIA	COLORADO	CONN.	DELAWARE	D.C.	FLORIDA	GEORGIA	HAWAII	IDAHO	ILLINOIS	INDIANA	IOWA	KANSAS	KENTUCKY	LOUISIANA	MAINE	MARYLAND
Adoption Services	●		●	●		●	●		●		●	●	●	●	●		●	●		●	
Case Management Services	●			●					●						●		●	●		●	
Chore Services			●	●	●			●	●		●	●	●	●	●	●		●			●
Counselling Services	●	●	●	●	●	●	●	●		●		●			●	●		●	●	●	●
Day Care – Adults	●		●	●	●	●	●		●	●	●	●		●		●	●	●	●	●	●
Day Care – Children	●	●	●	●	●		●	●	●	●	●	●	●	●	●	●	●	●	●	●	●
Day Care – Various																					●
Diag. and Eval. Services	●			●								●							●		
Educ. and Training Services	●		●	●	●	●	●	●		●	●	●	●	●	●	●	●	●	●	●	●
Emergency Services			●	●			●	●	●							●					
Employment Related Medical Services	●	●	●		●	●	●			●	●		●	●		●	●	●		●	●
Employment Services	●			●	●	●	●		●	●	●		●	●	●	●	●	●	●		●
Family Planning	●	●	●	●	●	●		●	●	●	●	●	●	●	●	●	●	●	●	●	●
Foster Care – Adults	●			●	●	●	●	●	●		●	●			●	●		●	●	●	●
Foster Care – Children	●		●		●	●	●		●		●	●	●	●	●	●	●		●	●	●
Foster Care – Various			●						●	●		●	●		●	●			●	●	
Health-Related Services	●		●	●	●	●		●	●	●	●	●	●	●	●	●	●	●	●		●
Home Deliv./Cong. Meals	●			●				●	●	●	●	●	●	●		●	●		●	●	●
Homemaker Services	●	●	●	●	●	●		●	●	●	●	●	●	●	●	●	●	●	●	●	●
Home Management	●		●	●	●	●	●		●	●	●	●	●	●	●	●	●	●	●	●	●
Housing Improvement	●		●		●	●	●		●	●	●		●	●	●	●	●	●	●	●	●
Information and Referral		●		●			●		●											●	●
Legal Services	●			●	●	●			●	●	●		●		●	●			●	●	●
Placement Services		●		●					●	●	●			●	●		●		●		
Protective Services – Adults	●		●	●	●				●	●	●	●	●	●	●	●					●
Protective Services – Children	●	●	●	●	●				●	●	●	●	●	●	●	●					●
Protective Services – Various						●	●	●		●		●				●	●	●	●		●
Recreational Services	●			●		●			●	●	●		●			●	●	●			●
Res. Care & Treatment	●		●	●		●	●		●		●		●	●	●	●	●	●			●
Unmarried Parents Services	●		●							●	●	●	●	●							●
Socialization Services	●		●	●	●			●		●				●	●				●		●
Sp. Svcs. – Alcohol & Drugs											●		●	●		●		●		●	●
Sp. Svcs. – Blind				●	●			●					●							●	
Sp. Svcs. – Child & Youth				●	●								●		●					●	
Sp. Svcs. – Disabled				●	●				●				●		●					●	
Sp. Svcs. – Juvenile Dels.	●								●		●					●		●			
Transitional Services				●																	
Transportation	●	●	●	●	●	●	●		●	●	●	●	●	●	●	●	●	●	●	●	●
Vocational Rehab.	●			●		●	●	●	●	●			●	●			●	●		●	●
WIN Medical Exam.	●		●	●	●	●			●				●	●			●	●	●	●	●
Other	●			●	●		●									●	●	●		●	●
TOTALS	29	9	19	29	29	19	21	12	24	24	22	23	22	25	22	27	20	25	23	26	29

Source: Reports from the 50 States and the District of Columbia to DHEW

shows services provided under the Child Welfare Services program (Title IV-B) and WIN (the Work Incentive program under Title IV-A) as well as services provided under Title XX (all titles from the Social Security Act).

Questions about services being provided by States should be addressed to State and local social services agencies.

MASS.	MICHIGAN	MINNESOTA	MISS.	MISSOURI	MONTANA	NEBRASKA	NEVADA	NEW HAMP.	NEW JERSEY	NEW MEXICO	NEW YORK	NORTH CAR.	NORTH DAK.	OHIO	OKLAHOMA	OREGON	PENNA.	RHODE IS.	SOUTH CAR.	SOUTH DAK.	TENNESSEE	TEXAS	UTAH	VERMONT	VIRGINIA	WASH.	WEST VA.	WISCONSIN	WYOMING	TOTALS
•	•	•	•	•	•	•	•	•		•	•	•			•	•	•	•	•	•	•	•	•	•	•		•	•	•	•	43
•			•	•				•									•								•	•			•	•	12
•	•		•		•		•	•	•		•	•	•	•		•	•		•		•	•	•	•	•		•	•		•	35
•	•	•	•	•	•	•		•	•	•		•	•	•	•	•	•	•	•	•	•		•		•	•		•	•	•	41
	•	•	•		•			•	•	•	•	•	•	•		•	•		•		•	•		•	•	•			•		37
•	•	•	•	•	•	•	•	•	•	•	•	•	•	•	•	•	•	•	•	•	•	•	•	•	•	•	•	•	•	•	51
						•				•								•	•										•	•	6
		•	•						•			•			•		•	•		•		•			•				•		13
•	•	•	•	•	•	•	•	•	•	•	•			•	•	•		•	•		•	•		•	•	•	•	•	•	•	46
•										•	•	•		•	•		•	•		•	•		•	•					•	17
	•	•		•	•	•	•		•	•	•	•		•	•		•	•		•	•	•		•		•		•		•	33
•	•	•	•	•	•	•	•	•		•	•		•	•		•	•	•	•	•	•	•	•	•	•	•	•	•	•	•	39
•	•	•	•	•	•	•	•	•	•	•	•		•	•	•	•	•	•	•	•	•	•	•	•	•	•	•	•		•	51
•	•			•	•	•	•		•	•	•		•		•	•	•	•		•		•	•	•	•					•	32
	•	•			•	•	•	•		•	•	•		•		•	•		•		•	•	•	•	•	•				•	39
•		•		•	•	•	•		•		•		•		•		•		•	•	•	•		•		•				26
•	•			•	•	•	•	•	•	•	•	•		•	•	•	•		•		•	•	•	•	•	•	•	•			45
	•	•	•	•	•		•	•		•		•	•	•	•	•	•		•	•		•	•		•	•	•		•		32
•	•		•	•	•	•	•	•	•	•	•	•		•	•	•	•	•	•		•	•	•	•	•	•	•	•	•	•	48
•	•		•	•	•	•	•		•	•	•		•	•		•	•		•	•	•	•		•	•	•	•	•	•	•	43
•	•	•		•	•	•		•	•	•	•	•		•	•	•		•		•		•	•	•	•	•				43
	•			•	•						•				•	•	•		•			•	•						•	17
•		•			•	•		•		•	•	•		•	•	•	•		•		•	•	•	•	•	•	•	•	•		32
•	•				•	•		•		•	•	•		•		•			•		•	•	•			•		•		23
•	•	•		•	•	•		•	•	•		•		•		•		•		•	•	•	•	•	•	•	•		•		34
•	•			•	•	•		•	•	•	•		•	•	•	•			•		•	•	•	•	•	•				35
	•		•	•		•	•		•	•			•	•	•			•	•		•	•		•		•		•		23
•		•	•	•		•	•	•		•		•				•	•	•	•			•		•		•		•		25
•		•	•	•	•		•	•						•	•			•		•	•	•	•	•	•					26
					•						•	•								•	•			•						14
	•			•					•		•	•	•	•		•	•				•	•	•		•		•		•		25
							•					•						•	•					•						11
							•					•						•		•	•			•						10
												•						•		•	•									7
			•								•			•				•		•				•						12
				•				•			•						•				•				•					11
																		•		•										3
•	•	•	•	•	•	•	•	•	•	•	•	•	•	•	•	•		•	•	•		•	•	•	•	•	•	•	•	•	48
•	•		•	•	•				•	•	•						•			•	•		•	•	•	•	•	•		32
	•		•		•	•	•			•	•	•		•	•		•		•	•		•	•	•	•	•	•		•	31
	•	•	•	•	•				•	•	•		•	•		•		•	•		•								•	20
20	21	21	19	26	24	25	20	21	22	17	24	31	20	25	21	26	26	22	27	21	26	24	22	24	30	28	18	23	17	

Council following standards of national standard-setting organizations, and out-of-home care is provided in facilities licensed by the state or by an Indian Tribal Council and meet specified provisions of the 1968 Federal Interagency Day-Care Requirements and specified day care staffing standards given in the regulation.

Educational services: When not generally available from public educational agencies to state residents without cost and without regard to their income.

Institutional services: Only when services are not normally provided by institutional staff or contractors. These include prisons, skilled nursing facilities, intermediate care facilities, and hospitals.

Foster family homes: Only when a resident requires an identified special service because of a physical or mental health condition, an emotional or behavioral problem not available in the home.

Emergency shelter: Only for a child threatened by abuse, neglect, or exploitation, as approved by state or Indian Tribal Council authority not in excess of 30 days in any 12-month period.

Cash payments for a service: Only to reimburse an individual for such services provided in the state service plan.

Procedures

Families and individuals are free to accept or reject social services; acceptance of a service under the program may not be a prerequisite for the receipt of assistance payments or other services, except for (1) protective services for children and adults, or (2) registration for work and training under the WIN program. An individual recipient basic data file is maintained for each family, child, and adult recipient who requests and requires services. It contains identifying information about the recipient, his basis of eligibility services provided, goal to which services are directed, provider agency or staff for each service, and other pertinent social, family, and economic information. The data file is not required for persons requesting information about services who are referred to other community resources.

Each individual may apply for service in writing on a state social services form to establish eligibility. The application may be filed by the applicant himself, or his authorized representative, or where incompetent or incapacitated, by someone acting responsibly for him. Applications must be acted upon by the state or local agency within 30 days and notice of its approval or denial given promptly, and if denied, with information about his right to request a fair hearing. If his eligibility is based on receipt of income maintenance, this fact is verified by agency personnel from documentation on his income maintenance status. Applications based on income status, rather than public assistance, shall be supported by documentation supplied by the applicant of his family monthly gross income.

Redeterminations of eligibility are initiated by agency personnel when information is received by the agency of changes in the individual's personal or financial situation which may make him ineligible. The review takes place within 30 days of the information. Otherwise, redeterminations are made periodically but not less frequently than every six months.

An eligible individual with a service problem is assigned to a social service worker for problem identification, diagnosis, counseling, arrangements for followup services, and supervision to provide help and encouragement to the individual and his family. Since this worker–client relationship may involve personal, psychological, family relations, social or economic conditions, the full range of social work analytical skills is required in the process. Changes in the individual's status are noted in a continuous service record kept by the worker and progress towards reaching the service goal is noted quite thoroughly by the worker. Barriers or other problems which arise in the course of time are dealt with to the extent possible by action of the social worker and agreement of the individual. The success of this process is dependent upon a number of factors: the close, confidential relationship between worker and client, the availability of community services and resources to turn to for help, the resourcefulness of the worker, and the inherent desire and drive of the client for self-improvement.

CHILD WELFARE SERVICES PROGRAM

The objectives of child welfare services program are

1. to prevent or remedy, or assist in the solution of problems which may result in the neglect, abuse, exploitation, or delinquency of children;
2. to protect and care for homeless, dependent, or neglected children;
3. to protect and promote the welfare of children of working mothers; and
4. otherwise to protect and promote the welfare of children, including the strengthening of their own homes where possible, or, where needed, the provision of adequate care of children away from their homes in foster family homes or day care or other child care facility.

Background

Public social services for the protection of children, strengthening family life and promoting the welfare of children were provided by state and local governments since before the turn of the twentieth century. Children's institutions, foster care placements, services to handicapped and retarded children, mothers aid programs and services for unmarried mothers were in operation prior to the passage of the Social Security Act of 1935. The organization of the Children's Bureau in 1912 and its activities subsequently reflected the federal government's recognition for the support of programs for children and their families through advocacy, research, studies and reports, and convening White House Conferences on Children and Youth.

The Social Security Act authorized the child welfare services program as the federal/state grant-in-aid program to help establish, extend, and strengthen state and local child welfare agencies through formula grants based on the child's population in each state and inversely with average per capita income. The 1967 Social Security Amendment transferred the program from Title V, Grants to States for Maternal and Child Welfare, to Title IV, Grants to States for Aid and Services to Needy Families with Children and specified that states designate the state agency responsible for administering or supervising the administration of the AFDC program to be made responsible for the child welfare services program, unless on or prior to January 2, 1968 they were administered separately and the state decided to retain their separateness. The 1972 Social Security Amendments authorized increased appropriations with the intent to apply them to increased foster care and adoption services. However, D/HEW budget requests for the late 1960s and 1970s remained at a level of spending of $46 million. It is estimated that the $46 million comprises 10 percent of total state and local child welfare service expenditures. However, this appropriation is supplemented by Title XX social service expenditures for AFDC children under child welfare supervision. State and local welfare agencies assign as much of the services costs as possible associated with providing child welfare services to the AFDC social services program in order to authorize their resources and provide additional services when their child services funds are exhausted. Estimates are that between half to three-fourths of state child welfare services caseloads are comprised of AFDC children.

Administering Agencies

The Children's Bureau, D/HEW Office of Human Development Services administers federal grants to states. The program is administered by a state agency through district and county offices in 33 jurisdictions and administered by local agencies with state supervision in 20 jurisdictions. In Illinois, child welfare services programs continue to be administered separately from the Title XX Social Services program. In Ohio, Pennsylvania, and Oregon, this separation exists at the local level.

Caseloads

Three million children received child welfare services in 1974.[2]

Total	3.0 million*
In home of parents or relatives	2,590,000

*Of this number, DHEW estimates 400,000 children in 220,000 families receive public services and services of voluntary child welfare agencies and institutions.

In independent living arrangements	11,455
In foster family homes	247,238
In group homes	4,532
In institutions	65,772
In adoptive homes	44,771
Elsewhere	13,344

Eligibility Requirements

There are no income or resources limitations for eligibility for the state child welfare services program. These services are available on the basis of need for services in the neglect, abuse, exploitation, or delinquency of children, or the protection or promotion of the welfare of children. Services may not be denied on the basis of financial need, legal residence, social status, or religion. Children and families receive services under one of two conditions: they may apply or be referred to the state or local agency voluntarily, or they may be referred to the agency by a court or other juvenile or family relations authority and be placed legally under the agency's supervision. If the latter, the agency acts as agent of the judicial authority and its services carry the sanction of that authority, that is, they are mandatory upon the child and/or his family until discharged by the authority.

Services

As a minimum, child welfare services are available to children in their own homes and in the provision of foster care. They include but are not limited to the following:

1. Foster care in foster family homes or institutions when children must be removed from their own homes.
2. Adoption placement services to provide a permanent family home for children who have lost their parents or whose parent's rights to them have been legally terminated.
3. Emergency care and protection of children reported to be abused, neglected, abandoned, or exploited by parents or guardians.

4. Services and assistance for unmarried mothers and their babies, including education and training of the mothers and family planning services.
5. Homemaker services to care for children in their own or a foster home during the absence or incapacity of parents or to help parents improve child care and household practices in order to prevent family disintegration.
6. Counseling children and their parents in relation to behavior problems, parent-child conflicts, physical and mental handicaps, and emotional and social adjustment.
7. Recruitment and licensing of child care facilities.
8. Day care services to care for children whose mothers are temporarily absent from the home and for children who need day care for such reasons as training to compensate for a physical or mental handicap.

Procedure

Each child referred to a child welfare agency undergoes diagnostic evaluation to determine the nature and causes of his social, psychological condition, the family/child relationships, the child's self perceptions, and other factors contributing to the problems of the child and his family. A case plan is drawn up and a treatment program developed with the cooperation of the child, his parents, or caretakers. Frequent review of the case plan and treatment program is made, changes in the child's and family's behavior patterns and relationships are noted, the success of placements in foster and other home settings is evaluated, and the outcomes of other services are measured in terms of the child's functioning and his present and future growth and development.

IN-KIND PROGRAMS

One of the more distinctive characteristics of the public welfare system is that it provides tangible products for needy persons in addition to money payments and social services. These are medical care, food, job training, and employment. Not unlike national programs in other aspects of American life, these came into existence under different acts of Congress at different times to deal with specific national problems which surfaced in public discussions and Congressional debate and enactment of federal law. Three programs of in-kind services resulted: Medical Assistance Program (Medicaid), Food Stamp Program, Work Incentive Program (WIN).

These in-kind programs have some common characteristics:

1.   They are intended to supplement, not replace, other income maintenance and social services benefits available to low-income persons;

2.   They have added responsibilities to state and local public welfare agencies and have expanded the responsibilities of the Departments of Health, Education, and Welfare; Agriculture; and Labor.

3.   They authorize additional federal grant-in-aid funds to state and local agencies and require matching of state funds for such purposes. (For the Food Stamp Programs, this pertains only to state/local administration, for Medicaid and WIN programs, it applies to program costs as well as state/local administration.)

4.   They required adoption of new administrative and program mechanisms, processes, and methods by public welfare agencies.

5.   They set up new relationships between public welfare agencies and other government agencies at the three levels of government.

6.   In Medicaid and Food Stamp programs, they created new categories of eligible persons and thereby enlarged the responsibilities of the public welfare system for a larger segment of poor and near-poor populations.

MEDICAL ASSISTANCE PROGRAM (MEDICAID)

The objective of Medicaid is to enable each state, at its option, to furnish (1) medical assistance on behalf of needy families with dependent children and needy individuals who are aged, blind, or permanently and totally disabled, and (2) rehabilitation and other services to help such families and individuals attain or retain capability for independence or self-care.

Background

The program was enacted in the present form in 1965 as Title XIX of the Social Security Act. Amendments in 1967 limited federal financial participation to payments on behalf of certain categories of persons whose income does not exceed 133 1/3 percent of the highest amount payable to a comparable AFDC family, and withdrew federal financial participation in medical assistance costs that would have been covered under Medicare, Part B, if eligible beneficiaries had been enrolled.

Prior provisions for medical assistance, under an amendment to the Social Security Act in 1950, provided for federal financial participation in direct vendor payments for medical care for public assistance recipients. An amendment to Title I in 1960 authorized additional federal matching for medical care payments for OAA recipients and also authorized programs of medical assistance for the aged which provided for medical care payments in behalf of medically needy aged who were not receiving public assistance. By the end of 1965, all states and jurisdictions had programs of vendor payments for medical care (limited to types of care and amounts specified by each state) for public assistance recipients, with a few states limited to the OAA category only, and 47 states had programs of medical assistance for the aged. By 1970, all states and jurisdictions, except Alaska and Arizona, had initiated Title XIX Medicaid programs which replaced the vendor payment and medical assistance for the aged program. Alaska initiated a Medicaid program in 1973. Federal participation in medical vendor payments under the public assistance titles was terminated after December 31, 1969.

The 1972 and 1973 Social Security Amendments amended

the program primarily to improve its fiscal and administrative controls, to clarify technical requirements and to remove potential abuses by health service providers and users of the services. The 1972 Amendments (P.L. 92-603) provided the following changes:

—instituted utilization review programs for institutional services (hospitals, nursing homes, institutional care facilities) as well as private practitioners effective July 1, 1973;

—effective January 1, 1973, required states which cover the medically indigent to impose monthly premium charges, graduated by income, and permitted states to require payment of the medically indigent of nominal deductibles and co-payment amounts in sharing medical care costs. States are also permitted to impose deductibles and co-payment amounts for medical costs of optional services received by cash assistance recipients such as drugs, hearing aids, and to exclude from this provision services required by federal law, namely, inpatient and outpatient hospital services, other x-ray and laboratory services, physician services, and home health services;

—termination of Medicaid eligibility is delayed four months for an eligible person or family losing eligibility because of increased earnings from employment;

—optometric services provided by an optometrist for eye care could be covered under a state Medicaid program;

—effective January 1, 1973, federal financial administration in reimbursement for skilled nursing homes and intermediate care facilities would be limited to 105 percent of per diem costs;

—states would be allowed to develop their own methods and standards for reimbursement of the reasonable costs of inpatient hospital services;

—a common definition and standards are to be established for "extended care facilities" under Medicare and "skilled nursing homes" under Medicaid, and the term "skilled nursing facilities" would be applied to both;

—reimbursement rates for skilled nursing facilities and intermediate care facilities would be based on a reasonable
cost-related basis using acceptable cost-finding techniques and methods approved by the Secretary of
D/HEW;

—professional standards review organizations (PSRO)
would be required in local areas to assume responsibility
for the review of professional care and services under
the Medicaid and Medicare programs. Professional
standards for institutional and noninstitutional care
and services would be developed and applied in such
reviews.

The 1973 Amendments (P.L. 93-233) clarified Congressional intent to assure that any new SSI recipients and essential
persons would obtain eligibility for the Medicaid program. Institutionalized persons in need of a supplementary payment if their
income is within 300 percent of the SSI benefit level applicable
to a noninstitutionalized person with no other income would be
carried under Medicaid. For persons not receiving an SSI federal benefit payment, but receiving a state supplemental payment, Medicaid eligibility is optional at the discretion of the
state.

Administering Agencies

The Health Care Financing Administration of the D/HEW administers grants to states. In 41 states and Guam the responsible
state agency is the same agency which administers or supervises
public assistance programs. In three of these states responsibility for administration of medical aspects of the program is con-
tracted out to the state health department. In eight states,
Puerto Rico, and the Virgin Islands, the agency responsible for
administration of the medicaid program is the Department of
Health, or, in one state, a medicaid commission. In these states
eligibility for medical assistance is determined by the public
assistance agency. Arizona is the only state electing not to participate in the program.

Caseloads and Costs

Over nine million persons received health care under the Medicaid program in December, 1975, 6.9 million or three-fourths of whom were cash payment recipients and 2.1 million or one-fourth other medically indigent persons (Table 4.2). It is estimated that, over a year's span, about 25 million different individuals receive health care under the program.

During December, 1975, $1.2 billions was paid for medical services for the nine million beneficiaries, making the program one of the largest of all health care programs in the nation (Tables 4.2 and 4.3).

Over half of the recipients are AFDC families and other low-income families with children eligible for state Medicaid programs. However, payments in their behalf represent only a third of total Medicaid payments. In contrast, aged, blind, and disabled beneficiaries are a third of total beneficiaries but payments for care account for more than half of total payments (Tables 4.3 and 4.4). This pattern has been consistent from the beginning of the program and is attributable to the higher costs for hospital and other institutional care provided the aged, blind, and disabled and the higher incidence of chronic illnesses among them. Table 4.5 reveals that over a three-month period, January to March, 1975 over 70 percent of payments made were for inpatient hospital care, skilled nursing facility, and intermediate care facility services.

Eight states with the largest medical vendor payments and caseloads in the aggregate constituted 60 percent of payments and one-half of all cases in December, 1975, as follows:

Basis of eligibility	Payments (in millions)	Percent	Case load (in millions)	Percent
Age 65 and over	$ 446	37.2	2.0	22.2
Blindness	7	.5	.1	1.2
Permanent and total disability	307	25.6	1.3	14.4
Family with children	366	30.5	5.0	55.5
Other Title XIX recipients	74	6.2	.6	6.7
Total	$1,200	100.0%	9.0	100.0%

	Payments (in millions)	Recipients (in thousands)
New York	$289	1,242
California	124	1,082
Michigan	61	454
Texas	58	339
Pennsylvania	56	245
Massachusetts	53	422
New Jersey	43	288
Ohio	42	384
Total	$726	4,456
Totals, December, 1975	$1.2 billion	9.0 million
Percent to Total	60.5%	49.5%

Eligibility Requirements

All states and jurisdictions opting to provide Medicaid programs must provide medical assistance for specified medical services to at least three groups: (1) Recipients of categorical money payments (under SSI, OAA, AB, APTD, and AFDC); (2) persons who would be eligible for money payments except for an eligibility condition or requirement that is prohibited under Title XIX, such as a lien imposed on the property of an individual prior to his death; and (3) children under 21 who would be eligible for AFDC except for an age or school attendance requirement.

In addition to the above mandatory components of Medicaid programs, states have elected to include categorically needy groups. These are defined as persons who are eligible for a categorical money payment or would be except for eligibility conditions prohibited under Title XIX, state-imposed eligibility less liberal than permitted under federal regulations, or residence in a medical institution. States may also include as categorically needy essential spouses of SSI recipients and children under 21 years of age who are financially eligible regardless of whether they meet the test of deprivation of parental support because of the death, incapacity, or absence of a parent, unemployment of the father, or whether they are living with a specified relative as required for eligibility to receive an AFDC money payment. Under this option, the children may receive Medicaid

Table 4.2 Recipients With Medical Vendor Payments by Basis of Eligibility of Recipients and by HEW Region and State (December, 1975)

BASIS OF ELIGIBILITY OF RECIPIENT

HEW REGION AND STATE	TOTAL	AGE 65 OR OVER	BLINDNESS	PERMANENT AND TOTAL DISABILITY	MEMBERSHIP IN FAMILY WITH CHILDREN UNDER 21	OTHER TITLE XIX RECIPIENTS
TOTAL REPORTING STATES	9,041,802	2,078,677	45,549	1,300,027	5,017,260	600,258
REGION I	644,610	151,668	2,922	69,517	379,362	41,141
CONNECTICUT	96,765	22,529	195	13,308	56,975	3,758
MAINE	53,747	13,878	367	7,566	31,738	198
MASSACHUSETTS	422,497	92,371	1,546	38,160	253,441	36,579
NEW HAMPSHIRE	19,210	6,057	252	2,098	10,648	155
RHODE ISLAND	52,391	16,833	162	8,385	26,560	451
REGION II	1,858,507	269,285	3,277	200,067	1,026,189	360,089
NEW JERSEY	288,002	38,174	636	32,222	209,162	7,808
NEW YORK	1,242,165	230,318	2,485	154,150	677,920	177,292
PUERTO RICO	326,655	701	155	13,383	138,718	173,698
VIRGIN ISLANDS	2,085	92	1	312	389	1,291
REGION III	663,216	119,677	2,636	88,863	371,564	80,476
DELAWARE	16,873	2,725	162	1,986	11,655	345
DIST. OF COL.	62,751	6,973	135	7,047	47,449	1,187
MARYLAND	156,168	26,930	249	19,524	87,144	22,272
PENNSYLVANIA	244,605	36,930	865	29,495	121,640	55,675
VIRGINIA	134,297	35,656	984	20,202	76,616	839
WEST VIRGINIA	48,482	10,414	241	10,609	27,060	158
REGION IV	1,256,465	458,657	11,496	251,702	528,744	5,839
ALABAMA	167,751	81,598	1,443	33,330	51,380	---
FLORIDA	160,349	56,388	1,221	36,815	65,925	---
GEORGIA	216,307	71,694	1,583	42,304	100,726	---
KENTUCKY	161,715	45,395	1,197	27,662	83,895	3,566
MISSISSIPPI	135,460	56,619	1,008	19,887	57,811	135
NORTH CAROLINA	165,543	53,943	2,882	38,285	69,063	1,339
SOUTH CAROLINA	95,975	36,574	1,358	18,948	38,375	720
TENNESSEE	153,265	56,446	804	34,471	61,569	79

154

REGION V	2,033,341	310,722	6,482	247,337	1,445,486	23,314
ILLINOIS	787,425	62,541	1,127	84,452	635,186	4,123
INDIANA	104,176	21,456	784	14,731	67,205	---
MICHIGAN	454,208	67,054	1,039	57,785	319,870	8,460
MINNESOTA	119,513	32,451	492	15,580	62,875	8,515
OHIO	383,706	78,750	2,324	48,025	254,607	---
WISCONSIN	183,905	48,470	716	26,764	105,743	2,216
REGION VI	713,831	314,344	4,804	122,404	263,385	8,894
ARKANSAS	113,047	45,933	1,010	20,092	43,874	2,138
LOUISIANA	180,009	74,986	1,119	35,512	67,764	628
NEW MEXICO	29,536	5,737	171	6,374	17,254	---
OKLAHOMA	51,503	26,612	286	7,664	10,813	6,128
TEXAS	339,736	161,076	2,218	52,762	123,680	---
REGION VII	380,776	100,118	3,291	41,963	208,290	27,114
IOWA	79,246	21,111	749	8,014	47,287	2,085
KANSAS	102,935	18,939	441	11,478	54,083	17,954
MISSOURI	166,022	49,401	1,940	17,377	90,305	6,999
NEBRASKA	32,573	10,667	161	5,094	16,615	36
REGION VIII	130,100	38,122	499	21,104	65,535	4,840
COLORADO	66,718	20,347	202	10,559	31,623	3,987
MONTANA	17,086	4,536	144	3,476	8,930	---
NORTH DAKOTA	8,929	3,628	17	1,311	3,835	138
SOUTH DAKOTA	12,851	5,798	55	1,890	4,818	290
UTAH	24,516	3,813	81	3,868	16,329	425
REGION IX	1,136,149	270,634	8,960	217,554	601,382	37,619
CALIFORNIA	1,081,820	262,939	8,801	213,324	569,636	27,120
HAWAII	44,127	4,887	68	2,881	26,102	10,189
NEVADA	10,202	2,808	91	1,349	5,644	310
REGION X	224,403	45,450	1,182	39,516	127,323	10,932
ALASKA	3,642	390	9	626	2,617	---
IDAHO	18,389	4,231	50	3,436	10,672	---
OREGON	74,932	11,815	695	10,288	45,611	6,523
WASHINGTON	127,440	29,014	428	25,166	68,423	4,409

Source: Medical Assistance (Medicaid) Financed Under Title XIX of the Social Security Act. December 1975. DHEW Publication No. (SRS) 76–03150, NCSS Report B–1 (12/75), issued April 1976.

155

Table 4.3 Amounts of Medical Vendor Payments by Basis of Eligibility of
Recipients and by HEW Region and State (December, 1975)

HEW REGION AND STATE	TOTAL	BASIS OF ELIGIBILITY OF RECIPIENT				
		AGE 65 OR OVER	BLINDNESS	PERMANENT AND TOTAL DISABILITY	MEMBERSHIP IN FAMILY WITH CHILDREN UNDER 21	OTHER TITLE XIX RECIPIENTS
TOTAL REPORTING STATES	$1,198,788,287	$445,741,908	$7,024,749	$306,955,700	$265,327,326	$73,660,564
REGION I	83,725,607	40,407,952	495,738	17,976,760	21,035,799	3,805,358
CONNECTICUT	14,029,792	6,921,970	44,061	3,237,609	3,345,673	480,480
MAINE	6,666,204	2,577,060	16,032	1,414,342	2,656,068	2,702
MASSACHUSETTS	53,434,006	25,687,974	358,054	11,212,422	12,896,224	3,279,334
NEW HAMPSHIRE	2,526,171	1,518,057	56,191	403,458	541,338	7,127
RHODE ISLAND	7,069,431	3,702,891	25,400	1,708,929	1,596,496	35,715
REGION II	339,691,994	142,908,641	1,087,840	66,876,547	51,026,945	37,792,021
NEW JERSEY	43,126,533	23,926,981	109,835	4,830,075	12,934,460	1,325,182
NEW YORK	289,312,180	118,882,425	973,825	61,791,295	35,748,873	31,915,762
PUERTO RICO	7,142,736	96,725	4,157	243,313	2,325,692	4,472,849
VIRGIN ISLANDS	110,545	2,510	23	11,864	17,920	78,228
REGION III	98,716,487	32,572,179	510,612	21,969,117	21,357,687	12,306,852
DELAWARE	1,367,544	435,367	12,419	248,443	659,991	11,324
DIST. OF COL.	7,152,553	724,553	22,387	1,630,424	4,422,568	352,621
MARYLAND	15,232,465	4,650,805	22,419	2,593,819	5,583,055	2,382,367
PENNSYLVANIA	55,729,259	19,716,643	319,018	12,182,209	14,329,787	9,181,602
VIRGINIA	15,506,922	6,068,492	117,373	4,285,658	4,739,691	295,708
WEST VIRGINIA	3,727,744	976,319	16,996	1,028,564	1,622,595	83,270
REGION IV	106,661,474	47,298,346	1,025,339	30,079,406	27,727,029	453,214
ALABAMA	11,855,295	6,422,041	101,658	2,513,420	2,818,176	---
FLORIDA	14,239,193	7,325,936	92,015	3,392,089	3,428,153	---
GEORGIA	21,547,096	8,732,157	133,087	6,820,788	6,261,064	
KENTUCKY	16,778,220	3,493,990	97,838	3,480,846	3,465,279	240,267
MISSISSIPPI	8,343,064	4,377,729	63,028	1,710,210	2,183,864	8,233
NORTH CAROLINA	15,532,236	6,101,742	322,511	4,899,258	4,046,028	84,557
SOUTH CAROLINA	8,416,265	4,044,690	133,342	1,992,864	2,132,987	112,382
TENNESSEE	15,550,105	6,800,061	80,860	5,269,931	3,391,478	7,775

156

REGION V	252,878,244	73,182,172	1,261,863	72,524,641	101,457,785	4,451,783
ILLINOIS	66,674,588	14,258,966	166,735	19,878,179	21,985,811	385,297
INDIANA	15,720,010	6,410,692	164,177	4,488,661	4,959,480	----
MICHIGAN	61,150,160	15,682,019	144,557	14,311,065	25,608,376	1,404,103
MINNESOTA	33,735,574	11,985,449	149,328	13,009,132	6,411,287	2,184,778
OHIO	42,214,942	12,667,135	335,702	9,377,261	19,834,845	477,605
WISCONSIN	33,378,169	12,480,911	301,324	11,460,343	8,657,986	
REGION VI	96,751,222	43,372,465	623,603	33,742,184	16,399,362	2,613,708
ARKANSAS	9,198,607	4,215,051	96,904	2,515,627	2,126,096	244,929
LOUISIANA	16,014,034	7,197,949	104,087	5,150,279	3,528,716	33,003
NEW MEXICO	2,715,159	697,357	41,148	986,378	950,276	----
OKLAHOMA	10,557,105	5,598,551	55,649	1,963,108	1,004,025	----
TEXAS	57,866,413	25,663,557	325,615	23,126,792	8,750,249	2,335,776
REGION VII	40,597,596	14,123,667	317,274	7,794,904	13,873,122	4,888,629
IOWA	8,159,662	4,689,216	85,385	1,170,529	2,064,455	150,077
KANSAS	17,398,613	3,641,509	74,041	3,642,141	5,558,598	4,042,324
MISSOURI	11,101,742	3,587,730	124,244	1,976,905	4,721,926	690,937
NEBRASKA	4,337,579	2,205,212	33,604	1,005,329	1,088,143	5,291
REGION VIII	19,181,174	8,163,031	140,395	5,615,581	4,544,291	717,876
COLORADO	9,076,555	3,695,793	77,776	2,834,746	2,004,567	463,673
MONTANA	2,842,641	1,100,016	31,701	971,333	739,591	----
NORTH DAKOTA	2,042,622	1,240,192	9,427	339,309	383,900	69,795
SOUTH DAKOTA	1,914,257	1,101,596	7,615	428,081	357,388	19,577
UTAH	3,305,098	1,025,434	13,876	1,042,112	1,058,845	164,831
REGION IX	129,943,817	33,919,809	1,246,548	41,566,151	47,955,773	5,255,536
CALIFORNIA	123,505,370	31,879,135	1,221,397	40,471,544	45,693,847	4,239,447
HAWAII	4,586,047	1,485,391	7,701	515,820	1,596,818	980,317
NEVADA	1,852,400	555,283	17,450	578,787	665,108	35,772
REGION X	30,240,672	9,793,646	311,537	8,810,409	9,949,533	1,375,547
ALASKA	756,283	302,174	4,244	260,308	189,557	----
IDAHO	2,325,723	851,371	4,667	886,422	543,263	----
OREGON	10,590,004	2,826,365	255,762	3,250,507	2,854,812	398,558
WASHINGTON	16,568,662	5,773,736	42,864	4,413,172	5,361,901	976,989

Source: DHEW Publication No. (SRS) 76-03150), NCSS Report B-1 12/75.

157

Table 4.4 Distribution of Participants and Dollars by
Category of Assistance: Medical Assistance Program

Participants / Dollars a/

Participants		Dollars a/
17%	Aged	35%
9%		
28%	Blind and Disabled	26%
	AFDC Adults	
46%		18%
	Children under 21	
		21%

<u>a/</u> Although based on FY72 statistical data (the most recent available) it is
not expected that significant deviations from this distribution would
appear. Source: NCSS B-4 (FY72)
Source: 1976 House Appropriations Committee Hearings Subcommittee of HEW
and Labor, p. 81.

Table 4.5 Distribution of Amounts of Medical Vendor
Payments By Type of Service, January to March 1975

	Amount	Percentage
Inpatient hospital services:	$1,011,349,014	31.2%
In general hospital	893,816,860	27.6
In mental hospital	117,532,154	3.6
Skilled nursing facility services	713,783,838	22.0
Intermediate care facility services	554,509,072	17.1
Physician's services	314,255,642	9.7
Dental services	82,214,616	2.5
Other practitioners services	29,686,556	.9
Outpatient hospital services	89,967,082	3.0
Clinic services	96,967,082	3.0
Laboratory and radiology services	26,605,471	.8
Home health services	23,540,009	.7
Prescribed drugs	218,168,096	6.7
Family planning services	18,462,217	.6
Other care	59,769,289	1.8
Total	$3,238,451,465	100%

Source: DHEW Publication No. (SRS) 76-03150, NCSS Report B-1 (3/1975), Medical
Assistance (Medicaid) financed under Title XIX of the Social Security Act, March 1975.
National Center for Social Statistics, August 1975.

benefits but not the parents or other caretaker regardless of their medical need unless they meet all conditions for eligibility for AFDC. The following are covered by state programs:

> Persons in a medical facility who are not receiving financial assistance but who would be eligible for SSI, OAA, AB, APTD, or AFDC if they left the facility—47 states.
>
> Persons eligible for but not receiving assistance under one of the above categories—35 states.
>
> Essential spouse who is essential to the well-being of a recipient of SSI, OAA, AB, APTD—28 states.
>
> The parents or relatives living with dependent children who have been excluded from AFDC because of an age or school attendance requirement—25 states.
>
> Children under 21 in foster homes or institutions for whom public agencies are assuming some financial responsibility—34 states.
>
> All financially eligible individuals under 21—18 states.

Twenty-eight States, the District of Columbia, Guam, Puerto Rico, and the Virgin Islands also extend coverage to the medically needy, that is, persons meeting the basic eligibility conditions for coverage of the categorically needy (aged, blind, disabled, or families with children deprived of parental support) whose income and resources exceed the levels for eligibility for financial assistance but are insufficient to meet the cost of medical care. Groups excluded are nondisabled adults under age 65 and intact families with children with an employed father in the home (Table 4.6).

Income Test

INCOME LIMITS.   Recipients of money payments under programs of SSI, OAA, AB, APTD, or AFDC are automatically eligible for Medicaid (except in Arizona). For the categorically needy, income limits are the same as those set by the state for the receipt of cash benefits under the category of assistance to which the applicant is characteristically related. For the medi-

Table 4.6 Medicaid Services State by State, June 1, 1976[1]

Services provided only under the Medicare buy-in or the screening and treatment program for individuals under 21 are not shown on this chart.

Definitions and limitations on eligibility and services vary from State to State. Details are available from local welfare offices and State Medicaid agencies.

Additional services for which Federal financial participation is available to States under Medicaid.

Legend:

● offered for people receiving federally supported financial assistance

▲ offered also for people in public assistance[2] and SSI[3] categories who are financially eligible for medical but not for financial assistance

FMAP[4]	*BASIC SERVICES MEDICAID REQUIRED	State	Clinic services	Prescribed drugs	Dental services	Prosthetic devices	Eyeglasses	Private duty nursing	Physical therapy and related services	Other diagnostic, screening, preventive and rehabilitative services	Emergency hospital services	Skilled nursing facility services for patients under 21	Optometrists' services	Podiatrists' services	Chiropractors' services	Care for patients 65 or older in institutions for mental diseases	Care for patients 65 or older in institutions for tuberculosis	Care for patients under 21 in psychiatric hospitals	Institutional services in intermediate care facilities	
74	●	Alabama		●		●					●	●	●					●	●5/	AL
50	●	Alaska									●	●	●			●			●5/	AK
60	●	Arizona																		AZ
75	▲	Arkansas	▲	▲	▲	▲					▲	●				▲	▲	▲	●5/	AR
50	▲	California	▲	▲	▲	▲	▲		▲	▲	▲	▲	▲	▲	▲	▲	▲	▲	▲5/	CA
55	●	Colorado		●		●			●		●	●		●		●			●5/	CO
50	▲	Connecticut	▲	▲	▲	▲	▲	▲	▲		▲	▲	▲			▲		▲	▲5/	CT
50	●	Delaware	●	●						●				●		●	●			DE
50	▲	D.C.	▲	▲		▲	▲		▲	▲	▲	▲	▲	▲		▲	▲	▲	▲5/	DC
57	●	Florida		●							●					●	●		●5/	FL
66	●	Georgia		●		●				●		●		●		●	●		●5/	GA
50	▲	Guam	▲	▲	▲	▲	▲		▲		▲	▲	▲							GU
50	▲	Hawaii	▲	▲	▲	▲			▲	▲	▲	▲	▲						▲	HI
68	●	Idaho	●	●							●	●	●	●	●				●5/	ID
50	▲	Illinois	▲	▲	▲	▲	▲	▲	▲	▲	▲	▲	▲	▲		▲	▲	▲	▲5/	IL
57	●	Indiana	●	●	●	●	●	●	●	●	●	●	●	●		●	●		●	IN
57	●	Iowa		●	●	●	●		●		●	●	●	●	●				●5/	IA
54	▲	Kansas	▲	▲	▲	▲	▲	▲	▲	▲	▲	▲	▲	▲		▲	▲	▲	▲5/	KS
71	▲	Kentucky	▲	▲	▲	▲			▲		▲	▲				▲	▲	▲	▲5/	KY
72	●	Louisiana	●	●		●				●	●	●		●		●	●		●5/	LA
71	▲	Maine	●	▲		▲	▲		▲	▲	▲	▲	▲	▲	▲	▲		▲	▲5/	ME
50	▲	Maryland	▲	▲		▲	▲			▲			▲	▲			▲		▲5/	MD
50	▲	Massachusetts	▲	▲	▲	▲	▲	▲	▲	▲	▲	▲	▲	▲		▲	▲	▲	▲5/	MA
50	▲	Michigan	▲	▲		▲	▲			▲	▲	▲	▲	▲		▲	▲	▲	▲5/	MI
57	▲	Minnesota	▲	▲	▲	▲	▲	▲	▲	▲	▲	▲	▲	▲	▲	▲	▲	▲	▲5/	MN
78	●	Mississippi	●	●							●					●	●		●5/	MS
59	●	Missouri		●	●					●		●		●		●	●		●5/	MO
63	▲	Montana	▲	▲	▲	▲	▲	▲	▲	▲	▲	▲	▲	▲	▲	▲	▲	▲	▲5/	MT
54	▲	Nebraska	▲	▲	▲	▲	▲	●	▲	●	▲	▲	▲	●		▲	▲	▲	▲5/	NB
50	●	Nevada	●	●		●	●	●	●		●	●	●	●		●	●		●5/	NV
60	▲	New Hampshire	▲	▲		●	●		●		●	●	●	●		●	●		●5/	NH
50	●	New Jersey	●	●	●	●	●	●	●	●	●	●	●	●		●	●	●	●	NJ
73	●	New Mexico	●	●	●	●	●		●	●	●	●	●	●		●	●		●5/	NM
50	▲	New York	▲	▲	▲	▲	▲	▲	▲	▲	▲	▲	▲	▲		▲	▲	▲	▲5/	NY
68	▲	North Carolina	▲	▲	▲	▲			▲		▲		▲	▲	▲	▲	▲	▲	▲	NC
58	▲	North Dakota	▲	▲	▲	▲		▲	▲	▲	▲	▲	▲	▲		▲	▲		▲	ND
54	●	Ohio	●	●	●	●	●	●	●	●	●	●	●	●		●	●	●	●	OH
67	▲	Oklahoma		●	▲								▲	▲		▲	▲		▲	OK
59	●	Oregon	●	●	●	●	●		●		●	●	●	●	●				●5/	OR
55	▲	Pennsylvania	▲	▲	▲	●	●		▲	●	▲	▲	▲	●	▲	▲	▲	▲	▲5/	PA
50	▲	Puerto Rico	▲	▲	▲				▲	▲	▲	▲				▲				PR
57	▲	Rhode Island	▲	▲	▲	▲					▲	▲				▲		▲	●5/	RI
74	●	South Carolina	●	●		●			●		●	●	●		●	●	●		●5/	SC
67	●	South Dakota	●	●		●	●		●		●	●	●	●	●				●5/	SD
70	▲	Tennessee	▲	▲		▲					▲					▲	▲	▲	▲5/	TN
64	●	Texas		●	●		●				●		●	●			●		●5/	TX
70	▲	Utah	▲	▲	▲	▲	▲	▲	▲	●	▲	▲	▲	▲		▲	▲	▲	▲5/	UT
70	▲	Vermont	▲	▲	▲	▲					▲	▲		▲		▲		▲	▲5/	VT
50	▲	Virgin Islands	▲	▲	▲	▲	▲													VI
58	▲	Virginia	▲	▲			▲		▲		▲		▲	▲		▲		▲	▲5/	VA
54	▲	Washington	▲	▲	▲	▲	▲	▲	▲	▲	▲	▲	▲	▲	▲	▲	▲	▲	▲5/	WA
72	▲	West Virginia									▲	▲	▲	▲		▲	▲	▲	▲	WV
60	▲	Wisconsin	▲	▲	▲	▲	▲		▲		▲	▲	▲	▲		▲	▲	▲	▲5/	WI
61	●	Wyoming																	●	WY

Totals:

	● 21 / ▲ 32	Total 53																		
●	21			13	21	12	14	12	5	10	5	18	18	15	14	10	14	11	8	25
▲	32			29	30	22	27	24	14	22	17	25	25	23	23	18	27	19	21	25
	Total 53			42	51	34	41	36	19	32	22	43	43	38	37	28	41	30	29	50

Intermediate Care Facilities (ICF): P.L. 92-223 transferred the ICF program to Medicaid (Title XIX) as an optional service, effective 1-1-72. States may at their option include institutions for the mentally retarded, both public and private. See footnote five.

*BASIC REQUIRED MEDICAID SERVICES: Every Medicaid program must cover at least these services for at least everyone receiving federally supported financial assistance: inpatient hospital care; outpatient hospital services; other laboratory and X-ray services; skilled nursing facility services and home health services for individuals 21 and older; early and periodic screening, diagnosis, and treatment for individuals under 21; family planning; and physician services. Federal financial participation is also available to States electing to expand their Medicaid programs by covering additional services and/or by including people eligible for medical but not for financial assistance. For the latter group States may offer the services required for financial assistance recipients or may substitute a combination of seven services.

1/Data from Regional Office reports of characteristics to State programs and State plan amendments.
2/People qualifying as members of families with dependent children (usually families with at least one parent absent or incapacitated).
3/People qualifying as aged, blind, or disabled under the Supplemental Security Income program.
4/FMAP - Federal Medicaid Assistance Percentage: Rate of Federal financial participation in a State's medical vendor payment expenditures on behalf of individuals and families eligible under Title XIX of the Social Security Act. Percentages, effective from July 1, 1975, through June 30, 1977, are rounded.
5/Including ICF services in institutions for the mentally retarded.

Source: U.S. Department of Health, Education, and Welfare, Social and Rehabilitation Service, Medical Services Administration, Division of Program Monitoring, 1976.

cally needy, federal financial participation in Medicaid payments is not available for any member of a family with annual countable income which would ordinarily be paid by the state under AFDC to a family of the same size without any income or resources. In the case of a single individual, annual countable income may not exceed 133 1/3 percent of the highest amount which would ordinarily be paid to an AFDC family of two persons.

In states which provide medical assistance to the medically needy, income limits varying by family size are established which represent amounts considered necessary for basic maintenance needs. Federal regulations require that the income level must be at least as high as the most liberal money payment standard used by the state since January 1966, or the level at which federal participation is available, whichever is less. Persons or members of families with income at or below these amounts are eligible for the full cost of specified medical services provided under the state plan. Payments for medical assistance on behalf of persons with income above these amounts are reduced by the amount of the excess income. (See the following section on treatment of income.)

TREATMENT OF INCOME.

Categorically Needy.   All income is considered except for required and allowable disregards applied in each state in determining eligibility for cash benefits under the appropriate category of financial assistance (OAA, AB, APTD, or AFDC) and the SSI federal benefit level. All required services are provided free to cash assistance recipients. These include: inpatient and outpatient hospital services, other x-ray and laboratory services, physician services, and home health services. The states may impose a cost-sharing provision for other medical services. The effect for these services is a zero percent benefit reduction rate as long as eligibility for cash assistance is maintained. When a person is no longer eligible for public assistance, he generally faces a benefit reduction rate of over 100 percent in those states in which there is no Medicaid program for the medically needy, that is, when the additional income which makes him ineligible for public assistance is less than the cost of medical care he would have received under Medicaid.

Medically Needy. Total gross earned and unearned income, subject to any disregards or deductions allowed by the states and further reduced by the costs incurred by the individual or family for medical care, is considered as available in determining eligibility for Medicaid. The legal liability of third parties to pay for medical services arising out of injury, disease or disability, is also considered as a resource.

Federal regulations state that disregards of income applied by the states under each categorical cash benefit program are to be applied in determining eligibility for Medicaid.

Full Medicaid benefits are provided for individuals and families with incomes at or below the level established by the state as necessary for basic maintenance needs. Any excess income must be applied to medical care costs. This represents a 100 percent tax rate on income above the basic maintenance level. Under the 1972 Social Security Amendments, the medical care cost to the medically needy was further affected by the provision for requiring states to impose nominal premium charges and permitted states to impose deductible and copayment charges for cost sharing for medical expenses. Since earnings disregards and other deductions from income are allowed in determining eligibility for public assistance cash benefits but not for Medicaid for the medically needy in most states, total family income of assistance recipients in these states may exceed the income level for eligibility for the medically needy. Therefore, when a family becomes ineligible for cash assistance, or ineligible for Medicaid as categorically needy, tax rates up to 100 percent or more may apply before the family is eligible for any Medicaid benefits as medically needy. For instance, a state with cost standards of $3,600 for an AFDC family of four may have an income eligibility level of $4,800 for medicaid eligibility for a medically needy family of four persons. If the family's income is $5,000, they would be eligible for Medicaid payments when they have spent $200 for medical care. However, the AFDC family is eligible for Medicaid benefits as long as they receive AFDC. When the earnings disregard ($360 plus one-third of the remainder of annual earnings) is applied, the AFDC family is eligible for an AFDC supplement until earnings reach $5,800 a year or more depending on amounts allowed for work expenses. Therefore, if AFDC payments are discontinued when earnings reach $5,800, the family would have to spend $1,000 (in a year) before they are again eligible for Medicaid benefits.

ACCOUNTING PERIOD.   Only such income and resources will be considered as will be "in hand" within a period up to six months ahead, including the month in which medical services for which payments would be made under the plan were rendered.

Assets Test

CATEGORICALLY NEEDY.   Excluded resources and allowable reserves are the same as for determination of eligibility for money payments in the appropriate category.

MEDICALLY NEEDY.   Resources which may be retained must be at least as great as the highest level used in any money payment program in the state since January 1966, and the amount of liquid assets which may be held must increase with an increase in the family size.

The 28 states which provide medical assistance to the medically needy have established asset limits which are generally more liberal than those applicable to cash benefit recipients. In addition to various exclusions of the home, income-producing property, automobiles, and life insurance, the allowable reserve varies among the states from $250 to $4,000 for an individual and from $700 to $6,200 for a family of four persons.

Other Conditions

WORK REQUIREMENT.   There is no work requirement.

ACCEPTANCE OF TRAINING OR REHABILITATION.   There are no requirements for acceptance of training or rehabilitation.

CITIZENSHIP.   A state may not impose a citizenship requirement which excludes any citizen of the United States or a legally admitted alien.

LIEN, RECOVERY, OR ASSIGNMENT.   No lien or encumbrance
of any individual prior to his death may be applied on account
of medical assistance rightfully received or at any time if he was
under age 65 when he received such assistance, unless a court
decides benefits have been paid incorrectly. Nor may there be
any adjustment or recovery of medical assistance paid correctly,
except from the estate of an individual who was age 65 or older
when he received such assistance, and then only after the death
of his surviving spouse, if any, and only at a time when he has
no surviving child who is under age 21 or who is blind or permanently and totally disabled.

TRANSFER OF PROPERTY.   There is no federal provision; it is
optional with the states. Twenty-eight states apply such provisions to the AFDC category. Information on state practices in
respect to Medicaid eligibility is not available.

RELATIVE RESPONSIBILITY.   A state may hold only the following relatives financially responsible for the Medicaid applicant
or recipient: the spouse of the individual who needs medical
care or services, and the parent of the individual if such individual is under 21, or is permanently and totally disabled.

All states consider spouses to be financially responsible for
each other and parents to be responsible for minor children or
children under 21 years of age. In addition, 30 states consider
parents to be responsible for Medicaid purposes for children
over 21 who are blind or disabled but two of these specify that
the disability must have occurred during the child's minority and
have continued.

INSTITUTIONAL STATUS.   States may pay for institutional
care to aged, blind, and disabled persons who would otherwise
need cash assistance if they were outside the institution if income is within 300 percent of the SSI payment level. However,
Medicaid is not available to an individual who is an inmate of a
public institution (except as a patient in a public medical institution) or to an individual under age 65 who is a patient in an
institution for tuberculosis or mental diseases.

RESIDENCE REQUIREMENT.   A state may not impose a residence requirement which excludes any of its residents. Generally, states define this as a person who is living within its borders voluntarily with the intention of making his home there.

Treatment of Assets in Determining Eligibility for Medicaid for the Medically Needy, Based on the 28 States Operating Such Programs

HOME OWNED AND OCCUPIED BY APPLICANT.   In 19 states the value of the home is not considered in determining eligibility. In five states the value of home property is limited to amounts varying from $3,500 equity to $25,000 assessed value.

INCOME-PRODUCING PROPERTY AND OTHER REAL PROPERTY.

Six states exclude the value of income-producing property in determining eligibility without setting an amount of value. Two exclude income-producing property with values up to $5,000 and $10,000. Four states set value limits of from $2,000 to $5,000 on other real property which may be retained, and two set limits of from $225 to $3,000 on the combined value of income-producing and other real property which may be retained. Two states require that all real property other than the home may be put up for sale, and two others imply that such property may not be held because they detail the kinds of property which are included in the permissible reserve and do not mention real property other than the home. Five states include the value of all real property other than the home within the total allowable reserve.

AUTOMOBILES.   Fifteen states exclude the value of an automobile, five specifically include the value of automobiles within the allowable reserve, and four others imply it in the term "all other property."

LIFE INSURANCE OR BURIAL RESERVE.   Ten states exclude life insurance or burial funds up to specified amounts of from $600 to $5,000.

TOTAL   ALLOWABLE   NONEXCLUDED   RESERVE.   These amounts vary by family size in most states. The median allowable reserve is $1,000 for 1 person varying from $250 to $4,000.

The median reserve for a family of 4 persons is $2,400 with amounts varying by state from $700 to $6,200.

In 13 states the individual or family is ineligible for medical assistance if he possesses resources in excess of allowable amounts. In 11 states any excess resources must be applied to cost of medical care before any medical assistance payments are made by the agency.

Benefits and Services

CASH BENEFITS.   There are no cash benefits. Payments are made to providers of services.

IN-KIND BENEFITS.

Nature of Benefits. The benefits are medical care services, specified in the state's plan, for which full or partial payment is made on behalf of eligible beneficiaries (Table 4.6). States may also make per capita premium payments to a health insurance agency for coverage of specified medical services and may pay Medicare supplementary medical insurance premiums to the Social Security Administration on behalf of specified groups of eligible beneficiaries.

Primary Determinants of Amount of Benefit. The cash value of the basic Medicaid benefit is determined by the reasonable cost of medical care which may be reduced by a deduction reasonably related to the Medicaid recipient's income and resources as provided in state plans. No deduction may be imposed with respect to inpatient hospital services furnished to recipients of SSI and AFDC.

Relationship of Benefit Amount to Family Size. The benefit amount depends on the individual need for specified medical care services for which payment is made.

Relationship of Benefit Amount to Place of Residence. The benefit amount varies by state of residence because of the difference in the scope of services provided and in fees charged by medical vendors, as well as differences in groups of persons covered.

Required and Optional Medical Care Services

For the categorically needy, states are required to include provision for inpatient hospital services (other than in institutions for treatment of tuberculosis or mental diseases); outpatient hospital services; other laboratory and x-ray services; skilled nursing home services for persons age 21 or over, and home health care services to persons entitled to skilled nursing home services; physician's services; early screening, diagnostic, and treatment services for children under age 21, as provided by the Secretary's regulations; family planning services and, as of July 1970, transportation to obtain Medicaid care services. For the medically needy, states may provide the above or any combination of seven specified services.

Services may be limited in scope such as the number of days of hospitalization for which payment will be made or the number of physician's visits or maximum amounts paid for laboratory and x-ray services over a period of time; or outpatient hospital and physician's services may be limited to specified types of services.

Optional services provided under state plans include prescribed drugs, dental services, eye glasses, physical therapy, prosthetic devices, private duty nursing, nursing home services for persons under 21, care for persons age 65 or over in institutions for the treatment of tuberculosis or mental illness, and clinical services other than outpatient hospital services. The number and scope of optional services vary among the states as do the groups of persons eligible for the particular services.

As of January 1972, the payment for care of individuals in intermediate care facilities is included as an optional service under Medicaid. Such costs were previously met under financial assistance programs of OAA, AB, or APTD. Intermediate care facilities are defined as institutions providing health-related care and services to individuals requiring institutional care but not the degree of care provided by a hospital or skilled nursing home. In 1975 $2.5 billion were paid for intermediate care facilities.

Per Capita Payments to a Health Insurance Agency or Payments to the Social Security Administration for Supplementary Medical Insurance Premiums (Title XVIII, Part B)

As of January 1970, three states paid monthly premiums to health insurance agencies under contracts to cover the cost of specified services such as Medicare deductibles and coinsurance for persons over 65 or physician's services, hospital care, and other identified services for persons under 65 or recipients of categorical cash assistance. As of July 1971, seven states paid health insurance premiums for some beneficiaries.

As of April 1, 1972, 46 states had buy-in agreements with the Social Security Administration for payment of supplementary medical insurance premiums on behalf of specified groups of eligible beneficiaries. The buy-in agreement in 27 states covered all persons eligible for both Medicare and Medicaid, and in 22 covered only money payment recipients who were also eligible for Medicare. Four states had no buy-in agreements.

Procedures

Applications for medical assistance may be made at any state or local welfare office by mail, in person, or by telephone, or, when applying for SSI benefits when the state has an agreement with the Social Security Administration, to a branch or district Social Security office. The Social Security Act provides that the state agency responsible for the state plan for income maintenance be responsible for eligibility determinations for medical assistance. Income maintenance recipients are automatically eligible for medical assistance services. Other applicants apply to the agency on a medical assistance form with space for their personal and family information, amounts and sources of income, kinds and value of resources, medical expenses, and other information required by the agency to determine eligibility. Agency processes for verifying information, maintaining the confidentiality of information, appeals from adverse agency decisions on eligibility, the responsibility of the applicant for supplying complete and accurate information, and periodic redeterminations are the same as those described for the federally supported income maintenance programs. An average of 25,400 applications are received daily, 6,800 from non-payment recipients. Sixty-eight percent of the latter are found to be eligible under the states' medical assistance standards.[3]

Medically indigent (noncategorical) eligibles are required to pay monthly premiums set by the state medical assistance agency and pay service providers any required deductibles and copayments for services they receive. Welfare payment recipients are required to pay service providers any deductibles and copayments, if any, prescribed by the state agency for optional services they receive. Otherwise, their services are free of cost to them.

Medical assistance eligibles are given a medical assistance identification card for use in requesting medical services under the state plan. They are assured freedom of choice of any hospital, nursing home, physician, pharmacist, dentist, or other medical practitioner agreeing to provide services under the plan, and may request any service which is covered under that plan or refuse any service offered, from any medical institution or practitioner. The individual recipient is entitled to receive quality care and attention meeting the professional standards in the state. Service providers bill the state government for covered services they provide at prescribed rates, either by mailing or presenting the bill to the state agency which maintains its own fiscal and accounting program or to the fiscal agency which serves under contract to the agency.

FOOD STAMP PROGRAM

The objective of the Food Stamp Program is to improve the diets of low-income households and to expand the market for domestically produced food by supplementing the food purchasing power of eligible low income families.

Background

The program was enacted in 1964 to authorize the purchase of food stamps by eligible low income households according to their incomes and size of family and to receive allotment amounts of food stamps of greater value to enable them to purchase food to meet their nutritional needs. The program was amended in 1971 to nationalize eligibility requirements and benefits, and to permit certain elderly persons to purchase delivered meals with food stamps. Also, the 1971 changes allowed households with little or no income to receive coupons free. (Tables 4.7 and 4.8)

The Agriculture and Consumer Protection Act of 1973 (P.L. 93-86) amended the program further, as follows:

Implementation of a nationwide food stamp program by June 30, 1974.

Redefined eligible foods to include imported items and seeds and plants for home gardens.

Required semi-annual adjustment of the coupon allotment to reflect changes in food prices.

Retention of food stamps for SSI recipients if benefits from SSI and state supplementation are less than the sum of December 1973 welfare benefits plus current food stamp benefits. (However, the provision was postponed to June 30, 1974 by the 1973 Social Security Amendments and postponed again indefinitely by later amendments.)

Authorized a four-year extension of the USDA's authority to run the food stamp program, plus authority to carry over any unexpended appropriation from one fiscal year to the next.

Required issuance of coupon allotments at least twice a month and optional public assistance withholding for AFDC recipients.

Required that eligibility standards take into account actual housing payments received in kind from an employer but not in excess of $25 per month.

The Food Stamp Act of 1977, effective Fiscal Year 1978, was enacted to correct perceived shortcomings of the program: to remove barriers which prevent needy households from participating, to simplify and make program administration less cumbersome, to place limitations on gross income for eligibility determinations, to correct program inequities in permitting unlimited itemized deductions from gross income, and to create safeguards against fraud and abuse. Among its principal features were: the elimination of the purchase requirement; establishment of a single benefit reduction rate of 30% of net income; adoption of standard deductions from gross income and expenses; and provision of increased financial incentives for states to pursue abuse and improve administration.

Administering Agency

The Food and Nutrition Service of the USDA, through local and state welfare offices, are required to implement the food stamp program in every one of their political subdivisions no later than June 30, 1974. No jurisdiction is exempt from this requirement, unless the state can demonstrate that it is impractical to implement the program in a particular area.

Eligibility Requirements

Participation in the program is limited to those households whose income and other financial resources are determined to be a substantial limiting factor in permitting them to obtain a more nutritious diet. Victims of a major disaster who are in need of food assistance because of reduction in or inaccessability of income or resources resulting from the disaster are also eligible for benefits in food stamp project areas.

No individual who is a member of a household is eligible for a) three months after he has been found guilty of fraud in connection with the use of coupons or authorization cards by a state agency or b) for an additional six to 24 months if found guilty by a civil or criminal court or c) both.

Persons Included

All persons in a household are included, other than boarders, roomers, and unrelated live-in attendants necessary for medical, housekeeping, or child care reasons. Persons must not be residents of an institution or a boarding house and must be living as one economic unit sharing common cooking facilities and purchasing food in common. However, elderly living in congregate housing and drug addicts and alcoholics in residential treatment facilities are covered.

A household may include legally assigned foster children or other children under age 18 when an adult member of the household acts in *loco parentis* to such children. Also included in the household are single individuals living alone who purchase and prepare food for home consumption and certain elderly persons and their spouses (whether or not they have cooking facilities).

A boarding house is defined as a place where three or more individuals are furnished meals or lodging and meals for compensation. Residents of boarding houses are not eligible for food stamps.

A household which includes a tax dependent (a person 18 years of age or over claimed as a tax dependent by a parent or guardian with whom he is not living) is not eligible for food stamp participation unless (1) the household of the parent or guardian is certified as eligible for participation in the food stamp program, and (2) the household in which the tax dependent is living meets all the other eligibility criteria. A person is considered a tax dependent for the period claimed and for a period of one year after the expiration of that tax period.

Students are eligible if enrolled at least half-time in an institution of higher education and if they meet one of the following work requirements: 1) employed at least 20 hours a week or working in a Federally-financed work-study program 2) working and receiving the minimum wage equivalent of twenty hours a week 3) registered for work on a twenty-hour per week minimum basis 4) acting as head of a household and supplying more than one-half of annual support 5) exempt from general work registration requirement because of age, fitness, parental status or other authorized exemption.

Aliens are eligible if they have been granted extended or indefinite voluntary departure status or the Attorney General has declined to proceed with deportation.

Income Test

INCOME LIMITS.   The income standards of eligibility are the nonfarm income poverty guidelines prescribed by the Office of Management and Budget, adjusted annually.

DEFINITION OF INCOME.   All household income from whatever source excluding only 1) any gain or benefit not in the form of money payable directly to a household 2) any income in the certification period which is received too infrequently or irregularly to be reasonably anticipated, but not in excess of $30 in a quarter 3) educational loans on which payment is deferred, grants, scholarships, fellowships, veterans educational benefits and the like which are used for tuition and school fees 4) loans on which repayment is deferred 5) reimbursements which do not exceed expenses and are not a gain in benefit to the household 6) moneys received for care and maintenance of a person not a member of the household 7) income earned by a student under 18 years of age 8) lump sum payments such as income tax refunds, rebates or credits, retroactive social security or railroad retirement pension payments or lump sum insurance settlements (although they are counted as resources unless excluded by other laws) 10) any income excluded by other laws.

In computing household income, a standard deduction of $60 a month per household is allowed in 48 states and the District of Columbia. The Secretary of Agriculture is authorized to fix the standard deduction of Hawaii and Alaska (higher) and Guam, Puerto Rico and the Virgin Islands (lower) to reflect their different cost of living standards. Standard deductions are adjusted every July 1 and January 1 to the nearest $5 to reflect changes in the consumer price index for other than food items.

All households with earned income are allowed an additional deduction of 20% of all earned income to compensate for taxes, other mandatory deductions from salary and work expenses. Households are also entitled to:

1. a dependent care deduction for the actual cost of payments for the care of a dependent child or adult when such care enables a household member to accept or continue employment, training or education preparatory for employment. Or,

2. an excess shelter expense deduction for monthly shelter costs of over 50% of monthly household income after all other applicable deductions are allowed. This deduction is limited to no more than $75 monthly in the 48 states and the District of Columbia and higher limits for Hawaii and Alaska and lower limits in the three territories. The deductions are adjusted annually to reflect any changes in the non-food items in the cost of living index. Or,

3. a combined deduction for dependent care and excess shelter expenses of no more than $75 monthly.

Assets Test

The value of nonexcluded resources of a household may not exceed $1,750, except that for households of two or more persons with a member age 60 or over the total resources may not exceed $3,000.

Resources which are excluded in determining eligibility are the following: the home and lot; one currently licensed automobile and any unlicensed automobile; personal effects and household goods; cash value of life insurance policies; property which is producing income consistent with its fair market value and other property essential to self-support (for example, vehicles needed for employment, tools, equipment, etc.); and resources of roomers and boarders, live-in attendants, and household members (other than the household head or spouse) with a commitment to contribute only a portion of their income.

(If such contribution is less than the value of the monthly coupon allotment for one person, the member's total resources are counted.) Also excluded as resources are certain relocation payments, Indian lands held jointly with the tribe or which can only be sold with the approval of the Bureau of Indian Affairs, and money which has been prorated or averaged as income for self-employed persons or students.

Resources which are included in determining eligibility are the following: liquid resources such as cash on hand, savings or checking accounts, U.S. savings bonds, stocks and bonds; personal property such as boats, snowmobiles, excess automobiles, mobile homes, and aircraft for recreation; nonrecurring lump-sum payments from insurance settlements, inheritances, retroactive social security benefits, prizes, gifts, etc.; and any other resources which have not been excluded.

Accounting Period

Anticipated income is usually averaged over the period for which eligibility is certified. The monthly income immediately prior to the application is also considered in determining the income actually available to the household for the certification period. Certification periods for public assistance households coincide with the period of their assistance grant. For other households, the usual period of certification is for three months but may be one month for unemployed persons, persons on strike, and other households where a change in income is likely. The certification period may be six months for households which have stable employment or other income, and it may be as long as 12 months for households with unemployable members dependent on regularly received pensions or benefits, the elderly, and for households dependent on self-employment, farm labor, or farming. Scholarships, educational awards, and the like are averaged over the time they are intended to cover.

Nonrecurring lump-sum payments are considered as resources at the time of the next scheduled recertification or no more than 3 months following receipt of such payments. The amount which is actually available at the time of recertification is considered in determining eligibility at that time.

Other Eligibility Conditions

WORK REQUIREMENT.   Each able-bodied person between
the ages of 18 and 65 who is a member of a household, including
a person who is not working because of a strike or lockout, shall
(1) register for employment at the time of application and at
recertification (exceptions include: mothers or members of a
household who are caring for dependent children under 18 or
incapacitated adults; students enrolled at least half time in a
school or training program; and persons working at least 30
hours per week) and (2) accept a bona fide offer of suitable
employment, including reporting for interviews and supplying
supplemental information as necessary.

Employment is not considered suitable if wages offered are
less than the applicable federal or state minimum wage; union
membership or nonmembership is required as a condition of
employment; or work offered is at the site of a strike or lockout.
Suitability of employment for a particular registrant also includes a determination that the risk to health and safety is not
unreasonable; the individual is physically and mentally fit to
perform the employment offered; the employment is within the
individual's major field of experience unless, after a reasonable
period of time, it is apparent that such work is not available; and
the employment is not at an unreasonable distance from the
individual's residence. The whole household shall become ineligible for benefits if any member refuses to comply with the work
requirement. It shall remain ineligible until such member accepts employment or complies with the work requirement or for
1 year from date of refusal.

Benefits cannot be denied to a household solely on the
grounds that a member of the household is not working because
of a strike or lockout at his usual place of employment.

WIN registrants or enrollees and persons receiving unemployment compensation are exempt from the work registration
requirement.

ACCEPTANCE OF TRAINING OR REHABILITATION.   There is no
requirement, but persons engaged in recognized training programs are exempt from the work requirement.

CITIZENSHIP.   No requirement.

TRANSFER OF PROPERTY.   No requirement.

RELATIVE RESPONSIBILITY.   No requirement.

INSTITUTIONAL STATUS.   Residents of institutions are not eligible to receive benefits, except elderly in congregate housing and drug addicts and alcoholics in a residential drug or alcoholic program.

RESIDENCE REQUIREMENTS.   A beneficiary must be a resident of an area which participates in the food stamp program.

BENEFITS AND SERVICES

In-Kind Benefits

NATURE OF BENEFITS.   Families obtain stamps or "coupons" up to the allotment and use them to purchase any food in authorized retail stores. (Food means any food for human consumption except alcoholic beverages and tobacco).

Persons 60 years of age or over who are members of an eligible household or who live alone or only with their spouses (whether or not they have cooking facilities) and who are disabled to the extent that they cannot prepare their own meals may use their food stamps to purchase meals prepared and delivered to them by authorized meal delivery services.

Temporary emergency food stamp assistance is available to households that are victims of a disaster where normal commercial food distribution is disrupted. Food stamps are distributed to them without regard to the regular income or resources requirements.

CASH VALUE.   The value of benefits to the household is the value of the monthly coupon allotment they receive. The allotment varies by family size reduced by an amount equal to 30% of the household's net (after deductions) monthly income. For example, assume the monthly coupon allotment for a family of four is $166 a month, a household of four with $200 net income would receive $106 in stamps:

$106 = $166 − $60. The $60 is 30% of $200.

Prior to the Food Stamp Act of 1977, when eligible households purchased stamps, the household would have paid $60 to receive a $166 allotment. Pursuant to law, the Secretary of Agriculture has increased the allotments a number of times to reflect the economics of increased food prices and cost-of-living generally.

Procedures

AFDC, SSI* and General Assistance recipients are eligible for the food stamp program. All other persons apply to the state or

*Except in the four states which provide cash payments to SSI recipients in lieu of food stamps: California, Massachusetts, New York and Nevada.

local public welfare office in person, or by telephone and followup home visit. The applicant is requested to supply personal and household information, information on amounts and sources of income, kinds and value of assets, and other data as may be required to establish eligibility. The applicant signs an affidavit as part of the application representing him as head of the household or acting for the household in making application. The information is verified using methods and procedures of those for applications for public assistance. A decision on the application is made within 30 days. Presumptive eligibility for up to 30 days is approved for a household which reports little or no income and, on the basis of other information, appears to be eligible.

Adverse decisions of the agency are appealable and there is provision for fair hearings. Penalties for fraud in supplying false or inaccurate information, or concealing essential information, are prescribed. At the time of application and at least once every six months thereafter, every able bodied person between 18 and 65 who is a member of a household including a person not working because of a strike or lockout, must register for employment with the public welfare agency, such registration being forwarded to the Federal or State employment office. He must report for an interview with that office and accept a bona fide offer of employment to which he is referred.

Eligibles receive an authorization card from the public welfare agency showing the face value of the coupon allotment the household is entitled to.

Food coupons in various denominations are shipped by the Food and Nutrition Service to state and local agency offices, credit unions, post offices, banks, and other organizations under contract to the state public welfare agency designated in the State Plan of Operations.

Distribution of coupons also is made bimonthly by mail to public assistance recipients in amounts to which they are entitled, at their option.

Coupons are cashed in for food purchases in retail stores authorized by the Food and Nutrition Service and are accepted only if detached from the coupon book at the time of final purchase. Coupons are accepted at the same prices and on the same terms and conditions as cash purchases. If change in an amount of less than a dollar is required, the purchaser receives the change in cash. The stores redeem coupons at face value at their commercial banks for credit or cash, or with authorized wholesalers with whom they do business. These latter also redeem the coupons at their banks. The banks send their cancelled coupons to a Federal Reserve Bank for credit in their accounts.

Table 4.7   Food Stamp Program

Caseloads	September, 1975
Program Scope	
States and Territories	54
Projects	3,046
Participation	
Persons	18,524,477
Public Assistance	8,565,443
P.A. as % of Total	46%
Non-Public Assistance	9,959,034
*Coupon Issuance**	
Total	$703,623,277
Bonus	$427,776,228
Bonus as % of Total	61%
Average Bonus per Person	23.09

*Note: This report predates the Food Stamp Act of 1977 which ended the food stamp purchase requirement.
Source: Food Stamp Program Statistical Summary of Operations September 1975 Food and Nutrition Service, issued 11/24/75

Table 4.8 Food Stamp Program Statistical Summary of Operations
September 1975

REGION BY STATE	NO. OF PROJCTS	PARTICIPATION — CURRENT MONTH (NUMBER OF PERSONS)			PRIOR MONTH	MONTH % CHANG	COUPONS				FY TO DATE	
		P.A.	NON-P.A.	TOTAL			TOTAL VALUE ($)	BONUS VALUE ($)	B/PT % BONUS	AVG BONUS	TOTAL COUPONS ($)	BONUS COUPONS ($)
DELAWARE	3	20,010	17,593	37,603	37,764	.4-	1,442,955	904,828	63	24.06	4,343,440	2,739,715
WASHINGTON D C	1	87,797	39,165	126,962	126,892	.1+	5,188,767	2,871,073	55	22.61	15,618,713	8,711,525
MARYLAND	24	171,839	102,044	273,883	274,705	.3-	10,833,219	6,868,959	63	25.08	32,739,570	20,701,383
NEW JERSEY	21	327,583	206,552	534,135	535,107	.2-	21,408,906	12,220,343	57	22.88	64,442,968	37,059,233
NEW YORK	58	1,153,386	268,372	1,421,758	1,383,240	2.8+	53,224,026	23,975,539	45	16.86	154,363,871	69,325,242
PENNSYLVANIA	67	565,258	323,593	888,851	891,268	.3-	34,651,170	17,280,994	50	19.44	103,545,762	51,807,109
VIRGINIA	122	102,857	179,428	282,285	286,282	1.4-	10,171,985	6,154,474	61	21.80	30,915,537	18,933,688
WEST VIRGINIA	55	101,691	129,892	231,583	233,225	.7-	7,314,811	4,463,154	61	19.27	21,948,342	13,442,792
PUERTO RICO	9	207,685	1,298,622	1,506,307	1,530,755	1.6-	55,245,068	41,065,700	74	27.26	161,980,370	120,175,205
VIRGIN ISLANDS	2	1,935	23,055	24,993	24,582	1.7+	1,201,809	833,286	69	33.34	3,670,207	2,567,585
MID-ATLANTIC	362	2,740,041	2,588,316	5,328,357	5,323,819	.1+	200,682,716	116,638,350	58	21.89	593,568,780	345,553,477
ALABAMA	67	94,041	282,721	376,762	381,732	1.3-	14,045,763	9,235,659	66	24.51	42,696,465	28,213,417
FLORIDA	67	165,360	619,888	785,248	773,357	1.5+	30,524,030	22,823,991	75	29.07	90,431,994	67,866,526
GEORGIA	159	190,794	359,127	549,921	555,459	1.0-	20,442,240	13,123,311	64	23.86	61,938,179	39,952,265
KENTUCKY	120	103,725	310,621	414,346	435,102	4.8-	15,829,987	10,339,157	65	24.95	50,285,635	33,109,403
MISSISSIPPI	82	86,802	291,589	378,391	388,792	2.7-	14,096,138	9,459,884	67	25.00	43,078,388	29,171,650
NORTH CAROLINA	100	89,595	399,248	488,843	495,941	1.4-	18,621,279	11,876,984	64	24.30	56,669,713	36,435,367
SOUTH CAROLINA	46	65,919	324,373	390,292	396,834	1.6-	14,539,368	10,082,379	69	25.83	44,591,170	31,174,381
TENNESSEE	95	107,269	321,398	428,667	429,126	.1-	16,438,126	11,217,108	68	26.17	49,407,400	33,904,092
SOUTHEAST	736	903,505	2,908,965	3,812,470	3,856,343	1.1-	144,536,931	98,158,473	68	25.75	439,098,944	299,827,101
ILLINOIS	102	749,459	200,273	949,732	957,041	.8-	40,438,374	24,616,193	61	25.92	120,945,584	73,202,095
INDIANA	92	105,001	140,857	245,858	249,692	1.5-	8,905,611	5,625,523	63	22.88	27,563,199	17,395,297
IOWA	99	65,540	51,438	116,978	118,323	1.1-	4,321,074	2,377,341	55	20.32	13,154,805	7,281,924
KANSAS	105	37,414	24,853	62,267	63,737	2.3-	2,350,533	1,151,523	49	18.49	7,063,967	3,508,201
MICHIGAN	83	482,914	186,843	669,757	676,409	1.0-	24,315,212	11,729,077	48	17.51	73,302,664	35,613,825
MINNESOTA	87	90,601	90,548	181,149	186,826	3.0-	6,790,653	3,692,491	54	20.38	20,868,400	11,494,079
MISSOURI	115	149,610	142,544	292,154	293,585	.4-	11,498,554	7,229,617	64	24.75	34,611,811	21,889,546
NEBRASKA	90	24,039	26,867	47,905	49,080	2.4-	1,769,091	962,457	54	20.09	5,444,881	3,055,194
OHIO	88	508,895	405,454	914,349	924,493	1.1-	35,242,597	22,714,307	64	24.84	107,188,263	70,508,509
WISCONSIN	72	98,455	71,112	169,567	165,196	2.6+	6,194,042	3,064,029	49	18.07	18,100,251	9,263,511
MIDWEST	933	2,308,928	1,340,789	3,649,717	3,684,382	.9-	141,915,741	83,162,558	59	22.79	428,223,825	253,212,181
ALASKA	1	3,417	7,962	11,379	11,507	1.1-	600,707	449,205	75	39.48	1,808,189	1,356,683
ARIZONA	14	39,762	121,668	161,433	166,773	3.2-	5,747,976	3,988,427	69	24.71	17,594,431	12,277,137
CALIFORNIA	58	1,029,375	453,982	1,483,357	1,498,233	1.0-	55,587,910	31,119,820	56	20.98	168,074,694	94,399,721
HAWAII	4	56,411	30,779	87,190	87,259	.1-	4,478,435	2,428,048	54	27.85	13,380,654	7,318,110
IDAHO	44	16,017	27,337	43,354	43,754	.9-	1,689,149	1,113,955	66	25.69	5,084,508	3,370,310
NEVADA	17	8,054	24,469	32,523	33,641	3.3-	1,275,895	915,037	72	28.14	3,937,396	2,845,473
OREGON	35	87,356	96,799	184,155	190,668	3.4-	6,865,919	4,069,716	59	22.10	21,434,227	12,876,158
WASHINGTON	39	120,366	116,704	237,070	238,771	.7-	9,458,145	5,520,037	58	23.28	28,516,152	16,757,995
GUAM	1	1,503	13,072	14,575	14,827	1.7-	704,882	424,655	60	29.14	2,121,766	1,286,635
WESTERN	213	1,362,261	892,772	2,255,033	2,285,433	1.3-	86,409,018	50,028,898	58	22.19	261,952,017	152,488,222

Table 4.8 (Continued)

ARKANSAS	75	61,816	191,304	253,120	258,511	2.1-	9,726,694	6,262,053	64	24.74	29,769,546	19,355,321
COLORADO	54	75,804	83,314	159,118	158,792	.2+	6,131,031	4,205,816	69	26.43	18,699,042	12,952,488
LOUISIANA	64	168,988	327,413	496,401	499,008	.5-	18,745,306	12,490,862	67	25.16	56,676,348	38,141,235
MONTANA	55	12,053	19,962	32,015	33,809	5.3-	1,216,047	819,420	67	25.59	3,852,320	2,630,093
NEW MEXICO	29	42,685	102,427	145,112	146,772	1.1-	5,629,981	3,850,373	68	26.53	17,102,665	11,798,183
NORTH DAKOTA	51	4,578	11,804	16,382	16,867	2.9-	618,488	349,090	56	21.31	1,937,865	1,119,116
OKLAHOMA	77	54,504	122,036	176,540	178,742	1.2-	6,649,191	3,425,093	52	19.40	20,272,136	10,577,118
SOUTH DAKOTA	65	11,946	17,255	29,201	30,623	4.6-	1,106,448	626,606	57	21.46	3,433,554	1,965,976
TEXAS	254	247,257	785,727	1,032,984	1,039,234	.6-	37,827,310	25,040,791	66	24.24	115,389,914	76,405,918
UTAH	9	28,921	20,267	49,188	49,582	.8-	1,857,781	1,022,444	55	20.79	5,584,574	3,066,893
WYOMING	23	3,346	5,980	9,326	9,245	.9+	347,564	214,759	62	23.03	1,044,504	651,391
WEST-CENTRAL	756	711,898	1,687,489	2,399,387	2,421,185	.9-	89,855,841	58,307,307	65	24.30	273,762,468	178,663,732
CONNECTICUT	8	93,548	72,754	166,302	166,862	.3-	6,313,346	3,167,055	50	19.04	19,003,809	9,627,239a
MAINE	16	37,969	96,527	134,496	138,954	3.2-	4,924,886	3,000,591	61	22.31	15,327,760	9,455,067
MASSACHUSETTS	7	311,380	270,274	581,654	563,154	3.3+	21,482,148	11,438,457	53	19.67	62,952,583	33,582,426
NEW HAMPSHIRE	1	20,818	38,251	59,069	59,513	.7-	2,228,313	1,315,396	59	22.27	6,871,277	4,099,925
RHODE ISLAND	2	55,022	37,202	92,224	92,438	.2-	3,530,205	1,637,497	46	17.76	10,626,274	4,985,628
VERMONT	12	20,073	25,695	45,768	46,079	.7-	1,744,132	921,646	53	20.14	5,140,808	2,720,207
NEW ENGLAND	46	538,810	540,703	1,079,513	1,067,000	1.2+	40,223,030	21,480,642	53	19.90	119,922,511	64,470,491
**												
MID-ATLANTIC	362	2,740,041	2,588,316	5,328,357	5,323,819	.1+	200,682,716	116,638,350	58	21.89	593,568,780	345,553,477
SOUTHEAST	736	903,505	2,908,965	3,812,470	3,856,343	1.1-	144,536,931	98,158,473	68	25.75	439,098,944	299,827,101
MIDWEST	933	2,308,928	1,340,789	3,649,717	3,684,382	.9-	141,915,741	83,162,558	59	22.79	428,223,825	253,212,181
WESTERN	213	1,362,261	892,772	2,255,033	2,285,433	1.3-	86,409,018	50,028,898	58	22.19	261,952,017	152,488,222
NEW ENGLAND	46	538,810	540,703	1,079,513	1,067,000	1.2+	40,223,030	21,480,642	53	19.90	119,922,511	64,470,491
WEST-CENTRAL	756	711,898	1,687,489	2,399,387	2,421,185	.9-	89,855,841	58,307,307	65	24.30	273,762,468	178,663,732
U. S. TOTAL	3,046	8,565,443	9,959,034	18,524,477	18,638,162	.6-	703,623,277	427,776,228	61	23.09	2,116,528,545	1,294,215,204

Source: U.S. Department of Agriculture Food and Nutrition Service, Statistical Summary of Operations, Food Stamp Program, September 1975.

182

WORK INCENTIVE (WIN) PROGRAM

The objectives of the Work Incentive Program are to furnish AFDC heads of households and youth 16 to 21 years of age not attending school training, employment, child care, and other services to restore families to self-support and personal and social independence.

Background

The program was authorized by Title IV-C of the Social Security Amendments of 1967. It evolved from and replaced two prede- cessor manpower and training programs administered by state and local public welfare agencies: the Work Experience and Training Program authorized under Title V of the Economic Opportunity Act (EOA) of 1964 and the Community Work and Training Program under Title IV of the Social Security Act. The Title V, EOA Work Experience and Training Program autho- rized experimental, pilot, and demonstration projects for com- prehensive manpower training, employment, child care, and supportive social services for all federal categories of public assistance, not limited to AFDC families. The Community Work and Training Program under Title V of the Social Security Act was intended only for AFDC families. It preceded the Title V program and set the stage in many state and local jurisdictions for public welfare agencies taking on responsibilities for train- ing, job counseling and job finding of employable public assis- tance recipients.

   In 1967, the initial groups of WIN enrollees were largely AFDC transferees from the Title V Work Experience and Train- ing projects. With experience gained during the first two years of the WIN program, Congress amended the law in 1971, the so-called Talmadge Amendments, to require registrations of all AFDC heads of households and youth not attending school, except for specified categories of persons listed below under *eligibility requirements.* In addition, other significant changes were made: increasing federal funding of state employment and sup- port programs from 80 to 90 percent, and from 75 to 90 percent for child care and other social services for WIN enrollees, estab- lishing priorities for certification for training, providing a 20 percent tax credit against the wages of persons hired by private employees from WIN enrollees, providing employers other tax benefits, organization of a separate administrative unit in state and local welfare agencies to provide supportive services for the WIN program, and giving greater emphasis to public service employment, on-the-job training, and continual exposure of WIN participants to job market information.

Administering Agencies

At the federal level, the Public Services Administration, Office of Human Development Services, D/HEW and the Employment and Training Administration of the Department of Labor share responsibility for the program; the former for the provision of child care and supporting social services, the latter for registration, training employment, and placement activities. At the state level, the state welfare agencies are responsible for providing child care and supporting social services, the state manpower agencies, usually the state employment service office, are responsible for training and employment services. In September 1975, the registration function was transferred from state and local welfare offices to local WIN offices.

Caseloads and Costs[4]

EMPLOYMENT AND TRAINING.   There were over 839,000 new WIN registrants in fiscal 1975, an increase of 2.4 percent from the previous year. Of that number, over 555,000 were appraised by teams of local WIN and welfare office staff and about 328,000 were certified available for active participation in WIN employment or training components. About one-fourth of all participants in fiscal 1975 were volunteers.

Despite the rise in the national unemployment rate from 5.2 percent in June 1974 to 8.6 percent in June 1975, 170,641 WIN registrants obtained jobs during fiscal 1975—only 3.7 percent fewer than in fiscal 1974 and 25 percent more than in 1973. In both years, about two-thirds of the total reflected direct job entries, i.e., jobs obtained without the need for training or job experience under WIN auspices (Table 4.9).

Table 4.9   Win Employment and Training Activities,
Fiscal Years 1974–75

Program activity	Fiscal 1974	Fiscal 1975	Percent change
Employment:			
Obtained employment (unsubsidized)	177, 271	170, 641	−3. 7
Direct job entry	119, 834	113, 485	−5. 3
WIN/JOP (OJT) [1]	42, 154	37, 185	−11. 8
WIN/PSE [2]	12, 625	14, 404	14. 1
Completed job entry [3]	118, 540	113, 316	−4. 4
Deregistered	51, 627	52, 700	2. 1
Recycled [4]	66, 913	60, 616	−9. 4
Training:			
Skill	46, 890	35, 588	−24. 1
Other classroom	31, 897	26, 970	−15. 4
Work experience	20, 576	20, 387	−. 9
Suspense: [5]			
To training	16, 546	28, 206	70. 5
To employment	12, 633	19, 219	52. 1

[1] WIN-OJT is an employment opportunity in which a certified WIN registrant is hired and given training under a contract with an employer.

[2] PSE provides WIN registrants with subsidized employment with public and private nonprofit employers who are committed to retain the registrants in unsubsidized jobs at the end of the contract period.

[3] Job entry is the status of a WIN registrant during the first 90 days of permanent, unsubsidized, full-time employment.

[4] WIN participants who have found unsubsidized employment but who, because of low earnings, continue to be eligible for WIN services and some portion of their welfare grant are recycled back into the program.

[5] WIN participants who are assigned to a non-WIN-funded training or employment activity are placed in suspense status while in that activity.

Source: Employment and Training Report to the President, 1976. U.S. Departments of Health, Education, and Welfare and Labor. U.S. Government Printing Office, Washington, D.C. 20402, p. 117–120.

The higher national incidence of unemployment made it considerably more difficult to develop on-the-job-training (OJT) contracts with employers, and, as a result, there was a noticeable drop in OJT activity during the fiscal year. Nevertheless, this decrease was offset by corresponding enrollment increases of over 14 percent in public service employment and more than 52 percent in "suspense to employment"; i.e., assigned to a non-WIN-funded employment program such as the Comprehensive Employment Training Act (CETA). The end result, despite the slack labor market, was a slight increase (about 2 percent) in the number of people who completed job entry and earned enough to be able to leave welfare—a total of 52,700 individuals.

During the fiscal year, WIN job entries increased slightly in white-collar (professional, technical, managerial, and clerical) and service occupations. Reflecting the downturn in labor market conditions, however, entries declined in manufacturing, especially processing, machine trades, and benchwork. The last group accounted for 23 percent of all WIN job entries in fiscal 1974 but only 17 percent in fiscal 1975. Despite high unemployment rates, about one out of three WIN participants found a job in the growing service sector during the fiscal year. Within the broader service category, however, household work declined from 16 percent of all service jobs taken in fiscal 1974 to 14 percent in fiscal 1975.

Starting wage rates in these jobs reflected differences in sex, age, race, and education. In fiscal 1975, the average starting wage for male entrants was $2.94. About 44 percent were paid at least three dollars an hour, and over 14 percent earned four dollars or more per hour. Women job entrants received substantially lower wages than men, with an average hourly starting wage of $2.42. Only about 15 percent were paid as much as three dollars per hour, and only 3.1 percent received four dollars or more.

At least some of these differences in wage rates may be explained by variations in occupational distribution. Women predominated in the usually lower paid clerical, sales, and service jobs and in benchwork, while men filled largely the higher paid jobs in machine trades and structural work. In an effort to expand job opportunities for women, the WIN national office provided specialized training for regional, state, and local WIN staff during the year to promote the idea and techniques of providing nontraditional jobs for women.

In addition, a contract was signed with the Brotherhood of Railway and Airline Clerks (BRAC) to offer an experimental orientation and training program intended to prepare women for placement in nontraditional railroad occupations. Under this arrangement, BRAC is recruiting, screening, and training a total of 80 WIN women in order to place them in apprenticeship or other entry-level jobs expected to lead to high-paying jobs in shop craft, yard service, and maintenance-of-way work.

Age, race, and level of education also had an effect on earnings. Not surprisingly, persons in the prime working age group (22 to 39 years) had higher beginning wages than those under 22 or 40 and over. White participants started at an average wage of $2.68 per hour, compared with $2.52 for blacks. Wage rates also rose consistently with the level of educational attainment, with an average of $2.40 for those with less than an eighth-grade education and $3.04 for those who had completed more than 12 years of schooling.

The number of individuals in WIN-funded training decreased sharply during fiscal 1975. From fiscal 1974, the drop in enrollments in both skill and other classroom training totaled about 16,000 persons, but was offset to a considerable degree by an increase of nearly 12,000 in the number of individuals suspended to other training programs. Work-experience activity remained essentially the same (showing a decrease of less than one percent) for the same period. Overall, the number of individuals receiving training from WIN or other sources decreased by about four percent from fiscal 1974.

SUPPORTIVE SERVICES.   Supportive social services, provided by local welfare agencies, are an integral part of the WIN program, since they are often needed to enable an individual to accept employment or engage in training. Child care, for example, is provided for the duration of a WIN participant's involvement in training and continues for 30 days following the start of employment. Under the WIN regulations issued in September 1975, child care (as well as other supportive services) may be offered for an additional 60 days at the discretion of the state welfare staff. These services may continue even after the AFDC grant has been terminated because of increases in income earned from employment. In emergency circumstances, working registrants who are not receiving WIN supportive services may also qualify for day care for up to 30 days when the absence of these services would result in the loss of employment.

Other assistance besides child care is also available, including health and homemaker services, family counseling, family planning, and rehabilitation services. Wherever possible, supportive services available through existing federal, state, or local programs are used through arrangements with WIN in order to avoid unnecessary duplication of federal support.

During fiscal 1975, 112,000 families received child-care assistance. The number of families receiving home management services totaled 109,400; family planning, 64,200; vocational rehabilitation, 23,500; and remedial medical services, some 39,-800. In addition, WIN participants were given over 45,000 medical examinations.

Eligibility Requirements

Each individual in an AFDC family must register for the WIN program unless he or she is:

> under age 16
>
> between 16 and 21 years of age and attending school full-time
>
> ill and his illness or injury temporarily prevents his job training or employment
>
> incapacitated with a mental or physical impairment which prevents him from participating in job training or employment
>
> 65 years of age or older
>
> residing at a location remote from a local WIN project
>
> a caretaker in the home who is required to care for another ill or disabled household member
>
> a mother or other caretaker relative of a child under age 6
>
> a mother or other female caretaker of a child in a home where the father is registered in a WIN project.

Also, any of the above AFDC family members may volunteer for WIN training and employment services.

Registrants are selected, appraised, and certified to participate in the following priority order:

1. All unemployed fathers
2. Mothers who volunteer
3. Other mothers and pregnant women under 19 years of age who are required to register
4. Dependent children and relatives who are at least age 16 not in school or already engaged in work or training

Services

All eligible persons may receive any of a broad range of services which contribute to reaching the objective of self-support through job placement and personal and economic independence. Mandatory social and supporting services which state public welfare agencies must provide under the WIN program are:

child care

family planning

health-related services

homemaker services

home management and other functional educational services

housing improvement services

transportation as needed to make self-supporting services accessible

selected vocational rehabilitation services which cannot be provided by the vocational rehabilitation agency

employment-related medical and remedial care and services not included under the Medicaid program

The following are mandatory employment training and employment services which state WIN designated manpower agencies must provide under the WIN program:

registration

appraisal of employability potential and needs, if any, for manpower, self support, and job placement services testing, remedial educational services, counseling, and placement for on-the-job training

institutional training and work experience training

public service employment

postplacement job counseling

job finding

employer counseling

manpower planning

WIN enrollees are entitled to various allowances: incentive allowances not to exceed $30 a month; training-related allowances of two dollars per day for lunches and transportation; subsistence allowances of eight dollars per day when they are assigned to a training facility beyond daily commuting distance from their homes (ten dollars in Alaska); a transportation allowance to a training facility located beyond commuting distance for the cost of the initial trip to the facility and for his final trip home at the conclusion or termination of training; allowances for nonrecurring expenses such as to report for an appraisal interview; relocation assistance for WIN participants and families to relocate to become permanently employed, including transportation costs and movement of household belongings. The above allowances are disregarded in figuring the AFDC assistance payments made.

Procedures

Referrals of AFDC family heads and youth are made by the state public welfare agencies to state WIN offices. Their names and records are placed in a registrant pool to await appraisal and placed in training or referred for a job. They are screened for employability by a team comprised of WIN project and welfare office staffs. An employability plan for each person is drawn up in consultation between the appraisal team and the participant. Testing may be utilized to the extent it is required to determine whether or not the individual is employable. The employability plan is designed to lead to appropriate employment and contains a definite employment goal attainable in the shortest time period consistent with the participant's needs and qualifications, project resources, and job market opportunities. All information which has a bearing upon his vocational objective is included in the employability plan. It specifies the steps for the participant to reach the goals established in the plan, identifies the major barriers to employment or training and proposes remedial action. The plan is reviewed periodically and modified as circumstances warrant. From the pool of registrants, individuals are certified by the WIN project staff as openings for training or job slots become available. Recipients then receive on-the-job training, institutional training, work experience, and-/or placement in private employment or public service employment. A WIN participant may go through one or a combination of these services.

SPECIAL POPULATION GROUPS

CUBAN REFUGEE ASSISTANCE PROGRAM

The objective of the Cuban Refugee Assistance program is to achieve the successful resettlement of Cuban refugees as permanent residents towards a gainful, productive life in the United States.

Background

Enacted in 1962, the Migration and Refugee Assistance Act (P.L. 87-510) provided financial assistance, health, education, and welfare services, and resettlement assistance to needy Cuban nationals granted asylum in the United States and registered with the Cuban Refugee Center in Miami, Florida. Refugees from Cuba were arriving in Miami at the rate of about 1,700 a week when the missile crisis occurred in October 1962 after which this number of arrivals decreased by about 90 percent. On October 3, 1965, the President announced that the United States would permit the orderly influx of refugees allowed to leave Cuba under a more liberal refugee policy adopted by the Cuban Government. In December 1965, a new influx of refugees started with the inauguration of freedom flights—the airlift operated by the United States as provided for in a United States-Cuban Memorandum of Understanding negotiated through the Swiss Government.

About 42 flights brought approximately 3,500 refugees to Miami each month between December 1965 and August 1971 when the Cuban Government began a series of interruptions in airlift operations. Only 26 flights had occurred during calendar year 1972 until December 11, 1972 when the airlift resumed. At least 40 flights bringing 3,400 refugees into Miami took place before another interruption occurred and an additional small number came since then.

The anticipated cessation of airlift activities and other considerations led the Department of Health, Education and Welfare to plan a phaseout of the program to begin July 1, 1973 with complete termination of the program projected for June 30,

1977. Subsequently, Congress passed and the President signed continuing appropriations (P.L. 93-52) which authorizes expenditures for the program at the fiscal year 1973 level, which nullified the plan and caused the Secretary to suspend the phaseout for the time being. The five-year policy recognized the minimum time for refugees to have become American citizens and to have overcome the most serious aspects of their adjustment to this country; in most states the Cuban refugees transferred to regular welfare programs will constitute a small portion of the state's total welfare caseload. Some modification of the plan was contemplated for Florida due to the large concentration of refugees there. When the SSI program went into effect January 1, 1974, a large number of refugees in the United States less than five years became eligible for that program as legally admitted aliens.

Administering Agencies

The program is administered by the Office of Family Assistance, Social Security Administration, D/HEW through state and local agencies administering categorical public assistance programs; through the State of Florida or Dade County health offices (for special health services in Dade County, Florida); or through one of four private agencies sponsored by Protestant, Catholic, Jewish, and nonsectarian groups (as selected by the beneficiaries) for resettlement services.

Eligibility Requirements

Cuban refugees entering the country by airlift and other means registering with the Cuban Refugee Center in Miami. No income or resources limitations apply.

Benefits and Services

Benefits and services include the following:

> health services, including medical screening upon arrival, clinic services, maternal and child health and school

health services, and care for tuberculosis and mental illness in Dade County

education and training services for children and adults

social services

financial assistance

employment services, including counseling and placement

resettlement services, including transportation and followup services

medical assistance

Procedure

The Cuban Refugee Center in Miami is the central registration and services agency for Cuban refugees. Services are provided by county and state health, education, and welfare agencies in Dade County and the state government of Florida under arrangements with the Federal Center while the refugees are in Miami. Upon resettlement to other parts of the country, state and local public welfare agencies assume the provision of financial assistance and social services on their behalf up to the time when they become eligible for citizenship or become self-supporting and no longer require such benefits and services.

REPATRIATED U.S. NATIONALS ASSISTANCE PROGRAM

The objective of this program is to provide temporary care and assistance to U.S. citizens upon arrival from a foreign country because of destitution, mental or physical illness, or because of war, threat of war, invasion, or other crises.

Background

Two Federal laws authorize this program: The Social Security Act, Title XI Sec. 1113: *Assistance For United States Citizens Returned From Foreign Countries* (Sec. 302 75 Stat. 142, sec. 1102, 49 Stat. 647, U.S.C. 1313, 1302) for destitute, ill U.S. citizens, or because of war, threat of war, invasion, or similar crisis; and P.L. 86-37, *An Act To Provide For the Hospitalization, at Saint Elizabeths Hospital in the District of Columbia or Elsewhere of Certain Nationals of the United States Adjudged Insane or Otherwise Found Mentally Ill in Foreign Countries.*

Administering Agencies

The U.S. Department of State (Office of Special Consular Services) and the Office of Family Assistance, Social Security Administration, D/HEW are the responsible agencies. State and local public welfare agencies with ports of entry into the United States are responsible for providing assistance and services to incoming U.S. citizens.

Caseload

An average of 600 to 800 citizens are aided annually by this program of whom approximately 100 to 150 are mentally ill. Most citizens return from Europe and Canada.

Eligibility Requirements

U.S. citizens in a foreign country certified by the Department of State to be returning because of mental or physical illness, destitution, war, threat of war, invasion, or other crises.

Services

Services include temporary care, hospitalization, if necessary, transportation, food, lodging, funds, and other goods and services.

Procedure

The responsible D/HEW officer (the Repatriate and Refugee Office, Office of Family Assistance) is notified by the Department of State about the time and place of arrival of the U.S. citizen and is provided information on his condition, plans, and the kind of help he may need. The D/HEW officer notifies the appropriate welfare agency of the arrival time and place at the port of entry or debarkation. The state or local agency representative receives the citizen and makes arrangements for his temporary care, treatment, and assistance. This may include arrangements for physical examination, hospitalization, provide notification of his legal guardian, spouse, or next of kin, appointment under state law of a guardian if the citizen is mentally ill, provide for food and lodging, funds, transportation to his home, other goods and services. Repayment of the cost of such temporary assistance to the U.S. Government is required in accordance with the financial ability of the individual.

NOTES

1. Spindler, A. On decision-making and the social and rehabilitation programs. *Public Welfare,* 1971, 307–315.

2. Estimated from "Children Served by Public Welfare Agencies in DHEW Publication No. (SRS) 76-03258 NCSS Report E-9 3-74, NCSS, SRS, DHEW Washington, D.C., issued December 1975.

3. Applications and Case Dispositions for Public Assistance, April–June 1972. DHEW Publication No. (SRS) 73-03106 NCSS Report No. 9.

4. Employment and Training Report to the President, 1976. U.S. Departments of Health, Education and Welfare and Labor, U.S. Government Printing Office, Washington, D.C. 20402, 117–120.

Chapter 5

PUBLIC WELFARE ORGANIZATION

The organization of the federal/state public welfare system is a product of 40 years of historical change in societal and economic conditions, in public welfare policies, political philosophies, public attitudes, revisions in federal/state laws and relationships, new technology, and changes in the number and characteristics of public welfare beneficiaries. *Organizational change is a constant.* Today's patterns of public welfare agencies are different from those of a decade ago, which were different from the preceding decades and will likely differ in the years ahead. We can be assured that any new reforms in public welfare will bring new organizational alignments.

The present organization of the system is comprised of federal, state and local governmental units represented in every political jurisdiction in the United States and its territories. Under our federal/state constitutional system, the President as administrative head of the Executive Branch of the Government is the top federal public welfare official responsible for carrying out federal public welfare laws and regulations, and the U.S. Congress legislates the federal laws governing the federal participation in public welfare. The federal judiciary, with the U.S. Supreme Court at its apex, and its system of appellate and lower courts, is the separate and equal partner for deciding constitutional questions and controversies arising from the public welfare system.

There is no *supreme national public welfare executive* with total responsibility, accountability, and authority for the administration of a national all–encompassing public welfare system. One American official does not have it within his power—as the ultimate authority—to control, manage, supervise, plan, and make decisions for all public welfare programs.

Under the state constitutions the chief executives (Governors) exercise authority over the organization of state and local public welfare programs, and, in the 20 states which authorize local government operations of such programs, county and city executives have this authority. Moreover, state legislatures and, in the locally administered programs, local legislative bodies exercise jurisdiction over the organizational arrangement of their public welfare activities. Their respective judiciaries also become involved in state and local constitutional questions and controversies covering public welfare programs. With so many political jurisdictions, there is a diversity in organization with the federal government organization of public welfare programs having no counterpart in state and local governments, and state and local public welfare organizations largely dissimilar one from another.

THE FEDERAL GOVERNMENT ORGANIZATION[1]

The Executive Branch (Chart 5.1)

The President is empowered to carry out all federal public welfare laws and regulations and has the power to appoint Executive Branch officials and nominate, by and with the advice and consent of the Senate, and appoint heads of departments and delegate to them appointive authority for subordinates. The "advice and consent" provision applies in the public welfare system to the Secretaries of Agriculture; Health, Education and Welfare; and Labor, and to the Administrator of the Social Security Administration.[2] The President has the authority to develop

Chart 5.1 Organization Chart Federal Government Organization for Public Welfare Responsibilities

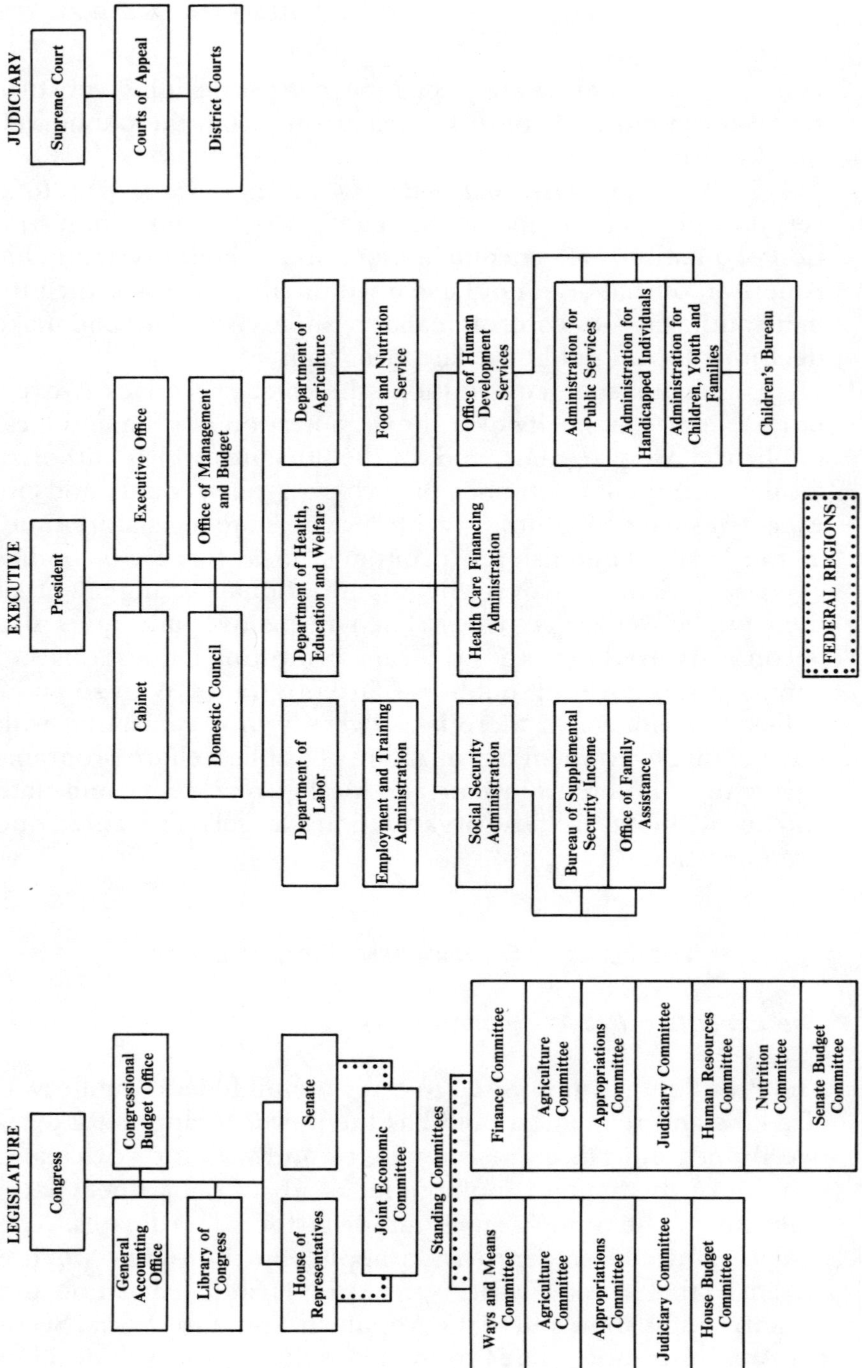

JUDICIARY

- Supreme Court
- Courts of Appeal
- District Courts

EXECUTIVE

- President
  - Cabinet
  - Executive Office
    - Domestic Council
    - Office of Management and Budget
  - Department of Labor
    - Employment and Training Administration
  - Department of Health, Education and Welfare
    - Social Security Administration
      - Bureau of Supplemental Security Income
      - Office of Family Assistance
    - Health Care Financing Administration
    - Office of Human Development Services
      - Administration for Public Services
      - Administration for Handicapped Individuals
      - Administration for Children, Youth and Families
      - Children's Bureau
  - Department of Agriculture
    - Food and Nutrition Service

FEDERAL REGIONS

LEGISLATURE

- Congress
  - General Accounting Office
  - Congressional Budget Office
  - Library of Congress
  - House of Representatives
  - Senate
  - Joint Economic Committee

Standing Committees
- Ways and Means Committee
- Finance Committee
- Agriculture Committee
- Agriculture Committee
- Appropriations Committee
- Appropriations Committee
- Judiciary Committee
- Judiciary Committee
- House Budget Committee
- Human Resources Committee
- Nutrition Committee
- Senate Budget Committee

and put into effect Presidential Reorganization Plans for executive departments and agencies, subject to disapproval of either House by a majority of those voting within 60 days of the date of transmittal by the President. He may not abolish any executive departments or agency created by statute, or to transfer or eliminate its functions (Reorganization Act of 1974). This latter proscription in public welfare is applicable to the Departments of Agriculture; Health, Education, and Welfare; Labor and to the Children's Bureau created by law in 1912.

Annually, the President submits to Congress his State of the Union Message which gives his report and appraisal of the American domestic and foreign status; its social, economic, international and environmental condition and outlines his measures for dealing with the nation's problems. Traditionally, this message includes the President's policies and recommendations for the federal role in the public welfare system. In addition, the President submits to the Congress the Federal Budget for the fiscal year requesting federal appropriations to implement the policies and programs outlined in the State of the Union Message.

To assist him in these duties within the Executive Office of the President in the public welfare area are the Domestic Council, the Office of Management and Budget, and the Cabinet. Because of their close relationship to the President, these organizations understandingly wield substantial influence over public welfare policy formulation and planning.

Three executive departments are responsible for federal public welfare program administration: the Department of Agriculture for the Food Stamp Program, the Department of Labor sharing with the Department of Health, Education and Welfare responsibility for the Work Incentive Program, and the Department of Health, Education and Welfare for all other federally funded and administered public welfare programs. The Food and Nutrition Service (Chart 5.2) is the agency within the Department of Agriculture administering the Food Stamp Program. The Administrator of the Service, who reports to the Assistant Secretary for Marketing and Consumer Services, is also responsible for the food distribution and child nutrition

Chart 5.2 Food and Nutrition Service Organization Chart

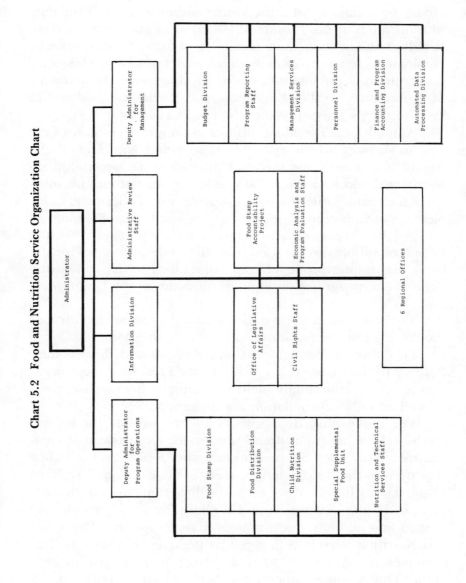

programs. The Employment and Training Administration (Chart 5.3) of the Department of Labor is responsible for training and employment services for AFDC-WIN registrants. It is directed by the Assistant Secretary for Employment and Training and administers a broad range of other programs including the Comprehensive Employment and Training (CETA) program, OJT, employment services, employment development programs, unemployment insurance, apprenticeship and training, and the Job Corps.

The Social and Rehabilitation Service of the Department of Health, Education and Welfare had primary responsibility until 1977 for the AFDC welfare payments and social services programs, the Work Incentive Program, the Medical Assistance Program, the Cuban Refugee Assistance, and Repatriated U.S. National programs. A major departmental reorganization effective March 8, 1977 abolished SRS. A new Health Care Financing Administration was created with joint responsibility for the Medical Assistance Program (Medicaid) and the Health Insurance For the Aged and Disabled Program (Medicare). The AFDC assistance payments, Cuban Refugee Assistance, and Repatriated U.S. Nationals programs were transferred to the Social Security Administration, already responsible for the SSI Program (Chart 5.4). The Title XX Social Services, Child Welfare Services, and Work Incentives Programs were transferred to the Office of Human Development Services. (Chart 5.5)

Special mention should be made of the role of the Rehabilitation Services Administration (placed in the Administration For Handicapped Individuals, July 1977) of the Office of Human Development Services. It is responsible for administering the vocational rehabilitation project for services to public assistance recipients through state vocational rehabilitation agencies and for the operation and financial support of state disability determinations units for determining eligibility of SSI applicants because of disability or blindness.

Finally, the Office of the Secretary, D/HEW, has major coordinative, policy, planning, and evaluation responsibilities for public welfare programs within the department.

Chart 5.3 Employment and Training Administration Organization Chart

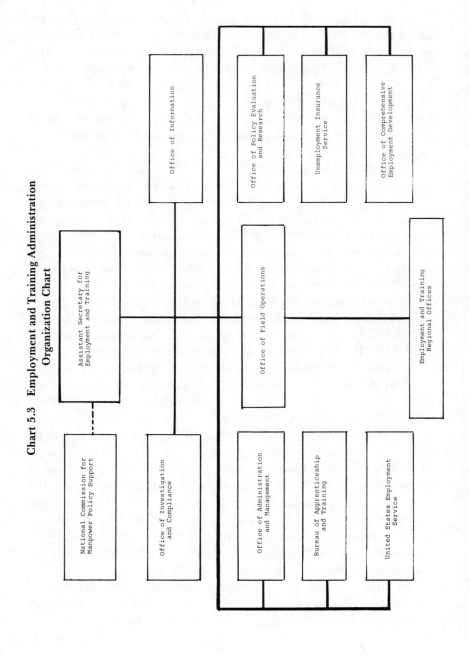

National Commission for Manpower Policy Support

Assistant Secretary for Employment and Training

Office of Information

Office of Investigation and Compliance

Office of Field Operations

Office of Policy Evaluation and Research

Unemployment Insurance Service

Office of Comprehensive Employment Development

Office of Administration and Management

Bureau of Apprenticeship and Training

United States Employment Service

Employment and Training Regional Offices

Chart 5.4   Social Security Administration
Organization Chart

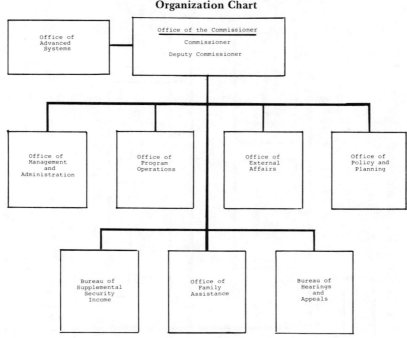

Field Organization

The federal government maintains regional offices with responsibility for maintaining contact with state and local governments
in administering public welfare programs. The Departments of
Health, Education and Welfare and Labor have 10 regional
offices with common locations and regional boundaries (Figure
5.1): Boston, New York, Philadelphia, Atlanta, Dallas, Kansas
City, Chicago, Denver, San Francisco, and Seattle. The Food
and Nutrition Service of the Department of Agriculture has six
field offices in Burlington, Massachusetts; Princeton, New Jersey; Atlanta, Chicago, Dallas, and San Francisco (Figure 5.2).

Each executive department maintains an office in each city
under a regional director appointed by the Secretary of his
department staffed with program and other technical field representatives to serve the state and local government jurisdic-

Chart 5.5 Office of Human Development Services Organization Chart

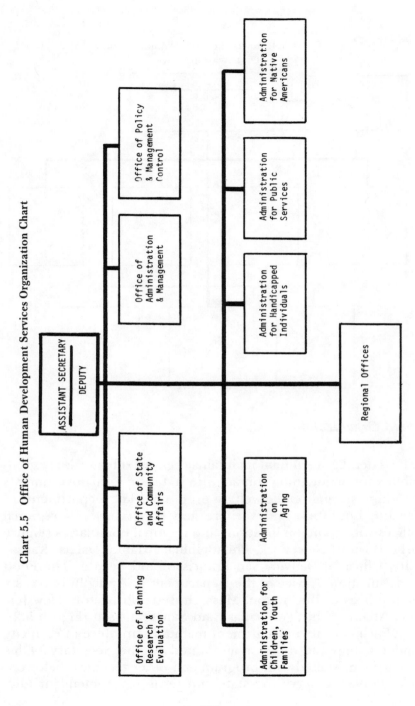

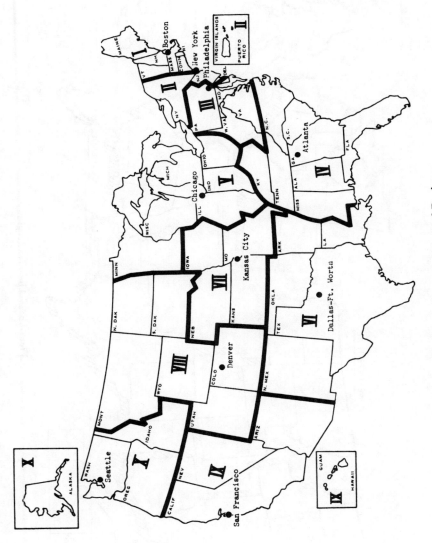

Figure 5.1 Standard Federal Regions

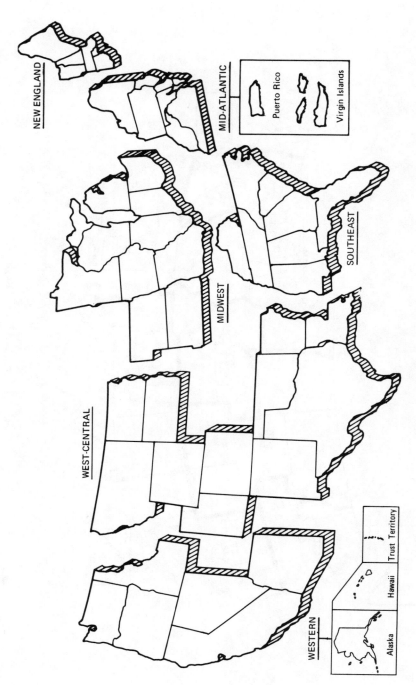

NEW ENGLAND

MID-ATLANTIC

Puerto Rico

Virgin Islands

MIDWEST

SOUTHEAST

WEST-CENTRAL

WESTERN

Alaska

Hawaii

Trust Territory

Figure 5.2 The FNS Regions

208

tions in their assigned regional boundaries, with activities in program coordination, program planning, monitoring and evaluation, technical consultation, assistance, and information and reporting. The regional staffs of the respective departmental administrations and offices are headed by regional commissioners who report to their regional directors and simultaneously to their central office counterparts: for the Social Security Administration, in Baltimore, for all other offices, in Washington, D.C. Their authority includes approval of state plan amendments initiated by state agencies administering federal/state programs, including the AFDC income maintenance program, social services and child welfare services programs, the medical assistance program, and the rehabilitation services programs.

The Social Security Administration administers its programs through a network of 1,200 local offices, supervised by the Social Security Administration regional commissioners in the D/HEW regional office in their geographic location. Each local office is responsible for providing general information, receiving, verifying information, and processing applications for all social security programs, including Supplemental Security income, and being of assistance to beneficiaries in explaining their entitlements and benefits and correcting payment errors, obtaining replacements for lost checks, and making referrals to other social agencies for their services and benefits. The Administration also maintains payment centers in four cities to maintain records and process payments to beneficiaries: Birmingham, Philadelphia, Chicago, and Richmond, California.

In the Department of Labor field organization of ten regions, the regional employment and training administrator is responsible to the DOL regional director and to the Assistant Secretary for Employment and Training for planning, coordination, administration, and evaluation of the Work Incentive program and other manpower training and employment programs in the states and localities in his region.

The Legislative Branch

The two houses of Congress exercise the legislative functions of the federal government dealing with the public welfare laws through the committee system of standing and select committees. The House of Representatives has several standing committees with public welfare jurisdiction. The Ways and Means Committee has substantive responsibility over all programs in the Social Security Act as well as tax and other revenue legislation. The House Agriculture Committee has jurisdiction over the Food Stamp program and other nutrition and food distribution programs as well as other agriculture legislation. It operates through ten subcommittees of which the Subcommittee on Domestic Marketing and Consumer Relations is concerned with the Food Stamp, nutrition, and food distribution programs. The House Appropriations Committee, Labor-D/HEW Subcommittee has jurisdiction over appropriation bills for the federal public welfare programs, except for the Food Stamp program, covered by the Subcommittee on Agriculture, Environment and Consumer Protection, and the Cuban Refugee Assistance program, covered by the Subcommittee on Foreign Operations. The House Judiciary Committee, Subcommittee on Immigration and Nationality has jurisdiction over Cuban Refugee Assistance program legislation.

The Senate has several standing committees with public welfare jurisdiction. The Senate Finance Committee is the Senate counterpart to the House Ways and Means Committee, with substantive responsibility over programs authorized in the Social Security Act. It has six subcommittees. The Senate Agriculture Committee is concerned with the Food Stamp program and its Subcommittee on Agricultural Production, Marketing and Stabilization of Prices has that program under its jurisdiction. The Senate Appropriations Committee and its Subcommittee on Labor-HEW deals with federal public welfare programs except for appropriations for the Food Stamp program, handled by the Subcommittee on Agriculture, Environmental and Consumer Protection, and the Cuban Refugee Assistance program, handled by the Subcommittee on Foreign Operations. The Senate Judiciary Committee, Subcommittee on Refugees and Escapees is responsible for legislative oversight of the Cuban Refugee Assistance program. The Senate Human Resources

Committee is concerned with measures relating to education, labor, and public welfare generally, exclusive of those provided for in the Social Security Act. Among its nine subcommittees are several with special public welfare interests: the Subcommittees on labor, handicapped, health, employment, poverty and migratory labor, children and youth, and aging. The Committee's specific jurisdiction in public welfare includes such matters as: child abuse, family planning, job training, health services, health maintenance organization, health care facilities for aged, blind and disabled, public service employment for the unemployed, adoptions, and child care.

Other committees in both Houses of Congress may be concerned with legislation having direct effect upon the public welfare system from time to time, for example, the House and Senate Committees on Government Operations in considering legislation for the reorganization of the Executive Branch and intergovernmental relations, or the House and Senate Post Office and Civil Service Committees, regarding legislation on civil service matters.

Both the House and Senate are represented in various Joint Committees, Commissions, and Boards, one of which, the Joint Economic Committee, has been concerned particularly with the study of public welfare policies, problems, and administration. Its Subcommittee on Fiscal Policy has developed national studies, reports and held hearings directly concerned with this subject.

The General Accounting Office is an independent agency in the legislative branch conducting audits and review of federal agencies and programs as well as those of state and local governments and quasi-governmental and private organizations which are recipients of federal funds. The office maintains a full time staff of accountants, auditors, and other specialists assigned to each of the executive departments and augments this with special staffs conducting analyses and reviews and making recommendations for improvement of governmental operations, including those of the federal/state public welfare system. It also is responsible for determining the legality or propriety of payments of federal funds, issuing Comptroller-General's decisions which are legally binding on executive agencies, and settling claims for or against the United States.

The Library of Congress, in addition to its collections and library services, maintains a Congressional Research Service for House and Senate members and committees. Its Education and Public Welfare Division performs legislative research studies and provides advisory assistance in the legislative process in these areas.

The Congressional Budget Office, the newest of the Congressional staff agencies, was created by the Congressional Budget and Impoundment Control Act of 1974 (P.L. 93–344). Its professional staff provides assistance to the budget committees of both Houses and the other committees concerned with financial matters as well as to individual members. It concerns itself with reports on fiscal policy, estimates of revenues and expenditures for the budget, national budget priorities and alternative ways to allocate budget authority and budget outlays. It is the central analytical legislative agency for appraising national public welfare policies and programs and recommending courses of strategy for federal legislation in this and other domestic and foreign policy spheres.

The House and Senate Budget Committees for their respective bodies perform parallel revenue and expenditure analysis functions in review of Congressional Budget Office recommendations and in making budget determinations to their respective houses.

The Judicial Branch

The authority of the Federal Judiciary is stated in Article III, Section 2 of the Constitution to include controversies to which the United States shall be a party, controversies between two or more states, between a state and citizens of another state, and between citizens of different states. The Appendix: *Supreme Court Decisions Affecting Public Welfare* reveals the significant position of the Judiciary in molding public welfare as a system of laws, in correcting abuses and excesses, and in influencing the relations between the federal and state governments and between government and the individual.

State/Local Public Welfare Organization

There is no "uniform" or "typical" or "standard" organization of state or local government public welfare agencies. There are many variations, in fact, no two state agencies, no two local agencies, are precisely alike in the 50 states, the District of Columbia, and territories. However, there are basic similarities agencies share which enable us to consider them as a group (Chart 5.6). These are:

A single state agency designated by state law to be responsible for administering or supervising the administration of the state plans for income maintenance under Titles I, IV, X, XIV, XVI of the Social Security Act and/or social services under Titles IV and XX of that act. All states, the District of Columbia, and territories designate the same agency for both income maintenance and social services programs, with 5 exceptions:

Illinois has a State Department of Public Aid for income maintenance and a separate State Department of Family and Children Services for social services.

Massachusetts has a separate Commission For The Blind to provide financial assistance and social services to the blind.

Ohio and Pennsylvania have separate organizations of county child welfare service agencies.

Oregon has a separate State Children's Services Division and State Public Welfare Division within the State Department of Human Resources, with separate field and local agencies of the two divisions.

A policy making and/or advisory authority, that is, a public welfare board, commission or committee of citizens usually appointed by the Governor, many with the consent of the state legislature.

A chief public welfare administrator responsible and accountable for administering or supervising the administration of public welfare programs under state law.

Chart 5.6 Typical Organization Chart of State Welfare Agencies

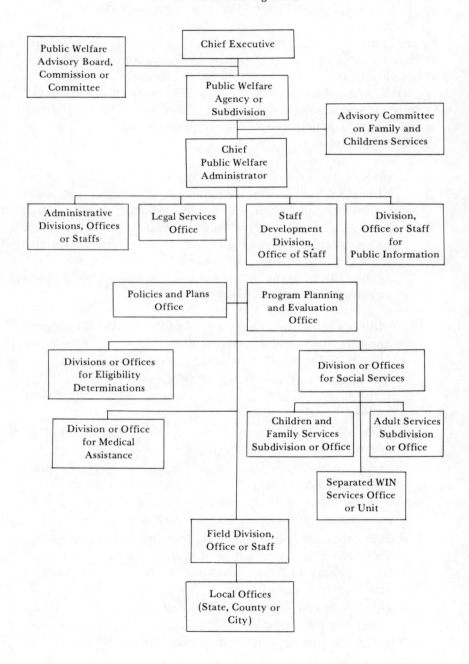

Divisions or offices of the public welfare agency responsible for eligibility determinations for income maintenance, social services, food stamps, medical assistance programs; supervision and direction of those functions and activities throughout the jurisdiction; administering the quality control program, monitoring compliance with the state plans, and planning and evaluation of the eligibility determinations programs.

An advisory committee on family and children's services, comprised of professionals, civic leaders, and recipients appointed by the chief executive.

Divisions or offices of the public welfare agency responsible for social services, including procedures, methods, standards, contracts, and agreements for social and child welfare services for eligible children, families, and adults; supervision and direction of all service functions and activities throughout the jurisdiction. These divisions or offices have subdivisions for children and family services, adult services and separate WIN services offices or units for AFDC/WIN registrants and families, and for maintaining liaison with state WIN manpower agencies.

Divisions, offices, or staffs of the public welfare agency responsible for all internal administrative functions, including budgeting, accounting, disbursements, auditing, research and statistics, personnel operations, procurement, space, supplies, equipment, printing services, planning and evaluation.

A staff development division, office, or staff of the public welfare agency responsible for training and staff development functions.

A public information division, office, or staff of the public welfare agency responsible for public media contacts, public information inquiries, releases, reports, and other communications.

Divisions, offices or staffs of the public welfare agency responsible for exercising supervision and control over decentralized field offices geographically dispersed within the jurisdiction.

Local offices responsible for eligibility determinations, social services, medical assistance, and food stamps provided under state and local law.

In the 41 states which assign responsibility for administering medical assistance program to the public welfare
agency, divisions, offices, or staffs with responsibility for
procedures, methods, standards, contracts, and agreements for the medical assistance program; and for planning, evaluation, and monitoring the program and
controlling costs throughout the jurisdiction.

Federal laws and regulations play an important part in influencing state/local public welfare organizations as well as substantive matters. Federal requirements impose specified functions
and activities and, in some instances, dictate creation of separate
organizational units (as WIN services units), or combinations of
organizational entities (combining social services under Title
XX of the Social Security Act with child welfare services under
Title IVB of the Act). But the most important of these requirements is designation of the single state agency responsible for
the basic federally supported programs discussed in earlier
chapters. This provision requires there to be a clearly identifiable public welfare organizational entity in each state, the District of Columbia, and the territories. Under the Social Security
Act, this entity must:

administer or supervise the administration of the federally
approved state plans for income maintenance and/or
social services.

insure the confidentiality of information concerning applicants or recipients.

maintain or supervise the maintenance of records necessary for the proper and efficient operation of the plan,
including records regarding applications, determination
of eligibility, the provision of financial or medical assistance or social services, and administrative cost; and statistical, fiscal, and other records necessary for reporting
and accountability required by the Secretary of D/HEW,
and to retain such records for such periods as are prescribed by the Secretary.

make rules and regulations governing the administration of the plan on a state-wide basis binding on all political subdivisions.

provide for eligibility determinations for federally supported income maintenance, medical assistance, social services, and food stamps.

provide or arrange for the provision of federally mandated social services and child welfare services.

exercise final authority over social services included in the state plan performed by other state or local agencies or other service providers.

assure that state public welfare policies, standards, procedures, and instructions are carried out in all political subdivisions in the state through monitoring and evaluations by regular visits of state staff, reports, controls, and other methods.

assure that state funds are utilized in both administration, assistance payments, and/or social services and apportioned equitably among the political jurisdictions.

maintain an accounting system and supporting fiscal records to assure that federal requirements are met.

establish and maintain methods and procedures for properly charging the costs of activities under the state plans in accordance with requirements.

establish, maintain, and monitor standards for office space, equipment and facilities that meet effectively program and staff needs.

designate the state authorities responsible for standards for institutions used by individuals receiving financial or medical assistance.

assure compliance of state and local public welfare agencies with merit system standards of personnel administration.

provide a staff development program for all state and local public welfare agency personnel.

provide an adequate number of full-time staff assigned to social services functions.

establish and support state advisory committees on family and children's services and at local levels where social services are locally administered, with professional, civic, and recipient representations.

establish a state advisory committee on day care as a separate committee or part of the state social services advisory committee.

employ subprofessional personnel and volunteers in social services programs.

maintain a leadership role in developing adequate community service resources to be able to administer the state plans.

administer a program for establishing paternity for children born out-of-wedlock and for securing financial support for them and for all other AFDC children deserted by their parents or legally liable persons.[3]

The many organizational differences of state and local agencies show their leadership exercises a high degree of individual self-determinism in choosing the pattern of organization for their jurisdiction despite, but not in conflict with, this impressive list of federal requirements. These differences are the product of many factors, many influences operating simultaneously, sometimes in a planned effort to reorganize, other times by chance, creating the conditions for retention of the existing organization or change and reorganization to another. In most states since 1935, there has been not infrequent organizational change in the search for the *ideal* arrangement of public welfare functions and activities, and this process can be expected to continue. Experience in this field is basically no different than other fields in the universal absence of agreement on the "one best way" to organize large, costly, sensitive, governmental programs such as public welfare. In many respects, the "trial and error" thesis applies. ("Let's try this. It appears plausible. See how it works. Change it later if we need to for something better.")

State and local government leaders make the decisions on organization usually as a compromise between opposing viewpoints, based on the facts before them, the urgency for change, their personal attitudes, the opinion of their advisors and of the public media, public opinion, the views of administrators and professionals, the current organizational principles then in favor, the weight of historical precedents, some of the foregoing in agreement, others in conflict. The search will go on.

Inevitably, these are the factors considered in state and local public welfare organization:

the federal requirements to be met.

the size and complexity of state and local public welfare programs, their cost, diversity, availability of services and resources, the size of the public assistance caseload.

the political philosophy of the leadership in the state or local jurisdiction towards social welfare, governmental expenditures and size, taxation, poverty, income redistribution, and related social and economic issues.

the financing of public welfare programs by the state and/or local governments, the state of their respective budgets, and prevailing pressures for government economy.

the attitudes of chief executives, public welfare administrators and other influential persons towards modern principles of organization and administration, such as services integration and new technology (computers, telecommunications).

the historical, social, cultural and economic background of the state.

the incidence (alleged or proven) of public welfare scandals, fraud, or other illegalities associated with public welfare programs.

the geographic dispersion of the state and its urban/rural character.

the state constitutional provisions affecting public welfare, their degree of flexibility or rigidity in organizing public welfare programs.

the leadership qualities of public welfare administrators in state and local administration.

public opinion and sensitivity towards public welfare and confidence in its administration.

the activities of professional, public interest, and other groups representing the poor, disabled, and minorities in pressing for public welfare reform.

State public welfare organizations fall into three broad descriptive groups:

Group A. The public welfare organization is a separate major state or local agency with responsibility for income maintenance and/or social services. Its commissioner or director reports and is responsible to the Governor or a state official in his office, or, if a county or city agency, to the chief executive of that jurisdiction. The state agency is the designated agency for administration or supervision of the state plans for income maintenance and/or social services under the Social Security Act. Six states have agencies which fall into this group. They are typified by the organization of the Welfare Department of Connecticut shown in Chart 5.7.

Group B. The public welfare organization is a separate major subdivision of an "umbrella" agency with responsibility for other major human services programs at state, county, or city government levels. The "umbrella" concept is to bring together under one administrator reporting to the chief executive closely related or overlapping human services programs formerly under separate administrators reporting to the chief executive. Twenty-nine states have "umbrella" agencies with public welfare subdivisions. Chart 5.8 illustrates the organization and functions of one such agency, the District of Columbia Department of Human Resources.

Group C. The public welfare organization is a subdivision of a major state, county, or city agency having responsibility for one or more other human services programs. This type of organization is not as encompassing as "umbrella" agencies in the variety and scope of the programs they include. Usually, it is designed to facilitate the coordination of one or two other human services programs with close ties to public welfare, either in the similarities of services provided or in the preponderance of welfare recipients, the poor or disabled who are served. Nineteen states are included in this group. The Iowa Department of Social Services as shown on Chart 5.9 is a typical state agency for this group.

State Organization For Medical Assistance

State governments have the option of assigning responsibility for administering the medical assistance program under Title XIX of the Social Security Act to any state agency, but require placement of medical assistance eligibility determinations functions with the public welfare agency responsible for similar func-

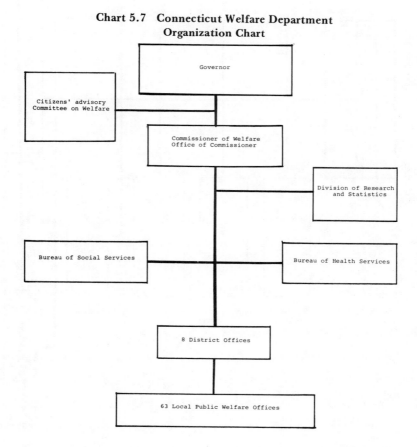

**Chart 5.7   Connecticut Welfare Department
Organization Chart**

Governor

Citizens' advisory
Committee on Welfare

Commissioner of Welfare
Office of Commissioner

Division of Research
and Statistics

Bureau of Social Services

Bureau of Health Services

8 District Offices

63 Local Public Welfare Offices

Chart 5.8 District of Columbia Department of Human Resources Organization Chart

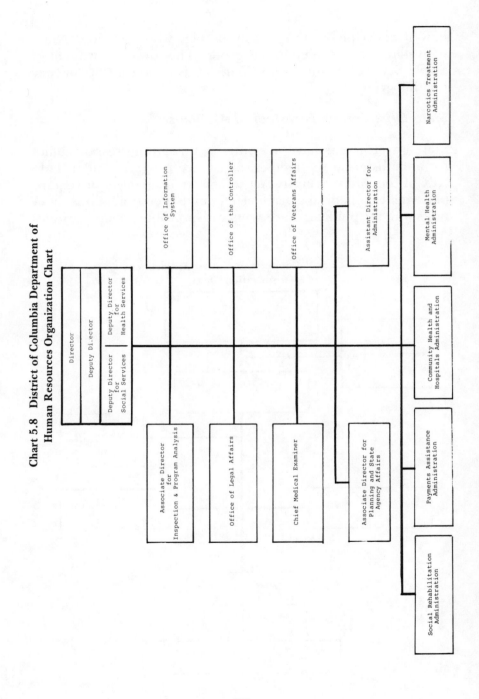

Chart 5.9 Iowa Department of Social Services
Organization Chart

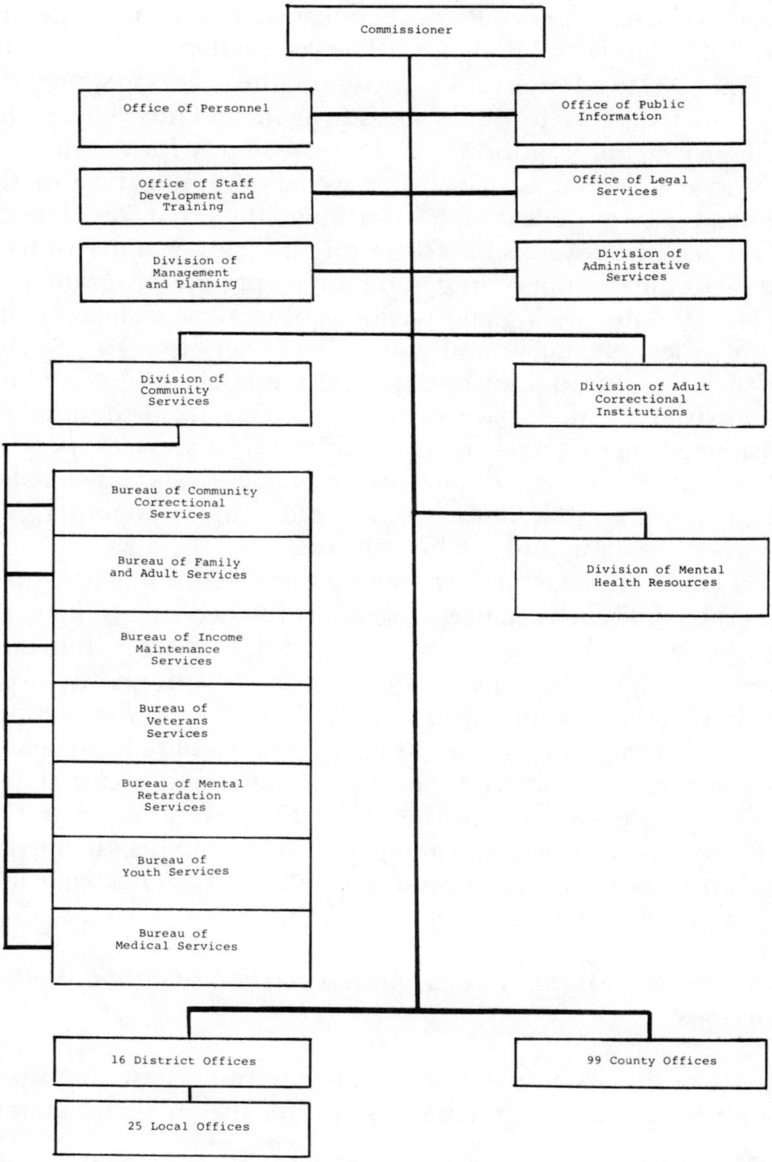

```
                          ┌──────────────────┐
                          │   Commissioner   │
                          └──────────────────┘
                                   │
   ┌──────────────────┐            │           ┌──────────────────┐
   │ Office of Personnel│──────────┤           │ Office of Public │
   └──────────────────┘            │           │   Information    │
                                   │           └──────────────────┘
   ┌──────────────────┐            │           ┌──────────────────┐
   │ Office of Staff  │            │           │ Office of Legal  │
   │ Development and  │────────────┤           │    Services      │
   │    Training      │            │           └──────────────────┘
   └──────────────────┘            │
   ┌──────────────────┐            │           ┌──────────────────┐
   │   Division of    │            │           │   Division of    │
   │   Management     │────────────┤           │  Administrative  │
   │   and Planning   │            │           │    Services      │
   └──────────────────┘            │           └──────────────────┘
```

Division of Community Services		Division of Adult Correctional Institutions

- Bureau of Community Correctional Services
- Bureau of Family and Adult Services
- Bureau of Income Maintenance Services
- Bureau of Veterans Services
- Bureau of Mental Retardation Services
- Bureau of Youth Services
- Bureau of Medical Services

Division of Mental Health Resources

16 District Offices	99 County Offices

25 Local Offices

tions of eligibility determinations for income maintenance. Eight jurisdictions opt for separate agency administrations: Alabama, Arizona, Puerto Rico, Tennessee, Virginia, Virgin Islands, Maryland and Mississippi. The last established a Medicaid Commission to administer the program, the others assigned the program to the state public health agency. Thus, except for these jurisdictions, authority and responsibility for the medical assistance program is placed in a separate subdivision of the public welfare organization to coordinate the provision of medical services; be responsible for setting policies, standards, fees, and procedures; supervising and monitoring the program, particularly the processing and payment of medical claims and assuring the adequacy and quality of services to eligible beneficiaries. In addition, public welfare agencies have added administrative and social work loads arising from the medical assistance program in such functions as social services, personnel operations, training, data processing, reports, office space management, public information, planning, budgeting, accounting, auditing and quality control.

A controlling factor determining these additional pressures from the medical assistance program is the decision to contract out the medical claims processing and payments function. Twenty-six states have fiscal agent contracts with private organizations to act for the agency, e.g., Blue Cross and indemnity health insurance companies. Agency responsibility for overseeing this contract function is vested in a state medical assistance division, office, or staff. In the other 27 states which maintain their own claims processing and payment operations, their organization places this responsibility directly on agency staff in a claims processing unit set up for that purpose.

State Administration vs. Local Administration of Public Welfare Functions

Twenty of the 54 state public welfare programs* are organized so that the counties and cities administer income maintenance

*New Jersey, New York, Maryland, Virginia, Alabama, Georgia, North Carolina, South Carolina, Indiana, Minnesota, Ohio, Wisconsin, Kansas, Nebraska, Montana, North Dakota, Colorado, Wyoming, California, Oregon.

and social services functions under state supervision. The effect of this is to change not only relationships between state and local governments, but also their organizations.[4] The contrast between a state-administered program and a locally administered, state-supervised program is best illustrated in New Hampshire and Alabama. The former is state-administered, the latter, locally administered. New Hampshire's Department of Health and Welfare administers public welfare programs through eleven district offices, each for an assigned geographic area. The director of the Division of Welfare appoints the district directors and is responsible for all other staff appointments of the district offices under the state's merit system. All are employees of the State Department of Health and Welfare, funded by the state government.** Alabama's Department of Pensions and Security has statewide supervision over public welfare functions which are administered by the state's 67 county governments. Each county has a pensions and security board and public welfare staff, all of whom are county employees appointed by county commissioners subject to the state merit system. All expenses incurred by the board and county employees are provided from county income. On the other hand, the state agency is comprised of state employees under the control of the State Commissioner of Pensions and Security. All state agency personnel are paid out of state funds.

In both states, federal and state laws, policies, standards, and regulations are carried out and the responsibility for federally supported public welfare programs rests with the state public welfare agency.

Five factors distinguish the two types of organizations:

location of the appointing authority for local personnel

local participation in meeting the costs of local administration

location of authority for making investigations of public assistance eligibility and maintaining contact with individual recipients

**However, general assistance is locally funded and administered autonomously by counties and cities by county and city employees.

location of responsibility for eligibility decisions and
amount of assistance payments

place of preparation of assistance checks[4]

The organization of a county public welfare department
with local administration is shown in Chart 5.10. The Minnesota
Hennepin County Welfare Department, has all the features of
a fully operational and responsible state agency. The executive
director reports to a county welfare board. It maintains staff
offices for planning and evaluation and legal counsel as well as
a separate, fully functional administrative organization. Its two
operating arms provide specialized services and maintenance
payments functions, prepared to cover all major public welfare
programs authorized in the state.

Separation of Services and Assistance Payments

Traditionally, prior to 1973, the financial assistance and social
services components of public welfare agencies have been administered as one program. However, since 1966, a number of
state and local agencies experimented with several forms of
organization separating the two with the objectives of strengthening both functions by eliminating confusion about the relationship between them. For example, persons needing services
refrained from applying because of the popular stigma to being
known as a welfare client. Separation would also help in improving administration, increasing effectiveness of agency personnel, and most importantly, encouraging agencies to expand
social services. On January 1, 1973, a statewide separated service system was mandated by the Department of Health, Education and Welfare.[5] Thus, separate lines of authority, divisions,
and offices within state and local agencies were established, each
reporting to the chief public welfare administrator. This is apparent in the county organization chart shown in Chart 5.10.
Each line of authority has separate staff for social services and
for assistance payments, including separate policy and program
development, supervision of local operations and actual provision of services and/or payments to clients. However, in the case
of a sparsely populated geographic area, where such an arrange-

Chart 5.10   Hennepin County Welfare Department Organization Chart

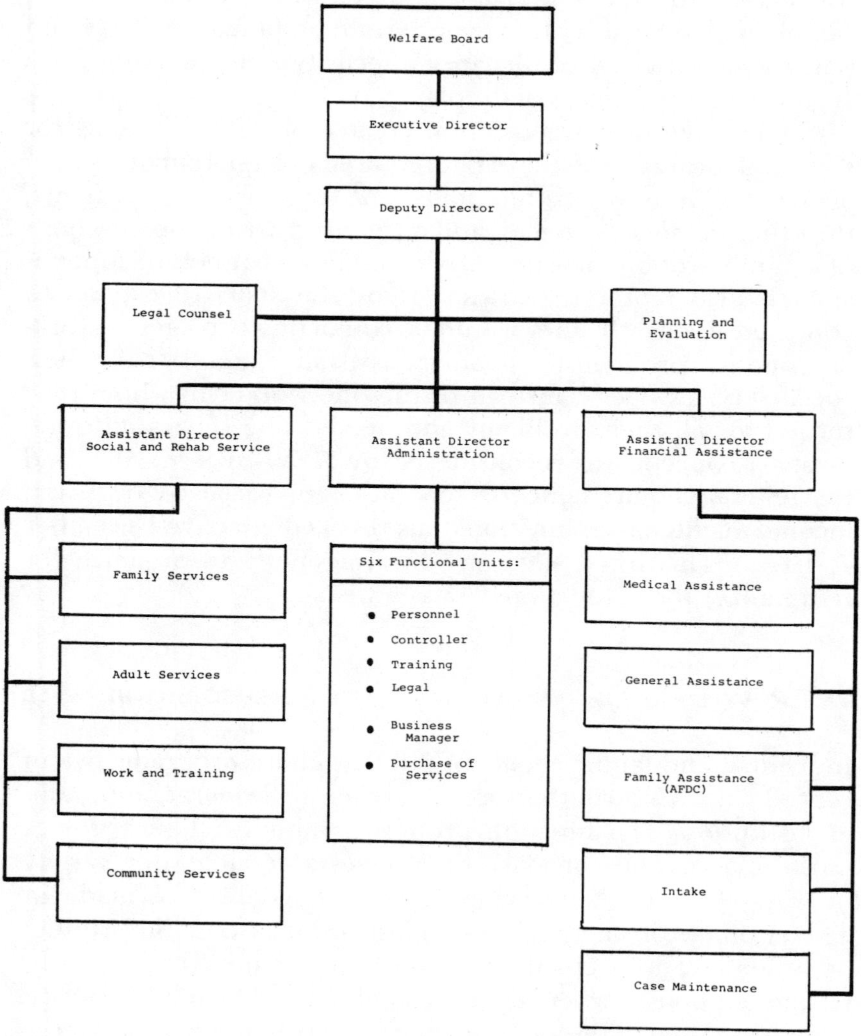

```
                          ┌─────────────────────┐
                          │    Welfare Board     │
                          └──────────┬──────────┘
                          ┌──────────┴──────────┐
                          │  Executive Director  │
                          └──────────┬──────────┘
                          ┌──────────┴──────────┐
                          │   Deputy Director    │
                          └──────────┬──────────┘
        ┌─────────────────┐         │         ┌─────────────────────┐
        │  Legal Counsel   │────────┼─────────│     Planning and     │
        └─────────────────┘         │         │     Evaluation       │
                                     │         └─────────────────────┘
  ┌───────────────────┐  ┌──────────┴────────┐  ┌──────────────────────┐
  │ Assistant Director │  │ Assistant Director │  │  Assistant Director  │
  │Social and Rehab Ser│  │   Administration   │  │ Financial Assistance │
  └───────────────────┘  └───────────────────┘  └──────────────────────┘
```

Assistant Director Social and Rehab Service	Assistant Director Administration	Assistant Director Financial Assistance
Family Services	**Six Functional Units:**	Medical Assistance
Adult Services	• Personnel • Controller • Training • Legal • Business Manager • Purchase of Services	General Assistance
Work and Training		Family Assistance (AFDC)
Community Services		Intake
		Case Maintenance

ment was impractical, continued joint operation by an agency is permitted.

This separated organizational arrangement was enhanced for services to aged, blind, and disabled with the coming of the Supplemental Security Income program on January 1, 1974 and passage of Title XX of the Social Security Act providing for a separate social services state plan.

The separated organization created several problems for state and local administrators: it required designation of a single agency staff into two distinct staffs, one for assistance payments, the other for social services, and it required setting up new lines of communication, new processes, and new channels of supervision. It also required extra effort by the staffs to explain to confused clients why they would be contacting two agency workers, one for problems in financial assistance, another for their social services needs, instead of the one worker to whom they turned for all their problems and needs. The separated organization concept was reconsidered by HEW-SRS in 1976 and the federal requirement for separation of social services and income maintenance functions was revoked effective December 7, 1976.[6] This freed state and local agencies to organize (or reorganize) these functions as they wish.

PUBLIC WELFARE ORGANIZATION AT THE NEIGHBORHOOD LEVEL

Individual and family clients of public welfare programs live in central cities, in suburban areas, on remote farms, at home, and in institutions. To function properly, public welfare agencies must be accessible, or make themselves accessible, in a variety of ways. Contact between agencies and clients are made in agency offices, in client homes, in institutions where they reside, or other locations, such as schools, community centers, and settlement houses where clients can be seen. The public welfare system has used different organizational arrangements and techniques for this purpose:

an agency worker from a local public welfare office is dispatched to the home of a disabled client for an emergency call or to determine possible eligibility for assistance payments

an agency worker on field assignment visits clients' homes or institutions on a regular schedule

an agency staff is assigned full time to a decentralized unit in a central location where large numbers of clients live

an agency staff has a regular assignment in a community action center, a public health clinic, a public housing development, or a township government office

an agency worker maintains office space in a nursing home or children's institution with planned, specified hours during the day or days during the week to interview applicants and assist clients

an agency-owned or rented bus or trailer follows a regular itinerary to offer assistance, information, and services to individuals and families along a publicized route

public welfare units are housed in multi-service neighborhood centers

Multiservice Neighborhood Centers[7]

The multiservice neighborhood center is the modern version of the settlement house movement founded in 1889 by Jane Hull. It is potentially the most rewarding organizational arrangement for client and program alike. The initial efforts to set up such centers in recent years were made under the Juvenile Delinquency and Youth Offenses Act of 1961, in which demonstration neighborhood centers were organized with public welfare representation, primarily child welfare social workers, to cope with juvenile delinquency. The concept was broadened greatly under the War on Poverty utilizing the community action program authority of the Economic Opportunity Act of 1964, under which an estimated 700 neighborhood centers were organized. The idea was also adopted as a key component of the Model Cities program sponsored under the Demonstration Cities and Metropolitan Development Act of 1966. In 1967, fourteen cities were chosen for a Neighborhood Center Pilot program to develop and test new and improved methods and organizations for such centers. The cities participating were: Boston, Chattanooga, Chicago, Cincinnati, Dallas, Detroit, Jacksonville, Louisville, Minneapolis, New York, Oakland, Philadelphia, St. Louis, and Washington, D.C. Their aims were to achieve maximum coordination of the many categorical human service programs for greater effectiveness, efficiency, and economy in rehabilitating the socially and economically disadvantaged.

Four types of organizations of varying sizes and complexity are in evidence throughout the country, a total estimated at more than 3,000:

THE ADVICE AND REFERRAL CENTER.   This center is the simplest arrangement with, for example, a store front location, a small staff, possibly only one or two workers, to inform people who walk in about available services and refer them to appropriate service agencies and programs. The staff answers questions, hands out forms, and makes appointments for clients, if they wish. The effectiveness of such centers is increased if usable, indexed information is available to the staff on federal, state, and local benefits and services, if transportation to agency offices is provided, and outreach, advocacy, and follow-up is included.

THE DIAGNOSTIC CENTER.   This provides, in addition to advice and referral, a professional interdisciplinary counseling staff to assume responsibility for diagnosing the problems of individuals and families, developing a comprehensive service plan with clients, scheduling appointments for them with the various specialized service agencies, designating a service worker to followup on referrals, provide advocacy back-up on behalf of clients and give continuing counseling to help them solve their problems. Such centers require the closest cooperation and colocation of representatives of the service agencies, with the public welfare agency providing eligibility determination workers for income maintenance, food stamps, and medical assistance services as well as social service workers for its various service programs. The effectiveness of these centers is enhanced by the adoption of unified intake and eligibility processes and common case records of the services represented.

THE ONE-STOP, MULTIPURPOSE NEIGHBORHOOD SERVICE CENTER. This center provides a service complex of specialist facilities and professional and support personnel in a wide range of human services to augment the advice and referral, and diagnostic and counseling services of the two preceding centers described. Multipurpose service centers may be located in a central city, a suburban area, or in a rural environment. They may be located in one building or in separate buildings within walking distance of each other, in close proximity to or in a school. They may contain health clinics, a day-care center, a senior citizens center, or other congregate group activity plus space for social workers, eligibility determination workers, manpower training, and employment counselors, rehabilitation workers, recreational and educational professionals, housing, aged, child welfare counselors, and space for group meetings and classes. Although the widest practicable range of services are available at the centers, referrals for specialist services for the more complicated cases external to the centers are made to such facilities as hospitals, mental retardation and mental health diagnostic and treatment institutions, and rehabilitation evaluation centers and schools. The effectiveness of the centers is conditioned not only on the cooperation of these latter organizations, but also on the degree of coordination which exists among the service components within the centers.

A NETWORK OR SYSTEM OF CENTERS. These provide a larger community area with a balanced service system with the one-step multiservice center serving at the hub and one or more outlying diagnostic centers serviced in turn by advice and referral centers. When operative, this community organization assures state and local public welfare agencies and other human service agencies a logical, economical, effective arrangement of services availability. However, a 1971 study[8] of approximately 1,000 multiservice neighborhood centers reported their potentials for public welfare programs failed to be realized. The study revealed that relatively few centers provide eligibility determinations, child welfare services, or social services to public assistance families and adult recipients. Referrals were routinely made by center personnel to the nearest public welfare office. The study concluded that these agencies "have not yet found a way to use the mechanism of the multiservice center as a means of significantly extending services to broader groups of potential users."

THE FUTURE OF PUBLIC WELFARE ORGANIZATION

The public welfare organization described in this chapter has all the attributes, strengths, and weaknesses of large-scale organizations and management everywhere plus those peculiar to a socially dynamic and sensitive sector of our national life. Its purpose is to coordinate the authorized activities and services to meet the needs of the eligible poor and disadvantaged. If it does so with effectiveness, efficiency, and economy, it achieves this purpose. If it interferes, or makes more difficult the delivery of services or the performance of activities, it needs changing. If it confuses, is unclear, wasteful in use of financial and other resources, if there is duplication of work, loose supervision, ineffective delegation, confusion of purpose, conflicts of policy, if there are gaps or overlapping authority or responsibility, if there is dissatisfaction among beneficiaries, government administrators, and leaders and public alike, the public welfare organization, and the system of which it is a part, needs review and, perhaps, a search for a better way.

Continuing welfare reform will undoubtedly change roles and relationships between federal, state, and local governments and result in significant organizational change as well. If federal assumption of income maintenance for the adult categories in 1974 through the SSI program is indicative of national policy, it is well within reason to assume a federalized income maintenance program for families with children, leaving to the state and local governments responsibility for social services and child welfare services. Moreover, if the debate for a national health services program culminates in a new program with the features of a federal administration, essentially reducing, if not bypassing, state and local administration for medical care, this, too, will bring about major organizational change at all government levels. The demise of the Cuban Refugee Assistance program in the next few years will play a part, although minor, in state and local organization and administration. This also applies to the food stamp program as now constituted which may be "cashed out" in an income maintenance package for families with money payments for food in lieu of food stamps, as was planned for in the original version of the SSI program in 1973.

The resultant shift in organizational responsibilities from state and local governments to the federal government for income maintenance and medical assistance programs and the other changes noted may accelerate another trend in organization already prevalent, namely that of *services integration,* or the movement to achieve the goal of better coordination of the many categorical human services programs. At state and local government levels, the organization of "umbrella" agencies in 29 states and numerous counties and cities marks a movement of historic proportions to accomplish these aims. Passage of a federal allied services law as proposed in 1972, but never approved, has the potential for further improvement in coordination of service programs. It proposed authorizing federal grants to state and local governments to develop plans for reorganizing human services and the funds to carry them and the transfer of federal grant-in-aid funds between service programs. It authorized the Secretary of Health, Education and Welfare to waive statutory and regulatory constraints of a technical or administrative nature which may impede coordinated human service programs. This proposal is one approach to the problem of organization. We will undoubtedly weigh others. For we need to be alert to organizational change yet to come in the public welfare system.

NOTES

1. The description of the Federal Executive, Legislative and Judicial Branches are from: Congressional Directory, 93rd Congress, First Session, 1973, U.S. Government Printing Office, Washington, D.C. Also from the U.S. Government Manual 1973–1974, Office of the Federal Register, National Archives and Records Service, General Services Administration, U.S. Government Printing Office, Washington, D.C.

2. The Social Security Administrator required Senatorial approval by the Reorganization Plan No. 1 of 1953 (67 Stat. 631, 5 USC 133–15).

3. 45 CFR 220, et al.

4. Spindler, A. Is it better to supervise or administer welfare programs. *Human Needs,* 1972, **1**:(6), 15–17.

5. 45 CFR 205 and *The Separation of Services from Assistance Payments: A Guide to State Agencies* Community Services Administration, SRS, DHEW, 1972, (SRS) 73-23015.

6. SRS-AT-76-144 (PSA:APA), September 8, 1976.

7. March, M. S. The neighborhood center concept. *Public Welfare,* 1968, 97.

8. O'Donnell, F. J. & Reid, O. M. The multiservice neighborhood center: preliminary findings from a national survey. *Welfare in Review,* 1971, **9**(3).

Chapter 6

STAFFING AND PERSONNEL ADMINISTRATION IN THE PUBLIC WELFARE SYSTEM

How well public welfare organizations perform is determined to a considerable degree by their employees, volunteers, and service providers: their numbers in relation to caseloads, their competence and experience, their dedication and morale, their effectiveness, honesty, the quality of supervision they receive, their training, and the salary and personnel benefits they earn. We can say that the most important resource in any service organization is its staff.

Since 1935, the size of the public welfare work force has grown year by year, gradually and consistently as public assistance caseloads increased and new public welfare programs came into being. The growth has been largest in county and municipal jurisdictions (primarily of eligibility workers and social services personnel). Lesser increases took place in federal and state agencies with public welfare responsibilities. About three hundred and forty thousand (342,775) employees and volunteers man the public welfare system and an uncounted number of additional persons are employed by other government and private organizations and self-employed professionals who provide services under contract or agreement with public welfare agencies. The federal government employs 27,075 and the state and local governments employ 315,700.

Over 27,000, or about 8 percent of the public welfare work force, are employed by the federal government, of whom an estimated 21,500 are Social Security Administration district and branch office personnel working in the SSI program. The others are federal employees in central and field offices of the Department of Health, Education and Welfare, the Food and Nutrition Service of the Department of Agriculture and the Employment and Training Administration of the Department of Labor. About 9% of the total or 32,000 employees, are in state public welfare agencies and over 283,000 employees, over 71 percent work in county and city public welfare agencies.

The more than 315,700 state and local public welfare personnel comprise the fifth largest body of public human services personnel, exceeded only by those in education, highways, police and fire protection, and hospitals.[1]

The federal bureaucracy employs a broad range of executive, administrative, planning, program, and management specialists and clerical aides in its central offices and a corps of professional and technical specialists and assistants in its regional offices. State and local public welfare agencies are administered at the top by over 19,000 administrators and managers and 38,000 supportive administrative personnel augmented by over 20,000 supervisors, 162,000 social service employees, eligibility workers, specialists, and consultants, supported by 47,-000 clerical aides and over 29,000 volunteers. These substantial numbers are a characteristic common to all large bureaucracies, in which every primary worker in contact with an applicant or beneficiary to provide payments or services is supported, controlled, held accountable to a hierarchy of other personnel, and the numbers of these support personnel increase with the size of the organization of which they are a part. The public welfare system is large, multitiered with local, state, and federal layers as we have seen in Chapter 5, and the overall personnel figures reveal a symbolic one-to-one ratio of primary worker to support worker.[2]

Somewhat less than half (46 percent) of state and local employees are assigned to social services, 42 percent to income maintenance, 7 percent to medical assistance eligibility determinations, and the remaining 5 percent to food stamp eligibility determinations. Over 40 percent have baccalaureate or graduate degrees; about seven out of ten employees are white, 15 percent are black, and the others are Spanish-surnamed, American Indians, and Orientals; three-fourths are women; and more than one-third are between the ages of 21 and 30, while another one-third, between 30 and 50 years of age.

Sixty-seven percent of state and local employees are employed by the 11 states having 61 percent of the AFDC caseload: California, Florida, Georgia, Illinois, New Jersey, New York, Massachusetts, Michigan, Ohio, Pennsylvania, and Texas.

New York and California, with combined staffing of 87,500 have 28 percent of all state and local public welfare personnel in the nation. The state-by-state distribution is shown in Table 6.1. Staffing of agencies in the large urban centers such as New York, Los Angeles, Chicago, and Philadelphia exceed those of most state agencies. In contrast, in rural areas, staffing to service sparse populations require few public welfare workers.

Table 6.2 shows the basic staffing pattern of state and local public welfare agencies. It helps us understand the great variety of public welfare workers, skills, and activities necessary to administer large-scale programs. An accurate personnel caseload comparison cannot be drawn among the states or between local governments from these figures because of organization, program, and geographic differences that impact on the size staffs reported by state and local agencies.

Organizationally, we have seen in Chapter 5 how agencies differ: the assignment of medical assistance program responsibility may be made to the public welfare agency or to another agency; the administration of public welfare programs may be retained by the state agency or decentralized to local agencies; the practice of contracting out may vary, so that social and medical services, medical claims processing, or other administrative activities, such as computer services, may be performed by other organizations, institutions, or private practitioners, or performed by agency personnel directly. For example, the county welfare agencies of the Health and Welfare Agency of California, with contracts with fiscal agents for claims processing and payment, do not maintain their own staffs, whereas, in contrast, the Welfare Department of Connecticut has its own staff

Table 6.1 Staffing of Public Welfare Functions, 1974–1975

Federal government

Program	Agency	Man years
All	SRS, OHD, Other offices of DHEW	2,370
SSI	Social Security Administration, DHEW	22,000
Food Stamps	Food and Nutrition Service, Agriculture	2,450
WIN	Employment and Training Administration, Labor	255
	Total	27,075

State and local governments

	No. in thousands		No. in thousands
Alabama	3.8	Montana	1.1
Alaska	.5	Nebraska	2.7
Arizona	1.7	Nevada	.7
Arkansas	1.7	New Hampshire	2.4
California	37.5	New Jersey	10.8
Colorado	3.4	New Mexico	1.5
Connecticut	2.6	New York	50.0
Delaware	1.1	North Carolina	5.8
District of Columbia	3.3	North Dakota	.8
Florida	7.8	Ohio	31.5
Georgia	4.7	Oklahoma	6.0
Hawaii	.5	Oregon	4.2
Idaho	.9	Pennsylvania	25.3
Illinois	15.6	Rhode Island	1.7
Indiana	5.1	South Carolina	3.5
Iowa	4.0	South Dakota	1.0
Kansas	3.1	Tennessee	4.5
Kentucky	4.2	Texas	11.6
Louisiana	5.0	Utah	1.0
Maine	.8	Vermont	.5
Maryland	4.6	Virginia	5.0
Massachusetts	7.5	Washington	4.6
Michigan	13.0	West Virginia	2.6
Minnesota	5.8	Wisconsin	6.2
Mississippi	2.2	Wyoming	.4
Missouri	6.0	Total	315.7

Source: 96th Edition, The Statistical Abstract of the United States, Table 443, p. 274.

Table 6.2   Basic Staffing Pattern of State Public Welfare Agencies

Public Welfare Advisory Board
Board Members
Executive Secretary
Clerk Typist

Office of Public Welfare Director
Public Welfare Director
Deputy Director
Secretary to the Director
Clerk Stenographer
Clerk Typists

Legal Services Office
Chief Legal Officer
Hearing Officers
Attorneys
Clerk Typists/Stenographers

Public Information Office
Chief Public Information Officer
Public Information Specialists
Editors
Information Clerks
Graphic Analysts
Clerk Typists/Stenographers
Volunteers

Staff Development Office
Chief Staff Development Officer
Staff Development Specialists
Staff Trainers
Clerk Typists/Stenographers

Program Planning and Evaluation Office
Chief Program Planning and Evaluation Officer
Program Planners
Program Analysts
Program Evaluation Specialists
Systems Analysts
Social Science Analysts
Clerk Typists/Stenographers

Table 6.2 (Continued)

Policy and Plans Office
Chief Regulations Officer
Policy and Plans Issuance Analysts
Clerk Typists/Stenographers

Office of Assistant Director for Administration
Chief Administrative Officer
Administrative Assistant
Secretaries
Volunteers

Administrative Services Division
Chief Administrative Services Officer
Purchasing Officers
Contract Specialists
Property and Supply Officers
Mail and Messenger Supervisor
Messengers
Mail Clerks
Duplicating Machine Operators
Property Custodians
Property Inventory Clerks
Travel Clerks
Communication Specialists
Space Analysts
Draftsmen
Central Files Supervisor
File Clerks
Clerk Typists/Stenographers

Budget Division
Chief Budget Officer
Budget Analysts
Budget Clerks
Clerk Typists/Stenographers

Research and Statistics Division
Chief Statistical Officer
Statisticians
Research Analysts
Statistical Assistants
Computer Programmers

Management Information Systems Specialists
Data Processing Supervisor
Key Punch Operators
Statistical Typists
Clerk Typists/Stenographers

Personnel Division
Personnel Director
Personnel Generalists
Recruitment Specialists
Classification Technicians
Wage and Salary Analysts
Personnel Interviewers
Volunteer Coordinators
Employee Counselors
Personnel Assistants
Personnel Records Clerks
Clerk Typists/Stenographers

Fiscal and Accounting Division
Chief Fiscal Officer
Systems Accountants
Financial Analysts
Fiscal Auditors
General Accountants
Accounting Clerks
Voucher Clerks
Ledger Clerks
Payroll Supervisor
Payroll Clerks
Payments Processing Supervisor
Payments Processing Clerks
Clerk Typists/Stenographers

Procedures and Methods Division
Chief Procedures and Methods Officer
Procedures Analysts
Organization and Methods Examiners
Management Analysts
Clerk Typists/Stenographers

Table 6.2   (Continued)

Eligibility Standards Specialists
Secretaries

Quality Control Division
Chief Quality Control Officer
Quality Control Investigators
Quality Control Reviewers
Quality Control Clerks
Clerk Typists/Stenographers

Public Assistance Eligibility Determinations Division
Eligibility Determinations Supervisors
Eligibility Determinations Workers
Case Aides
Receptionists
Clerk Typists/Stenographers
Volunteers

Medical Assistance Eligibility Determinations Division
Eligibility Determinations Supervisors
Eligibility Determinations Workers
Case Aides
Receptionists
Clerk Typists/Stenographers
Volunteers

Food Stamp Eligibility Determinations Division
Eligibility Determinations Supervisors
Eligibility Determinations Workers
Case Aides
Receptionists
Clerk Typists/Stenographers
Volunteers

Office of Assistant Director for Social Services
Assistant Director for Social Services
Deputy Director
Social Services Standards Specialists
Secretaries

Family and Childrens Services Division
Division Chief
Social Work Supervisors

Social Work Specialists
Child Welfare Specialists
Emergency Assistance Supervisor
Social Workers
Social Service Representatives
Community Resources Workers
Case Control Supervisors
Case Aides
Clerk Typists/Stenographers
Volunteers

Adult Services Division
Division Chief
Social Work Supervisors
Social Work Specialists
Social Workers
Social Services Representatives
Community Research Workers
Case Control Supervisors
Case Aides
Clerk Typists/Stenographers
Volunteers

WIN Supporting Service Division
Division Chief
Social Work Supervisors
Social Work Specialists
Social Workers
Social Services Representatives
Case Control Supervisors
Case Aides
Clerk Typists/Stenographers
Volunteers

Office of Assistant Director for Medical Assistance
Assistant Director for Medical Assistance
Deputy Director
Medical Assistance Standards Specialists
Medical Consultants
Medical Social Workers

Nursing Home Inspectors
Medical Claims Supervisors
Medical Claims Examiners

Office of Assistant Director for Eligibility Determinations
Assistant Director for Eligibility Determinations
Deputy Director
Medical Contract Specialists
Medical Program Analysts
Secretaries
Clerk Typists/Stenographers
Volunteers

Office of Field Service Director
Field Service Director
Field Representatives
Secretaries
Clerk Typists/Stenographers

Local Offices
Local Office Directors
Eligibility Determinations Supervisors
Eligibility Determinations Workers
Social Workers
Social Work Specialists
Social Services Representatives
Community Service Workers
Case Aides
Case Control Supervisors
Emergency Assistance Workers
Case Control Workers
Receptionists
Clerk Typists/Stenographers
Volunteers

for this purpose. In Ohio, the Franklin County Welfare Department maintains a custodial and maintenance unit for its own office buildings, functions usually supplied by county and city facility service departments elsewhere.

Program differences, especially in social services and medical assistance, whether narrow and conservative or broad and liberal have much to do with the size caseload and the diversity and complexity of services provided, which, in turn, determine the numbers and kind of staff needed. For example, the smaller social services staffs of the county public welfare offices of Mississippi provide a lesser variety of social services than the social services staffs of the county welfare departments of Wisconsin with their larger, more complex social services program.

The geography of the political jurisdiction affects public welfare staffing. The Department of Social and Rehabilitative Services in the geographically small Rhode Island does not require the extensive field organization of the Department of Social Services of North Dakota.

FEDERAL/STATE MERIT SYSTEM STANDARDS

The Social Security Act and other federal laws and regulations authorizing grants to states and local governments require them to establish and maintain personnel standards on a merit basis in the administration of their grant-in-aid programs. These standards were issued in 1971 jointly by the Secretaries of Health, Education, and Welfare; Labor; and Defense. A preamble to the standards explains their objective and coverage:

Standards for a Merit System of Personnel Administration

> These standards are promulgated by the Departments of Health, Education, and Welfare, Labor, and Defense to implement statutory and regulatory provisions requiring the establishment and maintenance of personnel standards on a merit basis in the administration of various grant-in-aid programs.
>
> The development of proper and efficient administration of the grant-in-aid programs is a mutual concern of the Federal, State, and local agencies cooperating in the programs. Proper and efficient administration requires clear definition of functions, em-

ployment of the most competent available personnel, and development of staff morale and individual efficiency. The cooperative efforts of merit system and program agency personnel offices in providing comprehensive personnel programs are essential. Such programs provide for analyzing and classifying jobs; establishing adequate and equitable salary, fringe benefit, and retirement plans; projecting manpower needs and planning to meet them; developing effective recruitment, selection, placement, training, employee evaluation, and promotion programs; assuring equal opportunity and providing affirmative action programs to achieve that end; protecting employees from discrimination, arbitrary removal, and political pressures; conducive positive employee-management relations and communications; and providing research to improve personnel methods. Personnel programs must be planned and administered in a timely, expeditious manner to meet effectively program and merit system objectives.

An integral part of the grant-in-aid programs is the maintenance by the State and local governments of a merit system of personnel administration for the grant-aided agencies. The Federal agencies are interested in the development and continued improvement of State and local merit systems but exercise no authority over the selection, tenure of office, or compensation of any individual employed in conformity with the provisions of such systems.

Laws, rules, regulations, and policy statements to effectuate a merit system in accordance with these standards are a necessary part of the approved State plans required as a condition of Federal grants. Such laws, rules, regulations, policy statements, and amendments thereto, will be reviewed for substantial conformity to these standards. The administration of the merit system will likewise be subject to review for compliance in operation.

Continuing application of these standards will give reasonable assurance of a proper basis for personnel administration, promote a career service, and result in increased operating efficiency and program effectiveness. Within these standards means are provided for the effectuation of national policies for structuring jobs and the training and employment of the disadvantaged.

In order to assist State and local jurisdictions in maintaining their merit systems under these standards, technical consultative service will be made available.

THE PERSONNEL SITUATION IN CRISIS

The personnel situation in the public welfare system suffers from a chronic nationwide shortage of social workers and workers of other skills, creating an unstable work force. The vacancy rate as last reported on June 30, 1973 and later periods was between nine and ten percent; annually there is a one-third rate of accession of new workers and a one-fourth rate of separations. Rarely does a state or local agency have its fully authorized staff complement, and the shortages have been greatest in the professional social worker ranks.

Widespread efforts are made to reduce the effects of these shortages. Federal/state plans require maximum employment of full- and part-time subprofessionals and volunteers. Agencies are encouraged to restructure jobs to make this possible, that is, to analyze duties, responsibilities, and qualifications and rearrange them to make maximum use of professional skills, relieve professionals of nonprofessional duties, and assign them to other workers with lesser qualifications. The differential use of staff as this process is named, has been widely studied and the use of subprofessionals and volunteers has increased greatly since 1967 when social services functions of public welfare agencies were expanded under the Social Security Act. This change was also stimulated by the new careers program authorized in the 1966 amendments of the Economic Opportunity Act to encourage hiring persons with varying levels of formal education, particularly among the poor and offering them opportunities for advancement.

The Department of Health, Education and Welfare developed guides to plan for the use of a range of personnel for social services. Qualifications for jobs were no longer related solely to educational credentials. Rather, the tasks to be performed, the knowledge and skills required for effective performance, the training required and the potential for development are the criteria for selection of staff. The guides describe the use of an analytical method called *functional job analysis* developed by Dr. Sidney A. Fine of the W. E. Upjohn Institute for Employment Research.[3] (Figure 6.1). The nub of this analytical process is the classification of tasks to achieve agency objectives along a range of scales from simplest to complex of (1) workers instructions, (2) worker functions covering things done, data handled, and relationships with other people; and (3) general educational development of knowledge and ability required for each task and objective.

I. BEGIN WITH SYSTEMS ANALYSIS

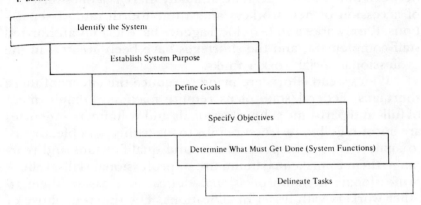

Identify the System

Establish System Purpose

Define Goals

Specify Objectives

Determine What Must Get Done (System Functions)

Delineate Tasks

II. USE TASK STATEMENTS FOR FUNCTIONAL JOB ANALYSIS

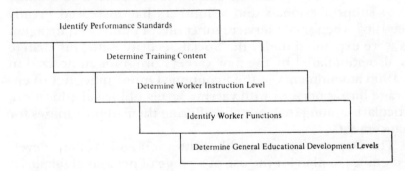

Identify Performance Standards

Determine Training Content

Determine Worker Instruction Level

Identify Worker Functions

Determine General Educational Development Levels

III. USE THIS INFORMATION FOR CAREER DESIGN

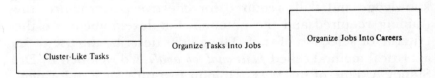

Cluster-Like Tasks

Organize Tasks Into Jobs

Organize Jobs Into Careers

Figure 6.1 Outline of Job Development Process

Social Work Classification

A classification of five levels of social work personnel is generally found in the federal/state system. They include[4]:

1.   The social service aide with high school education or less who, calling upon his native ability and the accumulated wisdom of life experience, assists in the interpretation and delivery of services with particular skills developed through on-the-job training. The social service aide is used in case finding, service interpretation, information and referral services. For social service programs to be effective and relevant, they will always need liaison personnel who can direct people to the right pathways for finding help, to search out and identify people in need of help, and to bring their needs to the attention of responsible bodies. Case finding in the social services can be as important as it has been in public health. People of the community can be trained to do these tasks in a short period. Aides can provide escort and protective services to the aged and handicapped and can serve as an essential link to the community in helping such people sustain their life situation and avoid hospitalization and institutional living unless they so choose. They can support and improve parental functioning and help in the development of homemaking and parenting skills.

2.   The social work technician with an associate in arts degree from a two-year technical program in the social services is used in fact finding, decision making, and service provision in agencies where the basis for service can be objectified and projected with a high degree of specificity. Social insurance programs, income maintenance programs, and certain of the environmental services—arranging for day care, summer camp, day-center membership for the aged and handicapped are examples of programs that can be wholly or partially administered by technicians. They can serve also as technical assistants to social workers, carrying partial or full responsiblity for service to certain individuals, families, and groups.

3.   The social worker with a baccalaureate degree from a four-year college, having completed an approved undergraduate social work program is prepared to serve individuals, fami-

lies, groups and communities in a wide variety of service programs. The social worker at this level of professional competence has a background of knowledge of human behavior, personality development, and the social system, and of the factors that contribute to normal development and strengthen personality, as well as the causes of social and individual breakdown. He has knowledge of social work purpose and process and skill in social work techniques and has integrated the values and ethical constraints within which the professional worker operates. Many of the supporting services for chronic or recurring problems can be provided at this level. These professionals understand the basics of determinants of behavior and the prescriptive norms of role enactments. The baccalaureate social worker is able to help people by eliciting and ordering pertinent information to identify and clarify the problem and by participating with the client or client community group as well as with a skilled social work consultant in arriving at an understanding of the nature of the problem, its causes or origins, and the course of action or intervention called for to alleviate or resolve it. The baccalaureate social worker is not expected to accomplish this diagnostic task without assistance from a certified social worker, nor, in most instances, should the mode of treatment or social action be arrived at by him and the client without such consultation. If the intervention action called for involves environmental services, clarification, and ego support, the baccalaureate social worker may assume full responsibility for working with the individual or group concerned.

If the interventive action is more complex, he may carry responsibility for certain episodes of service, moving in and out of activity with the particular family or community group, or work on a continuing basis with particular members.

4.   The certified social worker has completed graduate educational preparation leading to the Master's degree in social work in an accredited school of social work, and has been certified by the professional organization as capable of performing with professional competence and autonomy in practice.

The social worker at this level of expertise has mastered the knowledge of professional practice in the relevant subject areas in the humanities and sciences; has incorporated social work practice theory and developed a cohesive body of skills necessary to carry through complete social work processes in service to individuals, groups, or communities; and has broad knowledge of social policy and process, and the institutional organization of social services. He is able to offer consultation to social service aides and technicians and baccalaureate level social workers in determining proper utilization of such personnel in service to people. He is able to offer consultation to practitioners in other disciplines (medical doctors, employment counselors, judges in courts of law, etc.) in interpreting the social factors in a particular situation. Of great importance is the social worker's activities in administering the social services in terms of both personnel management and program design.

In practice, the certified social worker is utilized most economically as the team leader, participating only to the degree necessary in a particular case or situation in gathering and ordering of information, taking major responsibility in the definition of the problem, and determination of service goals and mode of intervention to effect these. Ideally, the certified social worker should engage in a direct service relationship only in instances where, because of the critical or complex nature of the problem, a high degree of treatment skill is required. Only the certified social worker should be sanctioned to function autonomously in private or group practice or as an agent of an organization.

5.   Social workers with advanced education leading to the doctoral degree are needed for:

     a.   The conduct of research. Inquiry and investigation are critically needed to provide knowledge of the etiology of social problems and the nature of social pathology, and to assess the effectiveness of social work techniques and services as applied to them.

     b.   Social planning and development. Social workers with broad knowledge of social and political process and depth of understanding of social systems and their operation are needed at all levels of government to assure consideration of social factors and to predict effects on the general social welfare of a wide range of developments in the public and private sectors.

    c.   Social workers with doctoral level education acting as teachers and specific preparation in the educational process are needed to prepare and keep up to date practitioners at all levels of practice.

SOCIAL WORKER RECRUITMENT AND PLACEMENT

The high turnover of staff and expanding social work manpower needs makes recruitment and placement a year round, continuous, and urgent personnel function. The sources for recruitment of social workers are primarily from fresh graduates of schools of social work, faculty members, and social workers employed in other social agencies and organizations, government as well as private. The more promising recruits are students who have completed field assignments in the agencies and are already familiar with the organization who have established a working relationship with agency personnel. The recruitment of social work personnel of other agencies is a common phenomenon, matched, however, by agency resignations and transfers of social work personnel to other organizations. Job dissatisfaction, limited promotional opportunities, desire for change, changes in family status (marriage, pregnancy), moving out of the area, and return to school for advanced education all contribute to the personnel turnover. The placement of new workers within the agencies is determined by existing job vacancies, employee qualifications, their preferences, and opportunities for promotion. An orientation program for new workers is a standard practice in all agencies to provide them with an understanding of agency mission, structure, functions, and personnel rules and regulations.

Subprofessionals

The output of graduate social workers has been unable to alleviate the chronic shortages in public welfare agencies. While the projected need for social workers in public agencies is expected to more than double by the year 2000, only 5,000 masters degree students and 7,000 baccalaureate students graduate in this country annually—thus the emphasis on the employment of subprofessionals. As they grew in number, agency administrators adapted their personnel program to provide for enlarged counseling programs for this group, career advancement training, and education to give them better job satisfaction, help in their promotion to more rewarding higher paid jobs and utilizing their skills and abilities more fully. In-service training in a broad variety of subject areas has been provided, their enrollment in formal education has grown through tuition payments and release-from-work arrangements, television and correspondence courses have become accredited to their earning college credits, day care, transportation, consumer education, tutoring, and counseling to encourage their participation in training have also been made available. Undergraduate colleges have cooperated with agency administrators and have been supportive of their educational needs by changing their entrance requirements for the subprofessional worker.[5]

Volunteers

There is a large and growing use of volunteers in the public welfare system, by definition, persons who contribute personal services to their communities through agency programs. One of every ten state and local public welfare workers is a volunteer. They are largely unpaid, although some are compensated for their expenses. Their use in public welfare agencies is as varied as agency activities themselves. They are commonly employed transporting children or adults to clinics and schools, visiting homebound elderly or ill persons, tutoring children, caring for infants in institutions, performing clerical duties, serving as receptionists or in the communities as outreach staff to locate elderly, disabled persons and families who need help. The more skilled and educated are employed in such specialized activities as organizing an agency library, studying agency methods, or providing group education to recipients. They may be working full-time or on a part-time and sporadic schedule as they prefer. In all cases, however, their services are conditioned by the agency's needs and agency rules and regulations. They may not replace or displace agency paid staff, they are supported by the agency in their work by the help of agency supervisors and staff, orientation, training, funds, materials, and equipment. Simple job descriptions are provided them in which tasks, job requirements and supervision are spelled out. Recognition of their services, worth, and status by the agencies is frequently given by awards, testimonials, identifying insignia, letters of commendation, and other signs of agency and community appreciation. They are recruited through established volunteer and public service organizations, newspaper, radio and television, and word-of-mouth contacts with friends and relatives. All socioeconomic groups are represented and all persons, from the little or no formal education to the highly educated, are encouraged to participate.

Agencies maintain one or more volunteer coordinators to administer the volunteer program, as shown on the basic staffing table (see Table 6.1) and the costs and expenses incurred by the program are a normal part of their administrative budget, financed by federal financial participation at a 50 percent rate for administration of eligibility determination functions and a 75 percent rate for social services.[6]

The Eligibility Determination Worker

The federal requirement for separation of state and local social services and assistance payments functions in 1973, discussed in Chapter 5, initiated in all jurisdictions the review and restatement of the role of eligibility determination workers in their status as workers in their own organizations parallel but not subordinate to the social services organization and personnel. These reviews and subsequent reorganizations entailed their duties, responsibilities, qualifications, supervision, training, classification, and career status.

Eligibility determination workers comprise the largest body of personnel in the public welfare system: In the Social Security Administration, they are claims representatives; elsewhere they are known as eligibility technicians, intake workers, financial eligibility clerks, or case aides. Their duties involve the acceptance and processing of applications for maintenance payments, social services, medical assistance, and food stamps, studying and verifying applicant information, determining eligibility and entitlement for agency payments, services, food stamps, giving information about the programs to applicants and beneficiaries, and recording and processing official records of actions taken according to the complex of laws, rules, and regulations in their jurisdiction. Their minimum qualifications usually include at least a two-year associate in arts degree, although many states and localities, and the Social Security Administration, require an undergraduate four-year college degree in one of the social or political sciences. They are required to complete an in-service orientation and training program to familiarize themselves with the laws, rules, and regulations and procedures for eligibility determinations. Their job classifications and salary are generally lower than agency social workers. Their lines of promotion are either to supervisory positions in eligibility determinations or, in state and local agencies, with additional training and educa- tion in social work, to join the agency's social services staff. As a group, they are the younger staff members of their agencies, have a shorter tenure, and have a higher turnover rate than social work and administrative staffs.

A recent study of their attitudes to their work and organiza- tion in two public welfare agencies revealed most of them to be highly interested in their work, found it challenging and reward- ing, regard their jobs to be a stepping stone or a chance to gain valuable experience for their future careers, but not necessarily to have a career potential. They feel the heavy work pressures and believe they are not receiving recognition for the special skills their job entails. They feel the salary differential between themselves and social workers are not fair.[7]

APPOINTMENT AND TENURE OF CHIEF ADMINISTRATORS

Chief administrators of state public welfare agencies are ap- pointed officials. In most states, the Governor is the appointing authority, often with the consent of one or both houses of the state legislature. In states which have umbrella agencies with a public welfare component, the chief administrative officer of the agency selects and recommends the chief public welfare appointments to the Governor. Several states place appointing authority in their public welfare commission or board. In Colorado, appointments to the position are made under the civil service merit system.

County public welfare directors in state-administered programs are appointed by the state public welfare director. In locally administered programs where authority and responsibility for administration is delegated to the local agencies, with state supervision, county and city public welfare directors are appointed by the county or city chief executive.

There is no federal requirement for minimal educational and experience qualification for state or local chief administrators, nor is there any requirement or practice for federal administrators to clear in advance or approve such appointments to these posts.

Federal public welfare executives, namely the Secretaries of the Departments of Health, Education and Welfare; Agriculture; and Labor, and the Administrator of the Social Security Administration are appointed by the President by and with the advice and consent of the Senate. The Food and Nutrition Service Employment and Training Administrators and Assistant Secretary for Human Development Services are appointed by their respective Secretaries. Subordinate officials of these agencies are secretarial appointments. All officials (federal, state, local) serve for unspecified terms at the pleasure of their appointing officers.[8]

TRAINING

The complex and changing requirements of public welfare programs, the volatile staff turnover characteristic of public welfare agencies and the public policy to maintain high performance standards has given impetus to a strong staff development and training component throughout the public welfare system. The chronic shortage of trained social workers and the infusion of unskilled and semiskilled personnel have added to the demands for all kinds of training within the agencies and the educational community. Since the 1963 amendments to the Social Security

Act, federal financial participation is available to states for costs of training public assistance staff or persons preparing for employment in public assistance agencies. Training programs include educational leave for employees, stipends for individuals preparing for employment, agency in-service training programs, and educational and training grants or contracts for training.

There are more than 1,060 training positions in state and local agencies to organize and execute training programs. Almost three-fourths of all employees (225,000) were reported in 1975 by state and local agencies to attend workshops and seminars. Over 4,000 received educational leave to attend specialized training in schools and colleges, of whom over 1,000 attended full-time and over 3,000 part-time. More than $68 million was spent by State and local agencies for training in that fiscal year. (Tables 6.3, 6.4)

The Social Security Act also provides (Secs. 705 and 707) federal financial participation for grants (1) to public and other nonprofit institutions of higher learning for training public welfare personnel or students preparing for such employment, (2) for special courses of study or seminars of short duration conducted for public welfare personnel by experts, (3) for establishing and maintaining fellowships or traineeships for such personnel at these educational institutions with stipends and allowances provided, (4) to public and nonprofit private colleges and universities and to accredited graduate schools of social work to meet part of the costs of development, expansion, or improvement of undergraduate programs in social work and graduate training of professional social work personnel.

Funding for these special grant programs was, however, discontinued in 1973 by the federal government in a change of policy to maintain the support of educational institutions through student fees and loans and private sources. The policy is based on the premise that federally-funded programs of general student aid are now available to assure that students are not deprived of higher education for lack of funds. These programs include scholarship assistance for needy students at the undergraduate level and guaranteed loans for other undergraduate students and for graduate study. Under this policy, the financial burden for the growth of professional social work education rests on the initiative of the states and localities to provide support, the educational institutions themselves, and the resources and initiative of individual employees and students to obtain educational funds.[9]

However, Title XX of the Social Security Act authorized federal financial participation at the rate of 75 percent for social services personnel training, including both short-term and long-term training at educational institutions. State and local public welfare agencies receive federal matching not subject to the social services allotment or other limitation for grants to such institutions or direct financial support to students enrolled in them. The federal financial support is not only given to agency personnel but also for training of volunteers and social service personnel of other public and private agencies under contract to the agencies. The grants to educational institutions are for periods of not more than three years to help them develop, expand or improve training curricula and resources for agency staff, volunteers or service providers.[10]

SALARIES AND PERSONNEL BENEFITS

The salaries and personnel benefits of public welfare personnel vary according to the general salary scales and kinds of personnel benefits provided public employees in the particular political jurisdiction. Studies prepared by the U.S. Civil Service Commission give comparative salary information in four job classifications of state director of social services, social services supervisor, graduate social worker, and social service worker. The range of annual salaries for the position of state director of social services is a low of West Virginia ($10,980–$14,820) to a high of $33,672 in Wisconsin, with the mean minimum salary of $19,545 and the mean maximum salary of $22,159. For the position of social services supervisor, the low annual salary is paid in New York ($6,700–$16,440) and the high in the District of Columbia ($16,682–21,686), with the mean minimum salary of $10,372 and the mean maximum salary of $13,863. The low annual salary paid to a graduate social worker is in Puerto Rico ($6,600–7,800) and a high in Alaska of $13,104–15,756. The mean minimum salary in all states is $8,124 and the mean maximum salary of $11,862. For a social service worker, the lowest salary range is paid in Indiana ($2,400–$10,800) and the highest in Alaska ($10,512–12,636). The mean minimum salary is $7,588 and the mean maximum salary is $10,309.

In recent years, there have been substantial increases in salaries and personnel benefits to reflect the inflationary times and, for the rank and file agency staffs, an increased militancy of public employee unions to raise salaries and provide more liberal personnel benefits. These latter include paid sick and annual leave, retirement pensions, group life and health insurance coverage, disability compensation, social security coverage, and unemployment compensation. (Since July 1, 1971 the mean minimum salary for state director of social services increased 28 percent by August 1973; that for a social service supervisor increased 18 percent.)

The federal government has led the way in increased salaries and benefits in most job classifications, although several of the larger states and cities have generally kept pace. The District of Columbia pays salaries and provides benefits under the federal civil service system. The salaries of state employees in Alaska are higher in most classifications to account for the unusually high cost of living there.

SOCIAL WORK EDUCATION

The formal education of social workers is a mixture of the theoretical and practical: classroom instruction and field experience. Placement in a social agency or organization to be exposed to a real life situation involves the student in the delivery of social services to individuals, families, and groups under supervision of a faculty member. Field placements are arranged for each of the two years of graduate study, usually on a three day a week basis.

To earn a master's degree of social work degree (MSW), the hallmark for professional status from the 79 graduate schools of

Table 6.3 Public Assistance: Aggregate Number of Employees Attending Workshops, Seminars, and Employees on Educational Leave, Fiscal Year 1975

State	Aggregate number of employees attending workshops and seminars	Employees on educational leave		
		Total	Full-time	Part-time
Total..............	1/ 225,482	1/ 4,141	1,027	3,065
Alabama.............	699	42	42	--
Medical Services Admin....	12	--	--	--
Alaska....	(1/)	(1/)	(1/)	(1/)
Arizona.............	1,436	--	--	--
Arkansas............	5,000	71	9	62
California..........	21,361	1,048	117	931
Health Care Services.....	2,100	--	--	--
Colorado...........	9,462	43	18	25
Connecticut........	155	--	--	--
Delaware...........	22	--	--	--
District of Columbia..	6,359	20	20	--
Florida............	12,457	145	24	121
Georgia............	8,504	1	1	--
Guam...............	229	2	2	--
Hawaii.............	506	--	--	--
Idaho..............	1,147	268	10	258
Illinois...........	14,124	189	11	178
Children & Family Services	800	4	4	--
Indiana............	(1/)	(1/)	(1/)	(1/)
Iowa 2/............	4,600	405	35	370
Kansas.............	3,612	26	26	--
Kentucky...........	(1/)	40	40	--
Louisiana..........	1,345	188	56	132
Maine..............	650	43	8	35
Maryland...........	(1/)	(1/)	(1/)	(1/)
Health & Mental Hygiene..	31	--	--	--
Massachusetts......	605	49	(1/)	(1/)
Comm. for the Blind......	94	5	3	2

260

Michigan	19,686	189	--	189
Minnesota	3,096	8	8	--
Mississippi	3,747	29	4	25
Medicaid Commission	33	--	--	--
Missouri	(1/)	33	33	(1/)
Montana	(1/)	160	(1/)	(1/)
Nebraska	3,265	(1/)	11	149
Nevada	574	--	--	--
New Hampshire	2,189	7	--	--
New Jersey	2,916	411	7	281
Medical Assistance & Health Services	227	--	130	--
New Mexico	2,933	122	6	116
New York	45,289	43	22	21
North Carolina	5,517	58	18	40
Comm. for the Blind	350	--	--	--
North Dakota	702	7	7	--
Ohio	7,423	67	67	29
Oklahoma	1,162	64	35	14
Oregon	2,041	14	--	--
Pennsylvania	1,212	29	29	(1/)
Puerto Rico	7,871	26	26	5
Medical Assistance Program	(1/)	(1/)	(1/)	--
Rhode Island	620	30	25	53
South Carolina	890	25	25	4
South Dakota	772	59	6	--
Tennessee	1,974	17	13	18
Texas	168	46	46	--
Utah	860	19	1	--
Vermont	150	--	--	6
Virgin Islands	525	--	--	--
Virginia	292	40	34	--
Medical Assistance Program	40	--	--	--
Comm. Visually Handicapped	10	--	--	1
Washington	3,109	36	36	--
West Virginia	2,780	10	10	--
Wisconsin	6,824	2	1	--
Wyoming	925	1	1	--

1/ Data incomplete. Reports not received from Alaska, Indiana, Maryland, and Montana. For Puerto Rico, no report was received from the Department of Health. Incomplete reports received from Kentucky, Massachusetts, and Missouri.

2/ Estimated.

Source: Expenditures for Staff Development and Training Activities, Fiscal Year 1975, DHEW Publication No. (SRS) 76-03252 NCSS Report E-3 (FY 1975), National Center for Social Statistics, Social and Rehabilitation Service, May 1976.

Table 6.4   Public Assistance: Total Expenditures for Selected Staff Development Activities, by state, fiscal year 1975

State	Total	Educational leave and preparation for employment	Salaries, travel, and employee benefits	Training sessions
Total....................	1/ $67,957,000	$5,388,000	$30,404,000	$3,800,000
Alabama......................	1,284,000	182,000	287,000	31,000
Medical Services Admin......	1,000	---	---	1,000
Alaska.......................	(1/)	(1/)	(1/)	(1/)
Arizona......................	312,000	---	154,000	---
Arkansas.....................	453,000	78,000	180,000	41,000
California...................	6,560,000	407,000	6,087,000	---
Health Care Services........	436,000	---	118,000	---
Colorado.....................	986,000	199,000	131,000	117,000
Connecticut..................	279,000	33,000	---	8,000
Delaware.....................	69,000	---	65,000	1,000
District of Columbia.........	678,000	---	598,000	80,000
Florida......................	1,999,000	191,000	627,000	12,000
Georgia......................	1,432,000	244,000	213,000	---
Guam.........................	33,000	4,000	20,000	---
Hawaii.......................	132,000	---	58,000	4,000
Idaho........................	314,000	67,000	134,000	90,000
Illinois.....................	914,000	57,000	656,000	55,000
Children & Family Services..	484,000	16,000	206,000	22,000
Indiana......................	100,000	(1/)	(1/)	(1/)
Iowa.........................	1,205,000	414,000	397,000	165,000
Kansas.......................	345,000	---	289,000	1,000
Kentucky.....................	1,382,000	247,000	11,000	---
Louisiana....................	1,559,000	259,000	142,000	65,000
Maine........................	202,000	21,000	34,000	1,000
Maryland.....................	2,471,000	---	551,000	---
Health & Mental Hygiene.....	1,000	---	---	1,000
Massachusetts................	715,000	433,000	273,000	9,000
Commission for the Blind....	44,000	29,000	13,000	2,000
Michigan.....................	1,418,000	---	262,000	7,000
Minnesota....................	1,408,000	38,000	499,000	138,000
Mississippi..................	765,000	29,000	87,000	---
Medicaid Commission........	7,000	---	---	7,000
Missouri.....................	1,645,000	280,000	846,000	118,000
Montana......................	(1/)	(1/)	(1/)	(1/)
Nebraska.....................	384,000	41,000	99,000	186,000
Nevada.......................	323,000	---	58,000	15,000
New Hampshire................	85,000	21,000	35,000	7,000
New Jersey...................	2,515,000	67,000	1,596,000	144,000
Medical Assistance & Health Services.................	52,000	---	46,000	4,000
New Mexico...................	716,000	51,000	197,000	167,000
New York.....................	14,458,000	---	8,558,000	1,449,000
North Carolina...............	969,000	96,000	367,000	---
Commission for the Blind....	6,000	---	6,000	---
North Dakota.................	330,000	39,000	34,000	51,000
Ohio.........................	1,770,000	339,000	549,000	86,000
Oklahoma.....................	513,000	221,000	62,000	17,000
Oregon.......................	591,000	1,000	406,000	113,000
Pennsylvania.................	2,742,000	65,000	1,239,000	159,000
Puerto Rico..................	481,000	142,000	327,000	8,000
Medical Assistance Program..	(1/)	(1/)	(1/)	(1/)
Rhode Island.................	426,000	269,000	97,000	---
South Carolina...............	919,000	104,000	192,000	102,000
South Dakota.................	276,000	52,000	25,000	40,000
Tennessee....................	544,000	75,000	93,000	23,000
Texas........................	4,236,000	252,000	1,651,000	7,000
Utah.........................	929,000	5,000	159,000	34,000
Vermont......................	63,000	---	30,000	33,000
Virgin Islands...............	29,000	---	21,000	---
Virginia.....................	764,000	139,000	150,000	15,000
Medical Assistance Program..	6,000	---	---	2,000
Commission for the Visually Handicapped......	21,000	---	20,000	1,000
Washington...................	1,255,000	28,000	505,000	---
West Virginia................	1,176,000	58,000	375,000	70,000
Wisconsin....................	1,631,000	87,000	533,000	86,000
Wyoming......................	114,000	8,000	36,000	6,000

1/ Data incomplete. Reports not received from Alaska and Montana. For Puerto Rico no report was received from the Department of Health. Columns do not add to the total because of omission of data on activities by Indiana.
2/ Less than $500.

All other staff development costs				
Total	Field instruction and experience	Summer training and employment	Teaching grants to schools	Other
$28,265,000	$1,855,000	$992,000	$15,490,000	$9,928,000
784,000	---	---	573,000	211,000
---	---	---	---	---
(1/)	(1/)	(1/)	(1/)	(1/)
158,000	---	---	148,000	10,000
154,000	---	---	148,000	6,000
66,000	---	---	---	66,000
318,000	30,000	---	---	288,000
539,000	141,000	---	302,000	96,000
238,000	---	---	---	238,000
3,000	---	---	---	3,000
---	---	---	---	---
1,169,000	---	---	873,000	296,000
975,000	---	---	912,000	63,000
9,000	---	---	---	9,000
70,000	53,000	---	---	17,000
23,000	23,000	---	---	---
146,000	---	---	2,000	144,000
240,000	200,000	---	---	40,000
(1/)	(1/)	(1/)	(1/)	(1/)
229,000	---	28,000	---	201,000
55,000	---	20,000	---	35,000
1,124,000	---	---	1,084,000	40,000
1,093,000	16,000	---	1,049,000	28,000
147,000	---	---	---	147,000
1,920,000	204,000	---	1,656,000	60,000
---	---	---	---	---
(2/)	---	---	---	(2/)
1,149,000	291,000	---	805,000	53,000
733,000	21,000	29,000	---	683,000
649,000	---	---	637,000	12,000
---	---	---	---	---
401,000	---	---	150,000	251,000
(1/)	(1/)	(1/)	(1/)	(1/)
58,000	20,000	---	14,000	24,000
250,000	---	---	250,000	---
22,000	---	22,000	---	---
708,000	---	---	---	708,000
2,000	---	---	---	2,000
301,000	---	---	---	301,000
4,451,000	---	---	---	4,451,000
506,000	---	---	490,000	16,000
---	---	---	---	---
206,000	16,000	22,000	89,000	79,000
796,000	32,000	229,000	535,000	---
213,000	20,000	---	88,000	105,000
71,000	---	---	---	71,000
1,279,000	47,000	266,000	806,000	160,000
4,000	---	---	---	4,000
(1/)	(1/)	(1/)	(1/)	(1/)
60,000	---	58,000	---	2,000
521,000	103,000	139,000	118,000	161,000
159,000	70,000	49,000	38,000	2,000
353,000	12,000	---	341,000	---
2,326,000	556,000	---	1,770,000	---
731,000	---	---	689,000	42,000
---	---	---	---	---
8,000	---	---	---	8,000
460,000	---	---	444,000	16,000
4,000	---	---	---	4,000
---	---	---	---	---
722,000	---	---	---	722,000
673,000	---	110,000	510,000	53,000
925,000	---	---	925,000	---
64,000	---	20,000	44,000	---

Source: Expenditures for Staff Development and Training Activities, Fiscal Year 1975. DHEW Publication No. (SRS) 76–03252 NCSS Report E-3 (FY 1975), National Center for Social Statistics, Social and Rehabilitation Service, May 1976.

social work, the student must first receive a bachelor's degree from an accredited college or university with a better than average academic record (usually a B grade or better), preferably with majors in the social sciences (sociology, psychology, history, political science). He must also exhibit in personal interviews and references, emotional stability and maturity, openmindedness, flexibility, and creative interest in social problems.

The general objective of the graduate school curriculum is to prepare students to be competent social work practitioners, to provide them with the insight, skills, and self-discipline that will enable them to affect other human beings and their environments creatively. Beyond transmitting knowledge and methodology, the schools try to develop attitudes in students that make for the sensitive use of themselves as helping persons, and to cultivate a spirit of inquiry and the capacity to test knowledge. About 90 percent of masters degree graduates enter full time employment, the majority in public welfare agencies. In recent years, many schools of social work have broadened their programs to prepare students for roles in social research and administration of social agencies in recognition of the enlarged demand for agency utilization of MSWs respectively in doing research on social problems and in the management of complex social services delivery systems. Changes were also made to relate education more closely to specific population groups and problems areas. Schools developed new courses of concentration on the aged, the mentally retarded, the juvenile and adult offender, and the physically handicapped. Emphasis has been given to the preparation of generalist social workers equipped to deal with a variety of tasks at the neighborhood and community level.

The proportion of minority groups is greater in graduate social work education than in any other discipline or professional education program. Social work education has been in the forefront of efforts to open opportunities for minority groups. In the 1973–1974 academic year over 25 percent of master's degree students and 10 percent of doctoral students in graduate schools of social work were from the five major ethnic minorities. Also, about 20 percent of all faculty in these schools are nonwhite. The curriculum is being enriched to help students learn more about the life styles, strengths, and problems of minority groups to enable them to work more effectively with them.[11]

Students are required to select one of several fields of concentration to prepare them for the social work careers they plan to follow. These vary by school, but they entail concentration for (1) clinical social work, that is, to serve as a caseworker or group work specialist; (2) community organization and social planning, that is, to work in planning and development of community-wide social programs and social institutions; and (3) research and social administration.

All students must complete designated basic courses and select other courses to suit their field of concentration and personal preferences.

Graduate study beyond the MSW degree towards a Doctor of Philosophy degree is available in 25 schools of social work to a small number of students to prepare them for research, teaching, consulting, or other professional roles in social welfare. Completion of three additional years of doctoral study and a doctoral thesis is required to earn the degree. Study programs, tailored to the individual student, usually involve university study in various disciplines and collaborating graduate schools. Only 90 students per year receive a social work doctoral degree from all universities.

A degree of Bachelor of Arts in Social Work is offered to interested students who completed their sophomore year successfully and devote their junior year to a social work curriculum in 200 colleges and universities. Over 7,000 graduate annually. The following basic course work is required, supported by electives in other social and behavioral sciences: Introduction to Social Work, Social Welfare, Intervention Methods, and Human Behavior and Social Responsibility.

In addition to the above, close to 100 two-year community college programs offer associate of arts (A.A.) degrees which help prepare community and social service technicians and offer continuing education programs to agency subprofessionals to improve their knowledge and help them earn promotions.

Employee and Professional Organizations

Public welfare workers as a group are, in general, sympathetic and sensitive to the human plight of their recipients. Their orientation, training, and daily exposure to poverty and its conditions tend to make them activists in seeking to remedy inequities and deficiencies in the program they administer, in their own roles, and in their relationship with their superiors. They join organizations which hold out promise of improvement in their working conditions as well as improvement in social welfare programs. Among the former are public employee associations; among the latter are professional social work associations. The most prominent of employee organizations are the following:

The American Federation of Government Employees (AFGE) affiliated with the AFL-CIO has an overall membership of 325,000 federal employees and is represented by Local 41 in the Department of Health, Education and Welfare in Washington, D.C.

The American Federation of State, County, and Municipal Employees (AFSCME), also affiliated with the AFL-CIO, has a membership of 700,000 in state, county, and city agencies and nonprofit agencies and institutions throughout the United States, Puerto Rico, and Panama as well as a small number of federal employees in the District of Columbia and Panama. It is organized into more than 2,400 local unions. Among them are locals of public welfare agencies, for example, Local 371, New York Social Services Employees and Local 580, Northern Minnesota County Welfare Employees as well as state, county, and city associations with public welfare workers as members, such as Local 829, San Mateo County Employees or Local 994, Little Rock (Arkansas) Public Employees. At its 19th International Convention in Houston, Texas, May 29–June 2, 1972, it passed a resolution to support continued state administration or the incorporation of strong employee-protection provisions in the event of federalization of welfare functions.

The National Federation of Federal Employees (NFFE) is an independent union with 100,000 membership of federal employees in 1720 local unions throughout the United States.

The programs of these organizations are generally to represent the interests of government and nonprofit public agency employees in such matters as promotion policies and practices, job security, fair hearings of grievances, wages, pensions, and other personnel benefits. An aim they share is the promotion of strong, fairly administered civil service systems. They engage in collective bargaining and support labor legislation beneficial to the interests of their membership and other civil servants.[12]

Four national professional organizations have representation among public welfare workers. They are:

The National Association of Social Workers, Inc. (NASW) with 60,000 members, mostly graduate social workers, is the largest organization of social workers in the world. It is exclusively a member organization, rather than one with agency or organization memberships. It maintains local affiliated organizations throughout the country.

The American Public Welfare Association (APWA), with 8,000 members nationally has representatives of all federal, state, and local public welfare agencies. It maintains close contact with all segments of the public welfare community through the National Council of State Public Welfare Administrators and the National Council of Local Public Welfare Administrators. Its newsletters cover current developments in public welfare legislation and administration and are the most thorough, widely read, and authoritative publications of their kind.

The National Council on Social Welfare (NCSW) is an organization of individual and agency members, including 70 national organizations, representing all aspects of health and welfare in the United States. Its major function is to conduct an Annual Forum, attended by 4,500 to 8,000 people, for the critical examination of basic welfare problems and proposed solutions.

The Child Welfare League of America (CWLA) serves the child welfare field in the United States and Canada. It is representative of over 400 affiliated child welfare agencies. It sponsors 8 regional educational conferences a year, reaching more than 12,000 child welfare workers. It is an accrediting body, setting and enforcing professional standards for child welfare agencies.

These professional organizations have extensive programs to improve the skills and knowledge of their membership through professional development activities including sponsoring workshops, seminars, symposia, special training and educational projects, and publications. They also endorse and support professional standards in public welfare and other social organizations. They engage in lobbying activities and issue policy papers for more liberal social welfare legislation and effective administration of social welfare programs. They initiate legislation proposals and seek the support of legislatures, executives, and the public for their adoption. In short, they serve as the collective voice of the social welfare professions.

TRENDS AND EXPECTATIONS

In perspective, the manpower situation in the public welfare system is far from satisfactory and is not likely to improve in the foreseeable future. Staff shortages, particularly of social workers, are chronic and the social work educational output of graduates is unable with present and planned resources to meet the needs of public or private social agencies.

This is a widely recognized condition and the social work professional leadership is searching for solutions. Strong support is given to the differential use of social work manpower, the simplification of eligibility determination processes to improve their efficiency (see Chapter 8), expansion of social services contracting out, and other measures to stretch agency manpower utilization and effectiveness. An area of contention concerns the emphasis of social work practice upon casework, that is, the diagnosis and treatment of problems of a client on a one-to-one basis or upon community development. This refers to the diagnosis and treatment of social, economic, and physical conditions which cause and make more difficult treatment of individual client problems, or some workable combination of the two.

> Over sufficient spans of time the pendulum swings from primary concentration on the individual, with the limelight falling on him

STAFFING AND PERSONNEL ADMINISTRATION   269

against a rather blurred social background to the limelight falling
on the social scene with the multitude of individuals as—dare I say
it?—rather cardboard one dimensional figures.

So, one of my questions to you about the future of social work
is whether these two approaches, the one individual/personal, the
other social/community are compatible, whether in the last resort
they are manifestations of different temperaments in those who
espouse the one or the other, or whether the two can be encom-
passed within the one profession of social work. This is to ask
whether the active dislike of casework by many young social workers on ideological grounds is a temporary phenomenon—a mani-
festation of that familiar process by which we often have to clarify
our own ideas, find our own identity, by hitting out at something
very near to us—or whether both casework and community work
are part of a wider spectrum. To me this seems so obvious that I
find it difficult to conceive that the swing of the pendulum process
is not bound sooner or later to result in some much wider range
of social work practice than that which we know today.[13]

The trends and potentials for the public welfare system
indicate continued program and organizational instability which
can only exacerbate the uneasiness of administrators and workers alike. The one constant (relatively) is the size of the public
assistance caseload, the poverty population from which it derives, and the needs of that caseload. However, further changes
in administration and responsibility for public welfare programs
which loom on the horizon in public proposals under consideration in national health insurance, family income maintenance,
and food stamp programs mean corresponding effects on manpower needs.

If the outcome of national health insurance is a federal
program administered by the Social Security Administration replacing the federal/state medical assistance program, the following can be expected to occur: (1) termination or transfer to
other duties of state and local medical assistance eligibility determination personnel and medical program administration,
continued employment of personnel required if a residual medical services program is retained for persons excluded from a
national program; (2) termination or transfer to other duties
under the new program of Department of Health, Education,
and Welfare regional office medical assistance personnel; (3)

termination or transfer to other duties under the new program of D/HEW medical assistance personnel; and (4) increases in personnel in the headquarters bureaus and offices of the Social Security Administration and its 1,200 district and branch offices.

If the outcome of a family income maintenance program is a federal program administered within the D/HEW with similar features to the Family Assistance Plan of 1971, the following can be expected to occur: (1) termination or transfer to other duties of state and local AFDC eligibility determination and payment processing and administrative personnel, continued employment of personnel required if a residual family income maintenance program is retained for families excluded from a national program; (2) termination or transfer to other duties under the new program of the D/HEW regional office AFDC income maintenance personnel; (3) termination or transfer to other duties under the new program of D/HEW assistance payments personnel; and (4) increases in personnel for the new D/HEW organization to be created, including both headquarters and regional office staffs. If the outcome is a negative income tax or other family allowance program, the termination of federal, state, and local public welfare personnel could be expected in even greater numbers and a staff increase will be required in the Internal Revenue Service or other federal agency vested with responsibility for computerized payments administration.

If the food stamp program is discontinued, central office and regional personnel of the Food and Nutrition Service of the Department of Agriculture will be terminated or transferred to other duties and the same actions will be taken in regard to the food stamp personnel in state and local public welfare agencies.

The net effect of these potential changes is significant staff reductions in state and local public welfare agencies and staff increases in the federal public welfare establishment. Under the Family Assistance Plan proposed in 1971, federal planners recognized the desirability of transferring experienced state and local public welfare personnel to fill federal posts in the new program and the mechanisms for doing so were explored in detail. The policy for such action was officially endorsed in a personnel amendment to H.R. 1, the Administration's bill for the Family Assistance Plan, submitted to the Senate Finance Committee which was considering the bill. The amendment sought authority for the federal government to appoint eligible state and local public welfare personnel to the competitive federal civil service within 90 days of date of enactment of the new programs and to fix their compensation at the rates they received under their previous positions. The bill also provided them credit for the length of their previous state or local service for purposes of career tenure, probationary period, annual leave accruals, group life or health insurance, and retention credit in reductions-in-force. It transferred state or local sick leave accruals earned and provided credit for state or local service on a formula basis towards a federal retirement annuity.[14] This policy may be the forerunner for national personnel policy should events result in the shifts in public welfare programs from state and local governments to federal jurisdiction.

THE SUPPLEMENTAL SECURITY INCOME PROGRAM EXPERIENCE

The recent experience of the organization of the SSI program is illustrative of the interrelation of program responsibility and staffing and a portent for the public welfare system.

More than a year before the SSI program's effective date of January 1, 1974, with the Social Security Amendments of 1972 under active Congressional consideration, Social Security Administration and Department of Health, Education and Welfare officials drew up plans for the new program and transfer of state/local aged, blind, and disabled caseloads to federal control. The decision was made to place responsibility for administering the different elements of the program to the Administration's existing bureaus and offices, rather than set up a separate, parallel organization to administer them. With a national work force of over 70,000 and an organization equipped to provide payments to over 28 million beneficiaries, the Administration concluded it could logically apply its organization, processes, and systems with some added personnel and funds to effective administration of the new, smaller program.

A new program and policy bureau of Supplemental Security Income in the Administration's central office was created to provide policy leadership, coordination, program direction, and overall program planning and evaluation. Field program staffs were added to the D/HEW ten regional offices to serve as regional liaison with state public welfare agencies regarding SSI activities, review SSI district and branch office operations and provide general oversight and assistance in the regions in administration of the program. New responsibilities and staff were added to the other SSA bureaus.

The same policy of assimilation of the SSI program was adopted for the district and branch offices. The processing of SSI applications was added to their responsibilities, additional positions were allocated to their personnel ceilings and new staff hired wherever necessary to cope with the new caseloads. The distribution of additional positions to individual district and branch offices was determined on a need basis by the number of SSI cases transferred from state and local public welfare agencies and the number of new eligibles expected to apply for assistance payments under the new income and resources standards. District offices with larger caseloads received larger personnel allocations. Those where the new caseloads were relatively small were required to absorb the added workload within their existing personnel allocations.

All SSA personnel—old and new, central office and field—were given intensive general and specialized training in the new program, tailored to their individual job requirements, before the January 1 deadline.

The basic staffing pattern of SSA district and branch offices did not change when the SSI program became their responsibility. No new types of positions had to be created for the new program; job increases were made to already existing positions. The staffing distribution in the Silver Spring, Maryland district office, a Class I office, and its two branch offices is illustrative of the numbers, general service grades, and relationship of the different positions. As shown in the chart on the following page:

		Silver Spring district office	Rockville branch office	Bladensburg branch office	Total
Manager	GS–14	1	GS–12 1	GS–11 1	3
Assistant Manager	GS–13	1			1
Operations Supervisors	GS–11	3			3
Claims Representatives	GS–10	12	3	3	18
Service Representatives	GS–6	8	2	1	11
Field Representatives	GS–10	2			2
Claims Development Clerks	GS–4	4	3	3	10
Data Review Technicians	GS–6	5	1	1	7
Receptionist	GS–4	1			1
Totals		37	10	9	56

The manager and assistant manager of the district office are responsible for supervision of all social security operations in the district. The branch office managers are subordinate to the district office manager and assistant manager and are responsible for supervision of branch office functions and personnel. The eligibility and claims activities of the branch and district offices are the same for applicants and beneficiaries living in the office nearest them. The three operations supervisors are employed in the district office to provide day-to-day supervision over the claims representatives and other personnel assigned to their alphabetical segment of the caseload of service applicants and beneficiaries. Claims representatives are responsible for determining eligibility of applications for all social security and SSI programs, including verification of information supplied by the applicant. Assignments are made alphabetically according to the applicant's surname. Service representatives are responsible for helping beneficiaries with claims payment problems and questions, such as, explanation of benefit amounts, changes in their status, lost checks, changes of address, and the like. Field representatives are employed to represent the district office in the community, speak to groups about social security and SSI programs, contact employees about their responsibilities for social security payroll deductions, and make home visits to assist homebound applicants. Claims development clerks are assigned to the claims representatives to provide them with clerical support in processing claims applications and maintaining case records. Data review techniques compute the amount of payment and review and prepare claims data for computer processing. The receptionist assists persons requesting information and assistance about social security and SSI benefits.

An additional 15,000 positions were authorized for the Social Security Administration in 1974 for the program, most for assignment to the 1,200 local offices. Relatively few of these were recruited from state and local public welfare agencies, although preference in hiring was given to state and local employees displaced involuntarily because of the program. The remainder were appointed through normal federal civil service processes, including competitive examination, certification and appointments from registers of eligibles, and transfers of federal government employees of other agencies. The relatively small number of state/local personnel recruitments is attributed to several factors: the unwillingness of employees to give up their accumulated rights and benefits earned in the state/local merit system to make the job change, the continued need for their services by state/local agencies, and their transfer within the public welfare agency to existing job vacancies.

The SSI legislation failed to provide the protective provisions for state/local personnel transfers to the federal civil service proposed in the Personnel Amendment of H.R. 1 for the Family Assistance Program described earlier. These provisions would seem to be prerequisite to the conversion of any state/local public welfare program to a federalized program where the experience and knowledge of state/local personnel are needed in the program. There are, however, other problems of organization, administration, and staffing to such conversion if the new program is made the responsibility of the Social Security Administration or other existing federal agency. Hard decisions will have to be made, for example, on (1) whether to assimilate the new program into the existing agency framework as was done in the SSI experience, create a separate self-contained organization for the new program, or seek some compromise arrangement of functions and personnel assignments between the old and the new; (2) how to rate the job experiences of state/local personnel to meet the federal job requirements standards of the new agency, considering the great variety and differences of personnel systems and organizational relationships in which such experience was gained; and (3) how to organize a large-scale orientation and training program to equip state/local personnel with the knowledge about the federal civil service system and the technical requirements of the new federal program to assure a high level of job performance. With change imminent in the public welfare system, these are among the pragmatic considerations to be given in deciding the shape of an improved system for the future.

NOTES

1. The Statistical Abstract of the United States 96th Edition, 1976. Bureau of the Census, Department of Commerce, U.S. Government Printing Office, Washington, D.C. Table 443, p. 274.

2. Public Welfare Personnel Annual Statistical Data, June 1973. DHEW Publication No. (SRS) 75-03251 NCSS Report E-2 (6/73). National Center for Social Statistics, March 1975.

3. Fine, S. A. Differential use of staff in family and child welfare services, a guide. Department of Health, Education and Welfare, Community Services Administration and the Office of Child Development, Washington, D.C. 1970.

4. Daly, M., Loeb, M. & Whitehouse, F. The social services and related manpower. Department of Health, Education and Welfare. Washington, D.C. U.S. DHEW Publication No. (SRS) 72-05300 pp. 17.

5. Gartner, A. The use of the paraprofessional and new directions for the social service agency. *Public Welfare,* 1969, 117.

6. E. G. Weller and E. B. Kilborne. Why volunteers: a guide for developing a volunteer service program. Alabama Department of Pensions and Security, mimeo 1969. Also, Weller, Kilborne: Citizen's Participation in Public Welfare Programs, Department of Health, Education and Welfare. U.S. Government Printing Office. Washington, D.C., 1956.

7. Schubert, M. The eligibility technician in public assistance. *Social Service Review,* 1974, **48**(1), 51.

8. Book of States, Council of State Governments, 1972–1973.

9. The Budget of the United States Government, Fiscal Year 1974, Appendix, Social and Rehabilitation Service, DHEW, Washington, D.C.

10. Social and Rehabilitation Regulations for the Title XX Social Services Program for Individuals and Families, Subpart H-Training and Retraining 40 CFR 72, DHEW April 14, 1975.

11. Wiest, B. J. The case for continued federal support of human resource services and social work training. Congressional Record, April 9, 1974. p. E2198-220.

12. Directory of National Unions and Employee Associations, 1971. Bulletin 1750. Department of Labor, Bureau of Labor Statistics 1972, U.S. Government Printing Office, Washington, D.C.

13. Younghusband, E. The future of social work. *Social Work Today,* 1973, 4(2), 33–34. Also Loewenberg, F. M. & Dolgoff, R. (eds.): *The Practice of Social Intervention: Goals, Roles and Strategies: A Book of Readings in Social Work Practice.* Itasca, Ill.: F. E. Peacock.

14. Personnel Amendment to H.R. 1 submitted January 28, 1972 by the Assistant DHEW Secretary for Legislation, Stephen Kurzman, to Senator Russell Long, Chairman of the Senate Finance Committee.

Chapter 7

PUBLIC WELFARE FINANCING AND BUDGETING

The $38.5 billion expenditures for public welfare programs in fiscal year 1975 is the third costliest social welfare program in the United States, exceeded only by those for education and social insurance. It represents 2.6 percent of the gross national product. Sixty-two percent ($23.8 billion) is funded by the federal government; 38 percent, or $14.7 billion, by state and local governments (Table 7.1).

Nine of every ten public welfare dollars goes for income maintenance and in-kind programs and the remainder mostly for social services. The Medicaid program has developed into the most expensive program ($12.8 billion) followed by the AFDC program ($9.5 billion), and the Supplemental Security Income program ($6.3 billion). The Food Stamp program with expenditures of $4.8 billion is the fastest growing program as a direct result of its outreach efforts and the socioeconomic effects of the mid-1970s recession.

TRENDS SINCE 1935

Since enactment of the Social Security Act in 1935, the cost of public welfare has risen sharply and steadily tenfold, from under $3 billion in 1935 to over $38 billion in 1975 and funding shifted

Chart 7.1 Public Welfare Expenditures by Program, Fiscal Year, 1975

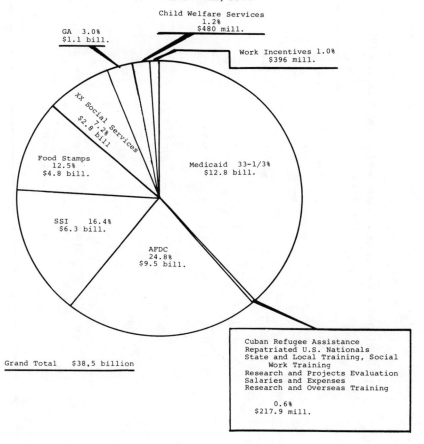

Child Welfare Services
1.2%
$480 mill.

GA 3.0%
$1.1 bill.

Work Incentives 1.0%
$396 mill.

XX Social Services
7.2%
$2.8 bill

Food Stamps
12.5%
$4.8 bill.

Medicaid 33-1/3%
$12.8 bill.

SSI 16.4%
$6.3 bill.

AFDC
24.8%
$9.5 bill.

Grand Total $38.5 billion

Cuban Refugee Assistance
Repatriated U.S. Nationals
State and Local Training, Social
    Work Training
Research and Projects Evaluation
Salaries and Expenses
Research and Overseas Training

0.6%
$217.9 mill.

279

Table 7.1 Public Welfare Expenditures by Program, Fiscal Year 1975
(in millions)

	Federal	% of Total	State and Local	% of Total	Combined	% of Total
Income Maintenance Program						
AFDC	$4,871.3	20.4	$4,661.0	31.8	$9,532.3	24.8
Supplemental Security Income	4,846.9	20.3	1,480.0	10.1	6,326.9	16.4
General Assistance	0	0	1,144.0	7.8	1,144.0	3.0
Subtotal	9,718.2	40.8	7,285	49.7	17,003.2	44.2
Social Services Programs						
Social Services	1,891.9	7.9	870.0[3]	5.9	2,761.9	7.2
Child Welfare Services	50.0	*	430.0	2.9	480.0	1.2
Subtotal	1,941.9	8.1	1,300	8.8	3,241.9	8.4
In Kind Programs						
Medical Assistance	6,966.4	29.2	5,832.0	39.8	12,798.4	33.3
Food Stamps	4,677.4[1]	19.6	146.0	1.0	4,823.4	12.5
Work Incentives	323.7[2]	*	72.0	*	395.7	1.0
Subtotal	11,967.5	50.2	6,050.0	41.3	18,017.5	46.8

Table 7.1 (Continued)

Special Population Programs						
Cuban Refugee Assistance	60.0	*	0	0	60.0	*
Repatriated U.S. Nationals Assistance	.9	*	0	0	.9	*
Subtotal	60.9	.3	0	0	60.9	.2
Research, Training, General Administration						
State and Local Training	53.2	*	18.0	*	71.2	*
Social Work Training Projects	8.9	*	0	*	8.9	*
SRS Research and Evaluation	9.2	*	0	*	9.2	*
SRS Salaries and Expenses	64.0	*	0	*	64.0	*
SRS Research and Training						
Overseas	3.7	*	0	*	3.7	*
Subtotal	139.0	.6	18.0	*	157.0	.4
TOTAL	$23,827.5	100%	$14,653.0	100%	$38,480.5	100%
Percent to total	61.9%		38.1%		100%	

*Less than 1%

[1] Revised estimate above the 1975 appropriation.

[2] Includes FY 1975 appropriations and program costs funded in prior years and excludes program costs to be expended in FY 1976.

[3] Includes $262 million estimated from general revenue sharing.

among the federal and state and local governments. In 1935, public welfare costs were borne largely by the federal government (80 percent) and only 20 percent by state and local governments. By 1950 there was a more even balance between them, with the federal government accounting for 43 percent and state and local government expenditures 57 percent of the total. By 1960, there was almost a 50–50 split between them. By the middle 1970s, the federal government's share grew to close to two-thirds and the share borne by state and local governments to about one-third.[1]

The long-term trends in public welfare expenditures cannot be attributed to any one reason. Rather, it is possible to detect the interaction of national growth characteristics in a rapidly changing world, and their influences. Among the more important of these are:

1. The 70 percent growth in national population from 126 million in 1935 to 215 million in 1975.

2. National and regional conditions which maintained large segments of American ethnic groups in economic poverty.

3. National social and cultural conditions which condoned poverty in American life.

4. A more liberal social policy of caring for the poor, of providing larger numbers of lower income groups with income maintenance to meet their basic needs and social and medical services.

5. The rising cost of living generally and expenditures for public welfare beneficiaries specifically.

6. The growing awareness among the poor and disadvantaged to their legal entitlement for public welfare benefits, spurred on by the community action programs of the 1960s.

THE INCREASING FEDERAL ROLE

The increasing role of the federal government in public welfare funding has roots in national social policies expressed in new programs and greater support of existing ones:

Recognition that poverty is a national problem requiring national solutions. The Medicaid program in 1959 and the Food Stamp program in 1964 are two examples of this policy.

Inability or unwillingness of state/local governments to assume all the financial burden of public welfare programs.

Use of Federal funding to offer "front end money" to stimulate state and local initiatives in starting or expanding their own programs, in organizing and training state/local staffs to administer welfare programs, to fund demonstrations for improvement of programs, to support research and developments into better ways to administer welfare programs, to evaluate and monitor how well programs are meeting needs of the poor and disadvantaged.

Federal legislation increasing federal financial participation (FFP) percentages to provide greater federal allocations to state and local governments to operate public welfare programs.

Nationalization of public welfare programs to make them more efficient and equitable, for example, passage of the Supplemental Security Income program to replace the federal and state program of Aid to the Aged, Blind and Disabled (except in U.S. Territories and Possessions).

STATE DISTRIBUTION

The state-by-state distribution of the $38.5 billion public welfare funds in 1975 reflects the population concentrations, size of beneficiaries caseloads, state payments standards and breadth of state services programs. The ten states with the largest welfare expenditures are New York, California, Illinois, Pennsylvania, Michigan, New Jersey, Ohio, Massachusetts, Texas, and Wisconsin. The five states with the lowest welfare expenditures are Wyoming, Nevada, Alaska, North Dakota, and Montana.[2]

Sources of Welfare Funding

Funds for public welfare programs are derived largely from general fund receipts of the respective governments, namely from taxes, fees, and charges. There are a few exceptions: Kansas, Oklahoma, Alabama, Connecticut, Louisiana, Montana, Tennessee, and Texas provide revenues earmarked for welfare programs from special taxes, such as ad valorum, sales, property or per capita taxes.[3] But these are not the only source of public welfare funding; three other sources can be identified: cost sharing by beneficiaries themselves, donated services from nongovernmental organizations, and so-called counterpart funds, that is, excess foreign currencies accruing to the United States through the sale of surplus agricultural commodities and other sources to support welfare research and training activities overseas. These sources are negligible in comparison with general government funding, but they do represent important public policies:

1.   that cost sharing by beneficiaries should be required to the extent of ability to pay even though the amounts are nominal to give them a sense of personal responsibility and accountability for the services they receive,
2.   that donations from the general community should be encouraged as recognition of its involvement in public welfare,
3.   that poverty and dependency are universal and the research and training efforts overseas should be studied for potential use in this country.

Examples of cost sharing are built into the Medicaid and social service programs. The Social Security Act of 1973 (P.L. 92–603) requires states with Medicaid programs which cover the medically indigent to impose nominal monthly premium charges graduated by size of income. The higher the income, the larger the monthly charges. Also, under Medicaid, states may, at their option, require payment by medically indigent of nominal charges to cover medical costs in the form of deductible (first charges) and copayment amounts. For example, for a hospital bill of $250, the medically indigent individual or his family may have to pay the first $50 and an added 10 percent, or $20 of the remaining $200 cost, a total of $70. A state also may require a public assistance beneficiary to pay a nominal share of the cost of optional Medicaid services, such as prescribed drugs or hearing aids but not the cost of the mandatory services the state must provide for it to receive federal funds (inpatient and outpatient hospital services, other x-ray and laboratory services, skilled nursing home services, physicians services, home health services, early and periodic screening, diagnosis and treatment (EPSDT) services for children and family planning services).

A similar cost-sharing provision for social service beneficiaries exists. Families must be charged fees for service if their monthly gross income is between 80 percent and 115 percent of the medium income of a family of four in the state, the amounts of income and fees adjusted by size of family. In addition, a state may impose a fee for service to any others whose monthly gross income is less than 80 percent of the medium income in the state for a family of four, adjusted by size of family.

In the same Title XX program of social services, the donation of funds and/or social services from private sources is permitted. The value of donations is accepted as another financial source for the State's social services program and is factored in when the federal financial share is computed.[4]

THE FLOW OF WELFARE FUNDS

Funds for public welfare programs flow from different sources which create different money streams of different volume before they reach their destinations. Public welfare dollars go for:

Monthly welfare checks
Cash payments to recipients
Payments to service providers (individuals and institutions)
  for services rendered
Funds for food purchased with food stamps
Salary checks to public welfare agency workers

> Payments by welfare agencies for employer contributions to retirement and insurance plans on behalf of their workers
>
> Payments by welfare agencies to grantees and contractors for supplies, goods and services

Sometimes a single source supplies all the funds (as a state government for the General Assistance program). At other times, two or more sources work in tandem (as in the Medicaid program, the federal government, a state government, and medically indigent recipients contribute to the cost of medical care). At times, one source must be available before another source is tapped and the dollars from the first determines the dollars from the second (as in the social services program where the amounts of state funds spent are matched by federal funds 75 percent to 25 percent up to a maximum formula allotment).

The multiplicity of sources is an important characteristic of the public welfare system. Money—its sources and uses—is the reality of the social commitment towards public welfare. The subtleties of funding limits, methods, and amounts translate the profound social welfare policies at work to the pragmatism of assistance payments and services to the poor and disadvantaged. For public welfare funds are, quite clearly, a powerful economic tool for the redistribution of the national wealth and income and the administration and direction of welfare financing is the sensitive barometer for expressing how much, in what ways, to what purpose, and for whose benefit this redistribution is to take place.

SOURCES

The following sources of funds and combinations are prevalent in public welfare:

Fully-funded Federal Appropriations

Public welfare programs or components where the federal government assumes 100 percent of costs. Examples are the free and bonus value of food stamps, the payments and services to

Cuban refugees, and some public welfare research and development grants and contracts to universities and research centers.

Fully-funded State Appropriations

Public welfare programs or components where the state governments provide 100 percent of costs. An example is a state-administered General Assistance program.

Fully-funded Local Government Appropriations

Public welfare programs or components where a county or city government provides 100 percent of costs. An example is a county or city General Assistance program wholly funded by the local government.

Federal/State Open-ended Matching Appropriations

Federal/state sharing programs or components where the federal government shares public welfare costs with state governments on an open-ended basis. Examples are the AFDC maintenance assistance and Medicaid programs. The open-end concept, simply described, is the legal obligation of the federal government to cover its matching share of the costs of state programs however small or large according to the applicable matching formula. Thus, if state X reports its AFDC assistance expenditures to be $50 million for July payments, $60 million for August, and $70 million for September, the federal government share would automatically increase according to the authorized formula method of determining the FFP rate. If state Y spends $200 million for Medicaid services a year, the federal government is obligated to meet the 50 to 83 percent of state Y costs of such services depending upon the federally-determined Federal Medical Assistance Percentage (FMAP), a formula designed to account for the difference among the states of their per capita income.

Federal/State Matching Formula Appropriations

Federal/state sharing programs or components where the federal government shares public welfare costs with state governments on a formula allotment basis. Examples are the child welfare services program and the Title XX social services program. In the child welfare services program the formula is as follows: each state receives a uniform $70,000 and an additional grant which varies directly with child population and inversely with average per capita income. In the Title XX social services program, each state receives an allotment on the basis of the state's population as a percentage of the total U.S. population. If a state fails to spend its share, that amount is available to Puerto Rico, Guam and the Virgin Islands. If a state spends more than the federal funds and state matching combined, the excess is funded from state funds.

Federal Funding/State Supplementation

Public welfare programs or components which are funded by the federal government and the state governments at their option agree to provide a supplement to add to the federal government's costs. The SSI program is one such program in which the national uniform assistance payments to the aged, blind, and disabled are supplemented by optional state payments in 38 states.

Revenue Sharing

Public welfare programs or components which are funded by general revenue sharing federal authorizations. These are distributed to state and local governments under the State and Local Fiscal Assistance Act of 1972 under a formula based on population, local tax effort, and per capita income. One-third of revenue sharing funds are allocated to state governments, two-thirds to local government units. Social services to the poor or aged, and health are authorized as two of the eight target areas for the program. The application of revenue sharing funds to the eight areas is made solely at the discretion of the individual state or local government, but they may not be used as the basis for federal matching to obtain added federal funds. The only federal proscription is that the revenue sharing monies may not be applied to a program which discriminates on the grounds of race, color, national origin or sex.

Other Sources

Public welfare agencies may, and do, supplement funds derived from the above sources through financial arrangements—compacts, contracts, agreements—with other public and private agencies. This initiates a separate flow of funds for welfare services, activities, individual and family benefits, and administration. (These are discussed more fully in Chapter 9.) They include funds from such agencies as community services, comprehensive employment and manpower training, community development, public housing, comprehensive health planning, juvenile delinquency prevention and control, vocational rehabilitation, developmental disabilities, services for the aging, and Indian affairs.

THE BUDGET PROCESS FOR PUBLIC WELFARE FUNDING

The budget process for the public welfare system is part of the general government budget process, basically the same in federal, state, and local governments. The United States Constitution, state constitutions, and local government charters require appropriation laws to draw monies from their respective treasuries, and their chief executives recommend to legislative bodies the government revenues and appropriations for the next fiscal year or years.[5]

Federal government appropriations for public welfare programs are for use of general and special funds drawn from the U.S. Treasury. Table 7.2 explains the federal appropriation structure for the programs. It shows that appropriations generally follow the prevailing organizational assignment of programs to the Social and Rehabilitation Service,* Social Security Administration, and Food and Nutrition Service. However, even within this general scheme, one finds inconsistencies. For exam-

*With the DHEW reorganization abolishing SRS, the appropriations for that agency will be organized to fit the new alignment of program responsibilities to the Office of Human Development Services, Health Care Financing Administration and SSA.

Table 7.2 Public Welfare Expenditures by Program, Fiscal Year, 1975

Program		Sub-Program	Public Law Authorization	Federal/State Ratio	Program Items Covered	Fiscal Year 1975 Amount (thousands)
Social and Rehabilitation Service						
Public Assistance	Maintenance Assistance	Adult Categories	Title I Social Security Act	49.6/50.4	Grants to reimburse welfare agencies for part of the cost of cash payments made to aged, blind, and disabled recipients in Guam, Puerto Rico, and the Virgin Islands. The SSI program appropriations (below) provides cash assistance for all other aged, blind, and disabled (in the 50 states and the District of Columbia) as of January 1, 1974, pursuant to Public Law 92-603 with the federalization of these programs.	$ 4,505
		Aid to Families with Dependent Children	Title IV Social Security Act	51.2/48.8	Grants to reimburse welfare agencies for part of the cost of cash payments made to families with dependent children. Also includes cash payments for foster care for AFDC children and vendor payments for home repairs for AFDC households.	4,325,232

Program	Sub-Program	Public Law Authorization	Federal/ State Ratio	Program Items Covered	Fiscal Year 1975 Amount (thousands)
	Emergency Assistance	Title IV Social Security Act	50/50	Grants to reimburse welfare agencies for part of the cost of cash payments made to families with dependent children for emergency care and medical assistance.	31,295
	State and Local Administration	Titles I, IV, X, XIV, XVI	50/50	Grants to reimburse welfare agencies for part of the cost of state and local administration of maintenance assistance programs.	514,738
	Assistance to Repatriated U.S. Nationals	Section 1113 Social Security Act	100/0	Payments to reimburse welfare agencies for the cost of financial assistance and services to U.S. Nationals repatriated from abroad because of illness, destitution, or international crisis.	882
	Adult Phaseout			Reduction in the costs due to transfer of SSI program.	-$ 14,725
					$ 4,861,927

Table 7.2 (Continued)

Program	Sub-Program	Public Law Authorization	Federal/State Ratio	Program Items Covered	Fiscal Year 1975 Amount (thousands)
Medical Assistance	Medical Vendor Payments	Title XIX Social Security Act	55.7/44.3	Grants to reimburse State agencies for cost of medical vendor payments for health care to recipients and other medically needy persons.	6,691,756
	State and Local Administration	Title XIX Social Security Act	56.9/43.1	Grants to reimburse Medicaid agencies for part of the cost of state and local administration of their Medicaid program.	274,619
				Total Medical Assistance	$ 6,966,375
Social Services		Title XX Social Security Act	75/25	Grants to reimburse welfare agencies for part of the cost of social services to recipients of public assistance and other persons.	$ 1,891,905

Program	Sub-Program	Public Law Authorization	Federal/ State Ratio	Program Items Covered	Fiscal Year 1975 Amount (thousands)
State and Local Training		Title I, IV, VI, X, XIV, XVI, XX	75/25	Grants to reimburse welfare agencies for part of the cost of training welfare personnel and persons preparing for employment in these agencies.	53,172
Child Welfare Services		Title IV Social Security Act	10.4/89.6	Grants to welfare agencies for part of the cost of services to promote the welfare of children, primarily through supplementation or substitution for parental care and supervision.	50,000
Research and Evaluation	Social Services	Section 1110, 1115, 426 Social Security Act	100/0	Grants to states and nonprofit organizations and contracts to nonprofit organizations to carry out research and development and evaluations of child welfare and social services programs.	2,725

293

Table 7.2 (Continued)

Program	Sub-Program	Public Law Authorization	Federal/ State Ratio	Program Items Covered	Fiscal Year 1975 Amount (thousands)
	Health Services	Sections 1110 and 1115 Social Security Act	100/0	Grants to states and nonprofit organizations and contracts to nonprofit organizations to carry out research and development and evaluations of the Medicaid program.	3,175
	Income Maintenance	Sections 1110, 1115, 426 Social Security Act	100/0	Grants to states and nonprofit organizations and contracts to nonprofit organizations to carry out research and development and evaluation of income maintenance programs.	2,775
	Social Security	Section 1110 Social Security Act	100/0	Grants to states and nonprofit organizations and contracts to nonprofit organizations to carry out research and development and evaluation of Social Security programs, including SSI, OASDI, and Medicare.	525
				Total Research and Evaluation	$ 9,200

Program	Sub-Program	Public Law Authorization	Federal/State Ratio	Program Items Covered	Fiscal Year 1975 Amount (thousands)
Training Projects		Section 707 and 426 Social Security Act	100/0	Grants to public and nonprofit institutions of higher learning for social service and child welfare training, including teaching, traineeship, and training grants.	$ 8,900
				Total Public Assistance	$13,841,479
Social and Rehabilitation Service Salaries & Expense		Section 703 Social Security Act	100/0	Federal administration of SRS programs: assistance payments, child welfare, social services, WIN, Medicaid, Cuban Refugees, U.S. National Repatriates.	$ 63,962
Work Incentives	Training and Incentives	Title IV Social Security Act	90/10	Funds transferred to the Department of Labor to provide grants to State manpower agencies for manpower and training activities for AFDC/WIN registrants, including intake services and Work and Training.	140,000

Table 7.2 (Continued)

Program	Sub-Program	Public Law Authorization	Federal/State Ratio	Program Items Covered	Fiscal Year 1975 Amount (thousands)
Child Care & Supportive Services		Title IV Social Security Act	90/10	Grants to State welfare agencies for part of the cost of child care and supportive social services for ADFC/WIN registrants to enable them to accept work or training.	70,000
				Total Work Incentives	$ 210,000
Social Security Administration					
Supplemental Security Income	Federal Benefits Payments	Title XVI Social Security Act	100/0	Payments to aged, blind, and disabled recipients of basic benefits.	$ 4,080,000
	Federal Contributions toward State Supplementation	Title XVI Social Security Act	100/0	Payments to aged, blind, and disabled recipients of mandatory supplement benefits by states; payments to recipients in states to carry out the "hold harmless" provision and Federal administration of payments to recipients in states electing Federal administration for mandatory supplement benefits and for optimal supplement benefits.	255,000

Program	Sub-Program	Public Law Authorization	Federal/State Ratio	Program Items Covered	Fiscal Year 1975 Amount (thousands)
Vocational Rehabilitation Services		Title XVI Social Security Act	100/0	Funds transferred to Rehabilitation Services Administration for allocation to state vocational rehabilitation agencies to meet their costs in providing services to blind and disabled SSI recipients referred by Social Security Administration offices.	48,853
Payments to Trust Funds for Administrative Costs		Title XVI Social Security Act	100/0	Transfer payments to the Social Security Trust Funds for reimbursement for federal administration of the SSI program.	473,249
				Total Supplemental Security Income	$ 4,857,102
Assistance to Refugees in the U.S.	Welfare Assistance and Services	Migration and Refugee Assistance Act of 1962	100/0	Payments to State and local welfare agencies to cover the cost of providing financial and medical assistance to needy Cuban refugees.	$ 47,000

Table 7.2 (Continued)

Program	Sub-Program	Public Law Authorization	Federal/ State Ratio	Program Items Covered	Fiscal Year 1975 Amount (thousands)
Education		Migration and Refugee Assistance Act	100/0	Payments to needy Cuban refugees to cover the cost of continuing education and training and to Dade County (Fla.) public schools system to cover the cost of educating Cuban refugee children.	11,300
Other Services		Migration and Refugee Assistance Act	100/0	Federal administrative costs of the program and contracts with voluntary resettlement agencies to provide pre and post resettlement services to Cuban refugees.	1,700
				Total Assistance to Refugees in the U.S.	$ 60,000

	Program	Sub-Program	Public Law Authorization	Federal/ State Ratio	Program Items Covered	Fiscal Year 1975 Amount (thousands)
Research and Training Activities Overseas	Special Foreign Currency Program		Agricultural Trade Development and Assistance Act of 1954 and the International Health Research Act of 1960	100/0	Grants to social welfare research centers in the U.S. and overseas research in income maintenance, social service, and health and to keep informed and disseminate information about such research.	$ 3,700
Dept. of Agriculture Food and Nutrition Service	Food Stamp Program	Bonus Costs	Food Stamp Act of 1964, as amended	100/0	Provides funds to cover the value of free and bonus food stamps issued to low income persons and families.	3,785,255

Table 7.2 (Continued)

Program	Sub-Program	Public Law Authorization	Federal/State Ratio	Program Items Covered	Fiscal Year 1975 Amount (thousands)
	Other Program Costs	Food Stamp Act of 1964, as amended	50/50	Provides part of the cost of administrative expenses of state and local welfare agencies incurred in the program, for the printing and distribution of food stamps and part of the cost of employment, registration, and counseling by state employment offices and the Department of Labor.	165,000
Operating Expenses		Food Stamp Act of 1964, as amended	100/0	Provides the cost of federal administration of the program.	34,285
Transfer to Dept. of Agriculture Office of Inspector General		Food Stamp Act of 1964, as amended	100/0	Provides for the cost of conducting audits and investigations of the administration of the Food Stamp Program.	5,245
				Total Food Stamp Program	$ 3,989,785

Program	Sub-Program	Public Law Authorization	Federal/State Ratio	Program Items Covered	Fiscal Year 1975 Amount (thousands)
			SUMMARY		
	Public Assistance				$13,841,479,000
	SRS Salaries and Expenses				63,962,000
	Work Incentives				210,000,000
	Supplemental Security Income				4,857,102,000
	Assistance to Refugees in the U.S.				60,000,000
	Research and Training Activites Overseas				3,700,000
	Food Stamp Program				3,989,785,000
	Total				$23,026,028,000

Source: 1975 Budget of the United States Government Appendix and the 1975 United States Budget in Brief.

ple, the Department of Labor's funding for the Work Incentive Program is not shown under that department's appropriation but is included under the Social and Rehabilitation Service and funds for the Training and Incentives component of that program, administered by the Department of Labor, flow from that appropriation. This arrangement, of course, is a Congressional and Presidential decision made when the Work Incentive Program was first set up as a joint departmental responsibility.

THE INTERGOVERNMENTAL NATURE OF PUBLIC WELFARE BUDGETING

The budget process of public welfare programs is a web of decisions and actions enmeshing federal, state, and local governments. Except for the few wholly federally funded appropriations, such as the Social and Rehabilitation Services Salaries and Expenses ($64 million), Social and Rehabilitation Service Research and Training Overseas ($3.7 million), and Social and Rehabilitation Service Research and Evaluation ($9.2 million), the federal budget estimates, particularly those of federal/state matching programs, depend upon estimates and forecasts of state and local spending financial reports, and estimates are requested of state and local welfare agencies for this purpose. In a like manner, state budget estimates depend upon county and city estimates and forecasts, especially of those which are locally administered programs to which funds from federal and state sources apply. Each level of government must know the estimates of service caseloads and costs of the others for the coming budget period to be able to present an intelligent budget statement of their own funds. They cannot be in conflict or inconsistent and all must use the same bases of caseloads, services, and costs. An over-or-under estimate such as a large discrepancy in predicting caseload levels or average costs by one level of government can place in jeopardy the funding of a given program at all levels. This has occurred in the past. Requests for supplemental funds by public welfare agencies are frequently attributed to miscalculations by the welfare agencies of the other government levels.

Timing is critical in budget formulation. The new federal fiscal year begins October 1.[6] The President is required to submit the Annual Budget shortly after January 1 when Congress convenes its new session. This allows both Houses of Congress time to hold appropriation hearings and deliberate, debate, and pass appropriation bills to be effective October 1. This requires the Executive Department and agencies—and the federal Judiciary and Congress as well—to begin work in April or May of the previous year to develop their budget needs and justifications. To guide executive agencies, the Office of Management and Budget (OMB) issues Presidentially-approved policy and target budget limits. Agencies respond with budget estimates by September 30. During the fall of the year, an intense period of negotiation and reconciliation follows, with agency officials and OMB examiners meeting to iron out differences, referring final decisions to the President.

The budget process is year-round. To be prepared for the initial period of fiscal planning and budgeting for public welfare programs and beyond, federal agencies request quarterly reports and estimates of state welfare agencies. These serve two purposes: to fix and justify advances of federal funds for which the states claim reimbursement, and to lay the groundwork for the next year's federal budget estimates. This information is submitted in advance each quarter to provide data on actual caseloads, services, and costs. Estimates are also given for each quarterly period to the end of the fiscal year as well as comparative information of the two preceding fiscal years. Thus, each new quarterly report revises and updates previous reports to give weight to the latest caseload, services, and cost experience. Reporting instructions to the states remind state agencies their estimates are made part of the record of Congressional appropriation hearings to justify the federal budget estimates.

State and local welfare agency budgets are drawn up from the same base of information about trends in caseloads, social services, and costs, following essentially the same budgetary process as that of the federal government. State welfare agencies begin to develop annual or biennial estimates of funds needed, with accompanying program and cost justifications from budget guidelines drawn up by the central state or local government budget agency approved by the Governor or local government chief executive about nine months before the beginning of their fiscal year(s). These estimates are submitted to the state or local government central budget agency for its review. Updating of budget figures as time progresses and reconciliation of differences with the central budget agency is a continuing part of the process, with chief executives making final budget and program decisions.

The state welfare budget is part of the Governor's budget submitted to the state legislature at the beginning of the legislative session. The same follows for local governments. Appropriation hearings are held by appropriation committees of the legislature and appropriation bills drawn up. Following passage by the legislature, appropriation bills are submitted to the Chief Executive for his review and decision to sign them into law or veto them to be returned for further legislative action. Throughout this executive and legislative process, the full measure of policy and political practice of conflict and compromise is evident. This process is duplicated in county and city jurisdictions where welfare programs are decentralized and local welfare funds are appropriated.[7]

The bases for forecasting the next year's welfare program funding needs are the insights of welfare officials into such varying factors as state and local social and economic conditions, government revenue and borrowing plans, and changes in welfare policies. Also taken into account are the previous year's experience in caseloads, services, and costs, and changes anticipated in state and local welfare legislation affecting maintenance payments, social and medical services, or welfare agency administrative budget limitations. Requests for new staff and fund allocations for eligibility determination reviews and audits, and such program factors as the effects of medical services utilization review in controlling Medicaid costs must be analyzed before final budget recommendations are made.

The uncertainties surrounding the budget estimating process exist uniformly in all federal, state, and local welfare programs. In recent years, only the two small welfare programs have not been beset by the same degree of uncertitude: the Cuban Refugee Assistance and Repatriated U.S. National Assistance Programs. Budget estimates for these are drawn up by the responsible D/HEW officials from caseload experience and policies affecting program costs.

The Form and Content of Public Welfare Budgets

The budgets of public welfare agencies are drawn up to show how many dollars would be needed the next fiscal year(s) by the jurisdiction to carry out each program of assistance or services. The assumptions for the dollar estimates are given to explain and justify them; comparisons of the amounts are made with amounts for the current year and the past year, e.g., for the fiscal year 1976 budget, comparisons are shown for fiscal years 1974 and 1975. For further support, estimates are also drawn up for up to five additional years in some jurisdictions to show longer range funding requirements.

In support of the dollars requested, estimates and explanations are given of expected caseloads, number of beneficiaries, types and costs of program activities to be carried on, objects of expenditure, changes in program and costs from preceding year(s) and any other useful explanations to convince legislative and executive decision makers—and the general public—of the validity of their money needs.

A standard budget classification of obligations of funds is prescribed uniformly for all federal agencies and programs.

    personnel compensation
    personnel benefits
    travel and transportation of persons
    transportation of things
    rent, communications, and utilities
    printing and reproduction
    other services
    supplies and materials
    equipment
    grants, subsidies, and contributions
    insurance claims and indemnities

With some modifications, state and local government budget systems follow this classification. The proportions spent by public welfare agencies for the different objects of expenditure vary by type of program. Income maintenance programs, with responsibility for issuing assistance checks, require large amounts for "grants, subsidies, and contributions." Social service programs require large amounts for "personnel compensation" and "personnel benefits" for their social work personnel and for "other services" for the service contracts made with private community service agencies. The "other services" classification is also applied in the Medicaid program for payments to contract fiscal agents for their payments to providers of medical services. Expenditures for food stamps are classified as "grants, subsidies, and contributions."

THE APPROPRIATION ACT AND ITS IMPLEMENTATION

Appropriation laws—federal, state, local governments alike—as the concluding instruments of the appropriation process, express the authorized spending limits for programs in total dollar amounts, sometimes with specific limits for named activities, purposes, or expense items. Quite often, language is found in the appropriation act placing restrictions upon the welfare agency or making mandatory adoption of a minimum standard for eligibility. This, of course, is use of the budgetary process to shape the substance or character of the program, a legislative tactic often used for modifying or controlling program content or its policies, priorities, and objectives.

Appropriation acts do not usually detail spending limits for each and every object of expenditures, activities, or program categories. To maintain financial controls to avoid spending more than is appropriated, and to carry out budget plans, a financial management and control system is applied by all governments for all programs, including public welfare. Once appropriations become law, each government agency or program director prepares estimates showing how the annual (or biennial) appropriation is apportioned quarterly so as not to exceed stated limits. These quarterly apportionments are submitted for approval to the central budget control agency (The Federal Office of Management and Budget, the state budget control agency, or the county or city budget control agency). The quarterly amounts need not be uniform, more frequently, they are amounts which reflect the latest quarterly estimates of caseloads, service needs, and cost trends. As in budget preparation, quarterly public welfare estimates of each government level need to be consistent with those of the others. Once approved by the central budget control agency, the public welfare agency director sets monthly or quarterly allotments of funds to each of its organization units. The apportionment is thus distributed to individual activities and objects of expenditure as controlling limits to the use of funds during the month or quarter.

Financial accounting and administrative controls are also imposed to assure these allotment limits are not exceeded. Personnel ceilings control the number of employees. Average grade ceilings control the civil service grade distribution in each organization unit. Travel ceilings are imposed. Personnel and travel records are kept for these controls. A system of allotment accounts are set up and all obligation documents, such as contracts and expenditure vouchers are recorded in their respective accounts and unobligated and unexpended balances are reported regularly to agency officials. These are studied routinely and with some anxiety when reported obligations and expenditures threaten to exceed budgeted allotments. At such times, welfare agency executives must, and do, spend hours and days of time, effort, and attention to devise ways and means to change financial plans and operating programs to avoid exceeding allotments. This financial management activity has been the normal pattern during the past decade of rising welfare caseloads, program changes, inflation, intensified public and legislative reaction to rising tax burdens.

APPLICATION OF PUBLIC WELFARE FUNDS

The flow of public welfare funds from government treasuries to their ultimate destinations of welfare recipients, welfare agency personnel, service providers, and others connected with the welfare system is indeed intricate. With controls exercised by interdependent governments for the different programs, it becomes essential to discuss individually each program's funding, amounts, rates, formulas, accounting and disbursing processes, appropriations and relevant program requirements which are applied from the point of authorization to actual application.

Aid to Families with Dependent Children Program ($9.5 billion)

Funds are derived from federal, state, and local governments to provide:

> monthly or semi-monthly assistance checks to AFDC families
>
> monthly checks to foster parents for the care of AFDC children
>
> vendor payments for home repairs of AFDC residences
>
> cash payments to AFDC families for emergency or medical assistance
>
> authorizations to state and local welfare agencies to pay salaries, personnel benefits, agency contractors, and suppliers of goods and services required to operate the AFDC program.

Three categories of the federal appropriation *Maintenance Assistance* apply to these purposes: the category *Aid to Families with Dependent Children, Emergency Assistance,* and *State and Local Administration.* The first authorizes matching funds for grants to welfare agencies for part of the cost of (1) cash payments to families with dependent children; (2) payments for foster care for AFDC children; and (3) vendor payments for home repairs for AFDC households. The second, Emergency Assistance, authorizes grants to welfare agencies for part of the cost of cash payments made to AFDC families for emergency care or medical assistance. The third, State and Local Administration, authorizes grants to welfare agencies for part of the cost of state and local administration of the AFDC program.[8] State government appropriations to its public welfare agency authorize funds for the state share of the program. Local government appropriations to the city or county welfare agency authorize funds for the program in 20 states where the program is locally administered.

The federal government pays five-sixths of the average monthly grant per recipient up to $18. Of the amount of the average grant above $18 and up to $32 (up to $100 for recipients of foster care), the federal government pays the "federal percentage," which takes into consideration per capita income of the states. States with an approved Medicaid plan may use the "federal medical assistance percentage" which varies from 50 to 83 percent with no maximum on the federal share of amounts based on the average grant. Separate provisions are included for computing the federal share of benefits in Puerto Rico, the Virgin Islands, and Guam. The federal government pays 50 percent of aid under the emergency assistance program under AFDC, with such assistance not to exceed 30 days in any 12-month period.

Vendor payments for the cost of home repairs for AFDC recipients are reimbursed by the federal government at a 50 percent rate not in excess of $500 for any one home, with state or local agencies required to pay the other 50 percent of costs and 100 percent of costs over $500.[9]

Federal funds are provided through an open-ended appropriation from general revenues. States are required to participate in financing, but local participation is optional. In 33 states, all financing of the nonfederal share is from state funds; in three states all nonfederal costs for assistance payments are from state and local funds with administrative costs from state funds. In 15 states, 50 to 85 percent of nonfederal assistance costs are from state and local funds with varying arrangements for sharing administrative costs between state and local funds.[10]

The "federal medical assistance percentage" is used in 30 states and the District of Columbia to determine the federal share of assistance payments. The proportions of federal, state, and local funds varies among the states. The federal share varies from 41.6 to 79.1 percent of total program costs and the state share from 15.5 to 54.1 percent. In 20 states, no local funds are used; in all states the local share is less than 1 percent and in 20 states, the local share varies from 1.3 to 24.3 percent of total program costs.[11]

State governments obtain federal grant-in-aid funds quarterly by an advance of funds based upon estimates of AFDC caseloads and costs submitted by state welfare agencies to D/HEW.

"Letters of Credit" are prepared for each state government, authorized by a responsible federal official. A Letter of Credit is an instrument certified by an authorized official of a grantor agency which authorizes a grantee (state or local government or other contractor) to draw funds when needed from the Treasury, through a Federal Reserve Bank and the grantee's commercial bank. They authorize a state government official to draw funds from the Federal Treasury through its regional disbursing centers and the state government's bank to be applied to the program. In state-administered programs, contracts, checks issued, cash drawn, and other obligations paid from its treasury for the program are processed through the accounts of the state welfare agency in accordance with the state government's accounting and disbursement procedures. When local governments contribute to the cost of the program, transfers of funds from the local revenue authority to the state treasury are made regularly.

In locally-administered programs, the treasuries of city and county governments are recipients of advance payments of program funds from the state treasuries. The amounts advanced are comprised of federal and state funds when state funds also share in the cost of the AFDC program. Contracts, checks issued, cash drawn, and other obligations paid from the city or county treasury for the program are processed through the accounts of the local welfare agency following local government accounting and disbursement procedures. Throughout, the federal government's accounting and auditing standards and requirements for the administration of grants as described above have to be met by state and local governments.[12] Checks and cash payments made to AFDC recipients and state and local agencies and other payees identify the governmental sources of funds.

Supplemental Security Income Program (SSI) ($6.3 billion)[13]

The SSI program funds are derived from federal and state governments to provide:

> monthly assistance checks to aged, blind, and disabled recipients of the program;
>
> authorizations to state vocational rehabilitation agencies to meet their costs in providing rehabilitation services to blind and disabled recipients;
>
> authorizations to the Social Security Administration to pay salaries, personnel benefits, agency contractors, and suppliers of goods and services required to administer the program;
>
> authorizations to state welfare agencies in 16 states which opt for state administration of supplemental payments to aged, blind, and disabled beneficiaries for use of state funds to pay salaries, personnel benefits, agency contractors, and suppliers of goods and services.

Two categories of the Federal Supplemental Security Income appropriation, *Federal Benefit Payments and Federal Contributions Toward State Supplementation*[14] authorize monthly payment checks to aged, blind, and disabled beneficiaries containing the basic Federal benefit and the additional amount for the "hold harmless" provision[15] for beneficiaries living in states choosing federal administration of their supplements. The state share of supplemental benefit payments is transferred from the state treasury to the United States Treasury in regular payments and credited to the SSI accounts.

Benefit checks from SSI are prepared and mailed by the U.S. Treasury from computer and mailing tapes supplied by the four Social Security Administration program centers. In the 16 states which elect state administration of optional supplemental payments, such payments are authorized from state treasuries. Regular monthly checks for the supplemental benefit are issued to aged, blind, and disabled beneficiaries charged to those accounts, thus providing them with two monthly checks, one federal one state. The administrative expenses borne by state welfare agencies for the optional supplemental benefit payments are authorized as part of the agencies' regular salaries and expenses.

To provide vocational rehabilitation services funds, transfers of funds are made by the Social Security Administration from the SSI appropriation to a special trust fund administered by the Administration For Handicapped Individuals, D/HEW.[16] Allocations are made annually by that agency to state vocational rehabilitation agencies on the basis of state agency estimates of caseloads and costs and adjustments are made during the year as needed. Federal vocational rehabilitation funds are provided to the states on an advance basis through transfers from Treasury regional disbursing centers to the state treasuries. These funds cover the full cost of services and administration incurred by the state rehabilitation agency and are applied to the salaries, personnel benefits, other administrative expenses, and vendor payments to agency service contractors, and other providers of vocational rehabilitation services. Regular monthly reports by the state agencies of caseloads and costs are submitted to the Administration for Handicapped Individuals.

Transfer payments are made annually from the SSI appropriation to the Social Security Administration to cover administrative costs by that agency of the SSI program. To authorize use of the Trust Funds for this purpose, an appropriation: *Limitation On Salaries and Expenses-Trust Funds* is provided. Because the administration of the program is integrated with that of other social security insurance payments activities, the costs of administration of these programs are carried in the same Social Security Trust Fund Salaries and Expenses appropriation.[17]

The Social Security Act authorizes advances from social security trust funds for the administrative costs of the SSI program. Repayment of this advance is made currently on an estimated basis with final accounting made after the year is over and actual data are available, including interest due the trust funds, if any.

The administrative costs of the Social Security Administration for the program cover the salaries, personnel benefits, travel, purchase of supplies and equipment, and other administrative and contractual expenses. A number of special items are also covered: the cost of paying state welfare agencies under contract for performing certain income level computations, contracts with state agencies (welfare and others) for determining the existence and continuance of a disability, and the cost of paying New York City to act as representative payee for the city's SSI beneficiaries who are drug addicts and alcoholics and to monitor their treatment.

General Assistance Program ($1.1 billion)

The General Assistance program is, as described earlier, a highly varied, characteristically distinctive social program of state, county, and city governments predating the Social Security Act, with no federal funding nor federal regulations and oversight which federally-funded programs impose. The individual states and local governments have gone their own ways to provide services and welfare payments where no other public welfare programs apply. In 18 states, only state funds are available; 16 states provide a combination of state and local funds; in 17 states only local funds are used.[18] The emergency characteristic of general assistance calls for quick on-the-spot decisions by local welfare offices usually requiring nominal sums for a one-time expenditure or temporary aid with a specified cutoff date. Program funds are appropriated to the program to state welfare agencies and to city or county welfare agencies where welfare programs for general assistance are locally administered. These funds are used to provide cash payments to individuals and families and vouchers issued to authorize services, commodities, or food stamps on their behalf. Such vouchers are accounted for and charged against the fund allocations made to the local welfare offices for such purpose.

Social Services Program ($2.8 billion)

Federal, state, and local governments fund the program of social services for public assistance recipients and other low-income persons authorized by Title XX of the Social Security Act. Also, for beneficiaries who can pay for specified services (such as for day care to children of families between 80 to 115 percent of a state's median family income for a family of four, adjusted by size of family), the cost of service is met by fees paid by the beneficiary. Further, to round out the description on funding sources for the program, donations of services are made by private sources without restriction as to how they are to be used by state and local welfare agencies.

Each government jurisdiction—federal, state, and local—which authorizes social services funds, does so through an appropriation act. At the federal level, the social services appropriation is a component of the public assistance appropriation. Each state has its social services appropriation, and each city or county in the states which administer and authorize funds for its program has a social services appropriation. This tri-level funding pattern is controlled by Title XX of the Social Security Act and the Federal Social Services Regulations.[19] This is a classic federal/state grant-in-aid program where federal financial participation provides the opportunity and imposes conditions on state and local programs, allowing for state and local flexibility in program design and administration.

Federal regulations specify the kinds, purposes, and FFP rates for social services expenditures under state and local plans. These cover the cost of services provided by state and local agencies directly, such as information and referral and counseling, those provided by other state and local government agencies, by private service organizations, and the costs of administration of the program.

Broadly classified, funds authorized for the program from all sources are applied:

    to provide for the cost of administration and services of state and local welfare agencies allocated to the social services program;

    to provide for the cost of social services provided by other government agencies through transfers of funds;

    to provide for the cost of social services purchased from private organizations;

to provide cash reimbursements to individual beneficiaries for services they obtain directly.

Title XX of the Social Security Act specifies that the Secretary of Health, Education and Welfare place a dollar limitation of the federal share for services for each state for the fiscal year (October 1 to September 30) on the basis of population: the ratio to $2.5 billion as the state's population of the 50 states and the District of Columbia. Each state certifies to the Secretary by October 31 whether and by how much the amount of the limitation is greater or less than the social services amounts needed by the state. To conduct this financial analysis, the state welfare agency costs out its social services plan and applies the rates for FFP to the kind and volume of services planned: 90 percent rate for family planning services, 75 percent for other services. If the limitation exceeds the state's needs, it is reduced and the excess made available up to a maximum of $15 million for Puerto Rico, $5 million for Guam, and $500,000 for the Virgin Islands.

At the outset of each fiscal quarter, funds equaling a fourth of the allotment are transferred by letter of credit from Treasury regional disbursing centers to the state government treasuries to be applied to the program. In state-administered programs, contracts, cash, vouchers for payment of expenses and services and other debits and credits are processed through the social services accounts of the state welfare agency and central treasury accounts in accordance with the state government's accounting and disbursing procedures. When local governments contribute to the cost of the program, transfers of funds from the local revenue authority to the state treasuries are made regularly. In locally administered social services programs, the treasuries of city and county governments are recipients of social services funds from state treasuries. Contracts, cash, and vouchers for payment of expenses and services are recorded in the local welfare agency accounts and controlled in the city or county treasury accounts. As with other federal/state grant-in-aid programs, the federal government's accounting and auditing standards and requirements must be met. Also, social services expenditures do not distinguish the different sources of funds from which they are derived.[20]

Child Welfare Services Program ($480 million)

Funds for this program are derived from federal, state, and local governments, but the proportions are unlike other grant-in-aid programs in that the preponderant financial support is from state and local sources, not the federal government. The latter has limited its appropriation to approximately eight to ten percent of total program costs. The federal child welfare services appropriation is a component of the public assistance appropriation. Funds are distributed to states on a formula basis. Each state receives a uniform grant of $70,000 and an additional grant which varies directly with the child population and inversely with the state's average per capita income.[21] State and local child welfare services funds are appropriated to the state and local social services welfare agencies.

Program funds from the 3 government levels are available for:

> payment for the cost of administration and services of state and local welfare agencies allocated to child welfare services;
>
> payment for the cost of child welfare services provided by other government agencies through transfer of funds;
>
> payment for the cost of child welfare services purchased from private service agencies and child institutions.

To distribute child welfare services funds to state and local welfare agencies, one-fourth of the annual allotment is advanced from the Federal Treasury regional disbursing centers to state treasuries by letter of credit. In state-administered programs, contracts and other obligations as well as vouchers for payment of expenses and services are processed through the child welfare services accounts of the state welfare agency and central Treasury accounts are maintained.

Because the Title XX social services and child welfare services are administered in all but a few states by a single services organization as discussed in Chapter 5, organization, funding, and accounting procedures are followed to maintain the fiscal integrity of the two programs, that is, to assure the two funds are kept separate and reflect accurately separate obligations and charges. State and local welfare directors are obligated to charge against each program's accounts the costs of administration and services to make full use of the federal allotment for each program. For example, temporary placement of an abused child from an AFDC family in a foster care home can appropriately be charged to either services program. The state or local agency may charge the cost to the Title XX program should the placement be made during the last fiscal quarter of the year when the federal allotment for child welfare services may be depleted and the 75 percent FFP matching rate would reduce the cost of the placement to the state or local government.

Medical Assistance Program ($12.8 billion)

The sources of Medicaid funds include the appropriation from three government levels and the cost sharing by individuals and family beneficiaries.* The Federal Medical Assistance appropriation as a category under the public assistance appropriation is subdivided into two categories: *Medical Vendor Payments* to provide grants to reimburse state medicaid agencies for part of the cost of medical vendor payments for health care to public assistance recipients and other medically needy persons and *State and Local Administration* to provide grants to the agencies for part of the cost of administering the program.[22]

State and local government appropriations to the designated medical services agency (the state welfare agency in 41 states; state public health or other health care agency in the other states) provide funds to cover the state share of the cost of the program.

Federal funds are appropriated from general revenues on an open-ended basis. The federal government pays the "Federal Medical Assistance Percentage" (FMAP) of the amount expended by a state as medical assistance. The FMAP ranges from 50 percent to 83 percent based on a formula which takes into consideration the state's per capita income. The federal govern-

*Not in Arizona, which does not have a Medicaid program.

ment also pays 75 percent of the costs of compensating and training skilled professional medical personnel and the staff directly supporting such personnel of public agencies and 50 percent of other necessary administrative costs. States may also claim 50 percent of costs of administration of medicaid benefits to groups, such as general assistance recipients, whose medical care costs under the state plan are wholly met from state funds.

In 33 states the total nonfederal costs of medical assistance payments are met from state funds; in 36, total nonfederal costs of administration are met from state funds; and in other states both state and local funds share in costs of payments and/or administration.[23]

Thirty states claim federal financial participation in administration of state-financed medical assistance payments to general assistance recipients or other persons ineligible for federally matched medicaid payments.

Federal matching is provided for the cost of designing, developing, and installing mechanized claims processing and information retrieval systems at 90 percent and 75 percent for operation of such systems. One-hundred percent federal reimbursement was provided to states for the survey and inspection costs of skilled nursing facilities and intermediate care facilities from October 1, 1972 through July 1, 1974.

Program funds from all sources provide the following:

authorizations for state agencies to pay salaries, personnel benefits, staff training costs, agency contractors, and suppliers of goods and services required to administer the program;

vendor payments to health service providers through fiscal agents or directly by state agencies;

insurance payments to "buy into" the Social Security Administration Medicare Part B (the Federal Supplementary Medical Insurance Trust Fund) for coverage of 65 and over beneficiaries;

premium payments to health maintenance organizations and other prepaid health groups for health services provided by enrolled beneficiaries.

Federal program funds are obtained by state governments quarterly by an advance of funds based upon their estimated need and availability of state funds. Overestimates or underestimates are corrected in subsequent quarterly grant awards. Letters of credit are prepared for each state government. State medicaid agencies issue contracts, obligate administrative funds, and process payment vouchers through their Medicaid accounts and the central Treasury accounts. When local government funds support the program, transfer of funds are arranged regularly from the local revenue authority to the state treasury. In the states where contract fiscal agents are employed to process and control bills from physicians, dentists, hospitals, nursing homes and other providers of health services, vendor medical payment funds are used to cover such payments and their contract fees. In the states where Medicaid agencies administer their own claims processing agency payments are made directly from vendor medical payment funds.

Food Stamp Program ($4.8 billion)

The source of funds for the Food Stamp program includes the three levels of government as well as payments made by some beneficiaries from their own resources for stamp purchases.* The federal Food Stamp appropriation is an open-ended appropriation.[24] It allocates funds separately for the bonus cost of stamps, costs for printing, and distribution of stamps, where 50 percent of the administrative costs are borne by state and local welfare agencies, and a portion of the cost of employment registration and counseling carried out by state employment office and the Department of Labor. A transfer of funds is also authorized to the Department of Agriculture Office of Inspector General for audits and investigations in connection with the program. State and local government appropriations are made to authorize their welfare agencies to meet their share of administrative costs in determining eligibility, controlling, issuing and accounting for food stamps.

*Discontinued with removal of the stamp purchase requirements under the Food Stamp Act of 1977.

Program and administrative Food Stamp funds provide for the following:

> paying the cost of federal administration, including salaries, personnel benefits of Food and Nutrition Service staff, its field staffs and staff of the Office of Inspector General, and contractors and suppliers of goods and services;
>
> paying for printing and distribution of food stamps;
>
> paying for the destruction of redeemed stamps by the Federal Reserve System by transfer of funds;
>
> paying the cost of state and local welfare agencies to administer the program, including their salaries, personnel benefits, staff training costs, travel, agency contractors, and suppliers of goods and services;
>
> paying for food stamps issued;
>
> paying for employment registration and counseling provided by state employment offices and the expenses of the Department of Labor to administer these services. This includes payment of salaries, personnel benefits and other expenses incurred in these activities.

Federal funds for operation and administration of the program by the Food and Nutrition Service is controlled by federal quarterly apportionment and allotment controls and Federal accounting and auditing requirements. Transfers of funds by that service are made quarterly to the Federal Reserve System based upon its estimates of its costs for the processing and destruction of redeemed stamps. Intradepartmental transfer of funds is made by the service to the Office of Inspector General to meet its expenses in conducting investigations and audits of the program. Federal funds are transferred from Treasury regional disbursing centers to state treasuries quarterly by letter of credit based on annual estimates of administrative costs submitted by state and local welfare agencies. These funds are applied to the payment of salaries, personnel benefits, and other costs incurred by the agencies for the program.[25]

Interagency transfers of funds between the Food and Nutrition Service and the Department of Labor are made quarterly to cover costs for employment registration and counseling. Part of these funds are further transferred by the Department of Labor to state employment offices based on estimates of caseloads and costs submitted by these offices. These funds are used to pay their staff's salaries, personnel benefits, and other costs for providing services to food stamp beneficiaries referred to them to obtain manpower training and counseling and to locate jobs.

At the point of use of food stamps, authorized grocery stores accept the stamps as payment for food purchase, and forward them to commercial banks for cash or credit at full face value. The stamps flow upward through the banking system to a Federal Reserve Bank for redemption out of a special account maintained by the U. S. Treasury Department.

Work Incentive Program ($396 million)

The Work Incentive program is funded from federal, state, and local government appropriations with a pronounced different pattern in the use of public welfare funds. Two factors make this so:

1. The dual agency responsibility of training and incentives, administered by the Department of Labor and state manpower agencies, and child care and social services, administered by Department of Health, Education and Welfare and state and local welfare agencies. Federal appropriations for the program are made to the Secretary of Health, Education and Welfare and transfers are made to the Department of Labor for the training and incentives component, about two-thirds of the appropriation. The funds then flow to state and local governments through two channels: manpower and training and public welfare to provide for their respective activities at the FFP rate of 90 percent.

2. State manpower training activities are provided by contract between the Department of Labor and the states. Appropriations made for a fiscal year are charged for these contracts but much of the counseling, training, and job referrals under these contracts do not end with the end of the fiscal year but continue on into the next fiscal year. This applies also to the

child care and social services but to a smaller degree. In accounting terms, the appropriated funds may be obligated and set aside for training activities during the year but some of their costs may actually be expended during the next year. Thus, during a fiscal year period, to plan for and cost out the program, one must analyze the manpower and training costs carried over from the last fiscal year, the costs during the year, and the costs carried over into the next year. The figures for fiscal year 1975 are (in thousands):

	DOL	DHEW	TOTAL
New Budget Authority	$175,000	$105,000	$280,000
Program Cost Funded Prior Years	+124,193	+23,068	+147,261
Program Cost Funded Subsequent Years	−69,861	−0	−69,861
Costs	$229,332	$128,068	$357,400

Federal Work Incentives program funds for child care and supportive social services are allotted by the Public Services Administration to state welfare agencies on the basis of state agency estimates of caseloads and costs, appropriation limits for such services, and the placement performance of state agencies, i.e., the state success rates in job placements of AFDC recipients. State funds—both federal and state shares—are further subdivided to local welfare agencies in those states which have decentralized service units.[26]

Federal manpower and training funds are distributed to state manpower agencies so that 50 percent is allocated on the basis of each state's percentage of registrants during the preceding January and the other 50 percent based on the state's placement performance.

State and local funds are appropriated to the respective manpower and welfare agencies for the 10 percent share of the costs of the program respectively.

Work Incentive program funds are applied as follows:

To pay the cost of state and local welfare agencies expenses to determine WIN eligibility, provide social work counseling, and arrange child care and supportive services to WIN referrals and registrants. This cost includes salaries of WIN employees, personnel benefits, travel, staff training costs, agency contracts for social services and suppliers of goods and services required in the program.

To pay the cost of state manpower agencies for registration of individuals, program orientation, testing, counseling, development of employability plans for each registrant, job referral services, job development, job training, work experience, direct job placement, and followup. The cost includes salaries of WIN employees, of the agencies' separate administrative units, personnel benefits, staff training costs, contracts with local employers, educational and training facilities for on-the-job training, subsidized public service employment, work experience and institutional training and suppliers of goods and services required in the program.

To pay the cost of federal administration of the program by the Department of Labor for overall program development, evaluation, research, and administration. This includes salaries of WIN staff in central and regional offices, personnel benefits, travel, purchase of supplies and equipment, and other administrative expenses.

To pay the cost of allowances to WIN enrollees for work incentives, training-related expenses (lunches and transportation) and relocation assistance.

Federal funds are transferred quarterly to state manpower agencies and state and local welfare agencies by letters of credit from Treasury regional disbursing centers to state treasuries. In state-administered welfare programs and state manpower agencies, contracts and other obligations and disbursements are processed through the accounts of the respective agencies. When local governments contribute to the cost of the welfare program, transfers of funds are made from the local revenue authority to the state's treasury. In locally-administered welfare programs, the treasuries of city and county governments are recipients of advance payments of WIN program funds for child care and social services from state treasuries. The amounts provided are comprised of federal and state funds when state funds also share in the cost of WIN services. Contracts and other obligations and disbursements by the local agency are processed through the agency's accounts.

Federal funds for operation and administration of the WIN program in the Department of Labor are controlled by federal government apportionment and allotment controls and federal accounting and auditing requirements.

Payments of allowances to WIN registrants are made by the state manpower agencies from WIN funds on an individual basis as authorized by WIN staff.[27]

Cuban Refugee Assistance Program ($60 million)

The Cuban Refugee Assistance Program is funded wholly by the federal government through a separate appropriation to D/HEW. Its funds apply primarily in Florida, particularly in Dade County. Some costs are incurred throughout the country by state and local welfare agencies to provide services to needy refugees in their jurisdictions who are not covered by other assistance and services programs.[28] The funds pay for the following:

> program and administrative expenditures incurred by state and local welfare agencies on behalf of Cuban refugees. These include payment of salaries, personnel benefits, and contracts for services to refugees
>
> assistance payments to needy refugees ineligible for other assistance programs
>
> payments to the Dade County, Florida public schools system to cover the cost of educating refugee children
>
> payments to needy refugees to cover the costs of their continuing education, including loans to needy college students
>
> contract payments to voluntary resettlement agencies for reception and resettlement services to newly arriving refugees and for help in resolving their post-resettlement problems, e.g., locating housing, job finding

program and administrative expenses for federal administration primarily to operate the Cuban Refugee Center
in Miami. This covers payment of salaries, personnel
benefits, cost of supplies and equipment, and other administrative expenses.

As with other federal funds, those to operate the Miami
Cuban Refugee Center are controlled by federal quarterly apportionment and allotment controls and federal accounting and
auditing requirements. This applies to their administrative expenses, contracts with voluntary resettlement agencies and payments and educational loans to needy refugees. Federal funds
are transferred to state and local welfare agencies to reimburse
them in full for assistance and services provided refugees on the
basis of regular reports to D/HEW. Such funds are transferred
by Treasury regional disbursing centers to state and local government treasuries. Separate accounts are maintained by state
and local welfare agencies of expenditures on behalf of refugees. Payments to the Dade County Public Schools System for
its services to refugees are made quarterly in advance from
estimates of students and costs submitted to D/HEW.

Repatriated U.S. Nationals Assistance Program ($.9 million)

Federal funds for this program are appropriated as a component
of the Maintenance Assistance category of the Public Assistance
Appropriation.[29] Such funds are applied not only for temporary
assistance payments to repatriated Americans but also to a variety of helping services for them, including transportation, hospitalization, food, lodging, as follows:

    payments to state and local welfare agencies at points of
        entry into the country for expenses incurred for repa-
        triated Americans such as for reimbursements to hospi-
        tals, hotels for temporary food and lodging, payment for
        cost of transportation to their homes;
    payments to repatriated Americans to provide them with
        emergency funds;

payments to Public Health Service hospitals and to Saint Elizabeths Hospital, D.C., to reimburse them for care for repatriated Americans.

Federal payments are made by transfer of funds to state and local welfare agencies and the public health service hospitals by reimbursement on the basis of records of costs of assistance and services, and detailed billings for hospital care on a case-by-case basis. Repayment of costs incurred under the program within a reasonable period is expected of the individual or his estate to the extent of ability to pay.

State and Local Training ($71 million)

Federal funds are appropriated for such training as a component of the Public Assistance Appropriation.[30] State government funds are appropriated for the state share of this federal and state program under the state welfare agency appropriation. Local governments which administer welfare programs appropriate training funds to cover their share of matching funds. Funds from all government levels are applied to cover the following costs:

State and local welfare agencies training costs, including payment of salaries for staff development personnel, personnel benefits, other training costs, such as for arranging seminars and workshops for employees, volunteers, providers of service under contract to the agencies and persons preparing for employment by the agencies, and the costs of educational leave for their employees.

Payments to schools, colleges, and other educational institutions for full- and part-time education of welfare agency employees. These payments may be for curriculum development, classroom instruction, and field instruction.

Stipends paid to welfare agency employees for job-connected educational courses.

Federal funds at the FFP rate of 75 percent are transferred quarterly to state welfare agencies in advance by letter of credit based on annual training plans they submit to D/HEW and quarterly training expenditure reports. The fund transfers are made by Treasury regional disbursing centers to individual state treasuries. State treasuries transfer training funds to local governments which administer their own programs in amounts which include federal and state shares. State and local funds are subject to accounting and disbursement requirements of their respective jurisdictions and must comply with federal regulations for the program. State and local welfare agencies disburse training funds to support their own training activities and to contractor educational institutions, service agencies, and stipends to individual employees.

Social Work Training Projects ($9 million)

This federal appropriation consolidates two separate training authorizations in the Social Security Act: Teaching grants for institutional support of social work education (Section 707) and child welfare education grants to institutions for higher education (Section 426).[31]

Training project funds are applied to meet the costs of:

colleges and universities with approved grants for social work education to compensate faculty, administrative personnel, and to make minor improvements of existing facilities;

student and traineeship stipends and allowances for education in the child welfare field.

Payments of grants are made to grantees on an advance or reimbursement basis from authorizations approved by the Public Services Administration and forwarded for payment by Treasury regional disbursement centers.

Social and Rehabilitation Service Research and Evaluation ($9 million)

Federal funds under this appropriation are subdivided into four categories: research and evaluation in social services, health services, income maintenance, and research and evaluation for

Social Security Administration programs, including Supplemental Security Income, Social Security, and Medicare. The latter category involves a transfer of funds to the Social Security Administration. The appropriation is applied to grants to states and nonprofit organizations and contracts to nonprofit organizations to carry out research and development and to conduct evaluations in the respective program areas.[32] Some grants and contracts are approved subject to the grantee or contractor meeting some of the costs.

The funds cover the following costs:

state and local agencies to carry out research and evaluations under federal grants, including employee salaries, personnel benefits, and other administrative and research costs;

nonprofit organization expenditures to carry out research and evaluations under federal grants or contracts, including employee salaries, personnel benefits, supplies and materials, and overhead costs.

Federal funds are made available in advance to grantees and contractors on the basis of approved cost budgets approved by the Office of Human Development Services, Health Care Financing Administration or Social Security Administration as part of the federal government contract and grant process. Payments are made from the Treasury disbursing centers. Uniform Federal grants and contract regulations, standards, and financial controls apply.

Social and Rehabilitation Service Salaries and Expenses ($64 million)

This federal appropriation applies to the support of the central office and regional office components of the ten D/HEW field office network. Funds are applied to the payment of salaries, personnel benefits, travel expenses, printing and reproduction, purchase of supplies and equipment, communication services, transportation, and other contractual services. Included in the latter are contracts for management services and for planning, evaluation, and systems development activities. Funds are applied to:

> payments to D/HEW departmental employees in headquarters and field offices;
>
> payments to private contractors for services, goods, and assistance provided to D/HEW;
>
> transfer payments to other federal agencies, e.g., General Services Administration for reimbursable services.[33]

Research and Training Activities Overseas (Special Foreign Currency Program) ($3.7 million)

The source of funds for this appropriation derives not from general revenues but from excess foreign currency balances from the sale of surplus agricultural commodities and other sources. The research and training activities are for the most part carried on in foreign countries with excess balances and payments applied to the support of the activities of other government agencies and private organizations, such as research educational institutions. Grants are also made to social welfare research centers for foreign research utilization, information dissemination, and domestic applications.[34] Thus, funds are applied to meet the following costs:

> payrolls, personnel benefits, and training organizations incurred by foreign research and training organizations;
>
> payrolls, personnel benefits, travel, and other expenses incurred by American research and educational institutions carrying out directed social welfare research.

Funds are made available and controlled through the Department of State, American embassies, and the foreign governments involved.

Implications for the Future

The diversity of public welfare funding sources, appropriations, FFP rates, applications of funds described here may be intellectually difficult to retain in all detail, and more difficult to administer, but it does represent national social policy accepted as part of American life. That this social policy is not clearly expressed, is not internally consistent, subject to varying interpretations, with uneven national application, and not universally agreed to, is a characteristic shared by the public welfare funding mechanism.

Welfare reform or improvement must include welfare funding and budgeting. Among the more obvious problem areas to be considered are the following:

> *Compartmented welfare funding.* By compartmentalizing welfare funds in so many different appropriations with different control authorities involving a *potpourri* of agencies and government levels, flexibility in their use is limited.
>
> *Overlapping spending purposes.* By providing different funding sources for the same purpose, for example, to reduce poverty, we have food stamps as well as food allowances in the AFDC family assistance payment and the SSI assistance payment, or for the same type of service, e.g., child care under the social services, child welfare services, or the work incentive programs (not to mention others outside the welfare system), coordination of programs to make best use of funds becomes difficult.
>
> *Different FFP matching rates.* By providing different federal matching ratios in different welfare programs, the temptation exists in administering them to maximize acquisition of federal dollars rather than concentrate on meeting the needs of the individual or family effectively. An example is the practice of terminating General Assistance (locally funded) aid to a family and requiring it to apply for assistance through the federally-matched AFDC program.
>
> *Tri-level funding.* By maintaining a tri-level government funding structure which is interdependent in financial planning and budgeting, dependence upon the rapid flow of caseload, services, and cost data becomes absolutely necessary but the coordinated information systems

for such data has yet to be developed. As we have seen, the federal level depends upon estimates from the states, which in turn depend upon estimates from local welfare agencies. Funding decisions at the top rung (federal and state) about public welfare operations at the bottom rungs (local) are made before hard data from the bottom rungs are processed through to state and federal levels.

Achieving basic welfare reform may well be conditioned by building in practices and requirements which:

reduce the complexities in funding and budgeting;

remove unintentioned but inequitable differences in FFP rates;

provide a simpler, more manageable appropriation structure;

simplify the flow of funds to the ultimate beneficiaries;

develop an information network to provide up-to-date reports and analyses of caseloads, volume of services, and costs;

expand support for evaluative techniques to measure progress in meeting the needs of beneficiaries—current and potential—and learning more of their unmet needs;

provide adequate support for research and analysis of effectiveness and benefits of public welfare programs in reducing the incidence of poverty in this country.

NOTES

1. Social Welfare Expenditures, 1950–1975. *Social Security Bulletin.* January 1976. Social Security Administration. DHEW, Washington, D.C., pp.3–20. Statistical Abstract of the United States, 1975. U.S. Department of Commerce, Bureau of the Census, 96th Annual Edition. Washington, D.C.

2. Ibid.

3. Ibid.

4. Title XX Social Services for Individuals and Families Regulations, 40 CFR 72 April 14, 1975.

5. Twenty states provide for biennial fiscal periods; all others and the federal government are for one year. The time periods covered by the fiscal year vary: The federal government in 1976 converted from the year beginning July 1 to the following June 30 to the year from October 1 to the following September 30 (Congressional Budget and Impoundment Control Act of 1974 P.L. 93-344). All but three states (New York, April 1–March 31; Alabama, October 1–September 30; Texas, September 1–August 31) maintain the fiscal year on the former basis July 1–June 30. For states with biennial fiscal periods, the beginning dates are July 1 and June 30 of the second year.

6. Prior to fiscal year 1977, the federal budget period was July 1–June 30. The dates were changed primarily because the Congress failed consistently to complete the appropriation process before July 1. Each year, as

July 1 neared, Congress passed and the President signed laws, known as "Joint Resolutions" which authorized continuation of the previous year's spending levels to permit federal departments and agencies to continue operations into the next fiscal year legally until the appropriations were approved. This created many problems for the Congress, the federal agencies, state, and local governments as well. Spindler, A. The way your money is controlled under a continuing resolution. *Human Needs* 1973, 1(8), 9–13.

7. Council of State Governments: Budgetary processes in the states. July 1975, Lexington, Kentucky.

8. The 1975 Budget of the United States Government, Appendix, p. 440–441.

9. The Social Security Act, as amended, Sec. 1119.

10. Handbook of public income transfer programs. Studies in Public Welfare Paper No. 2, Subcommittee on Fiscal Policy, Joint Economic Committee, U.S. Congress, October 16, 1972. U.S. Government Printing Office, Washington, D.C., pp. 136.

11. Ibid, pp. 137–138.

12. Federal Management Circular 74-7, Uniform Administrative Requirements for Grants-In-Aid to State and Local Governments, General Services Administration, September 13, 1974, as amended.

13. Maintenance assistance for aged, blind, and disabled recipients in Guam, Puerto Rico, and the Virgin Islands under Title I, X, and XIV of the Social Security Act is continued under the Public Law P.L. 92-603 setting up the Supplemental Security Income program. The flow of funds for assistance payments and administration in these three jurisdictions follows essentially the pattern descriptive of the AFDC program. Two categories of the federal appropriation *Maintenance Assistance* apply: Adult Categories Assistance and State and Local Administration. The former provides grants to reimburse the three jurisdictions' welfare agencies for part of the cost of cash payments to aged, blind, and disabled recipients; the latter to reimburse the welfare agencies for part of the cost of administration for maintenance assistance to these adult recipients.

14. The 1976 Appropriation Hearings on the SSI appropriation request Departments of HEW and Labor, House Appropriations Committee, Subcommittee on the Departments of Labor and Health, Education and Welfare, Part IV 94th Congress; First Session, U.S. Government Printing Office, Washington, D.C., 1976.

15. The law authorizing the SSI program included a "hold harmless" provision to the effect that states would not incur costs in excess of those incurred in 1972 for assistance payments to the aged, blind, and disabled, unless the state chooses to do so.

16. Ibid, The 1976 Appropriation Hearings on the SSI appropriation request, pp. 328.

17. Ibid, The 1976 Appropriation Hearings, pp. 399.

18. Ibid, Handbook of Public Income Transfer Programs, p. 329.

19. Title 45-Public Welfare, Chapter II, Part 228 Social Services programs for Individuals and Families: Title XX of the Social Security Act (Federal Register) Vol. 40, No. 125, Dated June 27, 1975.

20. Ibid, The 1976 Appropriation Hearings on Social Services, pp. 86–88.

21. Ibid, The 1976 Appropriation Hearings on Child Welfare Services, pp. 92–93.

22. Ibid, The 1976 House Appropriation Hearings on Medical Assistance, pp. 80–81.

23. Ibid, Handbook of Public Income Transfer Programs, p. 200.

24. The 1976 Appropriation Hearings on the Food and Nutrition Service, Department of Agriculture, Subcommittee on Agriculture and Related Agencies, House Appropriations Committee Part 4. U.S. Government Printing Office, Washington, D.C., p. 826.

25. Ibid, The 1976 Appropriations Hearings on the Food and Nutrition Service, pp. 86.

26. Ibid, The 1976 House Appropriation Hearings on the WIN program, pp. 128–171.

27. Ibid, The 1976 House Appropriation Hearings on the WIN program, pp. 144–171.

28. The 1976 Budget of the United States Government Appendix, the Cuban Refugee Assistance program, pp. 447–448.

29. The 1976 Budget of the United States Government Appendix, the SRS Maintenance Assistance program, pp. 440–441.

30. Ibid, The 1976 Budget of the United States Government Appendix, the SRS Maintenance Assistance program. pp. 72–79.

31. The 1976 Budget of the United States Government Appendix, the SRS Social Work Training budget estimate, pp. 442.

32. The 1976 Budget of the United States Government Appendix, the SRS Research and Evaluation budget estimate, p. 444.

33. The 1976 Budget of the United States Government Appendix, the SRS Salaries and Expenses budget request, p. 444.

34. The 1976 Budget of the United States Government Appendix, the SRS Research and Training Activities (Overseas) budget request, p. 444.

Chapter 8

PUBLIC WELFARE METHODS

Public welfare methods and processes are the daily actualities of public welfare policies, laws, and programs. They mirror the foibles, characteristics, strengths, and weaknesses of those same policies, laws, and programs and of the people who are of the system itself. They are complex, not always consistent or coordinated, subject to interpretation, bias, and error, applied differently in different circumstances and in different jurisdictions, often lacking equity, with varying degrees of efficiency and effectiveness.

Public welfare methods are criticized as "excessive red tape," a "flood of paperwork" and other labels of opprobrium.

> One result of these myriad eligibility requirements and program complexities is such a voluminous collection of manuals and supplementary directives that it is wholly unreasonable to expect staff at any level to keep abreast and to apply all of them properly with any degree of consistency . . .

> R. B. Shelton, Director, Wayne County
> Department of Social Sciences,
> Detroit, Michigan

The huge volume of rules, regulations, forms and paperwork involved in public welfare administration reflects the complexity of
payment policies and procedures. Local welfare agencies are supposed to follow directives which may fill a bookshelf 4 feet wide.
Recipients cannot keep up with the multitude of ever-changing
rules, and neither can caseworkers. To process one welfare applicant in Atlanta requires as many as 27 different forms; Detroit food
stamp workers are responsible for using 40 different forms. The
complicated forms necessitated by intricate eligibility requirements lead to inaccurate information and, as a Detroit caseworker
suggested, "entice borderline fraud cases to take advantage". In
addition, a welfare agency may keep several sets of records for the
same recipient. In New York, for example, the eligibility investigation section has one case folder, income maintenance has a second, social services a third, medicaid another, and food stamps yet
another.[1]

These criticisms are symptoms of dissatisfaction of our society to the management of the governmental mechanism it
created. Government laws have not provided a uniform definition of the persons entitled by need to government welfare
benefits, nor defined the social goals of independence and self-
sufficiency, nor established uniform, consistent eligibility requirements. The results are the present large bureaucracies with
large staffs, complex organizations, and volumes of welfare rules
and regulations. These spell out how the system applies to the
limitless spectrum of human conditions, when the combination
of conditions makes persons legally eligible for help, the kinds
and amounts of help the system is able to provide, with whose
funds, and how such help can be expected to result in independence and self-sufficiency. The system requires that an individual provide at first contact enough verifiable and verified
personal, family, and economic information to meet its eligibility requirements and provide from that point on information
about changes in his and his family's relations and economic
status. This is subject to close examination by the official agency
to check that (1) his eligibility remains unchanged and (2) the
help he is receiving is beneficial to his progress towards independence and self-sufficiency.

The interposition of government in the personal affairs of so many millions requires a lawful record of the initial contacts, the verifications to determine eligibility, and a continuing record of that relationship, producing information on the individual and his family, the basis for his continued eligibility, and the government's actions throughout the period of eligibility, often spanning many years if not a lifetime of agency/beneficiary relationship. Also, a large bureaucracy makes its own demand upon the public welfare system; the multiplicity of government jurisdictions, the thousands of public offices, community agencies, business suppliers, service and financial institutions of almost every type and size determine the methods applied in the system. They must direct, plan, supervise, coordinate, staff, fund, maintain, monitor, analyze, and report their activities regularly to function. The methods of public and business administration in all their sophistication, cost, and complexity apply to the public welfare system no differently from any other large-scale enterprise. Every office, institution, or other place of business in the public welfare system devotes a substantial proportion of time, energy, and attention to matters of administration and organizational relationships. In addition, the public welfare system applies methods unique to its societal role. They can be grouped logically into 5 categories:

1. Methods to establish and maintain the proper legal status of public welfare programs to enable agencies and programs to organize and use governmental funds to administer welfare services and activities.

2. Methods to learn more about the needs of the target populations of low-income and disadvantaged persons for assistance and services, the extent to which their needs are being met, and measures to inform them of the help they can receive through the system.

3. Methods to determine the eligibility (entitlement) of individuals and families for assistance and/or services provided by the system.

4. Assistance payments and services methods.

5.   Methods of accountability to assure that the laws, regulations, and goals of the public welfare system are met.

METHODS FOR PROGRAM LEGALITY

Our constitutional system of government by law requires every federal, state, and local public program to have a legal basis, an "organic" act, e.g., the Social Security Act, or a state or local government public welfare law, to define its public purpose and activities, to place responsibility upon a government agency for its administration, to give it authority to act, to define how it exercises its authority, to limit its authority, to authorize appropriations of public funds for its administration, and to hold it accountable for its actions. The constitutional provisions for enactment of laws by legislative and executive branches and judicial review processes apply equally to public welfare programs.

The federal and state grant-in-aid concept which governs most public welfare programs, described in Chapter 1, is the single most important controlling feature in determining the methods of public welfare programs, starting with the federal requirement that state agencies prepare plans describing how its programs meet federal requirements. An ever-expanding substantial body of laws, regulations, and judicial decisions and precedents covers the "who," "what," "when," "where," and "how" of this intergovernmental process.

Despite the de facto superior position of the federal government in dictating requirements, methods, processes, and standards of state and local welfare programs as conditions for FFP, the clearly expressed constitutional position of state supremacy prevails, as discussed in Chapter 1. State governments do decide whether and to what extent they are to provide for a public welfare program; what groups of individuals are eligible; which state agencies should administer the program; how the program should be organized; what state and local funds should be provided and from what revenue sources; what methods and processes should be used; how large the agency and programs should be and which state officials are to set policies and be held accountable.

Methods for Target Population Coverage

Demographic Analysis

The Decennial Censuses of Population, current population surveys, and special demographic analyses of the U.S. Bureau of Census are used extensively in poverty analyses, that is, to show the number and distribution of low-income individuals and families as shown in Chapter 2.[2] Other sources for low income population analyses are the Labor Department's Bureau of Labor Statistics data on urban family budgets for a family of four and the monthly Consumer Price Index. These are supplemented by state and local government-sponsored demographic studies and others published by research organizations, such as, the National Academy of Sciences, Brookings Institution, and the Urban Institute.

The National Center for Social Statistics produced periodically AFDC characteristics studies applying statistical sampling techniques to the data on AFDC caseloads. The Center also published characteristics studies of aged, blind, and disabled recipients but discontinued them when the SSI program replaced the federal/state adult category programs.

The National Center for Health Statistics of the Health Resources Administration publishes a series on health status and disability from its sample surveys. Periodically, state and local welfare agencies produce poverty population sample surveys for use in planning, forecasting, and budgeting of their AFDC and General Assistance programs. These become the basis of their budget estimates and AFDC caseload forecasts submitted to D/HEW as claims for federal reimbursement as described in Chapter 7, Funding and Budgeting.

Reliable welfare caseload estimates are difficult to make because state eligibility criteria vary as to such factors as income levels, inclusions and exclusions of family income, asset ownership, definition of disability and employability, and family and household composition. Each jurisdiction's trends in housing, economic conditions, family income, social mobility, and other population characteristics must be considered. Caseload forecasts are usually made from the month-by-month analysis of the trends in caseloads, the number of applicants, the reasons for application, applicants' socioeconomic status, the number of newly-approved applications, the number of cases closed, and the reasons for closings. Especially significant in such analyses is the proportion of families receiving assistance to all low-income poverty families by size of family and the dollar gap between the state's needs standards and payment levels to the poverty level.

Studies of the proportions of poor and disadvantaged persons who are potentially eligible for social, medical, employment training and food stamp programs are more difficult to make than forecasts of payments programs because of the additional factors which must be considered: (1) in social services, the Title XX program does not limit services to low-income persons and families but include for certain services those within 80 percent of a state's median family income and up to 115 percent of median family income for other services; (2) in Medicaid, the medically needy who are not cash recipients are eligible for services in most states according to the states' income and resources criteria; (3) in the WIN program, the employability potential of AFDC recipients must be determined in the provision of training and employment services; and (4) in the food stamp program, persons who may be above the poverty level are eligible to receive food stamps after reducing specified living and employment expenses. For all these programs, forecasting the number of eligibles must take into account not only income levels but also address the question of the actual needs of individuals or families for a given type of social, health, employment training service, or food stamps.

An illustration of the complexity of this problem may be seen in the Early and Periodic Screening, Diagnosis, and Treatment of Eligible Individuals under 21 (EPSDT program under Medicaid). The Federal Medicaid Manual[3] states:

Implementation of the regulation (for the EPSDT program) will necessitate an examination of the extent of the screening services needed by the young Medicaid population. Within any given population, individuals will differ greatly in their need for health care and medical services. Among children, some may never have seen a physician, and no assessment has been made of the state of health. These children should be drawn into a screening process to be followed by diagnosis and treatment, as necessary. Other children have apparent or obvious health problems but are not receiving treatment. They may need more definitive diagnostic studies and subsequent treatment, but screening might be unnecessary. Other young Medicaid recipients may already be receiving preventive and health assessment services in child health clinics or may be under the care of health practitioners. For this group it may be necessary only to make certain that an assessment of their complete health status has been made, and they are receiving the needed care.

To make caseload forecasts for planning purposes in the Title XX social services program, state and local welfare agencies have turned to such analytical techniques as surveys of neighborhood and private agencies, estimates of their clientele's needs for specified services, and special mail and personal interview questionnaire studies. To quote one state agency's experience in 1976[4]:

> In an effort to obtain data regarding human service needs beyond the information available through its direct service operations, the Office of Program Planning and Evaluation of the Maryland Department of Human Resources initiated a survey effort requesting information from 22 purchase of service vendors and 15 related service agencies, including State, regional, and local planning organizations . . .
>
> Data was requested regarding problem areas as seen by the various agencies, estimated number with problems, services to address needs, the estimated number serviced, the estimated number still in need, and the geographic area of the service needs. Responses with varying degrees of completeness were received as of June 6, 1975 from 16 vendors and 7 related agencies. Several agencies . . . could only provide partial responses . . . This analysis substantiates that human service planning is limited by the lack of a comprehensive viable needs assessment capability.

It is obvious the needs assessment techniques in public welfare are largely undeveloped. Survey research in this field is a significant untapped area.

Outreach Activities

Historically, public welfare programs have not conducted large-scale systematic efforts to publicize their benefits to encourage individuals and families to apply. The Social Security Act does not mandate programs of "outreach" as a federal requirement in income maintenance and social and medical services programs, nor have states and local governments done so, mostly for pragmatic financial reasons of greater costs which outreach brings. However, they do have public information programs designed to provide general information about the programs and how individuals may apply for benefits, directed to low-income and disadvantaged groups. Where there are substantial numbers of non-English-speaking people, information materials are published in the native languages. Much of the outreach activities came about through the community action programs of the Office of Economic Opportunity in the 1960s. The dramatic growth in welfare programs during the 1960s and 1970s is attributed to the success of their efforts.

Special outreach programs are in operation in the food stamp program, the EPSDT program under Medicaid, the child welfare services program and adult protective services; the latter two for the benefit of neglected, abandoned, abused children and helpless adults requiring assistance for their protection. The EPSDT program requires states to inform all AFDC families in writing at initial eligibility and each year thereafter of the broad range of services to children with instructions on how and where to receive services at no cost to them. It also provides a penalty of a reduction of one percent of their federal Medicaid reimbursements if they fail to do so.

In 1971, the Food Stamp program was amended to provide that states must take effective action "to inform low-income households about the program" and must "insure the participation" of eligible individuals.

In 1974, the Social Security Administration organized a national outreach program to encourage aged, blind, and disabled persons to apply for SSI benefits. During the early months of the program, it became evident that far fewer potentially eligible persons were applying than national data indicated. Special mailings were made and a massive publicity campaign was organized to reach former recipients of state programs who had failed to apply.

For other public welfare programs existing prior to the 1960s, the widely prevalent, implicit assumption was (and is) that (1) welfare benefits and programs are known generally to low-income and disadvantaged persons; (2) they apply to welfare agencies for assistance and services when they are in need; (3) they do not require outreach efforts of the agencies to inform them of their entitlement; (4) they should be encouraged to help themselves socially and economically without the intervention of government; and (5) as public policy, the growing financial burden of welfare programs should not be increased by caseloads expanded through outreach activities.

Outreach methods provide an organized publicity campaign of leaflets, pamphlets, and radio and television coverage targeted to low-income and disadvantaged persons and their neighborhoods. They may also call for employment of special paid and volunteer outreach workers, usually of former welfare recipients or other low-income persons to contact low-income individuals in their homes, patrol low-income neighborhoods or rural areas, locate and interview potential eligibles, organize group meetings where eligibility conditions are explained and applications for assistance and services are processed. Such workers may escort potential eligibles to the nearest welfare intake offices and give assistance in preparing applications. Special intake offices in low-income areas may be opened and staffed by agency workers during the business day, evenings, and weekends. These and other activities were the methods employed by community action agencies and continue to date. State and local welfare agencies also assign eligibility and social service workers to store front offices, churches, neighborhood centers, and other low-income locations to provide information and referral and eligibility determination services.

METHODS FOR INDIVIDUAL AND FAMILY BENEFICIARY ENTITLEMENT

The Intake Process

The intake process is the set of methods, paperwork, procedures, and contacts between the individual applicant and the welfare or social security agency for the purpose of providing him with information, establishing his eligibility for assistance and/or services, or, if ineligible, referring him to another public or private agency to obtain help. The initial point of contact in the intake process need not be in a welfare or social security agency office. It may be by mail inquiry, an application mailed to the agency or in the applicant's home if he is disabled and unable to travel to the agency office or institution. It need not require a person-to-person contact or interview between applicant and agency worker. For a disabled applicant unable to represent himself, a family member may apply in his behalf, or if there is no family member, a neighbor, friend, or other responsible individual acting for the applicant may represent him. The applicant may be assisted if he desires by an individual of his choice (who need not be a lawyer) in the various aspects of the application process and may be accompanied by him in followup contacts with the agency connected with his disability.[5]

The Application Form

The official applicant/agency relationship is initiated by a completed and signed application form. It serves 4 distinct uses:

1. It requests personal details about the applicant and each individual family member, the family's legal relationships, race, financial needs, income sources, work experience, education, housing conditions, eating practices, kinds and value of family assets, health and life insurance (even as to the future: potential family resources from insurance claims, inheritance, tax refund, back pay, and the details of family burial plans). The details in applications may vary among the different income maintenance and services programs, depending upon the eligibility factors involved in each program. For a blind or disabled

applicant for the SSI program, a Medical History and Disability Report Form requires him to give the details about his condition, its diagnosis and treatment. Food stamp applicants who are not receiving assistance payments are required to complete an application form designed for that program with personal, family, economic, housing, employment, and other details to determine eligibility.

2.   It requires certification by the applicant of the completeness, accuracy, and truthfulness of the information:

> I understand that all the information I give must be complete and accurate. I understand that under the law, withholding facts or giving false information for the purpose of obtaining assistance is punishable by fine, imprisonment, or both.
>
> Under penalty of perjury I declare, that to the best of my knowledge and belief, the information on this application for financial assistance and on any and all supplements thereto is true, correct and complete. I understand that I may be asked to bring in proof of these statements, or that a representative of the Department may get in touch with me or visit my home to request such proof.
>
> I will report promptly any changes in my income, resources, family members, needs, or change of address . . .

3.   It informs the applicant of his rights to a fair hearing and to obtain legal counsel if he is not satisfied with the agency decision.

4.   It may be used as an application for several welfare programs simultaneously (assistance payments, food stamps, medicaid, and social services) for which the applicant would also be eligible.

The applicant is requested to provide birth certificates, financial records, and an assortment of evidentiary documents to enable the agency to verify the information on the application. The variety of such documentation is illustrated by an information sheet "to Apply for Assistance" given to each applicant at time of application to the Burien Local Office, King County Regional Office, Washington State Department of Social and Health Services (Figure 8.1).[6]

Most applicants will not have assembled all the information at time of the first interview. The eligibility worker will offer

1. Sign in with the receptionist each time you come in to the office.
2. Plan to be here for several hours.
3. Bring the following with you:

Verification of Personal I.D. . . . . such as . . . birth or baptism certificate; divorce decree; valid driver's license; immigration or citizenship papers; passport; military I.D.
This is needed for all household members applying for assistance.

Verification of current address . . such as . . . rent receipt; lease or mortgage papers; current utility bills; current tax statement; house payment records

If you have . . .   *Bring In . . .*

Savings account . . . . passbook

checking account . . . . latest bank statement and check book

insurance policy(s) . . . . policy(s) or name of company and policy number(s)

stocks, bonds, marketable
securities, sales contracts,
or real estate . . . . proof of ownership and value

automobiles and other
vehicles . . . . registration or title

If you are working part/time or
full/time . . . . current pay stubs

If you receive money from Social
Security, retirement, Veterans,
Military allotments, Labor and
Industries . . . . award letter or last check

Unemployment Compensation . . . . U.C. booklet

Child Support . . . . proof of amount ordered and received

All other monies you receive . . . . proof of source and amount

If you are pregnant . . . . you will need verification of this from your doctor

If you cannot work for medical
reasons . . . . you will need a doctor's statement to this effect

If you are able to work . . . . you will need (1) proof that you have registered for work at Washington State Employment Service within the last 30 days
(2) proof of Unemployment Compensation benefit status

A reminder: Please complete all forms carefully and in ink. Answer all questions on the forms.
If you have any questions about completing the forms, please ask the receptionist.

Figure 8.1 To Apply for Assistance

advice on how to obtain the necessary documentation. All but a few well-organized Americans of any income level would have this same problem. Multiple interviews with the applicant are usually required.

Verification

The information is verified by eligibility workers by review of the documents provided and by home visits, telephone inquiries, inquiries of other official agencies, banks, public utilities, and other investigative techniques when verified documents are not available or raise questions of veracity, such as questionable home addresses, employment history, and family relationships. By count, more than 100 individual decisions are made in processing each application.

This process is expected to be completed promptly within a 45-day period for nondisability cases (and 60 days for disability cases) according to federal regulations, and the receipt of assistance payments is computed retroactively from the date of application. However, state and local welfare agencies have not been uniformly successful in meeting the 45-day rule, particularly with the added emphasis on quality control for reduction in errors in the intake process as is discussed later in this chapter. Delays in an eligibility decision may be caused by eligibility worker staff shortages, cumbersome procedures, failure of the applicant to provide verifiable information, delays caused by an examining physician, or an emergency not controlled by the agency.

THE SIMPLIFIED METHOD.   To correct this chronic inefficient, slow, and cumbersome process, D/HEW attempted in 1970 to moderate the requirements for verification by imposing a federal regulation that state and local agencies adopt the "simplified method" for aged, blind, and disabled applicants for the so-called adult category payments programs and to permit states the option of adopting it for the AFDC and Medicaid programs. This method relied almost wholly on a written self-declaration by the applicant as to the truth, completeness, and accuracy of his application. Verification of information was made only when the applicant's statements were incomplete, unclear, or inconsistent, or where other circumstances in the particular case would indicate to a prudent person that further inquiry should be made. Various difficulties arose, such as the large numbers of illiterate applicants and the difficulty eligibility workers had in reconciling inconsistent applicant information without substantial rechecking and—the most devastating objection—that the method contributed to errors and fraud. The "simplified method" was discontinued in August, 1973.[7]

The Application Procedures

The agency records generated by the application are the case control and management tools for the intake process. Different programs and jurisdictions may use different control methods but they basically serve the same purposes to record verification actions, findings, and dates for completion of the verification procedure, to locate files, to manage the process, and to prepare monthly reports of applications processing and decisions. The following is a description of the documentation and reporting in the Hennepin County (Minnesota) Welfare Department[8]:

> Basic responsibility for monitoring the progress of each case in the Hennepin intake system resides with the assigned Eligibility Technician (ET). Each ET has an individual system for keeping track of a case. Most use a card file or a spiral binder with a card or page for each case. They record the basic case information such as case number, home address, children, children's father, birthdates, etc. In addition, they might include critical milestones in the intake progress of the case with space available to record the date when each milestone is reached. Milestones include the first interview date, dates of major verification steps completed, date of Board action, date of transfer to case maintenance, and the name of the assigned case maintenance ET.
>
> For Intake Section overall management purposes, the transfer clerk maintains a file of cards which represents pending applications. This file, plus additions to it which represent new applications and the removed cards which represent disposed-of applications, is used for monthly reporting purposes. The clerk is able to prepare a report of section activity using the file and the cards pulled ... Because the card file is updated daily, it also provides an up-to-date reference concerning pending applications.

Unit supervisors use the monthly reports to reinforce their observations regarding which ETs are most productive, the size and average number of days pending of the application backlog, whether the various supervisory units are adequately sharing the new case workload, and the rates of application denial and withdrawal.

Information kept on the cards can also be used to generate additional reports or to check the information compiled in other reports. Periodically the file is used to prepare a "sixty-day list," a list of those cases not yet disposed of which have been on file for two months. The list is used to encourage ETs to remind applicants to submit missing verification documentation or to close the application. Other clerks collect additional data for monthly reports . . .

Confidentiality of Public Welfare Records

The Social Security Act expresses a broad social policy to protect the individual applicant and recipient from disclosure of the information he supplies to the government or his status as applicant or recipient. Types of information protected include:

names and addresses of applicants and recipients;

amounts of financial assistance provided;

information related to the social and economic conditions or circumstances of a particular individual;

agency evaluation of information about a particular individual;

medical data, including diagnosis and past history of disease or disability concerning an individual.

This protection takes the form of legal sanctions which all governments—federal, state, local—apply uniformly in the administration of welfare programs to the release of its welfare records. Such sanctions require enforcement of safeguards to the use or disclosure of such information only for purposes directly connected with the administration of programs, prohibit the publication of lists of names of applicants or recipients, and inform applicants or recipients that information about themselves may be disclosed to public officials who require it in connection with their official duties. However, mailing or distribution lists of applicants or recipients may be supplied for distribution of materials in the immediate interest of their health and welfare, such as announcements of free medical examinations, availability of surplus foods, and consumer protection information.

The release of information is considered legally permissible pursuant to a subpoena for the case record or for any agency representative to testify concerning an applicant or recipient in judicial proceedings related to welfare fraud, child support, child custody, conservatorship, guardianship, dependency, and juvenile court matters.[9]

Personal Identification

Different methods are used to identify applicants and recipients in maintaining records and processing actions of individuals, providing them official identification in cashing checks, to receive services, health care, food stamps, and other entitlements. Personal identification is also useful in cutting down on fraud for the protection of banks and businesses cashing checks and to service providers when individuals claim services or food stamps. A person's social security number is the primary mode of identification appearing in all agency case records. Applicants without social security numbers for themselves and family members are required to apply for them.

The use of photo-identification cards by recipients is another widely used method. A card is issued at time eligibility is granted. In some jurisdictions, to limit costs, cards are not issued to persons deemed capable of cashing their own checks.[10]

Under the food stamp program, eligibles receive an authorization card from welfare agencies.

Disability Determinations

Persons applying for eligibility to AFDC, Medicaid, SSI, and other welfare programs on the basis of blindness and/or disability are required to undergo a process of medical screening and, if necessary, a physical examination and review by an agency socio-medical team. The process for Medicaid eligibility is carried on by the state Medicaid agency, for SSI eligibility by the Disability Determinations Unit of the State vocational rehabilitation agency, for AFDC and General Assistance eligibility by the state or local welfare agency. The prevailing definition for blindness in most jurisdictions is that for the SSI program: "a person is considered blind if the vision in his better eye is 20/200 or less with the use of a correcting lens, or if he suffers from tunnel vision to the extent that his field of vision is no greater than 20 degrees.[11]

Disability is defined in Section 1614 a) 3) of the Social Security Act as "an inability to engage in any substantial gainful activity by reason of any medically-determinable physical or mental impairment which can be expected to last for a continuous period of not less than 12 months." Chronic alcoholism and drug addiction confirmed by medical findings are deemed to be disabling. Persons so judged are eligible for SSI payments if they undergo treatment of their condition at an approved facility.

The same definitions are applied for Medicaid eligibles, unless the state Medicaid plan, prior to SSI, defined blindness and disability more broadly.

Blindness or disability criteria under state or local General Assistance programs are not necessarily the same as for other programs, because GA programs provide temporary short-term assistance and services to persons with partial nonpermanent conditions. Applicants for AFDC assistance who claim eligibility because of illness or incapacity are required to undergo a physical examination. The results of such examination and an accompanying social report relating the disability or incapacity to employment of the head of household are submitted to the state or local welfare agency medical review team, comprised usually of a physician, social worker, and other professional personnel. A physical examination is not necessary when the applicant supplies the results of a recent physical or mental examination to support the claim of incapacity.

Under state Medicaid programs, an applicant for blindness submits to an examination by a physician skilled in eye diseases or by an optometrist selected by the applicant. No examination is required, of course, when both eyes are missing. The eye examination report is reviewed by the state agency's consultant ophthalmologist who makes the final eligibility decision. A disability applicant also must submit to a physical examination by a physician unless he supplies the results of a recent one. His medical report and social history are reviewed and acted upon by an agency disability determination team comprised of a physician, social worker, and other professionals. To receive eligibility approval, the medical report is required to show a substantiated diagnosis of permanent and total disability and social history information to relate the disability to the nonemployability of the applicant.

Under the SSI program, blindness and disability applicants are referred by the Social Security district or branch office at time of application to the nearest vocational rehabilitation agency Disability Determinations Unit. That unit, staffed with medical, rehabilitation, social, and other professionals, arranges for physical and/or mental examinations and completes a two-part review of each case; first, to establish whether the degree of blindness or disability falls within the respective legal definitions of eligibility for assistance and second, whether the individual is able to benefit from vocational rehabilitative services provided by that agency.

Presumptive and Emergency Eligibility

To reconcile the immediate, usually urgent, needs of individual applicants with the processing time needed to determine eligibility, the concept of "presumptive eligibility" is employed in the SSI and food stamp program. In the former, benefits not exceeding $100 (or $195 for a couple) are given to a presumptively eligible applicant faced with a financial emergency. Monthly payments not to exceed three months may also be made to presumptively disabled applicants otherwise eligible prior to the determination of disability.[12] In the food stamp program, a household is deemed presumptively eligible for up to 30 days if it reports little or no income, and, on the basis of other information, appears to be eligible.

Although these are the only public welfare programs which

provide assistance in advance of formal eligibility, other emergency aid methods are applied to meet an individual's prompt
needs. The Title XX social services program allows delivery of
services under emergency conditions with eligibility established
within five working days, rather than the 45 days normally required to process eligibility for social services.[13] Emergency
assistance for up to 30 days to needy families with children,
including migrant families, is provided for in the form of cash
payments and services to help the family cope with a crisis situation, particularly in the threat it represents to the destitution of
children. Food stamps are given in a temporary, emergency
situation to victims of disasters for up to 30 days. Eligibility for
an emergency food coupon allotment under the food stamp
program is determined at the disaster location on the basis of
immediate need for food assistance, the lack of funds to purchase food, and the breakdown of normal channels of food
distribution. Retroactive coverage of medical services is provided to Medicaid applicants who were otherwise eligible when
such services were received for up to three months prior to their
application.[14] Emergency assistance and services are also given
to Cuban refugees and repatriated U.S. nationals returning destitute or mentally ill from overseas.

Redetermination of Eligibility

An eligible individual household or family continues in an eligibility status for assistance payments and/or services under public welfare programs without a specified time limit, except for
the SSI and food stamp programs. In the SSI program, eligibility
continues for each quarter only. However, if the initial application is made in the second or third month of the quarter, eligibility is on a monthly basis for that quarter. In the food stamp
program, certification (eligibility) periods vary. For public assistance recipients (AFDC, GA, and SSI), the period coincides with
their payment eligibility. Other households are assigned three-
month certification periods based on predictability of income.
When frequent changes in income are likely, certification may be
less than three months. If there is little likelihood of change in
household status, the period may be for six months. In

households of unemployable persons and in otherwise stable circumstances, food stamp certification may be given for 12 months. Households deriving their income from self-employment, farm operations, or farm employment may be certified for 12 months.[15]

Eligible beneficiaries for assistance, social, and medical services are subject to a review of eligibility to determine whether their personal, social, and economic factors of need remain unchanged. This review entails examination of the individual or family case file by an eligibility worker and search for changes in family composition, residence, resources, or other eligibility factors and, if indicated, a recalculation of benefit need and payment amount. A review is made within 30 days from the time when the agency obtains information about a change in the individual household or family's circumstances which may affect his or their eligibility. Otherwise, a review is made not less frequently than every six months for AFDC eligibility and every 12 months for the Title XX social services and Medicaid programs. Continued eligibility for the WIN program is, of course, dependent upon AFDC eligibility.

Review of eligibility for the GA program is usually a process of determining the continued need of the individual or family for the emergency short-term or one-time assistance provided.

Under the SSI program, redeterminations are made by computerized means, i.e., a tape file called SSR (Supplemental Security Record) containing the basic data on income, living arrangements, and other characteristics to establish an individual's eligibility and compute his benefit amount. Changes in earned and unearned income, resources, payment amounts, and residential mobility are processed through the SSR tape file and the computer is programmed to detect ineligibles and make redeterminations automatically.

Recertification of food stamp eligibility of assistance payments beneficiaries is carried out as part of the redetermination process of state and local welfare agencies. Recertification of other households is made by a system of sampling under the Food and Nutrition Service quality control program.

DELIVERY MECHANISMS

Public welfare program methods to serve individuals are contradictory at one and the same time: often flexible to meet individual needs, at times inflexible in procedural requirements; sometimes imposed on the individual, often the epitome of reasonableness to provide aid or service; at times unresponsive to a personal inquiry for help due to a technicality, often giving essential, urgent service when help is neither requested nor its need recognized; at times unable to meet needs because of budget restraints, often sensitive to changing individual needs; at times intractable despite obvious need for aid or service because of organizational rigidities.

The program methods with these varied characteristics dictate how the amounts of assistance checks are determined; when and under what circumstances cash payments are made; when, where, and how social and medical services are provided; how food stamps are obtained; in what amounts; how they are exchanged in food purchases; the kinds of job training and job finding methods employed; and the special rehabilitative services rendered to Cuban Refugees and repatriated U.S. nationals.

There are many reasons for the contradictions: the programs are not designed to serve the needs of *all* Americans at all times without regard to their social and economic status or even to serve all of the needs of low-income Americans. Rather, as has been described in earlier chapters, public welfare programs serve some low-income populations who qualify individually as eligibles for benefits and services specified in different programs with different historical roots. The factors of size (the large numbers and diversity of beneficiaries and agency staffs), the geographic spread of the programs to every city, town, village, hamlet, and rural area of our large nation, and the multigovernment involvement all have a great deal to do with the strengths and inequities of public welfare methods. The following is a description of the more prominent methods.

Assistance Payments

NEED DETERMINATION IN ASSISTANCE PAYMENTS[16].   State and local welfare agencies for the AFDC program (and in Puerto Rico, Guam, and the Virgin Islands for their adult assistance payments (Old Age, Blind, and Permanently and Totally Disabled)) are required under the Social Security Act to determine who is financially needy. The states and territories establish a *standard of need* expressed in money amounts. This standard is expected to represent the cost of basic living needs of the individual or family recipient for food, clothing, shelter, and utilities. Some states also include household supplies, personal care items, transportation, and recreation. To this may be added special needs of an individual related to his health problems, for example, the need of a diabetic for special foods, or employment, such as the cost of a work uniform, or school attendance, for example, enrollment in a special school for handicapped children.

The money amount of the standard may be a flat amount by family size or it may be for a group of items or for each item included in the standard. No two states have established identical standards or money amounts and few, if any, have established similar amounts for groups of items in their standards. Federal regulations require a uniform statewide standard expressed in money amounts, except for area cost differentials for shelter.

All income and resources of the individual or family are taken into consideration in determining need and the amount of payment, unless certain amounts are to be disregarded, such as increases in social security benefits passed by Congress, public housing rent reductions, in AFDC, the first $30 and one-third of the remainder of gross earnings, the earnings of dependent children who are full time students, and the bonus value of food stamps. These so-called disregards are federally-mandated, others are optional for the states, such as disregarding the first five dollars of income per person per month. The states may specify limits on certain types of real and personal property as the value of a home, automobile, or personal effects as jewelry, or to retain up to $2,000 per person for reserve use.

State agencies use the budget method for determining financial eligibility and the amount of payment. Each family reports its expected gross income and expenditures for the month following their application to derive its available income. The difference between available income and the need standard represents the budget deficit. In 19 states and the Virgin Islands where all countable income is subtracted from the standard and no maximums or percentage reductions are imposed, need is described as being met in full. In 18 states, payments (the amounts of deficit provided for by the states) are limited by maximums of a specified amount by family size, or for all families alike, or for the number of persons in the household, or some combination of these. An example is the *specified maximum amount by family size* where the state agency regulation provides that the amount of assistance payment is the budget deficit or the following maximums, whichever is less, for example:

Family size	
1	$100
2	130
3	160
4	200
5	230
6	250
7	275
8	300
9 or more	325

If the budget deficit for a family of four was $250, the payment would be the maximum; if the budget deficit was $120, the payment would be the budget deficit $120.

Another example is the *specified maximum amount for all family sizes* where the state agency regulation provides that the amount of the assistance payment is the budget deficit or overall family (regardless of family size) maximum of $200, whichever is less. If we assume that the budget deficit is $250; the payment would be the $200 maximum.

Twenty-eight states, the District of Columbia, and Puerto Rico reduce either the standard of need or the budget deficit on a percentage basis because of insufficient funds.

Primarily the same "need," "available income," "deficit" concepts are applied in the SSI program to determine the amount of the federal benefit payment to aged, blind, or disabled beneficiaries and spouses. The state-by-state differences, if any, apply in the supplemental payments determined by the individual states.

METHODS FOR PAYMENT ISSUANCE.   Assistance payments are issued usually monthly by checks mailed to recipients. They may be issued bimonthly to larger families. In some states and cities, they may be distributed in person at the welfare agency or, in New York City, as an experiment, to provide an incentive for employment, at the local employment security office. In Pennsylvania, assistance checks are picked up at neighborhood banks in cities statewide. Checks are distributed by a computerized system and recipients are notified of the prescribed date of pickup. Other recipients in the state who do not live near a bank in the system continue to receive their checks by mail. In Nassau County, New York, payments are by cash rather than checks.[17]

In the SSI program, monthly checks are mailed to recipients, but they are offered an alternative of having their checks mailed directly to their banks, a practice initiated by the Social Security Administration for all Social Security beneficiaries.

Assistance payments from AFDC may be arranged so that checks may be made out for part payment to the recipient and part to an individual or other party for purchase of heating oil or payment of rent and utilities. AFDC payments may be made by states to a caretaker of a child under protective care or to a person furnishing food, living accommodations, or services to a child or his relative or other caretaker, but the federal regulation limits the number of such protective and vendor payments to ten percent of the number of AFDC recipients in the state for any one month. This limitation is designed to reduce the number of caretakers or other relatives living with an eligible child who fail to assign support rights or cooperate in securing support for themselves and the child.[18]

Protective and vendor payments to SSI beneficiaries also may be made to another person, or a public or private agency or institution caring for the beneficiary. Food stamp allotments may be issued to households at the face value of all, three-fourths, one-half, or one-quarter of the monthly allotment at their option.

PUBLIC WELFARE SOCIAL SERVICES.   Public welfare social services comprise by far the largest organized system of services operating under a common set of laws, rules, and regulations, represented in offices in every part of the country, with the largest composite staff of employee and contractor service workers, and the largest caseloads with the highest public social services expenditures.

Social service methods employed by this giant national resource of human services are as numerous, diverse, complex, and difficult to manage as the numerous, diverse, complex, and difficult to manage problems, situations, and severity of human conditions for which they are provided. Public social service workers play roles of advocate, mediator, broker, conferee, counselor, therapist, expediter, teacher, substitute parent, law enforcer, among others.[19] At times, they are required to be punitive, to use public authority to force clients to act for their own welfare, at other times they are a sympathetic, understanding friend and confidant. The service they provide may be dramatically tangible, at other times, tenuous. Progress towards a social services goal may be real, at other times, barely evident. The service may require working with the client to resolve his problem through the client's own actions, or change in behavior (to solve an intrafamily problem). At other times, it may require working with groups with the client as a group member (a class in home management). Sometimes, the service may involve the client's relationship with others in the community: a school institution, the police, his landlord, other service agencies. This may require action by others on behalf of the client (to apply for public housing or to make application for placement in a senior citizens home). Finally, the service may require efforts to change the client's social, economic, and physical environment to help solve his problem (creation of jobs, better housing, better access to medical care).[20]

The methods applied in the delivery of public social services are conditioned by many factors controlling the agency worker and his client. The conditioning factors impose definite responsibilities and accountability upon social service workers and give them specific governmental authorities. They are:

1.   The goals and objectives of the social services programs prescribe the target aims of services. The five goals of the Title XX social services program (to reduce dependency; to achieve and maintain self-sufficiency; to prevent or remedy neglect, abuse or exploitation of children, and provide family stability; to prevent or reduce institutionalization; to secure appropriate institutional care) are different than the supporting services role of the WIN program (to provide work, training, and employment to AFDC family members), the medical social services under the Medicaid program, or the special judicial/agency objectives of the child welfare services program to protect children and reduce juvenile delinquency.

2.   The particular governmental jurisdiction of social services programs authorizes the range of services which are employed. As we have seen, different states authorize different services, with varying service budgets, various allowances for staff and support of contract services in the community. The various eligibility requirements for services dictate the extent to which population groups in the jurisdiction are provided services or are turned away or referred to other community resources.

3.   The political, socioeconomic, and physical environment of the particular city, metropolitan area or region control the availability of community service resources upon which public social services depend, such as employment, housing, education, medical care, and transportation.

4.   The skills, attitudes, and numbers of social service personnel determine the choice of services, the effectiveness of service methods, the climate of empathy created with the client, the energies directed to community planning, and the adequacy of community resources, that is, to serve as agents of social change.[21]

5.   The relative authority and responsibility of the agency service worker and client in the particular social services program. In the Title XX social services program, the client has freedom to accept or refuse a service, unless it involves a protec-

tive or custodial relationship with a child or adult. In the latter, the client relationship with the agency is legally prescribed. In the child welfare services program for child abuse, delinquency, and child neglect cases, under court action, the services agency wears the mantle of an agent of the court with governmental powers to require the cooperation of clients which they may not deny under penalty of law. The provision of social services in the WIN program carries with it the authority to deny AFDC assistance to WIN registrants who refuse a training or employment-connected social service, whereas the medical social services under the Medicaid program are completely voluntary on the part of the client.

Social service methods for all public welfare programs may also be described by the different courses of action open to social service workers in relating to persons coming to the agency for help, to eligible service clients, to groups of clients, or in serving the general community.[22]

1.   Information and referral services are provided to persons inquiring about services but who fail to establish eligibility under the regulations of the program. They are given information about the eligibility requirements and available services of the agency and within the community, a brief assessment may be made of their problems to facilitate an appropriate referral to another service agency. When adequate information and referral staff is available, or time of social workers permit, followup action is also taken to learn whether the person referred approached the recommended agency and whether the referral was appropriate to the person's needs.

2.   The social service worker is involved with counseling with the client, problem definition, diagnosis, helping to set the client's service objectives, working with the client to remedy his problem, evaluating, and monitoring the client's progress in overcoming his problems.

3.   The worker is involved with perceiving the problem as common for a group, setting the client group service objective, working with the client group to remedy the problem, evaluating and monitoring progress to resolve the problem on behalf of the client and the group sharing the same problem. Examples are tenants in an apartment complex with property maintenance

problems; older persons in need of a neighborhood senior citizens center.

4. The worker is asked at times to perceive problems as social and community-wide requiring the support and action of the community-at-large, setting a service objective to resolve the problem, working with other government and community agencies and leadership, evaluating and monitoring progress in resolving the problem on behalf of the client and others with the same problem or need. Examples are inadequate housing or poor transportation for low-income persons.

5. Other worker requirements are perceiving the problems as requiring the action of other persons or organizations, setting the client's service objective, contacting and working with such persons or organizations to respond to the client's need, evaluating and monitoring progress towards the objective. An example is contacting drug stores on behalf of the client to have them stock a special prescription drug.

The judgment of the worker, the size of the caseload, and the limits upon time have much to do with the course of action and the quality of services. Under harassed conditions of staff shortages, large caseloads and limited community service resources prevalent in most public welfare agencies (as discussed in Chapter 6), social service workers, with rare exceptions, are able to take short-term emergency actions with their clients and deal with the symptoms rather than the causes of client problems. Solving the larger socioeconomic problems of low-income groups are generally beyond the means of public social service agencies in most instances despite their best intentions.

The following are the more common social services provided by state and local public welfare agencies:

Family planning services
Day-care services for children
Day-care services for adults
Foster care services for children
Foster care services for adults
Emergency shelter for children
Chore services

Educational services

Health-related services

Homemaker services

Home management and other functional education services

Housing improvement services

Legal services

Protective services for adults

Protective services for children

Special services for the blind

Transportation services

Health Services

The methods for the delivery of health services under state Medicaid programs are essentially the prevailing practices of the American health care system. Limited only by the coverage of services authorized by state programs, the receipt of services in hospitals, homes, skilled nursing facilities, intermediate care facilities, physician and dental offices, neighborhood health centers, health maintenance organizations is no different from those available to the population at large. The free choice by a Medicaid beneficiary of health practitioner and health institution, coupled with his freedom to request and accept medical care, is the same as that for all Americans. The difference lies not in health care methods and processes, but in the payments for them.

EARLY AND PERIODIC SCREENING, DIAGNOSIS, AND TREATMENT PROGRAM.   The Early and Periodic Screening, Diagnosis, and Treatment Program (EPSDT) for the children in AFDC and medically needy families is a special effort under the Medicaid program for providing health outreach and comprehensive, coordinated health services to eligible children under 21. It covers early and periodic screening and diagnosis to ascertain physical and mental defects, treatment of conditions discovered in this process, including the provision of eyeglasses, hearing aids, and other kinds of treatment for visual and hearing defects and dental care. During 1975, 1.8 million children were enrolled in the program, about 53 percent of whom were six years of age or older. About one-half the children screened had referrable conditions and four of every five were referred for diagnosis and treatment.

Screening is done in physician offices, neighborhood health centers, special screening centers, children, and youth projects.

Treatment services available within the state Medicaid program are provided promptly, within 60 days of diagnosis. Referrals of AFDC children for treatment not covered by the Medicaid program are made to other community health facilities, such as crippled childrens programs, community mental health centers, and voluntary health agencies. Children of medically needy families (not receiving public assistance) needing treatment but not covered by Medicaid are referred to private practitioners and other providers and bear the cost of such services themselves.

Food Stamps

The food coupon as a substitute for legal tender is a unique feature of the public welfare system. It has been called "funny money." It has value; it is negotiable; it comes in different denominations. It is widely accepted in the purchase of food. It is exchanged in financial transactions at face value. It is fully backed by the faith and credit of the United States Government. It is printed, distributed, controlled, and destroyed with the same care and in the same manner as money. It is safeguarded, stolen, and counterfeited as money.

We can interpret the printing, distribution, and control of food coupons as the only public welfare activity which makes the system part of the fiduciary organization of the federal government, basically a Treasury function. It is, however, not the only item of value in the public welfare system used for food purchases. Part of assistance payments in the AFDC and SSI programs is also intended for food purchases and is so used. This is also true of some GA payments made by state and local welfare agencies.

Work Incentives

Referrals of AFDC heads of households and other family members are made by state and local welfare agencies to the local WIN units (employment security offices or other employment and training facility approved by the Department of Labor). This precipitates the manpower training, job finding, and work incentive processes under the WIN program.[23] The goal is employment and simultaneous reduction in AFDC caseloads and payments.

WIN REGISTRATION PROCESS.   When AFDC individuals appear at the WIN office, they are requested to provide a complete work history and are given a description of the program. Their entitlements and responsibilities are explained and a form as proof of registration is furnished. Job market information from the local job bank is reviewed and a referral to available employment may be arranged on the spot if a reasonable employment opportunity exists. If an immediate job referral is not possible, the name of the registrant is placed in a "registrant pool" from which names are pulled in accordance with the workload of the WIN unit staff and the following order of priority: unemployed fathers, mothers who are volunteers for the program, other mothers, youth under 19 years of age, other youth and relatives, and finally, other AFDC registrants. Emphasis is placed on selecting those with the highest employability potential.

EMPLOYABILITY PLAN.   Each individual is given an appraisal interview at time of registration or shortly thereafter by a WIN unit counselor and a social worker of the separate administrative unit of the welfare agency. The outcome of this interview is an employability plan. Of a total of 816,000 new registrants in fiscal year 1975, 383,000 were appraised and had an employability plan.

The plan has two components: an employment and training plan and a supportive services plan. It contains a definite employment goal attainable in the shortest time period consistent with the individual's service needs for child care, his family responsibilities, attitudes, health condition, etc. Available training resources and job market opportunities are, of course, also taken into account in deciding his employment goal. The order of sequence of the plan—and the WIN program—is for immediate employment, intensive manpower services (special orientation to the world of work, compensatory education, job training, and job seeking methods), on-the-job training, public service employment, institutional training, assignment in any other manpower program or activity, or job training referrals.

Any job or training assignment must be related to the capability of the individual to perform the tasks on a regular basis. Any claim by the individual of its adverse effects on his physical or mental conditions must be based on adequate medical testimony from a physician or psychologist. Daily commuting time of the assignment from/to home and work or training site is not normally in excess of two hours. However, this may be exceeded if it involves transporting a child from/to a child care facility and a longer round trip commuting time is generally accepted in the community, as in a rural area.

Referral to a job may be made whether it is temporary, permanent, full-time, part-time, or seasonal. The hours of work, however, must not exceed those customary to the occupation. The wage rate in general must meet or exceed the federal or state minimum wage law, unless a lower rate for a job not so covered is normally paid in that labor market. However, WIN regulations require it to be at least 75 percent of the minimum wage rate of the Fair Labor Standards Act. Also, the sum of net wages and work allowances may not be less than the family's AFDC cash benefit to avoid penalizing the family.

Job referrals may not be to jobs vacant due to a strike, lockout, or other labor dispute, or if the job is not in accord with union regulations. Job training must be of such quality as to place the individual in a competitive position in the local job market and qualify him for a job.

ON-THE-JOB TRAINING.   This entails referral of a registrant to a private or public employer who agrees under contract to the WIN agency to employ him and provide individual job training, including increased supervision. The employer is reimbursed for any extraordinary costs he incurs for such supervision and training.

INSTITUTIONAL AND OTHER WORK EXPERIENCE TRAINING.
The registrant receives vocational or other classroom training
conducted by an instructor in a nonworksite setting. He may be
given work experience by an employer where he has the opportunity to develop work habits, to practice skills learned in classroom training, and to demonstrate skills to a prospective
employer.

PUBLIC SERVICE EMPLOYMENT.   All registrants who cannot
be placed in a regular job in the local labor market may be
offered a job in a state or local government agency, nonprofit
organization or Indian reservation, but not one which would
otherwise be performed by regular employees or displace a
regular employee.

Cuban Refugee Assistance

The methods of the Cuban refugee assistance program are
different from those of other public welfare programs largely to
reflect the special circumstances of the refugees and the objectives of the program to achieve resettlement in the United
States. The methods of intake, i.e., registration, counseling, the
provision of emergency assistance payments, social services,
medical services, educational and manpower retraining and employment are not, however, basically different. The 100 percent
federal funding for the program is different, the setting and
administration in the Miami area is different, the Spanish language orientation is different, and the trauma of personal and
family dislocation is more extreme than most low-income welfare applicants and beneficiaries.

The resettlement services provided refugees is unique to
the program.[24] Most resettlements are arranged through four
national voluntary agencies with offices in the Cuban Refugee
Center: Catholic Relief Services, Church World Service (Protestant), United HIAS Service (Jewish), and the International Res-
cue Committee (nonsectarian). Refugees choose a resettlement
agency along religious lines. Most Cubans register with the
Catholic agency.

Resettlements are made when local affiliates of these agencies undertake to sponsor a refugee family in their community.

Smaller and valuable roles in resettlement are also played by civic organizations such as the Jaycees, Kiwanis, Lions, and Rotary Clubs.

Repatriated U.S. Nationals Assistance

The emergency requirements for prompt temporary assistance to destitute or mentally ill citizens overseas dictate the place and variety of methods of this program. The most uncharacteristic features of the program within the public welfare system are (1) the urgent need for smooth communications among the principal agencies: Department of State, Office of Family Assistance, D/HEW, and the state or local welfare agency at the point of entry into the country; and (2) the availability of prompt followup assistance and services the individual and his family may need. An especially complicating requirement is immediate admission of a mentally ill person to a hospital or mental institution, the arrangement for his care and release to a relative for transfer to an appropriate mental health authority in the person's state of residence or legal domicile. When a relative or other responsible person to whom the mentally ill can be placed in custody cannot be located, the Secretary of D/HEW may be required to initiate judicial action to obtain a commitment to act on the person's behalf and authorize his transfer from one hsopital to another for his continued care.

METHODS OF ACCOUNTABILITY

Accountability in the public welfare system means being responsible and answerable for the administration of public welfare programs. It applies not only to public agencies and staffs but also to applicants and beneficiaries of payments and services and the individuals, organizations, and institutions which serve them. Each bears an obligation for honesty, integrity, objectivity, and impartiality to act to make public welfare programs provide the help they were designed to give to legally eligible persons.

The methods of accountability are methods of regulation,

control, supervision, review, auditing, accounting, investigation, standards setting, determining objectives, monitoring and evaluation, record-keeping and reporting, and the imposition of penalties. Their uses include such practices as prior approval of plans and actions, verification of information, spot checks of decisions, post review of actions, record checks, official reporting requirements, and auditing of funds. They also entail qualitative review of services, compliance with service and institutional standards, minimum professional standards for service workers, and licensing of workers and institutions. The regulations and mandatory requirements of organization, process, method of eligibility, and service delivery can also be regarded as accountability measures. The collective aim of these methods is the faithful execution of public welfare laws, a broad purpose of national significance and impact, commensurate with the billions of dollars invested, the millions of people affected, and the sensitive national socioeconomic issues of poverty and redistribution of income.

Most of the publicity, the greatest intensity of interest, the most vociferous debates about public welfare in the past decade has been about the need for and adequacy of accountability methods and their success in keeping the program efficient, effective, honest, and legally administered. The following are among the more important of these.

Individual and Family Eligibility

PUBLIC ASSISTANCE QUALITY CONTROL PROGRAM.[25]   This program is a system (1) for determining the extent to which those receiving AFDC assistance payments are eligible and receive payments in the amount to which they are entitled and (2) for assuring that rates of ineligibility and improper payments are held at minimum levels. Errors in eligibility encompass both ineligibility of assistance recipients and erroneous denials of assistance to applicants and recipients. Errors in amount of payment include both overpayments and underpayments. The program is used by states and the federal government to maintain a continuous and systematic control over the incidence of ineligible recipients and incorrect payments in the AFDC caseload.

It has been in operation since 1963 and has been revised and expanded since then. It is carried out in all states and territories in accordance with federally-established methods and processes.

Prior to May 1973, the program was applied to the Medicaid, Old Age Assistance Aid, to the Blind, Aid to the Permanent and Totally Disabled programs. However, a separate quality control program was adopted for the Medicaid program, and the adult assistance category programs, with the exception of those in Puerto Rico, Guam, and the Virgin Islands, were replaced by the quality assurance program of the Supplemental Security Income program. The quality control program described here is also being applied to the adult category programs in the territories. It is being used to review compliance with Title VI of the Civil Rights Act to detect evidence of discrimination on the basis of race, color, or national origin in state and local welfare agency eligibility determination processes.

The program seeks to hold the incidence of errors below preestablished tolerance limits of error: not more than three percent ineligibility rates and not more than five percent for over or underpayments. These standards were made effective for the July to December 1975 sampling period and for subsequent periods thereafter.* States which fail to meet these goals lose a proportional share of federal funds for the period in question to the extent of their overpayment and ineligibility rates. In the first quarter, fiscal year 1976 (July to September 1975), $97.1 million was withheld by D/HEW or ten percent of federal AFDC payments for that period.

Case reviews of sample cases include a field investigation by an agency quality control (Q.C.) reviewer, i.e., a visit to the home of the family; personal interview; corroboration of their family composition, income, and resources; and other eligibility factors, and contacts with relatives, friends, neighbors, and others who can provide verification of these factors. From this information, the reviewer redetermines the family's eligibility

*A U.S. District Court ruling barred DHEW from enforcing these numerical rates and cutting of federal funding for assistance payments (State of Maryland v. Mathews, United States District Court for the District of Columbia) May 14, 1976.

status and the amount of assistance payment, and changes in eligibility and/or payments are made accordingly.

Two general categories of errors are uncovered in the process of review: Agency errors and client errors. Agency errors are those where the eligibility worker:

1. failed to apply state policy correctly as to the facts at hand which resulted in incorrect payment or eligibility status;
2. made a computation or transcription error which resulted in an incorrect payment or ineligibility status; or
3. failed to take indicated action, such as failure to follow up on incomplete or inconsistent information supplied by the applicant.

Client errors are those due to the client, a friend, or relative acting for the client or the client's legal representative in providing incorrect or incomplete information or failure to report changes in the client's circumstances.

The focus of the program is on locating types of errors that occur with such frequency as to cause error levels in excess of acceptable tolerance limits and determining why they occur so that action can be taken to eliminate the causes. Among the more common types of corrective action taken by state and local agencies to strengthen eligibility processes are: increased verification, retraining of eligibility workers, increased staffing, improved supervision, adoption of mechanized methods in the process, development of a flat grant concept, and forms and procedures simplification.[26]

A federal monitoring staff conducts appraisals of state quality control operations. The federal appraisal consists of a continuing review of the administrative and operational aspects of the system and periodic rereviews by federal monitors of a sample of completed state quality control reviews.[27]

A major quality control campaign was initiated by the Social and Rehabilitation Service in January, 1974 when it was discovered that four out of ten (41.1 percent) of the 3.1 million families then on the welfare rolls were either ineligible or receiving incorrect payments. At that time 10.2 percent were ineligible,

22.8 percent overpaid, and 8.1 percent underpaid. As of June 30, 1975, the states had lowered their error rates to 7.5 percent ineligible, 17.5 percent overpaid, and 7.3 percent underpaid, a total of 32.3 percent of cases with some error. A total of $411 million in federal and state funds was reported saved and about 270,000 ineligible recipients (109,000 cases) were removed from the rolls.[28]

MEDICAID ELIGIBILITY QUALITY CONTROL PROGRAM.   In 1975, SRS authorized a Medicaid eligibility quality control program for all state Medicaid programs paralleling the AFDC quality control program. For state and local welfare agencies, it required them to expand upon the already familiar quality control process in operation for AFDC eligibility, particularly for the medically needy not receiving assistance payments.

FOOD STAMP QUALITY CONTROL.   The Food and Nutrition Service of the Department of Agriculture requires each state and local welfare agency to provide a quality control program for food stamp eligibility, directed to the nonassistance households comprising 45 percent of the food stamp case load in 1975.

A random sample of such households is selected and all elements of eligibility are verified by field investigators and personal interview, including their legal eligibility, and correctness of food stamp allotments. State and local welfare agencies are required to initiate actions to tighten up eligibility processes to remedy the errors uncovered in the sample investigations. Fifty percent of the costs of this program are reimbursed by the federal Government.

In a sample period January to June 1974, 25,585 households with food stamps valued at $1.7 million were reviewed. Of these, 37.9 percent of eligible households received erroneous food stamp allotments or were charged erroneously. The dollar amounts in individual cases were, on the whole, small. Six percent additional households would have been eligible had the work registration requirement been met; 12.2 percent of the sample included ineligible households because of excess income.[29]

SSI ELIGIBILITY ACCOUNTABILITY.   The Social Security Administration does not maintain a separate quality control mechanism for the SSI program as does the federal/state AFDC, Medicaid, and Food Stamp programs. Instead, it utilizes its computerized eligibility and payments processes to assure the integrity of its systems, as discussed earlier in this chapter (redetermination of eligibility).

CHILD SUPPORT ENFORCEMENT.   The Social Security Amendments of 1974, Title IVD (P.L. 93-647, effective July 1, 1975) initiated a new child support enforcement program for a long-standing serious social problem of the estimated three million fathers who strand the women (wives and unmarried women) and their children, provide no support to them and their six million children and make most of them dependent upon AFDC assistance. The program places responsibility upon the wife or caretaker for assigning rights to the state for enforcement and collection of child support payments and cooperating in locating the absent parent and receiving such support. The program is not limited to AFDC families; it covers all families whose children need the financial assistance of the absent parent. Non-AFDC families may be charged a small application fee for services for the location of the man and collections for child support. The state agency may deduct the cost of collection from child support payments. Cooperating AFDC recipients received an incentive bonus of up to $20 monthly which did not affect their AFDC payments. This provision was valid until September 30, 1976. Under the program, a coordinated parent locator service (Federal Parent Locator Service) is administered by D/HEW.

All states, the District of Columbia and three territories are required to establish a child support enforcement unit in state and local welfare agencies (or set up a separate agency) to determine the paternity of children and to obtain child support for applicants. They also maintain a parent locator service, help other states collect support payments for which they receive incentive payments equal to 25 percent of the amount collected for the first twelve-month period and ten percent of the amount collected thereafter, use their parent locator service to channel all requests for information from the Federal Locator Service and cooperate with the courts and law enforcement officials in carrying out the program.

When a mother applies for the child support service, the agency checks with local sources, such as the Postal Service, past employers, the state employment service, and motor vehicle licensing agencies. If unsuccessful, it contacts the Federal Parent Locator Service and a search of its records will be made. It contacts other states of former addresses of the parent, as well as other federal agencies, such as the Social Security Administration and the Internal Revenue Service. Once an absent parent is located, a state may petition its courts to issue a court order for child support. An order for garnishment of wages could be obtained if he refuses to pay. Under the law, for the first time, federal employees are subject to garnishment for payment of alimony and child support.

The funds obtained from the parent are given directly to the head of a non-AFDC family, except for costs incurred by the state in making the collections. Families receiving AFDC will get only the support payments not needed to repay assistance payments received in the past; the state retains any excess to reimburse it for past welfare payments. Once past assistance payments have been repaid, all child support payments will go to the family. Continued eligibility for AFDC assistance will depend upon whether the child support payments are enough to make the family self-supporting according to the state's need and payment standards. The change in family income may also affect eligibility for Medicaid, food stamps, and social services. Federal reimbursement for 75 percent of child support enforcement costs incurred by the state and local agencies is payable as well as costs of cooperating courts and law enforcement agencies.[30]

LAW ENFORCEMENT INVESTIGATIONS.   Special prosecutors, district attorneys, special grand juries, public investigators, and other law enforcement and court agencies make investigations of fraud in public welfare programs, directed to allegedly illegal practices by recipients to obtain eligibility in assistance payments, food stamps, and Medicaid programs. These investigative efforts are authorized either under special state laws or are covered by the inherent statutory authorities of state judicial and law enforcement agencies.

DATA PROCESSING AND COMPUTER SYSTEMS FOR ELIGIBILITY PROCESSING.   The application of automatic data processing and computer systems to the eligibility process has become widespread throughout the public welfare system not only to process the volume of applicant and recipient information and agency actions which result in the regular eligibility process and the quality control program but also to verify their status and benefits they receive from other programs.

Data processing and computers are also commonly used intrastate and interstate to verify the status and benefits of applicants and recipients in other state and local social programs of possible impact on their eligibility. Federal reimbursement of 50 percent of the cost for systems design, installation, and operation of these systems for this purpose is provided.

Accountability for Services

UTILIZATION REVIEW OF INSTITUTIONS UNDER MEDICAID.
The Social Security Amendments of 1972 (P.L. 92-603) provided for a reduction of one-third of the state's federal Medical Assistance Percentage unless the state Medicaid agency adopted and maintained an effective program of control over the utilization of institutional services and required hospitals, mental hospitals, skilled nursing facilities, and intermediate care facilities. For such control, each facility under contract to the agency must implement utilization review programs of their own. The review program is based on the concept that the assurance of high quality medical care and the necessity and appropriateness of institutional care can be accomplished through peer (medical) review activities. The concept is applied also in the Medicare and maternal and child health programs.

The Federal regulations (45. CFR 250) require that state medicaid agencies maintain a state-wide surveillance and utilization control program that safeguards against unnecessary and inappropriate utilization of care and services to Medicaid beneficiaries, excess payments for service, and assesses the quality of such services. This program requires a continuous process of review of utilization of institutional care and services, evaluation on a sample basis of the need for, quality, and timeliness of services, the postpayment review of utilization to develop recipient utilization profiles, provider service profiles, and exceptions criteria under which individual cases fail to meet the accepted criteria for admission and care. In addition, the state agency maintains control to see that each participating institution has in effect a written utilization review plan which meets federal requirements. A key requirement is that the institution provides a control system for periodic review and evaluation of the necessity for admission and continued stay of each eligible patient by a team of medical and other professional personnel who are not themselves directly involved in the care of the individual or have a financial interest in the institution. Also, certification at time of admission by a physician that such admission is required must be provided. If application for Medicaid coverage is made by the patient while in the institution, the physician certification must be obtained before he is granted eligibility.

A written plan of care must be prepared by a physician and evaluation is to be given periodically by the physician and other professionals involved in the patient's care. Medical review teams are required to conduct an independent evaluation and on-site inspection of the care in mental hospitals, skilled nursing facilities, and intermediate care facilities to assure the appropriateness and quality of care and services and the plans for continuing care and discharge.

Each Medicaid hospital and facility is required to have a utilization review organization comprised of medical and other professional staff or a group outside the institution for this purpose, a set of written utilization control procedures to select categories of admissions to be subject to closer professional scrutiny, and to conduct medical care evaluation studies with authority to modify initially approved length of stay of individual patients and to establish norms for initial review dates for reevaluation of the patient's condition and his projected discharge date. Detailed utilization review records are kept by the committee or group of its activities.

Medical care evaluation studies are performed in each hospital or facility covering the efficient and effective use of health facilities and services consistent with patient needs and standards of health care. Studies emphasize identification and analysis of patterns of patient care and suggest possible changes in patient care and use of services. Admissions, duration of stay, professional and ancillary services (such as drugs and biologicals) are also analyzed.

Appropriate modifications in the utilization review organization and processes in mental hospitals and skilled nursing facilities for the mentally retarded are made to reflect their specialized professional personnel, services, and different modes of care.

PROFESSIONAL STANDARDS REVIEW ORGANIZATION (PSRO).

The national policy for utilization review to hold hospitals and other health facilities accountable for the quality and appropriateness of care is paralleled by a program for checking the medical necessity, adherence to professional standards of physician services, and the appropriateness of inpatient admissions to hospitals and facilities. The Social Security Act of 1972 provides for the establishment of PSROs consisting of a cross-section of practicing physicians in local areas to assume responsibility for the review of services covered under the Medicare, Medicaid, and maternal and child health programs. In about a dozen states, a single PSRO covers an entire state; more often there are two or more (some states have as many as 15). Over 200 PSRO areas have been designated by the Secretary of Health, Education and Welfare. The Utah Professional Review Organization was the first to be organized in 1974; it covers 38 hospitals in the state.

Each PSRO is expected to include approximately 1,000 to 1,500 physicians (doctors of medicine and osteopathy) to assure adequate representation of all specialty groups for peer review. State and local medical societies sponsor most PSROs. Although they are expected to expand the scope of medical services reviewed to include all those provided under Medicare and Medicaid, such as in physicians offices and outpatient clinics and health centers, they limit their activities initially to reviewing care provided in institutions, principally in acute general hospitals.

The organizations are nonprofit corporations with a Board of Directors of practicing physicians and representatives of consumer, public, and health industry groups. The Utah Professional Review Organization, organized by the Utah State Medical Association, has an executive director, other supervisory officials, and a staff of nurse coordinators and medical advisors, with six committees: the executive, quality evaluation, length-of-stay norms, medical education, constitution and by-laws, and committee on medical advisors. Practicing physicians and doctors of osteopathy in the PSRO area are encouraged to serve on these committees on a rotating basis and participate as reviewers of hospitals and other health care facilities.

Funding of PSROs is from a special federal experimental grant program and fees paid by participating hospitals and health insurers on a per-patient basis. The fees for Medicaid patients are subject to FFP. In practice, PSRO nurse coordinators review all hospital admissions, indicate the expected length of stay according to the admitting diagnosis derived from the norms established by the PSRO committee of length-of-stay norms, and monitor the treatment program in consultation with the PSRO medical advisor assigned to the hospital. They collect data on each patient. This becomes the basis for the PSRO evaluations of the quality of care at the hospitals. In Utah, sets of qualitative criteria or norms are developed from more than 100 diagnoses of 17 medical specialties. These are based on typical patterns of practice in the state which reflect differences in care, diagnosis, and treatment.[31]

Certified PSROs also have the authority to determine, in advance, elective admissions to a hospital or other health facility which do not require emergency care, where the patient's condition does not require immediate treatment, or where the diganosis indicates the need for extended or costly courses of treatment. As in utilization review programs, PSRO physicians are not expected to review cases in which they are involved or assigned to institutions in which they or their families have a financial interest.

Physicians, hospitals, or other health care facilities are subject to the decisions of PSROs. Noncompliance with their decisions, following reasonable notice and opportunity for discussion, are reported to the Secretary of Health, Education and Welfare with a complete report and may result in termination of provider agreements with the state Medicaid agency or the Medicare contract authority in the area. In addition, the Secretary may require a practitioner or institutional provider to pay to the United States an amount (not in excess of $500) of the cost of medically improper or unnecessary service.

The relationship of PSROs and utilization review organizations under the Medicare, Medicaid, and maternal and child health programs are evolving so that PSROs, when certified by the Department of Health, Education and Welfare, will assume responsibility for review functions and make decisions on the appropriateness and quality of services binding on hospitals and other facilities providing care under these programs. They will thereby replace the utilization review authority and responsibility of state medicaid agencies for participating institutions.[32]

STANDARD SETTING AND COMPLIANCE.   Interwoven in the federal regulations controlling the delivery of social, medical, employment training, and job placement services is the imposition of minimum standards for institutions, professional standards for service providers, and operational and quality standards. Their purpose is to assure beneficiaries that services provided meet generally accepted criteria of facilities, staffing, performance, and quality. The inherent assumption is that the services of the public welfare system are to be at least as good as (or better) than those available to the general population.

Service standards have not, however, been developed for the great variety of social, medical, manpower training, and other public welfare fields, generally because of the difficulty in reaching agreement among service professionals, consumers, legislative bodies, and the general public as to acceptable norms. Standards may represent *minimum* requirements, *ideal* requirements, or something in between as to each, all, or some of the characteristics of a service: safety, healthfulness, quantity, availability, appropriateness, quality, effectiveness, efficiency, costs, benefits, ethical, or moral value.

Standards provide a benchmark for evaluating the performance of professional services and are frowned upon by professional service providers, especially since they become measuring rods by which service performance can be compared and, more importantly, reviewed and monitored, ergo, making them accountable. Arguments against standard-setting usually rely upon the logic that human conditions are as intricately complex as human nature itself. Human services, therefore, cannot be susceptible of a standard unless it allows for an infinite number of exceptions. Nevertheless, in striving for accountability, the public welfare system has adopted some important standards of service for enforcement. These appear in several forms: in provision of state and local government laws authorizing issuance of licenses by duly authorized boards and agencies to service providers and institutions; in federal regulations specifying the service and institutional requirements to be met by state and local governments to qualify for FFP; state and local government codes setting minimum technical requirements for public health and safety in the construction and operations of physical facilities; in eligibility for membership in professional societies which have minimum professional education, minimum experience, or minimum combinations of education and experience.

CHILD CARE STANDARDS.   In 1967 the Office of Economic Opportunity (OEO) and the Department of Health, Education and Welfare organized a Federal Interagency Day Care Committee with representatives of OEO, D/HEW, and the Department of Labor, to develop a set of day-care program standards applicable to federally-funded programs, including AFDC social services, child welfare services, OEO youth programs, community action programs, migrant services, manpower and training programs with day-care components, and elementary and secondary education programs. In September 1968 these standards were approved and published as Federal Interagency Day Care Requirements.

The requirements define types of day-care facilities, grouping of children, licensing and approval of facilities, location of facilities, safety and sanitation requirements, suitability of facilities, the requirements for educational services, social services, health and nutrition services, the training of staff, and parent involvement. They also detail the approved standards of administration, coordination of day-care programs, and the periodic evaluation of compliance of day care facilities with the standards.[33]

The Requirements were adopted under the Title XX Social Services program with several amended requirements:

In-Home care.   When homemaker service is utilized for this purpose, it meets standards established by the state which are reasonably in accord with recommended standards of national standard setting organizations concerned with this type of home care for children. When other caretakers are utilized for this purpose, such care meets standards established by the state which, as a minimum, cover the caretaker's age, health, capacity, and available time to properly care for children; minimum and maximum number of children that may be cared for in the home at any one time; and proper feeding and health care of the children.

Out-of-Home Care.   Facilities used to provide day care outside a child's own home are licensed by the state or approved as meeting the standards for such licensing. Such facilities and care must meet the 1968 Federal Interagency Day Care Requirements, except that educational service requirements are recommended but not required. Required staffing standards for children under three in day-care centers and group day-care homes are: 1 adult for each child under six weeks of age; one adult to each three children ages six weeks to 18 months and one adult to four children ages 18 months through 36 months. A family day-care home serving children from infancy to age six may care for no more than two children under age three (infancy through 36 months) and no more than five children under age 14, including the family day-care mother's own children. Required staffing standards for school age children in day-care centers are: one adult to 15 children, ages six to ten and one adult to 20 children ages ten to 14.[34]

The Child Day Care Social Services Act approved September 7, 1976 (P. L. 94-401) recognized the difficulty of states in upgrading child care to meet the standards. It suspended federal staffing standards for day care of younger children six weeks to six years to October 1, 1977, provided $200 million additional federal funding to enable day-care providers to employ more welfare recipients and other low-income persons in day-care jobs, provided full federal funding rather than the 75 to 25 matching ratio for state child care expenditures. It also authorized state agencies to waive federal staffing standards for child care centers and group day-care homes which meet state standards if the number of children served represent no more than 20 percent of the total number of children served and transfer to a facility meeting federal standards is infeasible. It also amended the federal standard for family day-care homes by excluding the mothers own children six years of age and older from the limitation on the number of children served.

FOSTER FAMILY SERVICE STANDARDS.   A foster family home is a home licensed by appropriate state or local authority or an Indian Tribal Council to provide board and care, including parenting of children and oversight for adults. The licensing standards cover requirements of admissions policies, safety, sanitation, and protection of the civil rights of children or adults. National standards for foster family home services for adults have not been promulgated and efforts to mandate standards for children at the federal level have yet to be approved. However, standards for foster family services for children have been developed and refined by social work professional and governmental social agencies, principally the U.S. Children's Bureau. The most recent (March 1975) standards have been formulated by the American Public Welfare Association under contract to the Office of Child Development, Office of Human Development Services.[35] The caveat of the standards state clearly in bold type: These standards are not mandated by any Federal agency nor are they related to any legislation or funding, existing or pending. The use of these standards by individual State agencies to improve foster family services is completely voluntary. However, the Children's Bureau recommends a process for implementation of the standards which requires a cooperative planning and working relationship between the Children's Bureau and the responsible State agency.

Two levels of standards are set: (1) *Basic standards* are a set of criteria which reflect a level of performance below which services are questionable. The authors of the standards estimate that one-third of the public agencies meets or exceeds the basic standards and the other two-thirds should be able to attain them within a relatively short time. (2) *Goal standards* represent an optimal level of performance which public agencies can work towards meeting within a specified time period. They are designed primarily to be used in planning for future upgrading of services. The critical difference between the two sets of standards is the quality of service provided.

PROTECTIVE SERVICES STANDARDS.   For children harmed or threatened with harm by a parent or caretaker responsible for his health and welfare, the following services are prescribed for federal financial participation in federal regulations (45 CFR 228):

> identification and diagnosis of the child and his situation
>
> reporting and investigation of the sexual abuse, or negligent treatment or maltreatment received
>
> determination that the child is vulnerable or at risk of neglect, abuse, or exploitation
>
> counseling and therapy services
>
> special training for parents to change their attitudes and behavior towards the child
>
> legal representation for the child
>
> provision of appropriate social, medical, housing, and other services for the child and parent or caretaker to prevent and remove the threatening conditions

For adults unable to protect their own interests and harmed or threatened with harm through action or inaction due to ignorance, incompetence, or poor health of a responsible relative or caretaker, the following services are required:

- identifying such adults and determining they have no one else willing or able to become responsible for them
- prompt investigation of the neglect, maltreatment, physical or mental injury, deprivation of entitlements due them, or diminution of their resources
- diagnosing the individual's situation and service needs
- providing counseling to the adults, families, other responsible relatives, or surrogates on handling their affairs
- arranging for alternate living arrangements in the community or an institution
- assisting in the location of medical care, legal services, and other resources in the community
- arranging for guardianship, commitment, or other protective placements as needed
- providing advocacy to assure receipt of rights and entitlements due to adults at risk

MEDICAID FACILITIES CONTROLS.   Federal Medicaid requirements for nursing home care provide that states designate the state authorities responsible for establishing and maintaining standards for skilled nursing facilities and intermediate care facilities. This requires state authorities to keep on file and make available information of the types and kinds of such institutions in the state and the standards they apply for approval or licensing, including those relating to health (continuing physician and nursing services, dietary standards, drug controls, and accident prevention); humane treatment; sanitation; types of construction; physical facilities (space and accomodations per person); fire and safety; staffing (number and qualifications related to the purposes and scope of services); patient records; admission procedures; administrative and fiscal records; and the control by the individual, guardian, or protective payee, of the individual's personal affairs.[36]

SKILLED NURSING FACILITY STANDARDS.   Under the Social
Security Amendments of 1972 (P.L. 92-603), the Secretary of
Health, Education and Welfare is directed to provide a common
set of standards for skilled nursing facilities under Medicare and
Medicaid programs.

State Medicaid agencies are required to obtain certification
of their state health institutions licensing agency that the facility
meets the standards, prior to execution of any agreement to pay
for skilled nursing home services for covered Medicaid beneficiaries.

The standards provide explicit requirements in each of the
following areas:[37]

> compliance with federal, state, and local laws
> governing body and management
> patient care policies
> physician services
> nursing services
> dietetic services
> specialized rehabilitation services
> pharmaceutical services
> laboratory and radiological services
> dental services
> social services
> patient activities
> medical records
> transfer agreements (between institutions)
> physical environment
> environmental services
> disaster preparedness
> utilization review
> medical direction

These standards also define the minimum acceptable education and experience qualifications and licensing requirements

of 15 types of skilled nursing facility staff, covering key administrative and professional personnel.

Definitions of approved drugs and biologicals authorized under the Medicare and Medicaid programs, the requirements for controlled drugs, drug administration, and dispensing are also mandated under the standards.

In toto, this body of requirements creates a national standard or norm for nursing home facilities unprecedented in American health care experience. It should be noted, too, that the regulations rely, to the extent possible, upon the prevailing requirements of state licensing authorities, professional standards of national standard setting bodies, educational requirements of degree-granting academic institutions, and the membership requirements of professional and technical societies.

Special waivers dealing with the problem of the supply of nurses and physicians, largely in rural areas, are granted by authority of the Secretary of Health, Education and Welfare where access to and quality of patient care in the facility is not jeopardized and the facility continues in good faith to fill nursing personnel and physician positions. Waivers of the requirements of facilities to meet fire safety provisions of the Life Safety Code of the National Fire Protection Association—a standard requirement—have been approved by state Medicaid agencies when the provisions result in undue hardship of a facility, does not adversely affect the health and safety of patients, and the state has an effective fire and safety code to which the facility complies.

STANDARDS FOR INTERMEDIATE CARE FACILITIES.   These facilities provide care to individuals who do not need the services of a hospital or skilled nursing facility but who require a protected residential environment and a planned program of care and supervision on a continuous 24 hour-a-day basis. A common set of standards for this type of facility under the state Medicaid program is applied for institutions for the mentally retarded or persons with related conditions, and institutions for other persons. However, special requirements are applied to reflect the treatment and care of the mentally retarded. The

general standards which all intermediate care facilities cover
include:

> methods of administrative management of the facility
> transfer agreements with hospitals
> arrangements for purchase of professional services
> resident record systems
> fire and safety provisions
> environmental and sanitary conditions
> food services administration
> drugs and biological administration
> health services planning and supervision

For intermediate care facilities for other than the mentally
retarded, the following additional standard provisions are required:

> appointment of a licensed nursing home administrator
> designation of a resident services director
> provision of rehabilitation services
> provision of social services
> organization of a resident activities program
> health care supervision by a physician

For intermediate care facilities for the mentally retarded,
the following additional standard provisions are also required:

> admission requirements for pre- and postadmission evalu-
> ation by a professional team and certification of need for
> admission
> appointment of a licensed nursing home administrator or
> Qualified Mental Retardation Professional
> designation of a Qualified Mental Retardation Professional
> to be responsible for health care planning and supervi-
> sion
> provision of comprehensive resident living services, train-
> ing, and guidance

provision for a direct care staff for a resident living program

By 1977, the standards for intermediate care facilities for the mentally retarded are to be extended and intensified to require them to comply with standards for Residential Facilities for the Mentally Retarded established by the Accreditation Council for Facilities for the Mentally Retarded of the Joint Commission on Accreditation of Hospitals. These standards are substantially more explicit with regard to their operating under general policies and practices of the state comprehensive program for the mentally retarded.

State Medicaid programs are required to maintain a program of independent professional review of all intermediate care facilities covering the physical, emotional, social, and cognitive factors of individual need for institutional care. This review and evaluation process begins three months prior to admission, periodic on-site inspection by a professional review team (at least once a year) to assure the institution meets standards and that individual resident plans are executed as directed. A report and record of the inspections and evaluations are made to the state Medicaid agency and forwarded to the state health institution licensing agency. The state Medicaid agency is required to assure that inspection reports and recommendations of the inspection team are followed up promptly and corrective action taken by the facility.

HOME HEALTH SERVICES STANDARDS.   Standards have been promulgated for Medicaid and Medicare eligibles receiving health services in their own homes. This service is one of the mandatory services state Medicaid programs must provide for persons entitled to skilled nursing facility services to be eligible for FFP. The standards, therefore, are obligatory for home health service agencies under contract to state medical agencies. There are three mandatory provisions: (1) services in the home by a registered nurse or licensed practical nurse under the direction of the patient's physician; (2) home health aide services; and (3) the provision of medical supplies, equipment, and appliances. In addition, state programs may provide at their option physical therapy, occupational therapy, or speech therapy by an agency licensed by the state to provide medical rehabilitation services. Service agency standards specify minimum requirements in these areas:[38]

> agency qualification specification for home health services for Medicaid and Medicare patients
>
> compliance with appropriate federal, state, and local laws
>
> written statements defining the organization, services, and administration of the agency
>
> appointment, membership, and role of an advisory committee
>
> rules concerning acceptance of patients, medical services, and supervision provided
>
> patient nursing services supervision and evaluation by a registered nurse and duties of a licensed practical nurse
>
> specification requirements for physical, occupational, and speech therapy services
>
> assignment, duties, and supervision of home health aides
>
> requirements for clinic records
>
> utilization control and home health evaluation studies by a professional team

Certification by the state Medicaid agency of home health services are generally valid for a one-year period or for a lesser time if the agency needs to improve its operations to meet these standards. Agencies are given up to 60 days to make improvements. Penalty for noncompliance with standards is disallowance of continued FFP for services provided by the agency.

AUTOMATIC DATA PROCESSING AND COMPUTER SYSTEMS FOR SOCIAL SERVICES.   Machine processing and computers are used in state and local welfare agencies not only for eligibility processes but also in the delivery of social and child welfare services. Mechanical systems are designed to record, summarize, report, analyze, and control social worker assignments; the diagnosis, treatment and outcomes of service clients; the allocation of social service resources; the kinds of services provided; and the community service agencies involved. Such statistical record and reporting systems are necessary because it is impractical and costly, perhaps impossible, to hand record and process information on the large volume of social services, the large numbers of agency service workers and service contract agencies employed, the many geographic locations of agency service units, and the variety of services.

State and local agencies must, as a matter of good management sense and public accountability, exercise proper supervision and direction of their social service programs. The use of readily available data processing and computer systems is standard throughout the public welfare system. Some states and cities have their own machine equipment; others have time-sharing agreements with other agencies. The agencies, however, do not use uniform components nor employ uniform record-keeping and case control methods and processes, but they do have the common objectives of social services control, administration, and the production of information. Since computerized record systems contain common elements of social worker, contractor service agencies, service clients, service organizational units, service goals, services delivery, service outcomes, and service costs, they are not all that different.

During the years 1967 to 1970, the Community Services Administration of SRS (renamed the Public Services Administration), in cooperation with state welfare agencies, developed a prototype social services control system called Case and Administrative Services System (CASS). It was designed to be modified to reflect state and local differences and, with foresight, to be sufficiently flexible to be adapted to such new requirements as are found in the Title XX social services program. Its principal features are widely in use among state and local welfare agencies. The system has three components: a case schedule, a reporting system, and an administrative plan for control and reporting of the social services program. The system encompasses all levels of the social services organizations: the case worker, the social service supervisor, and the social service administrator.

MEDICAID CLAIMS PROCESSING AND INFORMATION SYSTEMS.
The large volume of claims for payment by hospitals, physicians, and other health care providers under Medicaid, the billions of dollars processed, and the need to acquire information about the kinds of services and persons receiving them mandated the use of mechanized data systems by state Medicaid agencies. Liberal federal reimbursement of 90 percent of costs was authorized in the Social Security Amendments of 1972 to encourage states to design, develop, and install such systems and 75 percent reimbursement of the cost of operating them. To help state agencies, the Medical Services Administration of SRS developed a five-volume set of standard specifications called the Medicaid Management Information System—General Systems Design (MMIS-GSD). These are minimum requirements for state systems. They provide for a standard input of 111 items for each claim, including the claimant's name (physician, hospital, pharmacist, other provider) and ID numbers, individual beneficiary patient, diagnoses, amount of claim, sources of payment of claim, kind of service provided, dates of service, billing and payment, place of service, Medicare eligibility, and other descriptive information.[39]

FRAUD IN THE MEDICAID PROGRAM.   State Medicaid agencies are required to exercise diligence in detecting possible fraud by a provider medical practitioner or health care institution. This is, of course, applicable to all government agencies and to all service and supply contracts entered into by state and local welfare agencies. The special provision made for the Medicaid program reflect the potential for fraud in the multibillion dollar service costs, the great variety and number of health care providers and institutions, and the millions of claims for payment processed annually.

State agencies must investigate suspect cases of fraud and report their findings to state law enforcement authorities for possible prosecution. The state agency is required to designate a staff individual or unit to carry out these responsibilities. Reports of cases of alleged fraud referred to state legal authorities and their disposition are made to the Health Care Financing

Administration. The name of the service provider or institution involved is not revealed in such reports; they are identified by a number or letter to protect those found innocent.

Medicaid provider claim forms bear the statements:

> This is to certify that the foregoing information is true, accurate, and complete.
> I understand that payment and satisfaction of this claim will be from Federal and State funds, and that any false claims, statements, or documents, or concealment of a material fact, may be prosecuted under applicable Federal or State laws.

They may alternatively provide for the following statement to appear on the reverse of checks (or warrants) payable to all providers above the claimant's endorsement:

> I understand that endorsement hereon or deposit to the accounts of the within named payee is done with the understanding that payment will be from Federal and State funds and that any false claims, statements, or documents, or concealment of a material fact, may be prosecuted under applicable Federal or State laws.[40]

Accountability for Administration

The methods for accountability used in public welfare agencies are designed to give assurance that public welfare administration has proper legal status and is administered responsibly, efficiently, and effectively to achieve social and economic objectives of the various programs. The methods are varied and complex, made so by the public responsibilities common to all government bodies and by the special character of human service programs. By what standard of measurement shall public welfare agencies be judged? By the *reduction* in the size of public assistance caseload, or by an *increase* in caseloads? By the *reduction* in the numbers of poor people in this country? By the *reduction* in assistance payments through a *reduction* in payment levels below the need standard or by an *increase* in such payments to reflect inflationary factors? By the *reduction* or *increase* in the numbers of public assistance recipients who become self-sufficient and are removed from assistance dependency? By the *increased numbers* of poor people who use Medicaid services or by a *reduction* in such numbers? By the *reduction* in the numbers of people receiving food stamps, or by an *increase* in their numbers? By the *increased numbers* of WIN registrants from AFDC families, or a *decrease* in their numbers possibly reflecting self-reliance in job finding? By the *increase* in the number of institutionalized aged or disabled, or a *decrease* in their numbers?

All of the above are goals and objectives of the public welfare system explicitly stated in law or implied in its administration. A logical sequence of reasoning can be applied to the opposites of the social targets expressed, depending upon one's attitude towards government support of low-income and disadvantaged people. An *increase* in the numbers helped may show that government programs are succeeding in giving welfare assistance and services to the people in need. A *decrease* in the numbers may show that government programs are not helping as many. An *increase* may also mean that those in need are able to be self-reliant and do not need government support. All of the above are apart from the question of strict policing of eligibility standards to weed out ineligibles and assumes the divergent views are directed to the dependency or self-sufficiency of eligible persons, that is, those entitled to government services and assistance.

The nub of this introduction is to explain the difficulty of the general public, legislators, chief executives, and others to satisfactorily reconcile the operations of the public welfare system with social goals and objectives of public welfare law in holding public welfare administration accountable. This poses a dilemma for public welfare administrators: whether to have operational objectives for increasing eligible beneficiaries for legally authorized assistance and services to which they are entitled, or for achieving a reduction in their numbers. This dilemma is real and pervasive. It affects public opinion and confidence in public welfare agencies. It affects the outcome of budgets for administration of the agencies, to provide operating and service funds for personnel, administrative expenditures, contract funds to employ private service agencies, health care providers, and assistance payments. As is discussed later in Chapter 10 on issues and problems, for any welfare reform to be successful it must resolve this dilemma in the ambiguity of social goals and operational objectives.

Methods of accountability for administration of public welfare agencies include:

development, review, and updating of state plans

preparation and review of annual and biennial budgets

merit system requirements under civil service applied to public welfare agencies

case-by-case identification and assessment of social service goals

auditing of public welfare agencies by independent authorities

regular public reporting of program operations and costs

evaluation, monitoring, and research in public welfare programs

PROGRAM AND FINANCIAL PLANNING.   The federal/state grant-in-aid system of state plans, described in Chapter 1, is a federal requirement imposed upon the states to receive federal funds. State plans are required in the AFDC, Title XX Social Services, child welfare services, Medicaid, and food stamp programs. They are descriptive of state programs to give assurance to the federal government of their compliance with federal regulations and other programmatic and procedural requirements. They are the basis for federal agency oversight activities, including program reviews of federal regional representatives and federal auditors.

Program and financial planning is another method for holding public welfare agencies accountable. Under the Title XX social services program, annually-updated state social services program plans are directed to the five service goals of the program. In most jurisdictions, joint social services and child welfare services plans are drawn up. Their service goals are equally compatible to both programs, particularly the goal for preventing or remedying neglect, abuse, or exploitation of children and preserving, rehabilitating, or reuniting families.

The program plans describe the numbers and categories of individuals to be served, kinds and amounts of services provided, kinds and amounts of agency and community service resources to be used, service fund allocations to be made, evaluative methods to be used to judge the efficiency and effectiveness of services to the stated five goals, and reports to be provided to the public, elected officials, and the federal government. The methods for coordinating the service plans with other human service programs are also outlined in them. Maximum publicity, including public hearings throughout the state, is given to the plans prior to final approval. Community leadership involvement in plan preparation is provided for to include representatives of ethnic and low-income groups, public interest groups, professional groups, and community service agencies and providers.

The formal structure, specificity, and coverage of program plans for other public welfare programs are not as definitive. Planning of programs and operations are conducted as an integral part of the budgetary process at all governmental levels as described in Chapter 7 on funding and budgeting. At the federal level, budgeting for FFP amounts is derived from national welfare caseloads and budget estimates projected from those supplied by the states.

Estimates of caseloads and expenditures are made to the federal departments annually and quarterly for the AFDC, Title XX social services, Medicaid, and food stamp programs for preparation of the federal budget for public welfare programs and to claim federal reimbursement for state and local program and administration expenditures. These estimates, in the aggregate, give the anticipated program and financial levels based on best-judgment estimates. Budgetary review of these estimates by chief executives and legislators probe and weigh the legitimacy of the estimates. Their approval is extremely important in reflecting the degree of confidence public leaders have in the administration of public welfare programs.

OPERATIONAL PLANNING (MANAGEMENT-BY-OBJECTIVES).
Wide use by public welfare agencies is made of operational planning, commonly known as Management-By-Objectives

(MBO). Both terms are used to describe a method to commit an employee-unit-section-division to specific tasks within a given time period to accomplish designated objectives. The method converts annual or biennial program and financial plans to daily, weekly, and monthly work targets. Welfare directors, supervisors, and individual workers decide upon these targets or objectives, to organize and plan their operations to produce the desired ends. The system places the focus directly on results-oriented management. Its principal features are:

Definition of measurable objectives to be achieved by each organizational level, creating a hierarcy of objectives from those of the public welfare director to those of the first, second, third, and lower levels of organization and finally to the objectives for individual workers. The objectives of the worker are components of the objectives of his unit, those of the unit are components of the objectives of its section or branch which, in turn, are components of the objectives of a division.

Setting operational plans for each objective, specifying the kinds of actions to be taken, the dates when each action begins, and when it should be completed.

Making monthly reports and holding meetings with supervisors to review progress made in meeting target dates. Such meetings are scheduled for each level of organization from discussions between supervisor and worker, to the unit level to the next higher levels and finally at the agency director's level so that each level reports on progress during the month on its objectives, from the lowest to the highest level of organization.

Surfacing existing and potential problems for completing operational plans and working to resolve them.

Analyzing progress made to achieve the desired results and, if necessary, modifying plans, specifying new actions, or setting new target dates to achieve the objectives.

Coordinating operations of workers, units, sections, and divisions to improve their work assignments to make better progress towards the objectives.

Evaluating performances of workers, units, sections, and divisions to determine what measures to be taken for improvement, e.g., training, changes in organization, methods, processes, personnel ceilings.

AUDITING OF PUBLIC WELFARE PROGRAMS.   Every governmental jurisdiction has an independent auditing agency to investigate all matters relating to the receipt, disbursement, and application of public funds, to determine whether public funds are efficiently and economically administered and expended, and to review and analyze the results of government programs and activities. These agencies maintain an independent status and usually report to the legislature rather than to the chief executive. Their reports are almost always public; they not only describe their methods and findings but also frequently recommend action to correct deficiencies uncovered. The audit of public welfare agencies has been a high priority in recent years as public welfare budgets and costs have risen so sharply and the urgent concerns of the public and elected officials are expressed.

Two types of audits are performed: *fiscal audits,* which are concerned with the legality and appropriateness of accounting and fiscal operations and government expenditures; and *program audits* which are applied to the efficiency, effectiveness, and benefits of the content and administration of governmental programs. At the federal level, the General Accounting Office has performed both types of audits but the Comptroller General has given policy emphasis during at least the past decade to the conduct of program audits. Such audits have dealt with various aspects of public assistance, social services, Medicaid and Food Stamp programs, and their administration at federal/state and local levels, for example, quality control, intake processes, Medicaid claims and social services effectiveness. The Departments of Health, Education and Welfare; Labor; and Agriculture also have departmental audit agencies regularly assigned to their public welfare programs. Under federal law, these agencies are authorized to audit state and local operations of federally-supported grant-in-aid programs and state and local governments are obligated to open their books and accounts to federal auditors. The frequent news accounts of state and local audit agencies—and the separate audit divisions within state public welfare agencies—in the investigation of welfare programs accurately reflect the national concern to make them more effective in eliminating ineligibles and providing services more effectively and economically.

REPORTING AND PUBLIC WELFARE INFORMATION SYSTEMS.
Public reporting by government bodies is an inherent function common to all public welfare agencies. The only proscription to the public's right to know is the confidentiality of persons in the system and their rights to privacy as applicant, assistance recipient, food stamp, and Medicaid beneficiary and social service client guaranteed them under the Social Security Act and other laws. This requires each agency to safeguard the use and disclosure of information on applicants and recipients.

Public welfare agencies maintain a public information office as a federal requirement. They also issue regular monthly, quarterly, and annual reports of their activities: local agencies report publicly and to state agencies which, in turn, report to the public and to the federal government. Federal reports to the public are issued from this information flow. All three levels of agencies report regularly to their respective chief executives and legislatures. Federal regulations of public welfare programs mandate state and local reports "as the Secretary may prescribe." They must maintain records

> necessary for the proper and efficient operation of the program, including records regarding applications, determinations of eligibility, the provisions of services, and administrative cost; and statistical, fiscal, and other records necessary for reporting and accountability required by the Secretary; and shall retain such records for such periods as are prescribed by the Secretary . . .
> The State agency shall make such reports in such form as the Secretary may from time to time require, and comply with such provisions as he finds necessary to assure the correctness and verification of such reports.[41]

Broad-based comprehensive information systems are prominent in all public welfare agencies to comply with their public reporting responsibilities as well as to serve the needs for administration, supervision, control, and direction as noted earlier in this chapter. State and local agencies have offices of Research and Statistics or other differently named statistical and reporting units. The D/HEW National Center for Social Statistics served this same function. The Office of Research and Statistics of the Social Security Administration, the management information systems office of the Labor Department, and the Program Reporting Staff of the Food and Nutrition Service for the food stamp program are the central statistical and reporting units in their respective programs. The content of the regular periodic reports issued by these agencies do not vary greatly. They cover 4 areas of information:

1. Program expenditures and funding sources, for example, those for assistance payments, vendor payments, Medicaid claims, the value of food stamps, social services expenditures, WIN training expenditures, and administrative expenses incurred in the respective programs.
2. Recipients and beneficiary individuals and families by type or category of eligibility or service provided, the number of persons discontinued assistance (by reason of discontinuance).
3. Applications made and results of the intake process, for example, the number of eligibles, ineligibles, fair hearings by type or category of applicant.
4. Quality control processes and outcomes, for example, the number of cases reviewed, the number of errors found (by type), the percentage of cases of ineligibles, overpayments, and underpayments.

Special detailed studies and tabulations of socioeconomic characteristics of individual and family beneficiaries have been produced from time to time, such as the 1973 AFDC Characteristics Study made by the National Center for Social Statistics. State and local agencies also produce similar studies of the caseloads in their jurisdictions to gain insight into poverty-producing factors, the extent of need of low-income and disadvantaged persons, the nature of the problems confronting them, and the services they require.

The routine reports do not usually cover the number or percent of potential eligibles in the population, the effectiveness of services or benefits in rehabilitating individuals or families to self-support or improved living status, improvement in or maintenance of health status resulting from Medicaid services, or the economic savings resulting from the assistance or services they received. This information, vital to a belief in the social and economic value of public welfare services and benefits, is not a common product of public welfare reporting. It is produced to a limited extent in a largely uncoordinated effort by evaluations and special research studies conducted by universities, private research organizations, and the research units of state and local welfare agencies.

PROGRAM EVALUATION AND RESEARCH.   Program evaluation in the public welfare system is the process of examining and analyzing program objectives, operations, organization, and use of personnel and other resources of welfare agencies to provide information to decision-makers in and outside the system on the effectiveness, efficiency, quality, and availability of assistance and services. It is a widely used method of accountability, both to analyze how the programs are administered and what alternatives there are to the status quo.[42] The search for effective welfare reform to change the system is an example of program evaluation in its broadest sense. Evaluation asks this question:

> Is the program achieving the objectives sought by Congress and the executive branch and is it achieving it at the lowest practical cost? Arriving at a satisfactory answer presents difficulties, since the evaluation approach taken can influence the outcome tremendously. Whether the assessment is based on a political test or that of a possible more objective researcher, the results are often difficult to pin down. In the social area few observers approach the task with neither purely political nor no-political biases. The challenge is to provide decision-makers with the best analysis possible within the current state of the art.[43]

Acting Commissioner Michio Suzuki, Public Services Administration, acknowledged that

> The social services community has long recognized the need for ways by which to objectively measure the effectiveness of services upon the individuals, families, and children who receive those services. This need has been particularly strong among the managers of Federal and State social service programs who must make major decisions in the areas of budgeting, resource allocation, program development, and policy formulation . . .
>
> Unfortunately, although there has been much research and technological development in cost effectiveness, cost benefit analysis, predictive models, movement scales, etc., hard data on what social services actually do for people were at a minimum. Also, several current studies which seek to measure the effectiveness of social services are long-term efforts; they will not produce usable data for several years. Therefore, despite the recognized need, despite the methodological development, no generally accepted system existed for determining the impact of social services provided or purchased by public social service agencies for poor and disadvantaged people.[44]

PUBLIC WELFARE RESEARCH.   Public welfare research is supported by the federal government under the Social Security Act by: Special Demonstration Projects under Section 1115, Cooperative Research and Demonstration Projects under Section 1110, Section 1875 Health Care Prospective Reimbursement Experimental and Demonstration Projects.

Research in employment and training of low-income persons, including WIN program research, is supported under the Manpower Development and Training Act of 1962 (42 USC 2571) and its successor, the Comprehensive Employment and Training Act of 1973, as amended (87 Stat. 839) through Manpower Experimental and Demonstration Projects, Manpower Research-Doctoral Dissertations Grants, and Manpower Research-Institutional Grants and Projects.

Section 1115 Special Demonstration Projects are designed to develop and improve methods of public welfare assistance and service programs and their administration and training provisions. State and local welfare agencies are eligible to submit applications for demonstration projects of the following types:[45]

projects of special significant to one state, a group of states, or of national significance

pilot or experimental projects which introduce new methods or approaches to delivery of assistance and services

projects which test whether a method successful in other fields can be applied to an assistance program or can be made more effective when used in such program

methods of reducing dependency through provision of assistance to needy people who would not otherwise be eligible, or an increase in the level of assistance payments or provision of social services not otherwise available

testing new patterns for delivery of medical or social services

testing new methods for improving administration

testing new approaches to staff training

The Secretary of Health, Education and Welfare is authorized to waive compliance with other Social Security Act provisions necessary for the state to carry out a project. FFP is provided for approved projects to cover project costs which would not otherwise be included as public assistance expenditures under the regular reimbursement formulas. Grants are also made to state agencies of special federal project funds to finance all or part of a project not covered by payments under the welfare assistance, medical, and social services programs of the Social Security Act.

Section 1110 Cooperative Research and Demonstration Projects provide grants or contracts for research and demonstrations relating to the prevention and reduction of dependency, to aid in effecting coordination of planning between private and public welfare agencies, or to help improve the administration and effectiveness of public welfare programs. State welfare agencies, other public agencies, and private nonprofit agencies and organizations are eligible for contracts.[46] As with Section 1115 projects, FFP is available for part or all of contract funds except construction or major renovation of buildings. Grants and contracts have been granted for state welfare agencies, university-based research centers, and private nonprofit community service agencies for a wide range of projects in child care experiments, social indicators, cost-benefit studies of job training programs, income maintenance experiments, effectiveness of the EPDST program, experimental services integration projects, effect of earnings exemptions on AFDC recipients, employability of AFDC mothers and fathers, impediments to employment, and prevention of family breakdown.

Health Care Prospective Reimbursement Experimental and Demonstration (Section 1875) Projects are designed to test various methods of prospective reimbursements to providers of health services under the Medicare, Medicaid, and maternal and child health programs. It authorizes experiments and demonstration projects to increase efficiency and economy involving:

1. negotiated rates of charges of health providers;
2. use of rates established by a state for administering its laws for payment to health facilities;
3. alternative methods of reimbursement with respect to services of residents, interns, and supervisory physicians in teaching settings; and
4. payment for noncovered services incidental to covered services furnished by organizations providing comprehensive, mental, or ambulatory health care services or other institutional services which may be substituted for hospital care.

It authorizes experiments to determine whether coverage of intermediate care facilities and homemaker services would provide suitable alternatives to posthospital benefits under Medicare and experiments with use of fixed price or incentive performance contracts.

Among other projects funded are demonstrations to determine the most appropriate and equitable methods of compensating for the services of physicians assistants, where such services are performed independently and where not prohibited by the state medical and other professional practices acts. Experimentation in the provision of day-care services to persons entitled to Medicaid and Medicare is provided for. Projects in these and other areas in health care are in progress.

Manpower and Training Research and Evaluation projects and grants provide support for development of new ideas and improved techniques, for demonstrations of the effectiveness of specialized methods in meeting the manpower, employment, and training problems of particular disadvantaged worker groups. Funds are administered by the Employment and Training Administration, Department of Labor, and that Department's Office of Policy, Evaluation, and Research. The subject areas targeted for research and evaluation in recent years have been the WIN program, public service employment, comprehensive employment training program, and migrant worker program. Those directed to public welfare research in 1974–75 included an in-house pilot evaluation study of the work registration requirements of the Food Stamp Program; an evaluation of a welfare demonstration program which experimented with targeting public service employment to welfare recipients in 12 governments in four states, and the impact of the WIN program.

Welfare research is not, by any means, limited to federally sponsored projects. Among other research efforts are the studies and reports generated by state and local welfare agencies, by Congressional committees and committees of state legislatures (for example, the Studies in Public Welfare of the Congressional Subcommittee on Fiscal Policy of the Joint Economic Committee in 1972–1973) by private research organizations such as the Brookings Institution, the Urban Institute, and by many doctoral theses produced by candidates for a Ph.D., D.S.W., or Dr. P.H. degrees of schools of social work, public health, sociology, psychology, and other centers of learning.

PUBLIC WELFARE METHODS: UNIFORMITY OR FREEDOM OF CHOICE?

One cannot help but be impressed by the extent of federal government influence through its regulatory powers to mandate standards and processes as conditions placed upon state and local governments for FFP. Yet there are substantial differences in methods which reflect not only regional social, economic, and physical differences but even more the initiatives of state and local governments for self-determinism and independence in shaping their own programs. Even the differences in the choice of names for essentially the same welfare methods are indicative of this syndrome. This is not to denigrate state and local government independence in deciding how they administer their welfare programs. There is no reason to assume that federal government leadership in choice of methods is necessarily superior to that of the 50 states, the territories and the District of Columbia and thousands of local governments. In numbers alone, the talents, interests, and efforts of the tens of thousands of workers, leaders, and concerned citizens who comprise the public welfare constituency of counties and cities are a far greater resource than that of the federal government. And this resource is more attuned to local requirements and characteristics of its people in the administration of welfare programs. In conceiving utilization review as a method for holding accountable hospitals and other health care facilities, for example, the authors of the federal regulations must assume knowledge of the great variety and methods of health care institutions about which state and local officials have prior knowledge. To their credit, federal officials of these and other regulations involve state and local authorities, knowledgeable professionals in the field, and other interested parties in drawing up carefully worded and designed provisions to account for these vast differences and allow an opportunity for a period of review and criticisms which permit modifications in drafts prior to their final issuance. This careful balance between national interest in public welfare programs and local variations must be maintained in the design of any welfare reform efforts in the future.

This review process was enhanced in 1976 when then-Secretary of HEW Mathews announced a new requirement that a "Notice of Intent" be published 45 days in advance of any new or changed important regulations. This notice of intent would lay out the issues and options and the department's position in formulating the regulation. It would invite citizens' reactions through various public announcements, special mailings, open hearings, and other means. These would be reviewed in writing the proposed regulation. Accompanying the proposal would be summaries of comments received. After a second comment period, the final regulations would be published.[47]

NOTES

1. Studies in Public Welfare Paper No. 5 (Part 1): Issues in Welfare Administration: Welfare—An Administrative Nightmare, A Staff Study, Subcommittee on Fiscal Policy of the Joint Economic Committee Congress of the United States, December 31, 1972. U.S. Government Printing Office, Washington, D.C., p. 5.

2. Klein, D. P. Gathering data on residents of poverty areas. Monthly Labor Review, February 1975, Vol. 98 No. 2 Bureau of Labor Statistics, Department of Labor, Washington, D.C., pp. 38–44.

3. Medical Assistance Manual, Part 5 MSA-PRG-21 June 28, 1972, Par. 5-70-20.

.4. Maryland Department of Human Resources Comprehensive Social Services Program Plan 1975–1976, p. 24.

5. Section 206.10 Part 206 Chapter II Title 45 (37 CFR 16551), approved August 16, 1972.

6. Managing the Intake Process in Income Maintenance, a *How They Do It* Report, Assistance Payments Administration, Social and Rehabilitation Service, October 9, 1974, Washington, D.C., p. 9.

7. For a fuller discussion, see Issues in Welfare Administration: Welfare—An Administrative Nightmare. Paper No. 5 (Part 1) Studies in Public Welfare, Ibid, p. 5–11.

8. Ibid, Managing the Intake Process in Income Maintenance. *How They Do It* p. 51–52.

9.   Section 15.50 Part 205 Chapter LL Title 45 of the Code of Federal Regulations approved August 16, 1973 (45 CFR 205.50).

10. How To Do It: A Photo-Identification Card System for Welfare Recipients, Assistance Payments Administration, Social and Rehabilitation Service, September 31, 1974, APA-IM-75-5, Washington, D.C.

11. Section 1614 a) 2), Social Security Act, P.L. 62-603, January 1, 1974.

12. Section 1631 a) 4) P.L. 62-603, effective January 1, 1974.

13. Section 228.61 c) (45 CFR 228), April 14, 1975.

14. 45 CFR 206.10 a) 6), December 3, 1973.

15. Section 271.4 Certification of Households, Food Stamp Regulation 37 CFR 270. May 7, 1976.

16. This description is excerpted from Lotwin, G: Need determination in public assistance. Unpublished paper presented at the Second National Training Session on Public Assistance/Vocational Rehabilitation, New York City, December 6–8, 1972.

17. Peiper, C. M. The way to establish "no-check" welfare. Human Needs, 1972, 20–23.

18. Assignment of Rights to Support (45 CFR 232.11).

19. Middleman, R. R. & Goldberg, G. *Social service delivery: A structural approach to social work practice.* New York: Columbia University Press, 1974, pp. 54–80.

20. Combs, A. W., Avila, D. L., & Purkey, W. W. *Helping relationships: basic concepts for the helping professions.* Boston: Allyn and Bacon, pp. 272–288.

21. Ibid. pp. 81–150.

22. Ibid. pp. 18–24.

23. WIN Regulations, Department of Labor 40 CFR 182, September 18, 1975.

24. DHEW: The Cuban Refugee Program. Welfare in Review Vol. 1, No. 3, September 1963, Washington, D.C.

25. 45 CFR 205 et. seq.

26. Schutzman, F. How quality control cuts AFDC errors. *The Social and Rehabilitation Record,* 1974 1(3), pp. 18–22.

27. For further details, see the Quality Control Manual: Quality Control in Public Assistance, issued by Assistance Payments Administration, SRS Revised June 1972, SRS 72-21205. Washington, D.C.

28. HEW Press Release, October 31, 1975.

29. Quality Control In The Food Stamp Program—Non-Public Assistance Households. January–June, 1974. Hearings Before the House Committee on Appropriations, Subcommittee on Agriculture and Related Agencies, 1976 Appropriations, 94th Congress, First Session, U.S. Congress. U.S. Government Printing Office, Washington, D.C. 1975, pp. 909–914.

30. Child Support Enforcement Program 40 CFR 124, June 26, 1975. Also see Svahn, J. A. Enforcing child support. *The Social and Rehabilitation Record,* 1975, **2**(5), 10–12.

31. The Utah Story—Public Accountability in Quality Health Care Delivery. Viewpoint, a publication of the Health Insurance Council, New York, January 1973.

32. Action Transmittal SRS-AT-75-42 (MSA): Relationship of PSRO Review Responsibilities to the Medicaid Program-Secretarial Decision of February 24, 1975, June 25, 1975.

33. Federal Interagency Day Care Requirements, republished by DHEW Publication No. (OHD) 76-31081, Washington, D.C.

34. Section 228.42 CFR 228, Social Services Program for Individual and Families, October 1, 1975.

35. Standards for Foster Family Services Systems. American Public Welfare Administration, March 1975.

36. Medical Assistance Program Standards and Provider Certification. 45 CFR 205.190, July 12, 1973.

37. Compliance with federal, state, and local laws as regards state or local skilled nursing facilities, 39 CFR 2238, Juanary 17, 1974.

38. 45 CFR 249.

39. Program Regulation Guide MSA-PRG-31, June 10, 1974 MSA Medical Assistance Manual.

40. Section 250.80. Fraud in the medical assistance program, 45 CFR 250, March 31, 1976.

41. Section 228.17 45 CFR 228 Social Service Program for Individual and Family Services, April 14, 1975. This language appears in all federally-supported public welfare programs.

42. D. L. Cornick, A. L. Sheppard, and D. F. Brezine (eds.): A model system for organizing separated social services—a resource manual. Washington, D.C.: National Catholic School of Social Services, The Catholic University of America, 1973, 136–138.

43. Staats, E. B.: Challenges and problems in the evaluation of governmental programs. *Interfaces,* 1974, **5**,(1), 25–32, The Institute of Management Sciences, Providence, R.I.

44. Social Services Effectiveness Study, U.S. Department of Health, Education and Welfare, Social and Rehabilitation Services Public Services Administration, 1976, Washington, D.C.

45. Special Demonstration Projects Under Section 1115 of the Social Security Act, 45 CFR 282, February 4, 1976.

46. Research and Demonstration Projects Under Section 1110 of the Social Security Act, 45 CFR 283, February 6, 1976.

47. *The Washington Post,* July 25, 1976.

Chapter 9

PUBLIC WELFARE RELATIONSHIPS

Public welfare programs have a common bond among them of organization, goals, objectives, and service to eligible low-income beneficiaries. They are administered in an interconnecting link of federal, state, and local agencies under common leadership, supervision, and responsibility towards maintaining and improving their social and economic status. The programs are the principal publicly-sanctioned means of providing assistance and services for this population, but they do not have exclusive jurisdiction for them. Other public social programs and agencies also provide low-income beneficiaries income maintenance, social services, health care, food, manpower training services, and other public welfare services. This is common knowledge to the public assistance recipient, medically indigent, food stamp recipient, WIN registrant, parents and caretakers of neglected or dependent children.

It is this country's social policy that there is no unitary system of programs for *all* low-income and disadvantage persons, nor for providing *all* the social health and economic needs of those eligible for welfare assistance and services. We *do* have a complex of categorical assistance programs which directly concern them in a criss-cross pattern of programs administered

411

by different organizations, separately authorized and funded, with a different emphasis: of *population group* (for example: aged, veterans, children); of a particular *problem* (mental retardation, juvenile delinquency); of *geography* (Appalachia or a ghetto neighborhood); of *political jurisdiction* (state or local government); of *type of service* (legal services); of *social need* (education, housing); of *funding source* (federal or state); of *professional group* (medical); of *process* (social casework); of *production* (agriculture).

The differences among programs do exist, but so do the similarities. Public welfare and the other social programs share responsibility and accountability for a common beneficiary group. In public welfare it constitutes the group of eligible low-income individuals and families, in other programs a substantial part but not all of their clientele are these same low-income individuals and families. They may be known variously as educationally deprived, economically disadvantaged, chronically unemployed, underserved populations, ghetto residents, the rural poor, or the socially and economically vulnerable. Public welfare and other social programs also share in many common helping services, in the legally-declared policy objectives for human betterment and independent living, in the use of common social and community resources and facilities, in the background, training, and relationships of the helping professions and in the federal, state, and local government funding relationships of most projects, grants, and support assistance.

To this complex of public programs we must add the panoply of voluntary, community, and privately funded and organized social agencies. They play a vital role in serving the needs of low-income and disadvantaged persons who are not immediately (or temporarily) eligible for public services or who require emergency assistance, unattainable from public programs. Among these are the United Way, the Salvation Army, Catholic Charities, Protestant church agencies, Jewish Social Service Agencies, the fraternal brotherhood organizations (Kiwanis, Lions, Elks, Masons, Knights of Columbus) and a host of other independent and affiliated agencies. Public funds through contracts, agreements, and other financial arrangements are a large measure of support of these agencies primarily for social, medical, and rehabilitation services to public welfare recipients and other poor. In this posture, the voluntary agencies have a legal, contractual relationship with public agencies. When their contracts are with public welfare agencies, they are constructively part of the public welfare system; they apply government regulations, standards, and methods and are held accountable for them. This has created a dilemma for them of no small proportion; how to maintain their independence and flexibility, yet retain their voluntary service character under their own charters when they are so largely dependent, financially and otherwise, for serving as agents of public welfare authority.

Public welfare agencies operate in this setting effectively if there is mutual confidence and cooperation between social agencies to blend their actions for the benefit of welfare recipients and nonrecipient beneficiaries of other agencies. For example, state aging agencies are concerned with all older persons in the state. Within this group are, of course, SSI recipients. The joint collaboration of aging and public welfare agencies in service plans for the aged is of benefit to the larger group of non-SSI recipients, poor and nonpoor alike, as well as SSI recipients. To be effective, their separate actions may not be inconsistent, may not ignore or be at odds with the needs of the one group in favor of the other. Thus, the ultimate aim of the relationship among social programs at all levels of government and in all socioeconomic jurisdictional settings is to coordinate the disparate organizations and programs for the benefit of their respective clienteles. This is nowhere an easy accomplishment, given the realities of the host of differences among them of laws, goals and objectives, policies, funding mechanisms, organizations, operational priorities, processes, and constituents.

Since there are never enough dollars for all social programs to meet all America's social needs, nor are there enough social and medical service resources, facilities and professionals, there is a natural competitive spirit among administrators and supporters of public welfare and other social programs for the available funds and resources and the power which they represent. The consequences of witting and unwitting, of unreasoning, and rivalry among programs and agencies, of noncooperation among administrators and staffs, or of overt hostility, are a waste of public funds and resources, duplicative and ineffective services, often to the detriment and confusion of beneficiaries, and lastly, to a loss of confidence of legislators, chief executives, the general public and the media. Although no definitive research has been done of the incidence and adverse results of such rivalry and noncooperation, there is little doubt they exist among the hundreds of social agencies in this country where the overlapping structure of categorical programs, goals, objectives, services, and clientele prevails. From time to time public investigations and legislative inquiries have reported instances of such conditions but more often they are unpublicized and undocumented policies and practices, known only within the bureaucracies affected. Elliot L. Richardson, then-Secretary of Health, Education and Welfare, expressed this concern before a meeting of the United Way of America in a speech in Chicago May 5, 1971:

> My observations have convinced me that both the government and the voluntary agencies themselves are going to have to make some fundamental changes in the way we deliver those services.
>
> What has impressed me most is the extensive fragmentation of the delivery system. The Department of Health, Education and Welfare now administers over 270 separate programs through six major agencies and a variety of smaller ones all designed to meet one essential need—the solution of personal, human problems. These programs compete with each other for scarce funds and skilled manpower. The proponents of each spend too much time arguing against competing programs instead of improving the one for which they are responsible. Accountability for results is almost impossible with dozens of different officials each charged with managing only a part of the solution to a complex social problem.
>
> State and local programs have fared little better. Petty jealousies, politics, waste, and duplication can be found at all levels of government-delivered social services. The voluntary agencies have not escaped these problems either.
>
> This fragmented delivery system has developed as a result of many individual, well-intentioned efforts to solve isolated social problems as, from time to time, they were perceived. Unfortunately, this approach overlooked one important factor: an individual seldom has only one problem. He usually needs the services of several of our programs, plus some of yours. When you include the needs of his family, all of which interrelate to his own, a wide variety of programs all working in a coordinated fashion may be

required to meet that family's needs. The individual may be lucky enough to find one of our programs that can help him with some of his problems, but he would have to be a master of Chinese puzzles to put together the combination of public and private programs that could effectively meet most or all his needs, and those of his family as well. Unfortunately, the person who administers the one program he has found will probably not be much help either. That person may know of some other programs in his own office, but what of another agency or department, not to mention the services of voluntary organizations.

Nevertheless, the coordinating mechanisms which have developed over time have sought to overcome the differences and competition and produce benefits to both welfare recipient and nonrecipient alike. These are evident under different programs with different coordinative arrangements. Special joint action programs are created such as the public assistance/vocational rehabilitation program in which state vocational rehabilitation agencies and state and local welfare agencies jointly work to screen and evaluate public assistance recipients for rehabilitation and provide intensive job-related rehabilitative services to make them employable. The offices of the two programs may be placed in a common location, such as a neighborhood center to be accessible to public assistance recipients and applicants. Automatic eligibility may be given public assistance recipients for other program entitlements, as in the national school lunch program. Priority for recipients may be granted to receive benefits of other social programs, as in public housing or elementary and secondary education. The income of other programs may be disregarded in determining assistance payments as the value of food stamps. Standards applied in other social and health programs may be accepted by public welfare social and health programs, as in those for the Medicare program adopted for state Medicaid programs. Federal funding may be distributed in the proportion of welfare recipients in the general population as in general revenue sharing. The costs of services and benefits received by recipients may be given special consideration, such as in public housing rents. Joint in-service training programs may be set up for public welfare workers and those of other social programs. Joint demonstrations of new procedures and methods may be sponsored by public welfare and other social agencies. Joint funds may be applied to common special programs. Agreements may be reached on the order in which charges and reimbursements for services would be made as in the "first dollar" concept when the state Medicaid program covers the cost of health screening of children under the ESDPT program, or the Title XX social services program reimbursements for child care in public day-care centers. Referrals of recipients may be made to other social agencies for follow up to provide services and treatment, as referrals to a law enforcement agency in suspected cases of child abuse, or a handicapped adult needing supervision in a protective environment.

The interprogram relationships may affect public welfare beneficiaries in different ways: some programs may help potential recipients retain their abilities to function independently without welfare assistance or services. An example is the successful job training and placement of a poor family head under one of the Department of Labor employment programs, or a woman's graduation from college made possible by a higher education work-study grant. Other programs may have the opposite effect. Economically independent persons may become welfare-dependent when benefits of other programs terminate, such as unemployment compensation benefits. Some programs may improve the effectiveness of welfare services and benefits. An anxious aged person treated in a community mental health center is able to function independently at home, making unnecessary his placement in an intermediate care facility under the state Medicaid program. Other programs may be successful in removing welfare recipients from dependency. An example is the rehabilitated alcoholic in an alcohol treatment program becoming employed and free of the need for public assistance.

In a broader perspective, public welfare beneficiaries are affected by and are part of every facet of American life: social, economic, environmental, ethical, moral, intellectual, religious. This population group directly and indirectly influences and is influenced by every public program, every development in American experience, domestic and foreign. There is in every governmental program a logical connecting link with public welfare, with the poor, sometimes as part of the "general welfare" other times as part of the "War on Poverty." Public welfare cannot be treated in isolation, nor can its programs and agencies be administered without considering their relationships to the larger national and world scene. Within this larger context, it is important to give recognition to programs more closely tied to public welfare than others.

The following is a description of these relationships in the areas of education, food and nutrition, housing, manpower and employment, health, law enforcement, aging and other social programs:[1]

EDUCATIONAL PROGRAMS

State and local welfare and education agencies in combination employ the largest number of public employees, have combined funding making up the biggest slice of state and local budgets and serving the largest combined clientele of children, families, and adults. There are over 18,000 public school systems nationally, employing over five million employees, with expenditures of over $110 billion and an enrollment of over 60 million children and adults in close to 90,000 public and private schools of all types.[2]

The more than eight million AFDC children, the millions of children of non-AFDC medically indigent families, food stamp beneficiaries, recipients of child welfare services and other public welfare programs, their parents and other family members are at some time part of the public and private educational systems. They are not grouped separately, segregated, or receive individual consideration as public welfare recipients per se. Rather, they are part of a larger group of persons deemed to be educationally deprived or disadvantaged for which special compensatory, supplementary, and intensive educational programs are provided. This larger group includes children and adults who are in low-income families; are physically handicapped, dependent, or neglected children; orphans, juvenile delinquents in institutions; migrant families; those who live in areas of high concentrations of low-income families; non-English-speaking persons, American Indians, and other minority groups.

The objectives of the special educational benefits are to compensate for the physical, economic, social, cultural, and psychological deprivation which handicap their education. The handicaps may discourage or prevent children or adults from enrolling in a school, because they may be without transportation to a school, not have parental guidance, do farm labor as migrant workers, be emotionally or psychologically immature or have a language barrier. The handicaps may impose barriers to maintaining learning progress at a satisfactory rate and be outside the normal capability of the education system to provide the special supplementary educational facilities needed. Examples are children or adults with a chronic learning disability with a nutritional deficiency, poor health or be in a disruptive family setting barring regular attendance. The handicaps may also cause early and premature dropouts because of social and economic dependency, physical or emotional illness, delinquent and criminal behavior, or other disruptive factors, including loss of interest in education.

The special educational programs for this group require the closest relationship between the public welfare and educational programs as well as the private educational systems. The relationship is of mutual interest, awareness and interdependence of each others domain: teachers, other educational personnel, and administrators must be knowledgeable of public welfare programs, their eligibility requirements, organization, personnel, services, and facilities. Caseworkers, eligibility workers, social work specialists, health care personnel, manpower training counselors, and welfare administrators must have a good understanding of the educational systems in their jurisdictions. They must maintain formal and informal day-to-day contact in the broader areas of policy development, program plans, priority and administration as well as in the individual case-by-case problems which thwart or interfere in the educational and social development of children and adults with which both agencies are concerned. The special educational programs for the "educationally deprived or disadvantaged" function within every educational level and target group: pre-school, elementary and secondary education, vocational education, higher education, adult education, minority group education, and handicapped children education.

FOOD AND NUTRITION PROGRAMS

The food needs of public welfare beneficiaries are met not only through food allowances in their assistance payments checks and in the purchase of food stamps but through federal/state surplus food distribution programs and special meal programs for children and the aged. These programs provide food through federal, state, city, and county agencies as well as private nonprofit agencies and institutions: (1) in schools operating nonprofit food service programs; (2) in nonprofit summer camps and service institutions for children, (3) in charitable institutions; (4) in state correctional institutions for minors, (5) in nutrition programs for the elderly; and (6) in the assistance of needy persons. Public welfare beneficiaries are participants as needy persons and as students or residents of the given school, camp, or institution.

The acknowledged official purpose of these food programs when they were put into effect was to prevent the waste of agricultural commodities in private stock or acquired through price-support operations of the Commodity Credit Corporation. However, subsequent food programs have a different emphasis: that of the importance of diet and nutrition and in support of programs to children and adults vulnerable to malnutrition.

HOUSING AND COMMUNITY DEVELOPMENT PROGRAMS

The need for decent housing and a safe, suitable community environment in which public welfare recipients and other low- and moderate-income persons live is accepted as broad government policy. The great variety of government assistance in programs for housing and community development is designed to carry out this policy to the extent other public and private investment sources fail.

Public welfare assistance in housing is in the form of (1) allowances for shelter costs and utilities provided in assistance checks to AFDC and SSI beneficiaries, estimated to be $1.1 billion annually; and (2) payments for major repairs to otherwise unliveable homes owned by a beneficiary. Social service counseling in home management and assistance to AFDC families and SSI recipients in locating suitable housing are widely provided. Social workers recognize the acute debilitating effects of poor housing and community conditions upon the attitudes of the poor, the loss of spirit, the inability to cope, making them less willing and able to help themselves to self-sufficiency and independence. This is where the interrelationship of welfare and housing agencies and programs becomes an essential ingredient for interaction. The priority of housing and community development towards low- and moderate-income needs create otherwise unavailable resources to public welfare programs in helping their clientele meet their social and economic self-improvement objectives. This was reaffirmed formally in an "HEW-HUD Memorandum of Agreement" in 1971 to provide federal leadership for coordinating housing and social services programs of the two departments.[3] A program of housing-welfare cooperation was agreed upon to:

> cooperate in policies and procedures for establishing equitable rents paid by public welfare recipients in public housing, resolving rent delinquency problems of such recipients, and furnishing social services to explore causes and seek remedies for them;
>
> promote cooperation of state and local welfare and housing agencies in such matters as setting welfare rent schedules, provision of comprehensive social services in public housing;
>
> cooperate in developing model programs for demonstration of joint social services/housing agency improvements and methods for collaboration between them; and

provide for joint evaluation of joint programs to improve the quality of services provided by welfare and housing agencies.

As in other social programs, housing programs exclusively for public welfare recipient groups do not exist. They are part —a major part—of the low-income population and of public housing and central city ghetto neighborhoods. These are the targets of housing improvement and community development assistance. The benefits gained by this larger population group accrue also to public welfare recipients. These include the availability of public housing, rental apartments, condominium and cooperative housing, single-family ownership, homes for the elderly and handicapped, mobile homes, and community facilities.

Housing and community development assistance comes in many forms: interest reduction payments to lower housing costs; interest subsidies to finance the acquisition and rehabilitation of housing; property and home improvement loan insurance; mobile home loan insurance; mortgage insurance; loans for low-income projects; public housing loans for acquisition, construction, and leasing; rent supplements; grants for community development projects; housing allowances to assist families in meeting rental or homeownership expenses. Except for the last, assistance is given to financial and real estate organizations in financing and supplying the property and improvements for low- and moderate-income households and their neighborhoods. The more direct recipients of housing and community development assistance, therefore, are banks, insurance companies, property owners, rental property landlords, the housing and building construction industry, and, finally, in the housing allowance program, individuals and families. This policy follows prevailing economic principles that conventional market practices require government inducements of loan guarantees and other legal, financial protections and guarantees to financial and real estate interests—before they apply themselves to housing and community development for low- and moderate-income persons. Without such inducements, protections, and guarantees, they would continue to meet the normal supply and demand of housing of higher income persons and give low priority to, or ignore altogether, the less affluent.

About one-third of public housing tenants are public welfare recipients. At least 20 percent of new public housing units are rented to families whose incomes do not exceed 50 percent of median income in the area. Rental for a dwelling unit may not exceed 25 percent of a low-income family's income. A maximum rent of 5 percent of gross family income or the portion of a welfare payment specified to meet housing costs is charged, provided that the aggregate rents of the local public housing authority equals 20 percent of the aggregate income of tenants. This last is to assure a mix of low- and higher-income tenants able to support at least some of the operating costs of the public housing property.

JOB TRAINING AND EMPLOYMENT PROGRAMS

The close working relationship in the WIN program is part of a larger relationship between public welfare agencies and labor and manpower agencies. Both agencies have a collaborative role in their respective programs to remove people from poverty, promote full employment, provide a labor force of competent, satisfied, productive workers earning wages to support themselves and families and provide adequately for their needs and wants. Both agencies provide services to help the disadvantaged and vulnerable in our society maintain self-sufficiency and independent living. In short, manpower and welfare agencies seek the same national social and economic goal of maximizing the value and productivity of people, our most important American resource. In combination, both agencies and programs provide in their respective spheres a comprehensive range of support services and assistance to:

> stimulate and encourage individuals to enter the labor force;
> prepare individuals for a productive life of work;
> help them find productive work up to their capabilities and the development of skills and abilities;

assure payment of adequate wages;

remove social, health, education barriers and barriers of discrimination to their receiving training, employment, and worker development;

provide a safe and healthy working environment;

provide financial assistance when unemployed or if unemployable; and

assure workers receipt of such benefits as sick pay, vacations, pensions, workers compensation and other work entitlements.

Public welfare recipients are not specifically designated for job training and employment services, except in the WIN program. They are part of the larger target population of economically disadvantaged unemployed or underemployed, or designated as persons living in areas of high unemployment. The success of manpower and labor programs measured in full-time job placements, earning an adequate wage—for public welfare recipients—has an add-on social benefit of simultaneously removing them from assistance rolls. From a different perspective, successful job placements also serve the socioeconomic purposes of keeping potential welfare recipients off assistance rolls, reducing the size of assistance payments by helping welfare youth, women, and men locate part-time and intermittent paid employment to provide earnings to offset part of their personal and household needs.

In general, the monetary value of training, support services, and other related allowances welfare recipients receive do not reduce the size of their welfare payments. The wages they receive from employment, however, are counted on a dollar-for-dollar basis in reducing their monthly assistance checks, unless legally disregarded.

HEALTH CARE PROGRAMS

The health components of the public welfare system are manifold: the Medicaid program, health-related social and child welfare services programs, those of the WIN program, health services provided Cuban Refugees, and repatriated U.S. nationals. But these health supporting activities are not isolated. They are part of a larger, multidimensional pattern of government-aided public health and medical care which concerns the health status of all Americans.

The common denominator of public welfare health services is the poverty of welfare individuals and families (with the exception of the nonpoor families with children receiving child welfare services). Public health policy gives them special status in promoting and safeguarding the public health and provision of public medical care, including the use of mainstream health providers and institutions. There is no public policy to set up a separate health and medical care system for the poor and one for the nonpoor.

Public welfare recipients are beneficiaries of a variety of health programs and services operated by agencies other than public welfare agencies. These are offered by public and private health agencies and facilities in a multitude of locations and settings. They may be a store front clinic in an urban ghetto, a community hospital, a health center, a physician's office, at home, in the street or a mobile van, in a skilled nursing facility, a halfway house, a detention center, in a school. They may be services to people with a special health problem, such as a physical handicap. They may be the target of a public health education or family planning campaign or subjects of a health research project, such as cancer detection. They may be eligible for health care because of their age, as Medicare or school health, be recipients of a general nutrition improvement or drug abuse program sponsored by a local public health department. They may receive health services as Indians, migrants, veterans, and armed forces dependents in a program designed for these special groups.

The social policy of government-aided health services as they apply to the poor and near-poor follows this pattern of logic: (1) Low-income populations are part of the general population towards which public health programs are directed. (2) Low-income populations are high risk public health groups with comparatively poorer health histories, poorer health practices, poorer health status, poorer health information, living in poorer home and neighborhood environments than the general (non-poor) public. (3) They are the targets of special public health and medical care programs with broad objectives to improve the general level of health. (4) They are less able economically to meet the costs of essential health services than other population groups. (5) Public welfare programs do not cover all the health needs of all low-income persons. They are mainly limited to health diagnosis and treatment of illness (except for the EPSDT program for children) and leave to other health programs the provision of health education, health prevention, such as disease control, food and drug purity and other public health services and activities aimed at the general population. Nor do the public welfare medical services meet the needs of nonwelfare, low-income groups, such as childless couples or individuals living alone and other poor living without welfare aid.

Coordination and cooperation in the health field on behalf of public welfare beneficiaries require an acute awareness by public welfare administrators and personnel and those of other health agencies and providers of the variety of health programs and the fostering of mutual understanding and collaboration among them. The close association of federal public welfare and most public health programs is facilitated somewhat by their organization in the Department of Health, Education and Welfare.

Coordination of state and local government public welfare and health agencies is aided in many jurisdictions by the close organizational association of programs within umbrella human service agencies. Continuing operating relationships are also maintained across government lines in the case of state Medicaid programs and the federal Medicare program, veterans health programs, Indian health services, and armed services dependents programs. The relationships among the public welfare/health agencies deal with matters of policy, processes, admissions, eligibility for service, service delivery, records exchange, use of facilities and personnel, cross-program training, and education. But the most sensitive subject of the relationship is in the matter of finances: which program(s) pay for services when the beneficiary is eligible under two or more health programs simultaneously. Each state or local government jurisdiction decides which funds are to be applied for health and other social programs funded entirely by its own jurisdiction, but the matter becomes more difficult when—as in most health and social programs—there is an infusion of federal dollars. Examples are an aged poor woman of 67 receiving hospital care who is a Medicare/Medicaid eligible; a child of four of an AFDC Medicaid-eligible family registered in a child health clinic supported by a federal maternal and child health grant; an AFDC mother receiving family planning services in a neighborhood health center which is a grantee of federal family planning project funds; a medically indigent man eligible for the state Medicaid program which covers mental illness receiving outpatient psychiatric services in a federally-supported community mental health center.

The attitudes of all executives, legislators, and administrators towards this question of financing of services are inherently the same: "Let the other fellow pay." In city and county government programs, the prevailing policy is to pass along program charges to the state and/or federal government wherever possible. In state government programs, the policy is not any different, to have the city or county, or federal government finance program charges up to legal limits. In the federal government, despite carefully drawn up regulations prescribing what program charges are and are not covered under federal financial participation, there is continuing dialogue and controversy with the states and other grantees about allowable costs and charges and covered program expenditures. This problem is exacerbated by the multiplicity of federally-funded programs covering the same service and the federal policy to avoid dual federal matching payments for a given program cost or charge. Although this problem faces all federally-supported programs and activities, it is an acute one for health and health-related programs, made so by the relatively large number of cross-cutting categorical programs, authorized under different federal laws which do not contain clear-cut guides. The key guiding principle on this question is that programs authorized under the Social Security Act are residual in the sense that individuals are expected to exhaust their own resources first before obtaining assistance and services from Social Security Act programs, including resources of other public and private social and health programs to which they are entitled.

VOCATIONAL REHABILITATION PROGRAMS

Vocational rehabilitation services are provided persons with mental and physical handicaps through a federal/state network of government agencies.[4] At the federal level, the vocational rehabilitation program is a responsibility of the Administration For Handicapped Individuals, Office of Human Development Services. State vocational rehabilitation agencies are in operation in all states as independent state agencies, or as divisions within the State Department of Education. The federal/state program includes diagnosis, comprehensive evaluation, counseling, training, reader services for the blind, interpreter services for the deaf, and employment placement. Medical and related services are provided, as are prosthetic and orthotic devices, transportation to secure service, financial assistance during rehabilitation, tools, licenses, equipment, and supplies. Services are also provided families of handicapped individuals when they are believed to contribute to rehabilitation progress.

All persons with a physical or mental disability are eligible to apply and receive vocational rehabilitation services if the disability is a handicap to employment and there is reasonable expectation that the services will render the individual fit for employment. The lack of money to pay for services is not a bar to the receipt of vocational rehabilitation services.

The rehabilitation of disabled public assistance recipients is a critical program priority. Its working principle is that poverty is a handicapping condition producing serious psychological, social, and cultural barriers to the attainment of a person's employment objectives to enable him to become self-sufficient. Rehabilitation towards employment can result in dual benefits to the individual and society, the former by having him function independently, the latter by removing him from welfare dependence and converting him from lower-income to middle-class (and taxpayer) status.

In fiscal year 1975 approximately one-third of a million public assistance recipients received vocational rehabilitation services of whom 87,800 were rehabilitated. Federal funds for this program are part of the general funds for the vocational rehabilitation program.

AGING PROGRAMS

Programs for the 22 million older persons reflect the national social policy to provide them with assistance and services to enhance the quality and productivity of their remaining years and support them with material and psychological social health, welfare, employment, and cultural services. Public welfare programs apply to the aged poor and near poor in the SSI assistance program, General Assistance programs, the Title XX social services program, and to the aged indigent and medically indigent of the Medicaid program and aged food stamp beneficiaries. Our national aged policy goes beyond these programs to serve also the nonpoor aged. Special aged programs, operated by public and community agencies and organizations, besides public welfare, have a unique role of service to the aged of all income levels. Since poverty is one of the most debilitating conditions which faces at least one-fourth of the aged, there is a deliberate general emphasis upon the problems of the poor aged: to prevent poverty from spreading among them during the nonincome producing part of their lives, to alleviate poverty causing physical, social, and mental deterioration and to supply the poor and nonpoor aged alike with the necessities for individual fulfillment. Thus, there is a natural affinity of programs and agencies among public welfare and aging bodies. To the extent public welfare agencies can sustain the poor aged through assistance payments, food stamps, social and medical services, the greater the opportunity for aging agencies to provide services to other aged groups in cities and rural areas. Reciprocally, to the extent aging agencies can support their clientele in meeting their physical, social, psychological needs, there will be less need among the aged for dependence upon public assistance and welfare services.

ADMINISTRATION OF JUSTICE PROGRAMS

Crime and delinquency statistics reveal a disproportionate percentage of poor and disadvantaged offenders and victims. For example, 54 percent of all jail inmates in 1972 had a prearrest annual income of under $3,000 and over 80 percent did not graduate from high school.[5] In 1973 crime rates for violent crimes in larger inner cities were double the rates of cities of smaller population.[6] Public welfare programs necessarily regard crime and delinquency as serious barriers to their clientele's success in improving their socioeconomic status to become self-sufficient. Poverty is often both the cause and the result of crime and delinquency in a vicious cycle of need, deprivation, hostility to society, jealousy by the have-nots of the haves, and finally, delinquency and lawlessness. Conversely, delinquency and lawlessness beget social alienation, unemployment, income loss, and poverty. Moreover, illegal acts by poor youth and their incarceration occur at a critical time in their development, divert their efforts and energies to illegal, antisocial, or counterproductive activities and create an often irreversible behavior pattern operating to prevent their social and economic independence.

Public welfare programs are most directly associated with delinquency, crime, and administration of justice in the delivery of social and child welfare services and as important factors in the effectiveness of job training and placement services of the WIN program. Welfare services run the gamut of youth and family predelinquent counseling, delinquency prevention activities, placement in foster homes and children's institutions, counseling of families of prison inmates, legal services, drug abuse education, job and family counseling of parolees, cooperation with the police, parole officers, court personnel and others connected with the administration of justice and juvenile delinquency systems in individual cases and community services development.

INCOME SECURITY AND BENEFIT PAYMENTS PROGRAMS

The primary distinction between public assistance programs and other income security and benefit payments programs such as, Old Age and Survivors Insurance (Social Security) is in their different socioeconomic public policy basis. Both result in an income transfer among and within population groups. The first —AFDC, GA, and SSI—are measures of income support to the poor to help them meet their basic living needs until (or if) they become socially and economically independent through their own efforts. The second—the income security and benefit payment programs—are measures of income support to (1) contributing wage earners, employees, and the self-employed (and their dependents and survivors) during their later years of retirement or in periods of disability to replace income no longer available to them, and (2) veterans (their dependents and survivors) to compensate them for their sacrifices in the armed services of their country. As discussed previously in Chapter 3, public assistance and other income security and benefits payments are intertwined in the amount of payments welfare recipients receive, the overlapping of beneficiaries (for example, welfare recipients on veteran's benefits or social security rolls), and the close relationship of agencies and administrations responsible for the respective programs. The ultimate relationship between the two is, of course, in the common organization and administration of the SSI and social security insurance programs in the Social Security Administration. The very name of the former, Supplemental Security Income, was chosen to express the piggyback relationship of the program to the basic social security programs in which eligible poor, aged, blind, and disabled, unable to meet their needs from their own resources and earned social security benefits or unable to qualify for such benefits could obtain needed supplement support from the SSI program. In this program as in others, the financial benefits are paid to beneficiary individuals and families having dual eligibility, as for example, a deceased veteran's survivor family or a disabled longshoreman's or mine worker's family. Figured into the welfare recipient's need and payment level computations are the income from pensions and worker's compensation which offset family expenditures; the greater the amounts from pensions and worker's compensation, and the smaller the amount of welfare need.

OTHER DOMESTIC ASSISTANCE PROGRAMS

Other government programs in addition to the above are in operation which represent public and community resources to which public welfare agencies can turn to help clients cope with their problems. Individually, their relationship to public welfare agencies is no less important to the effectiveness of assistance and service programs to public welfare beneficiaries. These include community action programs, Volunteer in Service to America (VISTA) and other volunteer programs, the Legal Services Corporation, small business assistance aimed at minority enterprises and American Indian social programs.

Income Tax Policy and Provisions

Federal, state, and local income tax provisions are critically important to public welfare programs in reflecting social policies to limit the tax burdens of low-income individuals and families and provide equitable tax treatment to other marginal income persons to help them retain an independent status. These provisions are in the form of exclusions, exemptions, deductions, and graduated tax rates. For example, federal income tax laws provide a special low-income allowance of up to $1,700 for single individuals and $2,100 for married persons in the tax rate tables, thereby removing many low-income taxpayers from tax rolls.

AFDC, GA, and SSI assistance payments are excluded as taxable income, as is the value of food stamps or the value of public social, job-training, and medical services received by public welfare recipients. Social security disability and retirement benefits are not taxable, nor are unemployment compensation or worker's compensation payments. Amounts received by volunteers for reimbursement of out-of-pocket expenses are not regarded as income. This includes foster grandparents, retired senior volunteers, and older American Community Service volunteers. Foster parents income received from a public welfare or other childplacing agency to reimburse them for the expenses of care of children in their own homes are not taxable. However, payments for providing temporary emergency shelter care facilities to children in physical or mortal danger are taxable income. Unreimbursed expenses for volunteer services are deductible as a contribution to the public or private agency as is the value of property donated and other gifts to such agency.

Twenty percent of expenses for child care, care of a disabled dependent or a disabled spouse is not subject to tax if they are necessary to enable a head of household to work. Special federal tax treatment is granted private employers involved in the WIN program. They are entitled to a credit of 20 percent of wages paid to an employee under that program.[7]

State and local governments give generally comparable tax treatment to low-income persons, with income from public assistance and social security exempt from taxation. The income tax burden from these governments is, on the whole, only a sixth as large as that of the federal government, since they obtain about 85 percent of their revenues from property, sales, and other tax sources. On a per capita basis, the state and local income tax burden was $86 and that for the federal government $492 in 1973.[8] Twelve states imposed a flat income tax rate for all income levels in 1974. The others applied a graduated tax rate averaging about six and seven percent.

Tax rolls and public welfare assistance rolls are two of the largest national record sources on individuals. They include those of the Internal Revenue Service federal income tax files, state and local tax record systems, and state and local public welfare record files. Under federal and state laws, to protect their confidentiality and limit their disclosure, they are not available for routine cross-checking between tax and public welfare authorities, with one exception: in connection with official efforts of state and local public welfare agency searches for absent parents of families with children to obtain their financial support for their children. Such state authorities, specifically the State Parent Locator Service and the Federal Parent Locator Service may request a search of tax rolls—state, local, and the Internal Revenue Service—to locate the absent parent, provide his full name, social security number, his last named address, and place of employment. In addition, the Internal Revenue Service may be requested to make collections of child support obligations from the absent parent when other collection efforts have failed.

Barriers and Opportunities for Coordination

The foregoing reveals a complex of interactive and interdependent but independent organizations. From a broader global perspective, however, one may see them as components of a single national mechanism whose purpose is to help the poor and disadvantaged, whose efficiency and effectiveness is at times unexpectedly productive, at other times discoordinated, wasteful, and counterproductive, with neither its constituent organizations or observers able to know or predict when it is helping or harming the people whom it is designed to help.

The pattern of relationships is not unidimensional. Each social program has its own network of contacts with other agencies and programs, with responsibility for its own legally-mandated objectives and priorities. At one and the same time, a public social agency may be the principal sponsor and mover of a project involving several other agencies pursuing their own primary projects and interests, and a secondary source of support for those of other agencies. For example, an area aging services office may be planning and organizing a community services program for senior citizens with the help of an interagency committee of public and private agencies, be cooperating with the state department of public health in planning an immunization program while negotiating a joint agreement with the county public welfare agency for expanding protective services for the poor aged, and discussing the need for a new housing project for the elderly with the city housing agency. This pattern of interprogram contacts and cooperating activities translates into a maze of actions and interactions which constitutes the normal environment of all human service programs. There is little a public welfare or other agency or program can accomplish effectively alone without others participating. Likewise, there is little a public welfare or other agency or program can accomplish if there is foot-dragging, uncooperativeness, competition, or hostility in their relationships.

On reflection, one may recognize two kinds of barriers to improvement in public welfare relationships with other social programs and agencies: institutional barriers and attitudinal barriers. The former are the structural composition of the programs which fail to mesh with other categorical programs. Examples are the differing percentages of federal financial participation—90 percent, 80 percent, 75 percent, etc.—making it more financially attractive for state and local governments to maximize investment in a program with higher matching ratio than one which is less well supported by the federal government; or, a program which is administered as a large independent state department and another organized as a subdivision of a city or county; or, a program with an income and resources eligibility requirement proscribing its clientele and another open to all regardless of level of income or resources; or, a program operated centrally from its principal offices at the state capital and another operated on a decentralized basis in every county and city in the state; or, a program with a sophisticated computerized records system and the other with a hand-posted local office records administration. These and other program differences constitute the prevailing situation. They are built-in barriers to coordination which administrative leadership and program staffs deal with in their efforts to make things happen, to provide effective service and assistance to their clientele, or use them to postpone, delay, or obfuscate such efforts.

The second set of barriers are attitudinal, personal, and psychological, emanating from an innate need of individual administrators and program staffs to act independently and eschew cooperation with others.

The allied services provisions in proposed federal legislation sponsored by HEW referred to earlier (see Chapter 5) is a movement to remove some of the institutional barriers by providing incentives for state and local governments to organize and administer social programs by giving them flexibility in program decisions concerning federal funds to improve their efficiency and effectiveness. The action to federalize social programs is another effort to remove institutional barriers, as in organization of the SSI program replacing the state OAA, AB, APTD assistance programs. Of equal importance is the movement towards organization of state and local umbrella human service agencies.

The response to the attitudinal barriers is of another character. Here, we must deal with the individual administrator and employee and his relationship to his position, his self-image, his job expectations, and style of performance. These are found in the areas of the personnel selection process, performance evaluation, supervision, personal responsibility and accountability, availability of in-service training, and the possible redirection of professional education, all of which require sustained long-term efforts at change in motivation, attitudes, and personal adjustment. There is no ready solution to remove personality barriers to cooperative performance.

NOTES

1. Catalog of Federal Domestic Assistance published by the Office of Management and Budget, Executive Office of the President, Washington, D.C., 1976.

2. The Statistical Abstract of the United States, 1976 96th Edition, U.S. Bureau of the Census, Washington, D.C. pp. 108–122.

3. Information Memorandum CSA iM-71-15, June 30, 1971. Community Services Administration, HEW.

4. Rehabilitation Act of 1973. Public Law 93-112 as amended by Public Law 93-516 (1974) 29 USC 701.

5. Table 289. Reason for Retention and Selected Socioeconomic Characteristics of Jail Inmates by Race 1972. The 1976 Statistical Abstract of the United States, Bureau of the Census, Commerce Department 96th Edition, U.S. Government Printing Office, Washington, D.C. 0. 167.

6. Table 251. Crime Rates for Violent Crimes in Cities, by Size Group and for Selected Cities: 1960–1973. The 1976 Statistical Abstract of the United States. Ibid. p. 152.

7. The tax data and foregoing description are from the 1977 Edition, Your Federal Income Tax Publication 17, Internal Revenue Service, Department of the Treasury, Washington, D.C.

8. Table 416 Tax Revenues by Source and Level of Government 1950–1973 p. 252. The 1976 Statistical Abstract of the United States, Bureau of the Census, Department of Commerce, Washington, D.C.

THE PUBLIC WELFARE SYSTEM IN PERSPECTIVE: LOOKING AHEAD

The adage that the whole is more than the sum of its parts applies to the public welfare system. It can be better understood in a holistic perspective, as the chosen governmental instrumentality for treating the poverty condition. For it is from this perspective that the system is commonly judged by the public, the media, legislators, and chief executives. This concluding chapter provides this added dimension. What follows is: (1) a balanced assessment of the system; (2) the public policy options to shape the future in public welfare; (3) the public policy issues to be decided in effecting change; (4) the more widely discussed proposals in welfare reform, social services, and health care; and (5) the alternative poverty goals to be considered. And so we provide a springboard for the next chapter in public welfare yet to be written.

A BALANCED ASSESSMENT OF PUBLIC WELFARE

In the view of many, the present public welfare system is a national disgrace. It is beset with flaws and inconsistencies, waste and inefficiencies. Former Representative Martha Griffiths of Michigan said it this way: "An uncoordinated governance has produced uncoordinated programs with gaps, overlaps, cross-purposes, inequities, administrative inefficiencies, work and family support disincentives, and waste of taxpayers' money."[1] But a balanced assessment also leads one to acknowledge public welfare's positive attributes as well. The public welfare balance sheet provided at the end of this chapter serves this purpose (Figure 10.1). It strives for an evenhanded equitable listing of "assets" and "liabilities" of the system. The resultant "net worth" of the system is a value judgment weighing its positive and negative features. To what extent and in what ways do the benefits outweigh the disbenefits, or the disbenefits outweigh the benefits? How do we improve the system to produce a greater net worth? Do we declare bankruptcy and start anew to build another system? These are questions to be asked in policy discussions surrounding welfare reform, social services, national health insurance, full employment, and other social issues the country faces. For we know that the poverty problem is integral to the larger problem of preserving the nation's social and economic health.

The preceding chapters contain a thorough explanation of the public welfare system as it functions circa 1975–1976. The system was described in its organizational framework of federal, state, and local welfare agencies having responsibility for assistance payments, food stamps, social services, employment training and job services, medical care, and the two small refugee and repatriate nationals programs. As discussed in Chapter 1, this pragmatic organizational approach to the subject differs from other published research and discursive treatment by economists, social workers, political scientists, and others. Theirs have a problem and goal orientation, namely, income security, comprehensive social services or universal health care of general applicability to all Americans. In the search for ideal reforms and remedies, they cover such financial assistance and service programs outside of the public welfare organizational framework as Social Security programs, unemployment insurance, housing programs, employment and training, and comprehensive health programs. This distinction is important to keep in mind in that the issues and solutions proposed are directed to these different national goals.

Public Welfare Growth Projections

Growth of federal income assistance programs, including SSI, AFDC, food stamp, and Medicaid programs by the year 2000 was projected by the Congressional Budget Office in a 1975 study.[2] The Office made the projections on three bases: (1) No change in current law and adjusted for changes in the cost of living where mandated by law; (None of the four programs have this provision.) (2) benefits and eligibility in all programs would be increased for inflation; and (3) benefit and eligibility schedules for all programs were adjusted for both inflation and real wage increases. The results for the four programs are thought-provoking, to say the least (Table 10.1).

Table 10.1   Year 2000 Alternate Projections

	Fiscal year 1975	Current law	Adjusted for Cost-of-living	Adjusted for inflation and wage rate increases
SSI	$ 4.8*	$ 1.9	$ 2.0	$ 7.2
AFDC	9.7	2.3	8.8	18.7
Medicaid	12.4	24.0	26.3	41.5
Food Stamps	4.6	7.5	5.9	7.1
Totals	$31.5	$35.7	$43.0	$74.5
Costs as % of GNP	8.7%	1.1%	1.2%	10.1%

*Dollars in billions

PUBLIC POLICY OPTIONS FOR THE FUTURE

For the past decade or more there has been a national climate of unrest and unease about the apparent or assumed shortcomings of welfare programs. This has been shared by leaders, the public media, the social professions, administrators, clientele, consumer groups, and the general public. Changes in law have been made, new programs implemented, Presidential messages on welfare reform sent to Congress, income maintenance experiments tried, fully publicized Congressional hearings held. Welfare scandals, including those in Medicaid, spot the front pages of the daily press and news journals. Comparisons with welfare programs of other countries have been drawn, welfare clients have picketed welfare offices and legislators, welfare workers have struck, charges and countercharges of welfare abuse and fraud have been made in a heated passion to correct inequities and deficiencies. Whether and to what extent the criticisms are justified, in the final analysis, change appears imminent. The options are quite clear and explicit although in all certainty they are difficult to agree upon and implement. Four options are open to the American people:

1. Continue the present public welfare system fundamentally unchanged;
2. Continue the present public welfare system and effect changes to correct deficiencies within the existing structure of programs, organizations, federal/state/local government relationships.
3. Restructure the present system by revamping programs, organizations, responsibilities, funding, and relationships.
4. Conceptualize and implement a completely new public welfare system to replace the existing system, or create national, social, and economic mechanisms which preclude separated welfare programs or systems.

In option 1—to continue the status quo—our national leadership will be relying on the system to correct itself through the efforts of (1) welfare recipients, by their becoming more self-sufficient and less dependent upon welfare assistance and services; (2) welfare administrators, staffs, and service providers, by becoming more efficient and effective in their dedication, motivation, belief in ethical and moral principles, and the precepts of their training in the helping professions; (3) the general public and elected representatives, by giving increased attention to and, if needed, additional support and funds for welfare resources and their sustained pressure to improve public welfare.

This option may be a deliberate choice after weighing all factors. It may be an unwillingness of the national leadership to consider drastic overhaul of the present welfare system, or, it may be the failure of national leadership, despite its best efforts, to reach a majority consensus reconciling opposing liberal and conservative constituencies in this country. It may be none of these. Instead, it may be a considered judgment that in the long view, national, social, and economic conditions will improve, reducing much of the poverty which exists and welfare dependency with it.

In option 2—to remove deficiencies in the present system —our national leadership will be relying upon the correction of observable defects in the system to make it respond more effectively to the needs of the poor and disadvantaged. One example is tightening eligibility processes—quality control—to weed out ineligibles, and redirecting welfare funds and services to eligible individuals and families. Another example may be a revision in federal law and regulations to require state payment needs standards be adjusted to equal current federal poverty guidelines. The exercise of this option may be a deliberate choice to retain the present welfare system as the "one best way" to meet the needs of the poor and, by a piecemeal approach, improve its performance. However, as in option 1—this may simply be an unwillingness of the national leadership to impose major changes in public welfare, implying confidence in welfare programs, or, the national leadership may not be able to muster a majority consensus in support of drastic change.

In option 3—to restructure the present system—our national leadership will be acknowledging the serious deficiencies in public welfare and seek remedies in new programs, new eligibility standards for payments or services, new organization, possibly modifying the fundamental federal/state/local relationship in such areas as funding, authority and responsibility, and welfare administration.[3] The most recent example of such major change is adoption of the Supplemental Security Income program under federal administration in place of the state payments programs for the aged, blind, and disabled. The exercise of this option is a choice endorsing the social and economic principles and goals of the present system enunciated in the Social Security Act and other federal and state laws but changing the welfare mechanisms to carry them out.

In option 4—to conceptualize a new governmental approach to the social and economic conditions of poverty—our national leadership will be charting a new course, thereby asserting that the present welfare system has failed irrevocably to meet the needs of the poor. The exercise of this option calls for (1) a restatement or reaffirmation of society's role and responsibility in helping the poor and disadvantaged as well as the individual's role and responsibility towards his own self-sufficiency and independence; (2) the definition of the new governmental resources—its programs, services, activities, funds, organization, processes—to be committed to this purpose; (3) the delineation of the conditions placed upon the individual to benefit from the new direction the government is taking; and (4) the results expected from the new system, including its impact upon the incidence of poverty and upon national social and economic conditions generally. For example, in considering welfare reform, the Report of the Subcommittee on Fiscal Policy of the Joint Economic Committee expressed the need to balance the public's responsibility with that of the individual in a shared burden:

> All societies make arrangements, formal and informal, that cushion the impact of random events and economic irregularities on the less fortunate. But no society has promised subsistence without expecting or exacting a quid pro quo. Like other societies, ours is based on the principle that individuals should pull a share of the load.
>
> Much of the debate about income maintenance programs focuses on fundamental questions of public versus private responsibility. Provisions of public aid for part of the population implies that most of the rest must pay the cost. Thus, it is natural for policy-makers and the public to be uneasy about the potential impact of expanded welfare on work and other private choices. As a consequence, cash aid has been systematically withheld from certain groups—such as many of the able-bodied. But this has distorted recipients' choices about work, family structure, and behavior, and penalized or failed to reward socially desirable behavior . . . How to divide responsibility for basic income maintenance between the individual and society, that is, other individuals (is at issue). Individuals make choices for which they should be held responsible, at least in part. Some of their choices greatly affect their economic well-being: employment, place of residence, family size, family structure, and parental support of children . . .
>
> At the same time, much poverty is caused by random events, the structure of the economy, discrimination by age, race, sex, and

national origin, and human weaknesses, and that the public should help to cushion their impact. The public should help not only out of humanitarian concern or the fear of economic and social harm, but also because of the realization that it possesses the ultimate responsibility for income distribution. For, although the market is an efficient allocative mechanism, it is essentially a technical process and cannot make ethical judgments . . .[4]

PUBLIC POLICY ISSUES[5]

In considering change in public welfare, our national leadership must agree upon social, ethical, and moral principles, thus affirm the philosophical approach to social and economic problems and conditions, reexamine the features of present welfare programs and systems, and weigh their trust in public administration to be able to supply effective and efficient organization and mechanisms to the poverty phenomenon. Basic to these is the resolution of public policy issues in income maintenance, social services, health care systems, and other poverty-related measures.

The Choice Among Competing Goals

The goals sought in the search for the "one best way" for government to meet its responsibility for anti-poverty action are competing goals. Government, like individuals, must make choices, but the task is harder for government because it represents millions of individuals with varying interests and needs and, sometimes, conflicting goals. Compromise is necessary. In income maintenance, social services, health care, manpower training and employment, and other measures of aid, the following goals are sought:

> *Adequacy*—Program benefits plus other available resources and services should be sufficient to sustain life and health and provide basic amenities, maintain an intact family relationship.
>
> *Incentives*—Public benefits should not substitute for private, individual obligations. Programs should maintain incen-

tives for work, thrift, family stability, encourage individual initiatives towards self-sufficiency, and instill a desire for self-help and personal independence.

Equity—Benefits should be fair and uniform, so that people in the same circumstances are treated the same way.

Efficiency—Programs should be administered at the least cost commensurate with program integrity.

Least Cost—The least amount of public funds should be spent on benefits and services while achieving the previous goals.

CONFLICTING GOALS IN NONCASH AID TO THE POOR.   An illustration of conflicting goals may be seen in noncash aid to the poor. Two years after Congress passed the Social Security Act, it initiated a major program of low-rent public housing. The program offered grants and loans to local public housing authorities to help them finance construction, acquisition, and subsidized operation of public units.

Within the last decade there has been an explosion of other noncash benefit programs to provide help for needy recipients, including Medicaid, food stamps, free or subsidized services, such as day care, legal services, job training, new forms of subsidized housing, basic educational opportunity grants. Two kinds of restrictions limit the ability of the poor to gain these noncash benefits: categorical eligibility rules and closed-end appropriations. Of these benefits, only food stamps are universally available on the basis of income and resources.

Medicaid also illustrates the conflict in goals. Medicaid may be offered by states to near-poor families and individuals who fit the categories of AFDC and SSI, but only 32 states do so. In the majority of states, Medicaid benefits are cut off abruptly when counted income exceeds welfare eligibility limits. In these states a small increase in earnings of $10 can cause the "sudden death" of benefits valued at hundreds of dollars. Restricting coverage to only certain types of families and imposing rigid income limits on them saves money and concentrates benefits on some among the very poor but creates inequities and discourages work for those at the eligibility margin.

This goals conflict is also evident in day care. Day-care benefits have been too expensive and too scarce to be provided on an equal basis to all. Estimates from the D/HEW that governmental child care expenditures in fiscal year 1973 (federal and state) exceeded half a billion dollars and averaged about $1,090 per child. In addition, AFDC reimbursed welfare mothers for an estimated $80.1 millions spent on child care. Because costs preclude giving the same range and quality of services to all, comprehensive benefits such as Medicaid and developmental day care are provided free for some, but denied to others of equal or greater need. In general, noncash benefits are given, and given free or at nominal charge, only to those already qualified as "needy" by certification for cash payments or others of low income whose eligibility are sharply defined.

Coverage

Who is eligible? Most current programs for the needy limit income protection and services to specified groups, defined by conditions that represent a particular risk (of age, disability, etc.) or a particular family structure. This is inequitable to others in need and it creates incentives for people to change their behavior or their family structure to qualify. Administrative procedures are complicated by the need to check evidence of categorical eligibility. Nevertheless, when a program is targeted to the needy, how is it to determine which individual applicant is to benefit and which is not?

Recipient Unit Definition and Financial Benefit Structure For Income Support

One major objective of basic income supplements should be to promote family life. A broad-scale income supplement program cannot eliminate personal and social problems, but an income floor should provide an economic base for family life. Supplements should be designed to minimize: (1) financial incentives for family breakup or creation of one-parent families; (2) financial penalties for meeting parental responsibilities; (3) disincentives for work, savings, and other self-help measures; and (4) constraints on living arrangements and participation in family life. The choice of recipient unit and the structure of benefits will determine success in meeting these goals.

Benefit Level for Income Support

Adequacy of benefits is perhaps the hardest issue in any system for income supplementation. On the one hand, it is the essential reason for providing income benefits. On the other hand, adequacy is a most controversial quality to define, and once defined, it often proves to be immeasurable. To most people, income adequacy means enough income to assure some minimum level of living in our society. But there is little agreement on what constitutes the minimum. For example, how does one measure the adequacy of diet? By variation from an ideal standard diet? Whose standard? Similar difficulties arise regarding "minimum" shelter, health care, or clothing. Should a minimum standard of living make allowance for buying a daily newspaper, owning a TV, or eating in a restaurant twice a year? This question was discussed earlier in Chapter 2.

Kinds and Quality of Services

Shall the social, manpower training and employment, health care, and other services to the needy be of a kind, variety, and at a quality level less than, the same, or exceed those available to the general public? An argument can be made that the poor are in greater need of the best services that are available. This suggests a duality of service systems in this country: one for the poor, the other purchasable by the general public. Is this practicable or equitable? Also, to what extent should services assume a degree of self-help, of responsibility for personal decision making, much as the nonpoor decide for themselves when to seek a service and whether to follow the treatment proposed by the professional service provider? How much individual discretion is to be built into service programs?

Reduction in Income Maintenance Benefits as Earnings Rise[6]

In order to relate benefits to need, they must be scaled to income. The rate at which earnings (or other income) are subtracted from the maximum basic benefit (benefit-loss rate) has several crucial effects: Available research indicates that higher benefit-loss rates have a dampening effect on work effort, but benefit-loss rates which allow some increase in recipient income helps to reduce poverty. Most Americans accept the general principle that persons who work would be better off than those who do not. But no technical basis exists for providing how much better off workers should be than nonworkers or, conversely, to what degree benefit programs should narrow the gap. This is a question of fairness, and must be decided on moral grounds. The higher the benefit-loss rate, the less the income difference between workers and nonworkers, or among workers at various wage levels.

Who Pays for Income Maintenance Benefits: Federal or State Governments?

The issue arouses strong emotions not only because it entails large expenditures which influence budget and revenue policies for all governmental functions, not only welfare, but also because it is symbolic of regional relationships. Under a plan for 100 percent of federal funding, the people of the Northwest states are required to support the poor of Eastern and Southern states. A plan for state funding, in contrast, could assure them that their tax dollars support their own poor, a position far more amenable. However, with rising uncontrolled benefit payments helping to erode state and local government budgets, there is almost universal agreement among state and local government leadership to transfer more of the welfare fiscal burden, if not the entire burden, to the federal government. At the federal level, it is common knowledge that the problem of balancing the federal budget and of reducing the federal deficit, can be worsened by takeover of all or more of income maintenance costs. This confrontation in views is not to be confused with the setting of welfare policies and administration of welfare programs. State and local leaders are ambivalent on the subject: some would opt for federal administration of welfare to relieve themselves of any responsibility for it; others would wish to retain full control over the policies, programs, and administration of their own poverty caseloads, assuming federal funding of all or more of their cost. The debates on this issue at the July, 1976 National Governors Conference in Hershey, Pennsylvania revealed the differing positions of the Governors in funding and administration of income maintenance programs. They voted finally for an increase in federal funding of 75 percent of benefit costs with continued state and local administration of their own programs. An equity question is implicit in the federal state controversy: should the degree of responsibility for funding of a program be commensurate with responsibility for setting policy and making decisions on organization and administration? If the federal government provides 75 percent of the funds, should it control 75 percent of welfare policies and administration, or control *all* major policies and administrative decisions, or have state and local governments administer their own programs without federal intervention despite the federal financial participation? The discussions of these principles on revenue sharing and block grants are illustrative of the difficulty to resolve this issue.

Who Pays for Social, Health, and Other Welfare Services?

What is the equitable distribution of government funding support for service programs among the federal, state, and local governments. Shall funds for such programs be allocated to furnish the poor a larger proportion of resources in underserved areas, or in states and localities where the availability, quantity, and quality of services are failing to meet needs of the poor? What measuring rods shall be applied to make such fund distributions proportionate to the severity of service needs?

In regard to the equity of setting service charges for those able to pay, shall such charges be set to meet costs, or be raised above cost levels through subsidization to enable the poorest to receive free services? Or shall service charges be set below costs and the resulting deficits met from general welfare services appropriations? Another possibility for financing of service costs is found in other programs in the creation of trust funds or special earmarked taxes to be directly assessed for support of service programs. Restated, the issue concerning support of service programs for the poor centers around the question of whether the full burden is to be placed upon users, according to ability to pay, or whether all the people should support services through general government financing regardless of their use of publicly-supported services.

Universal Comprehensive Services or Separate Service System for the Poor?

Implicit in the proposals for universal comprehensive service systems in social services, health care and other human services is the belief in the commonality of need by both the poor and nonpoor. Adoption of a single standard of eligibility, availability, volume, variety, and quality of service is a prerequisite. Such proposals aim to fulfill the promise that the receipt of service is an American right available to all persons equally without regard to ability to pay. An assumption is made also that a universal comprehensive system of services in whatever social field can produce large-scale efficiencies and economies.

The issues revolve around the validity, practicality, and correctness of these assumptions, given the critical shortages in service manpower, facilities, institutions, and funds. It is argued that a universal comprehensive service program is impractical in the foreseeable future because of these shortages. Reliance must be placed upon the normal operation of the market place for control of service demand where ability to pay determines utilization of services. Besides, the service needs of the poor are believed greater and different than those of the nonpoor because their needs are more severe, their social, health, psychological, and environmental conditions and problems are unique (not shared by the nonpoor) and the poor have a greater dependence upon them to survive.

Utilization of services by the poor is greater, requiring separate service systems more efficient and adaptable to them. Such systems may be more responsive to their needs. Service workers and providers can, by concentration of service to the poor, gain experience and sensitivity in the background, conditions, and environment of the poor and thus give them more effective service. Finally, it has been argued that a universal comprehensive system of services once implemented will revert to a service system for the poor because the poor will utilize service facilities and resources disproportionate to their numbers and the non-poor will underutilize the system by use of paid services outside the system. An example is given of the British national health program. These are some of the more sensitive issue questions which need thought, debate, and resolution in proposing a universal comprehensive services program for Americans.

Adjusting Payments for Service Benefits as Earnings Rise

Unless we adopt a universal comprehensive system of entitlements for services, it is assumed that service programs for the poor will be provided free or at nominal cost. As earnings rise, shall they be expected to pay a fee graduated in relation to the rise in earnings or other income, or shall services be provided free or at nominal costs regardless of any earnings or income after they have established initial eligibility? Not all services are of equal importance to the needy individual or family. A cardiac condition is life threatening; heart surgery may be an absolute requirement; in contrast, enrollment in a group nutrition program is not. Is it equitable to require payment for the second when earnings rise while the first be provided to a poor person regardless of any increase in earnings or income? Which services fall into the category of payability as earnings rise? Shall payments be set at the cost of service or some amount tied to the account of earnings rise? These alternatives are parallel to similar circumstances of persons receiving income benefits as discussed above, with the added considerations of the relative need for the specified service.

Reducing Income Maintenance Benefits for Nonemployment Income

Many public welfare programs now treat earned income more generously for benefit computation purposes than "unearned" income from social security, unemployment compensation, rents, interest, dividends, alimony, and child support. Whereas federal AFDC rules require states to ignore the first $30 of monthly earnings, one-third of the remainder and all expenses reasonably related to work, in many states no portion of unearned income is ignored. This practice has the effect of making such income worthless to the individual family. It can be argued that this practice, however, reduces program costs and allows limited funds to be used for higher benefits for all recipients. But further explanation reveals that unearned income usually represents some earlier work or savings. Interest, dividends, and rents require conscious acts of savings or management. Insurance proceeds result from premiums or taxes paid by oneself, relatives, or one's employers. To obtain child support or alimony often involves legal proceedings and continued struggles. Thus, "unearned" income generally requires effort and some reward or recognition of this effort seem appropriate. At issue is the principle that persons in unequal circumstances should be treated unequally. Thus, should persons with "unearned" income be penalized in receiving income maintenance?

Asset Tests

Asset tests have been used in need-based programs to define the eligible population and to control welfare outlays. Allowable asset limits typically are low, permitting only very modest savings, and stated in flat dollar amounts. There are usually some exclusions of types of assets considered essential such as personal effects, household furnishings, an automobile, or a home owned by the applicant if within a specified value, and some types of income-producing property. The basic premise is that assets other than those considered essential represent wealth that should be utilized for living expenses before a person with low cash income is given public aid. But traditional asset limits have other effects. Savings are discouraged and the meager limits typically applied contradict commonly accepted social values of thrift, homeownership, and emergency planning. Flat dollar ceilings require evaluations and borderline decisions and make the difference between full benefit entitlement or no benefits at all. Moreover, exclusion of some categories of assets from limitation encourages transfer of excess amounts to excluded items rather than to use for living expenses.

The problem is to achieve greater fairness while still limiting benefits to the truly needy. The solution should recognize differences in need that are related to differences in assets, but it should not penalize thrift and it should avoid substitution of tax dollars for reasonable asset conversions for day-to-day needs or utilization of income from income-producing assets.

Income Accounting Period Where Income is a Test of Eligibility Status

Implicit in the design of all income-related programs is the need to relate payments to income of beneficiaries measured over some time period. Income accounting and reporting procedures help determine the costs and caseloads of income maintenance and services programs, as well as their administrative burden. Moreover, accounting procedures exert a subtle influence on the character of the program and help to shape the public perception of it as fair or unfair, rational or irrational. How much aid is received by two persons of identical *annual* but fluctuating *monthly* income depends on the choice of a monthly or an annual accounting period, and the difference can amount to several hundred dollars. A short accounting period favors sporadic work and fluctuating income; a long one is fairer to the steady worker. A short accounting period is immediately responsive to sudden need; a long one gives more recognition to individual responsibility for money management. Moreover, an income maintenance benefit program must calculate payments either on the basis of predicted future income or reported past income— prospective or retrospective reporting. And it must decide how frequently to require reports (the reporting period), to pay benefits (the payment period), and to adjust payments (the adjustment period).

The principle of equity requires that persons in equal need receive equal help. But one must decide over what time period need itself is to be measured. If the time chosen is a week or a month, a family may be found in current need although it received twice as much income in the previous six months as its nonneedy neighbor. It would seem more reasonable, perhaps, and more consistent with usual ideas of equity, to adjust benefits to income over some relatively long-term period.

Reporting and Verifying Income and Other Family Circumstances

In any program, welfare or otherwise, where individual eligibility status is based on criteria of inclusion or exclusion, there must be an administrative mechanism to apply them initially at time of application and subsequently to verify continued eligibility. Particularly in programs which have criteria of such a personally sensitive nature as family relationships, income, personal expenditures, and household conditions, the process should be organized and administered to obtain correct and complete information in a manner which is not demeaning to the individual or family beneficiary, does not constitute harassment, does not promote fraud, is conducted at low administrative cost, and assures the full confidentiality of the information supplied. At the same time, the process must not discourage applications of those who can benefit from it and be productive in keeping ineligibles from receiving benefits to which they are not entitled.

The issue arises in the design and administration of eligibility determination processes. To what degree shall the public welfare agency trust the information supplied by the applicant? With minimum or no verification or full field investigation? How frequently and in what depth should eligibility-critical information be verified once initial eligibility has been approved? What methods of verification shall be prescribed and which ones prohibited? For example, if checking rental payments with a beneficiary's landlord is permitted, is observation by a welfare investigator of his claimed use of an automobile for business purposes, or requiring him to undergo a lie detector test about his sources of income appropriate?

Work Requirements

There is widespread belief that strong financial awards should be provided those who work yet require income supplementation. But the question arises as to whether beneficiaries who can work but do not should be required to register for work and take jobs when available. To have a work-or-train rule in a benefit program, it is necessary to decide the following: who must work; what sort of jobs or training people may be required to accept, and at what pay, if any; on what grounds work may be refused; and whom to penalize and by how much in cases of work refusal.

One basic decision is who is employable and subject to the work rule. While the employable/unemployable distinction is clear in theory, in practice there are many borderline cases, for employability has little meaning apart from specific people and specific labor markets. When a large manufacturing plant opens or closes in a small town, the employability of specific individuals in that town will change overnight. When labor markets are tight, employers hire some of the so-called unemployables. When unemployment is up, personnel directors tighten their standards. They look for experienced, young, and healthy people. They are less flexible in terms of educational requirements and work hours. These processes have operated and will continue to operate regardless of the decisions of welfare program and WIN staffs about who is employable.

Federal Versus State Administration

A basic premise of welfare reform and other programs for the poor is that the government's treatment of the poor should be uniform. In considering state administration of a welfare program reformed by federal legislation, a dilemma arises: How could states be permitted to control programs through administration, yet be required to relinquish control over setting benefit levels and eligibility rules? This was discussed earlier in this chapter in regard to the ambivalent attitudes of governors towards financing. The advantage of using state agencies is that offices, payment systems, and personnel are already in place. But there are two major disadvantages, aside from the need for new administrative procedures to implement a new system. First, uniform administration of a national system requires central control over staff hirings and training. Second, modernized efficient payment and audit systems dictate use of a national or at least regional data processing system. In favor of state administration, is the illogic of administering a centralized payments/benefits program for the poor and multipurpose service programs administered by state and local governments for these same poor. There is little doubt this centralized/decentralized arrangement can function, but there is a serious question of the effectiveness, cost, and confusions which are expected to arise in the minds of workers, the clientele, the general public, and the leaderships in both federal and state governments. Illustrative of this point is the public criticisms of the SSI program— a federal program with uniform national standards—and its impact on state and local governments, the welfare constituencies, and the adverse effects upon agency workers and their relationships to recipients.

Is a New Agency Better Than an Old One?

Assuming welfare reform for a federal system with national standards, the advantage of creating a new federal agency is the desirability of starting off fresh. Offices and staffing could be optimally arranged. The latest information retrieval system and data processing technology could be utilized and the bureaucratic problems of grafting a new function to an old-line agency could be avoided. But what are the problems? The first is size. Although it would be a major undertaking for an existing agency to run a national system, setting up a new agency to run a new national system would require an even greater investment in buildings, staffs, training, and computers. The second issue is the compounding of overlapping bureaucracies. A goal of welfare reform is to reduce overlapping and simplify administration. With three other major agencies with large-scale national records systems (Veterans Administration, Internal Revenue Service, Social Security Administration), adding a fourth poses serious problems of economies and records duplication. A third issue is technical efficiency in administering a benefits program.

The closest existing program with such experience is the Social Security Administration with the SSI program. Some transferability of organization and techniques should be possible. However, this program has been relatively small compared with a welfare program four or five times the caseload. Further, the administrative problems of benefits to families are conceded to be far more complex than those of the aged, blind, and disabled. In the final analysis, the choice of a new or existing federal agency is a choice of compromises.

All of the foregoing appropriately relate to nationalization of social services, health care, or other human service programs. The issues have overtones of politics, economics, intergovernmental rivalry, administrative questions, questions of program effectiveness, efficiencies, of public and beneficiary confidence in the respective choice options, and in the decision-makers.

AGENDAS FOR PUBLIC WELFARE CHANGE

Public welfare is, as described here, a multifaceted combination of antipoverty programs. It is *not only* an income maintenance program for eligible poor. It is *not only* a health care program for indigent and medically indigent. It is *not only* a manpower training and employment program for AFDC recipients. It is *not only* a child welfare services program for neglected, dependent, delinquent children. It is *not only* a food stamp program for eligible public assistance recipients and other poor. *It is all of these.* Yet the national proposals for welfare change and improvement for the most part—with the exception of the program recommended by the Advisory Council on Public Welfare in June 1966—have dealt with the subject in piecemeal fashion. Welfare reform proposals offer change in the basic approaches to income maintenance to the poor to coordinate them with other income security programs. Proposed comprehensive social services programs suggest how we can overcome the shortcomings in social services programs. National health insurance proposals are ways and means to finance health care as a universal right. Full employment measures address the reduction in national unemployment and underemployment. What has been lacking thus far in these efforts for change is an integration of all helping mechanisms to achieve national goals to reduce the incidence of poverty through the application of the same diversity of helping programs as is now part of the present public welfare system. Nevertheless, the validity of the individual proposals is not to be denied. There is an implicit assumption, sometimes stated, that other welfare support and services components would continue to be supplied and improved, that the condition of the poor dictates a variety of governmental support as a precondition to the effectiveness of the proposal. For example, income security proposals reference the urgent need for social services, particularly day care, manpower training and employment services, health care for the poor as well as proper housing, community improvement, and a wide range of educational services. National health insurance proposals recognize the significant needs of the poor for income maintenance and social and job-related services. Proposed housing improvement programs for the poor implicitly rely upon the provision for social services, availability of health care and job training, and employment to meet their social and economic needs. This latter is clearly expressed in the goals of the Housing and Community Development Act of 1974.

The following provide a review of the principal proposals for public welfare change in income security (welfare reform), social services, and national health insurance suggested during the past decade. Their variety and intricacies, their potential impact on national social and economic conditions, their challenge to government's ability to govern, to governmental fiscal integrity, and the different political philosophies they reflect explain why a consensus is so difficult to achieve.

Welfare Reform

THE PROGRAM FOR BETTER JOBS AND INCOME: PRESIDENT CARTER'S 1977 WELFARE REFORM PLAN.[7]   President Carter submitted his Program For Better Jobs and Income to Congress in August, 1977 to replace the existing welfare program. He then stated:

... the welfare system (is) worse than I expected. Each program
has a high purpose and serves many needy people, but taken as
a whole the system is neither rational nor fair. The welfare system
is anti-work, anti-family, inequitable in its treatment of the poor
and wasteful of taxpayers' dollars ...

The Program For Better Jobs and Income has the following
elements:

Job Opportunities.   The federal government would assist workers
from low-income families to find jobs in the public and private
sectors. When such employment could not be found, up to 1.4
million public sector jobs would be created. The jobs would pay
the minimum wage or slightly above. Applicants will be required
to engage in an intensive five-week search for regular employment before becoming eligible for a public service job. Those
working in public service employment will be required to engage in a period of intensive job search every 12 months.

Work Benefit and Income Support.   The AFDC, SSI, and Food Stamp
programs would be replaced by a new work benefit and income
support program. Under the work benefit plan, two-parent families, single people, childless couples and single parents with no
child under the age of 14 would be expected to work full-time
and be required to accept available work, with cash supplements
to those whose incomes are $8,400 or lower. Income support
would be provided for those who are aged, blind, or disabled
and for single parents of children under 14. Single parent family
heads will be able to deduct up to 20 percent of earned income
up to an amount of $150 per month to pay for child care ex-
penses required for the parent to go to work.

Income Payments.   An aged, blind, or disabled person would receive $2,500 a year; a couple in this category would get $3,750,
slightly higher than their benefits under the SSI program. A
family of four eligible for full income support would receive a
basic federal benefit of $4,200 a year in 1978 dollars. Benefits
would be reduced 50 cents for each dollar of earnings and would
be phased out entirely when a family earned $8,400 in outside
income. No limits are placed on the rights of states to supplement these basic benefits. However, only if states adopt supplements which complement the structure and incentives of the
federal program will the federal government share in the cost.

Earned Income Tax Credit.   The current earned income tax credit program would be expanded to provide more tax relief to the working poor. The new program, which would apply to private and nonsubsidized public employment, would continue the current 10 percent credit on earnings up to $4,000 a year and provide a five percent credit on earnings between $4,000 and approximately $9,000 for a family of four.

State Role and Fiscal Relief.   Each state would be guaranteed at least a 10 percent reduction in its current welfare expenditures in the first year of the program, with substantially increased fiscal relief thereafter. Every state would be required to pay 10 percent of the basic federal income benefits provided to its residents except where it will exceed 90 percent of its prior welfare expenditures. The federal government will pay 75 percent of the first $500 supplement and 25 percent of any additional supplement up to the poverty line. State supplements will be required to follow federal eligibility criteria to help achieve nationwide uniformity.

Where states supplement the income support, they must also proportionately supplement the work benefit and public service wages.

There will be a three-year period during which states will be required to maintain a share of their current effort in order to ease the transition of those now receiving benefits.

States will have the option to assist in the administration of the program. They will be able to operate the intake function serving applicants, making possible coordination with social services programs. The federal government will operate the program's data processing system, calculate benefits, and issue payments.

The federal government will provide a $600 million block grant to the states to provide for emergency payments to recipients. The federal government will also provide 30 percent above the basic wage for fringe benefits and administrative costs of the jobs program, and will reimburse the states for costs of administration of the work benefit and income support program.

Implementation.   The new program would become effective in the fiscal year 1981, which begins October 1, 1980.

H.R. 1—THE NIXON FAMILY ASSISTANCE PLAN A (FAP), THE SOCIAL
SECURITY AMENDMENTS OF 1971.   This plan was submitted
by President Nixon in 1969 to the Congress; was revised by the
House and Ways Committee in 1971; passed by the House of
Representatives as H.R. 1, the Social Security Amendments of
1971. The bill contained many improvements and expansions of
the Social Security, Medicare, and Medicaid programs in addition to a new Opportunities for Families program and the Family Assistance Plan (FAP). It was referred to the United States
Senate and revised drastically by the Senate Finance Committee.
A new "workfare" provision was introduced in the revised Senate bill to deny AFDC assistance payments to needy families
having an employable adult and require him or her to obtain job
training and placement services to find employment in the labor
market or be offered employment in a new public service job
program. Unlike the House bill, the revision continued the
AFDC program and public assistance programs for the aged,
blind, and disabled under state administration. The bill failed to
be enacted that year. The following year, 1972, the two versions
of the bill were considered by the House-Senate Conference
Committee and an impasse resulted. The Joint Committee reported out the bill without the basic welfare reform package,
both Houses approved it, and H.R. 1, the Social Security
Amendments of 1971 was signed by the President on October
30, 1972 with substantial changes in Social Security, Medicare,
Medicaid, and social services financing. The law created the
Supplemental Security Income program, replacing state programs for aged, blind, and disabled.

The Original FAP Plan. The following is a summary of the principal features of the original welfare reform Family Assistance
Plan proposals[8]:

    1. The AFDC program would be discontinued. Low-
income families with a working father would be eligible for cash
payments. Thus, all needy families with children would be eligible for assistance. The aim would be to move every family in
which there are employable adults toward employment and economic independence. These families would be enrolled by the
Department of Labor in a new program: Opportunities for Families Program. Other families in which there was no employable

adult would be enrolled in a new program: Family Assistance Plan (FAP) under the Department of Health, Education and Welfare.

The Opportunities for Families program would emphasize work rather than welfare dependency through the use of incentives and requirements by providing:

a. registration for jobs or training, as a prerequisite to receiving benefits, of all able-bodied applicants (except mothers with young children);
b. reform of current job training programs by deemphasizing institutional training which "does not lead to jobs," by the creation of needed jobs through a major public service employment program, and by placing authority and responsibility on the Secretary of Labor for all aspects of the expanded work and training programs, including day care, family planning, and other supportive services;
c. a schedule of benefits and training allowances so that an individual will always have financial gain from effort expended in work or training; and
d. penalties through loss of benefits for those who refuse to register or to accept employment, training, or vocational rehabilitation services.

Needy families with no employable adult would be enrolled in the Family Assistance Plan. Individuals who were incapacitated would be referred to the vocational rehabilitation program and required to accept such services if offered. Family planning services would also be offered. As soon as any needy family included an employable adult, that family would be transferred to the Department of Labor Opportunities Program.

2. The plan would provide greater equity in welfare payments and improve administration of payments to families. The plan would provide:

a. a basic federal payment level for all needy families with children of $800 for the first two members of a family,

$400 for the next three, $300 for the next two, and $200 for the next one on an annual basis ($2,400 for a family of four);

b.   uniform eligibility requirements throughout the nation, including limitations on assets and uniform definitions of what constitutes income for purposes of eligibility;

c.   payments to families where the father was working full-time thus eliminating inequity and economic incentive for family breakup in the present system under which poor families in which the father was present and working were not eligible for help;

d.   federal administration of the payments procedures, with requirements in law which would assure that eligibility determinations were both strict and fair; and

e.   that deserting parents would be held responsible for federal payments made to their families, and that it would be a federal crime for a parent to travel in interstate commerce to avoid supporting his child.

3.   The state-administered programs of assistance to the aged, blind, and disabled would be replaced by a federally-administered program with state supplementation of benefits above basic federal levels (the Supplemental Security Income Program).

4.   Assistance payments beneficiaries would not be eligible for food stamps.

The Senate Version.   The following is a summary of the alternate welfare reform proposal developed by Senator Long of Louisiana, chairman of the Senate Finance Committee[9]:

1.   The AFDC program would be continued under state administration. Eligibility would be limited to the following classes of families:

families headed by a mother with child under age 6

family headed by an incapacitated father where a mother was not in the home or is caring for father

family headed by a mother who was ill, incapacitated, or of advanced age

family headed by a mother too remote from an employment program to be able to participate

family headed by a mother attending school full time even
if there was no child under age 6

child living with neither parent, together with his caretaker
relative(s), providing his mother was not also receiving
welfare.

2.   Each state would be permitted to establish its own level
of assistance payments, but it could not reduce payments below
the level of $1,600 for a two-member family, $2,000 for a three-
member family, and $2,400 for a family of four or more; or, if
payments were already below these amounts, they could be continued but could not be reduced.

3.   Needy families having an employable adult would not
be eligible for financial assistance. Instead, they would be assisted through a "workfare" program to be administered by a
newly created independent federal agency: Work Administration. A Bureau of Child Care would also be established within
that agency to be responsible for child care services for children
of parents working under this program. Job training and placement services would be offered for jobs in the regular labor
market or in a new public service employment program.

4.   Three types of work incentives would be offered heads
of families: a *guaranteed job opportunity* paying $1.50 per hour for
32 hours and with maximum weekly earnings of $48 (or $2,400
per year); a *wage supplement* for persons employed at less than
$2.00 per hour (but at least $1.50 per hour), and a *work bonus*
equal to ten percent of wages covered under social security up
to a maximum bonus of $400 with reductions in the bonus as the
husband and wife's covered wages rise above $4,000.

5.   The three state-administered programs of assistance to
the aged, blind, and disabled would be continued but with a
national minimum payment level of $130 for an individual or
$195 for a couple with no other income.

6.   Assistance payments beneficiaries would not be eligible
for food stamps. States which adjusted its payment levels to take
into account the food stamp losses would be reimbursed by the
federal government for this added cost.

TAX CREDITS AND ALLOWANCE FOR BASIC LIVING EXPENSES (ABLE): THE GRIFFITHS PROPOSAL.[10]   This proposal was the culmination of the three-year study of public welfare by the Subcommittee on Fiscal Policy of the Joint Economic Committee with Representative Martha Griffiths, Michigan, as chairperson. The proposal recommended replacing the income support programs based on family and individual income by establishing as part of the income tax a new federal system of tax credits and allowances. The suggested system was designed to increase the equity, strengthen the administration, and improve the adequacy of income maintenance programs, and to restore desirable social and economic incentives to the nation's system for income security. It was designed to alter the old welfare reward system by ending the penalties on work, marriage, and family responsibility.

The reform proposal was based upon both a reformed income tax system and a reformed welfare system. In the tax system, the deductions from income for personal exemptions were replaced with tax credits, which were deducted from tax liability with excess credits paid to the tax filer. Several current welfare programs (principally AFDC and food stamps) were replaced by a comprehensive system of allowances to poor people administered by the Internal Revenue Service.

As a result of this reform, people with little or no private income would receive full allowances and credits and pay no income tax. Those with very small incomes would still receive full credits but reduced allowances. Persons in the modest and middle-income range would not be eligible for allowances, but they would pay less income tax than is now the case. Some taxpayers in the high-income brackets would owe more taxes than now.

Tax credits. Everyone permanently residing in the United States, and anyone else required to file a federal income tax return, would be entitled to a $225 per person annual credit against income tax liability. If the total credits for a tax filer and dependent exceeded their tax liability, the unused credits would be paid to the filer. Much of the tax revenue lost through these credits would be recouped through the elimination of two present income tax features: the personal exemption and the low-income allowance. The personal exemption permitted a taxpayer to reduce taxable income by $750 for himself and each dependent. The low-income allowance sets a minimum floor of $1,300 on the amount by which each taxpaper could reduce taxable income through the standard deduction.

Allowance for Basic Living Expenses (ABLE).   This was a new system of allowances to be operated by the Internal Revenue Service to replace AFDC and food stamp programs. These allowances would be payable to qualified low-income families and individuals every month. Allowances would be uniform nationally and available to all the poor, except the aged, blind, and disabled and their dependents covered by the SSI program. The monthly amounts paid would be determined by subtracting a filing unit's income from its total allowances, based on the following schedule:

Member of unit:	*Annual allowance*
a) Married couple filing jointly	$2,050
b) Head of household filer	1,225
c) Single filer	825
d) Dependent age 18 or over	825
e) First and second child in filing unit, each	325
f) Third, fourth, fifth, and sixth dependent child, each	225
g) Seventh and successive dependent children	0

These allowances, when added to the personal tax credits, would constitute a federal floor under individual and family incomes. Thus, a couple and two children with no private income would receive $900 in tax credits and $2700 in ABLE grants for a total income of $3,600. A penniless mother of four would receive $3,450 ($2,325 from ABLE, $1,125 from credits).

STATE GOVERNORS FEDERALLY-ASSISTED WELFARE REFORM PROPOSAL.[11]   In July 1976, the 68th National Governors Conference adopted a proposal to replace the existing public assistance programs with a single, simplified national welfare system with the following features:

1. A national minimum level of income maintenance
    would be established with regional variations based on
    cost-of-living differences. State supplemental payments
    would be provided at the discretion of each State.
2. All poor unemployable persons would be eligible solely
    on the basis of financial need.
3. Able-bodied welfare recipients (ages 17 to 60) would be
    required to register for work and to accept jobs offered
    them at federal minimum wage standards. Excluded
    would be family heads with small children and those
    with older dependents.
4. State administration of assistance payments programs
    would be continued.
5. Full federal financing of the minimum welfare benefits
    would be provided as well as 75 percent of all state
    supplemental welfare payments and 75 percent of state
    administration costs.

FEDERAL ADMINISTRATION AND FINANCING OF PUBLIC ASSIS-
TANCE PROGRAMS.[12]   The Committee on Economic Development, a nonprofit research and educational organization of
corporate and university executives, proposed in July, 1976 that
full federal financing and administration of public assistance
programs be supported by diversion of proposed new general
revenue sharing funds under consideration at that time by Congress. The Committee recommended this action to achieve sizable efficiencies in administration and reductions in state and
local expenditures to offset the cut-off of general revenue funds.
National payments levels would be established to be more equitable to the recipients living in states with inadequate assistance
payments levels. Coincidentally, the Committee's recommendations were made the same day as that of the National Governors
Conference.

A COMPREHENSIVE PROGRAM OF BASIC SOCIAL GUARANTEES: A
PROPOSAL OF THE ADVISORY COUNCIL ON PUBLIC WELFARE.[13]
    The Advisory Council on Public Welfare of 12 national so-
cial welfare leaders was convened in 1964 by the Secretary of
Health, Education and Welfare to review and recommend im-

provements in the public welfare system. Its Report: *Having the Power, We Have the Duty,* deals with public welfare in its many programs and ramifications. Unlike most other proposals, it recommended a comprehensive, coordinated public welfare program, including public assistance, social services, child welfare services, health care, manpower training and work programs, and juvenile delinquency tied to the social security system. In this context, it recommended the following welfare payments improvements:

1. Adoption of a minimum standard for public assistance payments below which no state may fall.
2. Public assistance eligibility would be based solely on need. This would be intended to remove the barriers to assistance for families without children, single individuals, partially disabled persons, and other needy individuals.
3. Federal–state financial sharing in public welfare costs would be continued and recognition given to the relative fiscal capacity of the federal and state governments to finance public welfare programs. National standards for state financial support of comprehensive public welfare programs would be set by the federal government. Each state's share of the national standards would be specified with poor states, those with lower average personal income, required to finance public welfare programs at lower levels, while those with higher average personal income would be required to finance such programs at higher levels. The federal government would finance the balance required for a comprehensive program of public assistance and other welfare programs.

THE AMERICAN PUBLIC WELFARE ASSOCIATION RECOMMENDATIONS FOR WELFARE REFORM.[14]   On September 23, 1976 the American Public Welfare Association recommended a structure for welfare reform incorporating principles and practices espoused by others but packaged blending social objectives and administrative practicality.

The Association plan provides the following:

1. *Federal benefit floor.* A nationwide minimum payment funded fully by the federal government should be provided to all eligible participants. The level of this payment should be based upon a percentage of an objectively established and annually updated government poverty index.
2. *State supplementation.* States should be allowed to supplement the federal minimum payment at their own option, except that no participant should receive a lower payment than provided under current cash assistance programs.
3. *Universal eligibility.* Income maintenance should be provided to all persons (intact and single-parent families, childless couples, and single individuals) who qualify on the basis of their income and resources.
4. *Consolidation of programs.* Various programs that provide income maintenance (such as AFDC, Food Stamps, and General Assistance) should be consolidated into one cash payment program. The SSI program should continue as an independent program.
5. *Work requirement.* As a condition of eligibility, employable participants should be required to accept a bona fide offer of employment or training leading directly to a specific job. Age, disability, or defined socially productive activities, such as providing care for a child, disabled, or aged person, should each be a basis for exemption from the work requirement.
6. *Work incentive.* The "tax rate" applied to the earned income of program participants should be no higher than 50 percent.
7. *Administration.* Program administration should be the responsibility of the states, with federal supervision of the uniform eligibility criteria for the nationwide minimum payment. The states and federal government should share in the costs of administration.

DEMOGRANT PROPOSALS.[15]   A demogrant is simply a per capita benefit paid to persons regardless of the amount or sources of their other income. The grant amount can be structured in a number of different ways. For example, if paid only to children, the demogrant would be a children's allowance. Alternatively, the benefit could be paid to all persons but with a different amount paid to persons of different ages. Still further modifications could be introduced so that the first two children in a family receive higher benefits than do additional children. These are just a few examples of the many ways in which a demogrant program can be structured. Regardless of what criteria are chosen, the essential feature of a demogrant program remains unchanged; benefits are paid solely on the basis of some demographic feature of persons, and, once established, payments are made to qualified individuals as a matter of right and without any demonstration of need or means test.

Although the demogrant may seem new and radical to some people, tax provisions which serve in lieu of a demogrant program have existed in the United States since 1913 when the present federal individual income tax was adopted. Under current law, there is a $750 per capita exemption and a $2,400 to $2,800 standard deduction permitted when computing one's federal income tax liability.

Dr. Benjamin Okner of the Brookings Institution analyzed four different demogrant applications:

benefits of $1,500 to adults with no allowances for children;

$1,500 for each adult and $300 per child;

differential payments to individuals of different age groups ($1,500 to aged 65 years and older, $1,200 55–64, $1,000 to adults 18–54, $200 to children under 14, and $400 to children 14–17); and

$1,250 each for first two family members, $750 each for two additional members, $500 each for fifth and sixth, and $250 each for members after the sixth.

He concluded that most types of families fare extremely well when measured against poverty-income thresholds. Aged couples with no children receive payments above poverty-level incomes. Aged single persons receive 80 percent of their poverty income level except in the last category of variable payments analyzed. For the four-person family, payments equal 90 percent or more of their poverty-income threshold. Only under the last category of variable payments do benefits stay close to the poverty line as family size increases. However, in the first category of payments to adults and none for children, demogrant payments decline relative to the poverty level as family size increases. Adoption of this income transfer method is tied to revision of the income tax structure, virtually calling for elimination of all tax preferences, nonessential deductions, and personal exemptions. This is conceded to be an insuperable task under prevailing national conditions and political climate.

NONCASH (IN-KIND) PROGRAMS.[16]   Income supplements are paid in many forms. In addition to giving cash to some needy families, the government gives free or subsidized food, housing, health care, and day care. Many purposes lie behind the use of noncash (or in-kind) benefits instead of cash benefits to supplement incomes. Among them are: (1) a desire to earmark benefits so that recipients use government support only for socially approved items; (2) a judgment that the private market does not function well in the provision of certain goods in certain locations; (3) an effort to help specific industries by increasing the demand for their goods; and (4) a belief that some services such as medical care are so important that the government must assure their availability. These factors often bring greater political support to in-kind than to cash programs.

Economists long have argued that cash supplements are a superior way to raise the recipient's economic welfare, a way that lets the recipient define his own well-being. Noncash benefits have several drawbacks: First, they may cause recipients to consume much more of one item than they would if given an equal amount of cash. For example, in Mississippi, a welfare mother of three children receiving AFDC but with no other income was eligible to buy each month $150 of food stamps for $13, when the purchase requirement was in effect. This constituted over 76 percent of that family's total cash income plus food stamp allotment. One would expect that many of the families receiving food stamps would prefer cash payments, even smaller than the bonus value of stamps, if necessary. Empirical confirmation shows up in reports of black market sales of food stamps. Although recipients no doubt have to accept a significant discount to sell their stamps, some decide to do so anyway. Second, noncash benefits are economically inefficient because the cost of providing goods by the government often exceed private market prices, or the quality of government-provided goods is lower than that of private goods of similar cost. Third, recipients find a large difference between programs that constrain their choices to a general category, such as food stamps or housing allowances, and those that limit their subsidies to specific items, such as a particular public housing unit or a food basket from the commodity distribution program.

Persons favoring in-kind programs may argue that the government knows more about what is best for the poor recipient than he does, so that it is more helpful to give them goods than cash. One of the rationales for in-kind programs has been the fear that cash payments would be used frivolously, wantonly, or not in the best interest of children. Another reason for in-kind programs is failure of markets to supply the poor with goods and services, such as housing or medical care. Also, this ensures the receipt of goods and services of better quality than may be available to them. However, administrative considerations argue against the in-kind strategy. Noncash aid requires a larger number of programs than cash aid. Each in-kind program typically requires a separate administrative apparatus, including a separate income reporting and verification unit and a separate unit to verify that the benefits are used for the earmarked goods or services.

VOUCHERS VERSUS CASH PAYMENTS.[17]   The use of vouchers such as food stamps is another noncash option to consider. Vouchers are written authorizations to obtain a specified good or service. Vouchers have several advantages over cash: (1) They allow the welfare recipient freedom to select the supplier of the goods and often allow freedom to choose among a wide range of goods intended for the particular purpose. (2) They allow meeting individuals' special needs or tastes. For example, Medicaid payments are made only for those with particular medical needs and enable the individual to select a provider of the individual's choice. (3) They involve lower administrative costs in comparison with the direct provision of goods and services. Thus, vouchers are appropriate when society wants to encourage the utilization of a particular good or service available in the market beyond the level at which it would be consumed if a greater cash income was available to a recipient, or to provide benefits to recipients that are limited to a particular purpose. However, two things should be noted in connection with these goals. First, to the extent the voucher simply frees cash resources that the recipient would otherwise have spent on that particular good or service, the use of a voucher has not restricted consumption patterns any more than an equivalent amount of cash would have. Second, if the voucher value is sufficiently in excess of what the recipient would otherwise have spent for its designated purpose—such as for food—the worth of the transfer to the recipient is less than program outlays.

Universal Comprehensive Social Services

The goals of the Title XX social services program are comprehensive; their potential fulfillment, however, is compromised by the limitations of government funding; states providing an array of social services of uneven diversity, quantity, quality, and availability; shortages of social services manpower and resources; and in limiting eligibility for service largely to low-income persons. On the positive side, the program is more liberal than previous public welfare services programs in opening eligibility for other than low-income persons, albeit at a limit of 115 percent of the state's median income, and adopting the concept of fee-for-service for those able to pay. Proposals have been made to move further towards a universal social services system for all Americans without regard to economic status. The rationale for a universal system rests on both philosophical and pragmatic grounds.

> Continuing changes in modern life have sharply reduced the capacity of the family and the neighborhood to aid its members in dealing with a variety of social and family problems. The elderly, the sick, and the disabled, newcomers to urban life, youth, men and women seeking to adapt to a changed market for their labor,

members of minority groups, and in fact, most people are confronted at times with problems requiring a new type of community service. These problems are not restricted to persons of low income or of little education . . .

Financial assistance, while of primary importance in many instances, is but one answer to the variety of problems spawned by the rapidly changing patterns of modern society . . .

The anxiety and alarm engendered by family breakup, juvenile delinquency, alienation, mental illness, and other evidences of social maladjustment, are not limited to a single class, one economic level, any particular educational level, or any racial or cultural group. These are symptoms indicative of the stresses of modern life which put heavy pressure on people everywhere. They emphasize the need for an improved social environment better adapted to the needs of present and future generations. For hard-pressed families and children, specific social services are needed which can support, supplement, strengthen, and, if need be, substitute for the traditional parent–child relationship. The functions of social services become increasingly important as the variety of community services of many types confronts the individual with a complex maze of potential benefits and services. Increasingly, people need advice and counsel in finding specific answers for their problems. Many people are not familiar with the machinery of government and require the skilled guidance of the public social service agency in obtaining the help that is, or can be made, available to them . . .

People confronted with an emergency, isolated from the community, discouraged, overwhelmed by the confusion and demands of a new environment, people who see their jobs disappearing, their debts mounting, their family problems sharpening into seemingly insoluble conflict, the demands for new adjustment outrunning their experience to the point of panic—all need a source of support, encouragement, guidance, and direct help.[18]

The financial and administrative complexities and issues raised earlier for a universal comprehensive social services program must be dealt with if it is to become a reality. If one accepts the logic for such a program, one need question whether it can best function as part of a public welfare system, with its poverty orientation or treat it philosophically, organizationally, financially, as an independent, separate public service system for all Americans. This different context raises other questions about the imprecise definition of social services as distinct and separate from other human service programs. Several examples are child development programs, services for the aged, vocational rehabilitation services, juvenile delinquency services, all of which have a core of social services, all of which are available to all Americans regardless of financial need or status. Once a universal comprehensive social services program is divorced from its public assistance, low-income orientation, it is no longer a public welfare program in the present context. However, its proponents must face these other continuing barriers: (1) the widespread inadequacies of social work manpower and community service resources; (2) the knowledge gap in determining (and justifying) the effectiveness of social service methods to ameliorate or remedy the individual social, psychological, economic, and cultural problems which confront most Americans in one form or another; and (3) the acquisition of political and public support and confidence to provide the necessary authority, funds, and resources-building capability to achieve universal social services objectives.

COMPREHENSIVE CHILD CARE.   Progress towards such a system is becoming visible in the field of child care, primarily because it is a key adjunct to job training and employment of family heads and essential for early childhood development. Thus, universal comprehensive child care programs are sponsored by diverse political, labor, industry, social, educational, women's, and children's organizations. Such proposals have provision for free (or nominal charges) child care, voluntary in nature, of high quality, conveniently located in all communities for all children. They provide for national standards and requirements for early childhood education and diverse child care services. They call for coordination by public and community nonprofit agencies of a broad range of services for children, including health, nutrition, education, counseling, and other support services necessary for proper child development in a variety of settings, including family and group care homes. The involvement of parents is regarded as an absolute in all planning, programming, and operation of child care programs. At least a half-dozen comprehensive child care legislative proposals have been introduced in Congress during the past five years.[19] The most prominent proposal was S.1512 Comprehensive Child Development Act of 1971 introduced by then-Senator Mondale of Minnesota. It was approved by both Houses of Congress September 24, 1971, but vetoed by President Nixon. It amended Title V of the Economic Opportunity Act to authorize the Secretary of Health, Education and Welfare to provide financial assistance for child development programs. Authorized appropriations would have been allotted among the states, with 50 percent of the funds allotted on the basis of the number of economically disadvantaged children in the state, 25 percent on the basis of the number of children under age 6, and 25 percent on the basis of children of working mothers and single parents. Allocations among localities within a state would be made by the Secretary according to the same formula. Set aside funds for use of child care programs for children of migrant agriculture workers, children on Indian reservations, and for special model projects were also authorized.

Funds could be used for planning and developing child development programs and for operating programs to include:

physical and mental health;

social and cognitive development services;

food and nutrition services;

rent, remodeling, construction, or acquisition of facilities;

programs to meet the special needs of minority group, Indian, and migrant children;

diagnosis and identification of physical, mental, and other barriers to participation in child development programs;

prenatal services;

activities to identify and ameliorate identified handicaps and learning disabilities, including the operation of separate programs for handicapped children;

preservice and inservice training for professional and paraprofessional personnel;

training in child development for parents and youth;

use of child advocates; and

other specially designed health, social, and educational programs (including after-school, summer, weekend, vacation, and overnight programs).

The Secretary of HEW would designate prime sponsors of programs for particular geographic areas. The Secretary would provide financial assistance to any prime sponsor in any fiscal year only pursuant to a comprehensive child development plan. Such plan would set forth a program of services which would identify child development needs and goals and describe the purposes for which financial assistance would be used; meet the needs of children in the area, including provision for infant care, and for before- and after-school programs, but with priority to children under six, economically disadvantaged children, children of single parents, and working mothers. No charge for care for children of economically disadvantaged parents would be made and a fee schedule would be established for other children.

Federal funds would cover not in excess of 80 percent of the cost of child care programs. The nonfederal share could be in the form of goods, services, or facilities.

This and other proposed comprehensive child development programs remain as proposals. However, child care and early childhood development are being supported in the WIN program, the Title XX social services program, the child welfare services program, in preschool educational programs, in Headstart and other preschool child development programs, in the Comprehensive Employment and Training program, in the community development block grant program, and other federal, state, and local government and private nonprofit programs.

NATIONAL HEALTH INSURANCE

The widespread dissatisfaction with the country's medical care for all Americans also applies to the Medicaid program and the other health-related public welfare programs. The country spent $118 billion on health care in fiscal year 1975 or 8.3 percent of the gross national product. Yet this expenditure left 38 million people without health insurance coverage. Eighty percent of the population do not have health insurance for initial doctor visits in the home or physicians' offices. The Medicaid program is deemed generally to be uncontrolled and the variations in state plans in eligibility, kinds of covered services, and abuses in utilization and costs have been major criticisms of the program. National health insurance schemes have been proposed by such varied groups as the American Medical Association, American Hospital Association, the AFL-CIO, the health insurance industry, consumer groups, legislators, and the national administration. Consensus has not yet been reached on this subject but the dissatisfaction with present health care is so acute and widespread that it surely is a high priority issue. We can expect the proposal ultimately approved will mark serious change in public welfare medical care in any event.

The American Public Welfare Association developed a Statement On National Health Policy of 12 points in 1977 to form the guiding principles for health care reform.[20] It proposed that a national health insurance program should:

1. Provide coverage for all residents of the United States.
2. Cover a comprehensive scope of essential health care services, including (a) primary preventive care, (b) emphasis on health education so that the consumer has an active role in the maintenance of his own health, and (c) long-term care.
3. Impose no deductibles or coinsurance.
4. Be financed through earmarked federal revenues, to the maximum extent possible on a progressive basis.
5. Be enacted immediately.
6. Be administered by an independent federal agency, newly established.
7. Authorize use of regional, state, and local public and private organizations which, through contracts negotiated on a periodic and competitive basis, could be delegated the daily operation of the benefit payment process. Contracts with public agencies should be negotiated to assure regulation of delivery system performance and resource development.
8. Utilize the budgeting appropriation process as the basic expenditure control, with appropriations planned on a 5-year basis and subject to annual review.

9. Provide federal leadership and earmarked funding for research, planning, and development of resources.
10. Assure an open and participatory process of policy-making at all levels.
11. Allow states a major role in administration of the program, particularly in regulatory activities, but with no responsibility for financing.
12. Give priority in the first years of the program to coverage of children and primary preventive care while improving Medicaid, Medicare, and related programs.

The following are the major proposals put forth[21]:

HEALTH SECURITY S.3 AND H.R. 22-23 (93RD CONGRESS).
This is a plan for universal comprehensive health insurance for all Americans introduced in Congress in 1973 by Senator Kennedy of Massachusetts and then-Representative Martha Griffiths of Michigan and supported by major labor and consumer groups. Benefits cover the entire range of health care services, including prevention and early detection of disease, care and treatment, and medical rehabilitation. There are no cutoff dates, no coinsurance, no deductibles, no waiting periods. Some limitations on adult dental care, nursing home care, psychiatric care, and drugs are provided. Pilot projects are to be supported under the program for evaluating the benefits of home care for chronically ill and aged. A Health Security Trust Fund would be set up, as follows: 50 percent from general tax revenues, 36 percent from a 3.5 percent tax on employer payroll, 12 percent from a one percent tax on the first $15,000 of individual income, 2 percent from a 2.5 percent tax on the first $15,000 of self-employment income. The program would be administered in HEW through its 10 regions and newly-created 100 health subregional offices. A five-member Health Security Board appointed by the President would decide policy. This plan would absorb both Medicare and Medicaid.

MEDICREDIT. (S. 444; H.R. 2222 93RD CONGRESS).   This is a voluntary income tax plan sponsored by the American Medical Association. Tax credits would partially offset the cost of qualified private health insurance. The amount of the credit would be graduated by income. Medicare would be retained but Medicaid would be discontinued. A qualified health insurance policy would offer insurance against the expenses of illness, subject to deductibles, copayment and limitations. Benefits include payments for doctors and hospital care and dental services for children aged two to six. The government would pay all premiums for the destitute—individuals and dependents with no income tax liability. For others, the government would pay between 10 percent and 99 percent based on family or individual income. It would pay everyone's premium for catastrophic expense coverage. Coverage would be provided through private health insurance. Enrollment in prepaid groups would be permitted. An 11-man Health Insurance Board would be appointed to administer the program, including the HEW Secretary and the Internal Revenue Service Commissioner.

HEALTH CARE SERVICES H.R. 1 (93RD CONGRESS).   This plan is sponsored by the American Hospital Association. It provides comprehensive health care benefits for all Americans through a reorganized and coordinated health system. Hospital and doctor benefits would include insurance against the cost of catastrophic illness. Special benefits would be provided children up to age 12 and medical, dental, and eye care. Outpatient care would be emphasized. Primary reliance would be placed on state and local facilities. Employers would be required to purchase for their employees a comprehensive level of benefits, paying at least 75 percent of the premium costs. Registrants and Health Care Corporations (to be set up in each local jurisdiction) would be entitled to a ten percent federal subsidy on their health insurance premiums. Health services for the aged would continue to be financed through a combination of Social Security taxes and general federal revenues. The plan would establish a new Department of Health separated from the Department of Health, Education and Welfare. State health commissions would implement federal regulations and laws and would develop state health care plans, subject to the approval of the Secretary of Health. Health Care Corporations would administer the program in cities and counties. They would make available to everyone in their jurisdiction comprehensive health services, including health maintenance and catastrophic illness services. The Medicaid program would be discontinued.

HEALTH CARE S.1100 and H.R. 5200 (93RD CONGRESS).   This plan is sponsored by the Health Insurance Association of America. It provides tax penalties for employers failing to purchase broad standard health insurance coverage for their employees. It also provides creation of government-subsidized state insurance pools for private health insurance for the poor, near-poor, and uninsurables. Such insurance would cover physicians services (office, home, and health facilities), laboratory and x-ray expenses, general and psychiatric hospital services, home health services, dental care for children, prescription drugs, and catastrophic illness coverage. Most of these are to be subject to sizable deductible and coinsurance requirements. The plan would be financed through general revenues and Social Security. Tax incentives would be offered to encourage purchase of insurance policies by individuals and employers, with 100 percent tax deductibles if coverage meets federal standards. The very poor would pay no premiums. The near-poor would pay increasing amounts and the balance of premium cost would be financed by federal and state general revenues. The federal government would provide 90 percent and the states ten percent of these amounts. Medicaid would be discontinued.

CATASTROPHIC HEALTH INSURANCE S.1416 (93RD CONGRESS). This plan was introduced by Senator Long of Louisiana, Chairman of the Senate Finance Committee. It provides catastrophic health insurance for all persons now insured under Social Security, plus spouses and dependent children. Services provided under this plan would include those provided under Parts A and B of Medicare except that there would be no upper limit on hospital days. Benefits would be payable only after the 60th day of hospitalization and after the patient incurs $2,000 in other medical expenses. A maximum of $1,000 per family would be required as copayment for covered expenses. The plan would be financed through a Social Security tax of .3 percent on the first $9,000 of employees wages and a .3 percent tax on employers payrolls of the first $9,000 of each employee's earnings. It would be administered by the Social Security Administration using health insurers and intermediaries. Under this plan, Medicaid would continue and more of its coverage for catastrophic illnesses would be paid through the new program.

NATIONAL HEALTH INSURANCE PARTNERSHIP.   This plan is the Nixon Administration proposal submitted to the 92nd Congress. It proposed the Family Health Insurance Plan (FHIP), federally subsidized insurance for poor families, and a National Health Insurance Standards Act (NHISA) as a medical insurance program for employed persons under 65. This act would require employers to offer minimal health insurance to employees. Such insurance would include inpatient hospital, physician, and other services with deductibles and copayment provisions and well-child care with no copayment necessary. It would also provide 30 days of ambulatory and institutional care with deductibles and copayment requirements for all but the poorest. The plan would be financed through an increase in the Social Security tax base for catastrophic insurance. Employers would be required to pay 65 percent of employee's coverage the first two and one-half years, 75 percent thereafter with the employee paying the balance. The FHIP Plan would be financed from federal general revenues. It would be administered by the private health insurance industry. Medicare and Medicaid would be continued, the latter as a residual program for adult assistance recipients not covered under the FHIP or Medicare programs. The proposal would encourage development of health maintenance organizations through planning grants, start-up funds, operational grants in underserved areas, and loan guarantees for capitol costs and operations. It also calls for establishment of professional standards review organizations to review health insurance and HMO contracts and quality standards.

THE NEXT CHAPTER

It is obvious this country is at a crossroads in deciding upon the future of public welfare programs and seeking ways and means to make them more effective, efficient, and less costly. In decid-

ing which direction to take, there is no doubt the end results
would be enhanced by a fuller knowledge of the current public
welfare system in all its intricacies and eccentricities. This volume has sought to fill this need. But this is not enough.
Throughout, the debates on welfare reform, comprehensive social service, health insurance, etc. will be governed by the nation's goals toward the poor. These are not self-evident. They
are ethical and moral choices about the government's responsibility towards the poor and the individual poor towards himself.
On one extreme, the government may, within constitutional
and democratic principles, support all the poor without regard
to their own capabilities or interest in self-improvement. At
the other extreme, the government may assume a posture that
each individual shall decide to cope with his own problems using his own resources and chart his own fate without society's
intervention, as long as it does not interfere with or harm
others.

It is fair to say that prevailing policies accept neither of
these extremes. Rather, we as a people are searching for the one
best way to provide help and support to the poor in many ways
while maintaining that this group—individually and collectively
—must develop to its fullest capability to achieve self-sufficiency
and personal independence. But this broad policy leaves room
for further definition. Within this general policy framework we
recognize alternative poverty goals. The choice of goals will
help in framing the public welfare anti-poverty system of the
future. Do we as a society wish a public welfare system:

> to eradicate poverty in this country now and in the future?
>
> to reduce the incidence of poverty in this country to some
> arbitrary percentage below current population levels?
>
> to raise the social, economic, cultural level of the poor to
> at least that of the American middle class?
>
> to raise the social, economic, cultural level of the poor to
> a point where they can meet their basic needs for food,
> clothing, and shelter?
>
> to help the poor help themselves to reach whatever social,
> economic, and cultural level they can?

to help those poor who are willing or able to help themselves and not those unwilling or unable to do so?

to help those poor who are unable to help themselves and not those who can?

to provide the poor with income security and services at a national cost up to a fixed percentage of the gross national product, or a fixed dollar ceiling?

to help the poorest of the poor and assume the marginally poor can help themselves?

to obtain social and economic equality among all Americans?

to reduce the social, economic, and cultural drag of the poor upon all other Americans?

to create a utopian country of healthy, happy people where all share equally in the abundant life?

to erase the causes of poverty as well as the conditions of poverty?

to guarantee the children of the poor full opportunity for normal growth and development to become able to escape poverty in their adult years?

to guarantee the children of the poor full opportunity for them in meeting their basic needs for food, clothing, and housing?

These are the choices we have in the primary aims for public welfare. They are not all compatible. There may be others. Once we can reach agreement on the ones which most closely express what the people and its leadership feel and believe, we can form our public policies and proceed to the implementing steps of program design, federal/state/local government relationships, beneficiary eligibility, organization, methods, funding, and the myriad other characteristics needed to produce an equitable, effective, efficient, economical system for the poor.

Figure 10.1 Public Welfare Balance Sheet

Assets	*Liabilities*
Population coverage	
Assistance payments, social services, health care, food stamps, job training, and employment are provided to an aggregate of 25 million persons.	12.6 million poor who are members of families without children and poor single individuals who are not aged, blind or permanently and totally disabled are not helped by public welfare programs, except temporary General Assistance.
Public welfare programs and activities	
Programs and activities are provided with few exceptions in every one of the 54 states and territorial jurisdictions.	Payment levels in all but 4 or 5 states are below their basic support needs as determined by federal poverty guidelines.
Federal and state governments are committed through public welfare agencies to the principle of helping poor families, disabled, blind, and aged persons. This principle is mandated in federal and state constitutions and laws.	The quantity, availability, kind and quality of services fail in many jurisdictions to meet the needs of the people for whom they are intended. There are serious service gaps.
The concept of purchase of service by public welfare agencies recognizes that *all* services and facilities in the community should be made available to welfare clients.	Services for the prevention of social, health and economic problems and handicapping conditions are not generally available on a scale where they can be effective.
With some exceptions, e.g., protective services, child abuse, neglected and abandoned, delinquent children, child support; programs and services are available on a voluntary basis to those who apply and are eligible. Assistance payments may be used at the discretion of the recipients; services may or may not be requested or accepted.	Public welfare services are often separated from the services available to the nonpoor population, thereby creating a lower standard separated system.
	Public welfare service programs are not effectively coordinated and barriers to the provision of services exist because of excessive rules, regulations and limitations unrelated to the need for services.

Public welfare offices are located in practically every state, county, and city in the United States and Territories.

Public welfare agencies are organized in accordance with the constitution and laws of the 54 jurisdictions to reflect their individual characteristics and needs.

State public welfare agencies have been combined with other human service agencies in many states to achieve better coordination of service programs. There is a decided trend towards these umbrella organizations.

State and local organizations have adapted their organizations to help create neighborhood centers.

Most state and local public welfare agencies have been reorganized to reflect changing service needs or to recognize their deficiencies and seek improvement in their programs.

State and local public welfare agencies comprise the second largest group of public social organizations next to departments of education.

The federal government does not have an organization with responsibility for all public welfare programs and services.

The diversity of state and local public welfare organizations mitigates against effective planning, evaluation, understanding, development of standards and models for the most effective arrangement of welfare programs and activities.

The organizational separation of public welfare agencies from other human service agencies in federal and many state and local governments makes effective coordination of services difficult.

Public welfare agency staffing and personnel administration

The social work profession is recognized as the core discipline for meeting human needs. It has specialized courses of study, undergraduate and graduate degree status, schools of social work, professional standards and professional organizations.

There is widespread turnover of public welfare workers and poor morale among many of them.

The size of public welfare staffs has not risen proportionally to the rise in welfare caseloads and service needs of welfare clientele.

Figure 10.1   (Continued)

Public welfare agencies employ many paraprofessionals and volunteers.

A staff of more than 340,000 is employed in public welfare agencies to meet social, health and other service needs of welfare clientele.

Public welfare agencies maintain diversified staff training and education programs with shared federal/state financial support.

Public welfare agencies utilize social work specialists to give intensive service in such problem areas as nutrition, psychological testing and counseling, alcohol and drug abuse, foster care, adoptions, child welfare, housing assistance, financial management, family relations, family planning.

Large numbers of public assistance recipients are being employed in state and local welfare agencies and as volunteers.

Schools of social work do not have the capacity to train enough social workers for public welfare positions.

Widespread complaints are voiced about the overworked conditions of public welfare workers, such as excessive paperwork, excessive caseloads.

The public image of public welfare workers is tarnished by their inability to service applicants promptly, high error rates in processing applications, and complaints from welfare recipients.

Public welfare financing and budgeting

The public commitment to public welfare funding is evident in the $38.5 billion appropriated for this purpose, with financial commitments of all government levels.

The Social Security Act reflects the national policy that federal reimbursement for assistance payments and medical services for assistance

Public welfare costs have skyrocketed and are believed out of control.

Federal and state legislators have adopted restrictive laws and appropriations in light of adverse economic conditions to control rising welfare budgets to the detriment of welfare programs, services, and recipients.

recipients and the medically indigent are open-ended, that is, that state expenditures are reimbursed without a specified ceiling on federal matching funds.

Financial accounting systems and procedures are applied to process and control the flow of public welfare funds through government treasuries to recipients and service providers.

State and local public welfare agencies prepare budget plans for public assistance caseloads, social services, Medicaid, and WIN estimates for their own use and as the basis for federal budgeting of public welfare appropriations.

Welfare funds are grossly misapplied to large numbers of persons who are ineligible.

Data and methods for forecasting public welfare expenditures and caseloads are inadequate.

Assistance payments procedures to determine the amounts of monthly grants to recipients are complex, often requiring elaborate computations difficult to explain to recipients and subject to varying interpretations and error.

Federal matching of state and local welfare programs reward those which have a greater financial commitment, rather than greater payment and service needs of their poor population.

Public knowledge of welfare financial needs and purposes is inadequate and welfare budget decisions are subject to error as a result.

Public welfare methods

The Social Security Act expressly states the national policy that state and local welfare agencies "must provide such methods of administration to be necessary for the proper and efficient operation of the state plan."

Public welfare agencies as large bureaucracies employ administrative and program methods of planning, control, coordination, reporting, minotoring and evaluation. Federal and state governments maintain auditing programs to exercise oversight of these agencies.

Public welfare agencies are perpetrators (or victims) of a paperwork explosion which impedes rather than facilitates services and payments to recipients.

High error rates in eligibility determination processes indicate a poor level of quality control in such processes.

Imposition of elaborate verification procedures to check on the completeness and accuracy of statements by applicants and recipients is demeaning to most of the honest poor clientele.

Figure 10.1 **(Continued)**

Wide use is made in most welfare agencies of automatic data processing and computers.

The Title XX social services system and plan requirements are a good influence in developing uniform procedures and methods in all public welfare agencies.

The right of appeal by applicants and recipients and fair hearings to contest agency actions are protected as national policy under the Social Security Act.

The confidentiality of public welfare case records and actions protect individuals against disclosure of their welfare status.

The federal government encourages state and local welfare agencies to adopt goal-oriented social services planning, monitoring, and evaluation.

The federal government supports research and demonstrations and evaluation of public welfare programs.

Some welfare agencies continue to use wasteful and costly hand-written notes to record and process actions.

Widespread use is made of costly, time-consuming and unnecessary dictation methods to fill case files with trivia in social work practice.

Separation of social services and eligibility determination functions create separate case records and files worsening the quantity of paperwork and record-keeping.

The federal government imposes burdensome, complicated, and costly reporting requirements upon state and local welfare agencies.

With some exception, the federal government issues detailed regulations which leave little to the discretion of state and local agencies and fail to take into account local conditions of geography and social, economic, cultural differences.

There is insufficient information about public welfare. There is yet no information system comprehensive enough to detail and summarize the national scope and prevalence of the problems and service needs of the poor, the effectiveness and benefits of services, the types, quality, and availability of services, and the costs of services.

There is no national consensus about public welfare goals and objectives.

More and better research, demonstrations and evaluations of public welfare are needed and there appears to be no national commitment to provide the funds and organization for these purposes.

Public welfare relationships to other human service programs

Public welfare agencies at all government levels have established working relationships with other human service agencies.

There is a definite trend towards setting up human service agencies with public welfare a major component.

Interdisciplinary education and training programs are being expanded to develop trained employees for different human service programs.

The official and informal contacts of human service workers of public and voluntary agencies have helped develop a coordinative environment for more effective programs.

The large number of narrow categorical human service programs have created overlapping, duplication, and gaps in service, have confused the public and recipients, and have been more costly than necessary.

Services coordination has been impeded by conflicting and different eligibility requirements and funding arrangements of the different programs.

Public welfare agencies have not been able to function effectively because they do not control all the services their clients need, such as housing or education. Social services are fragmented among many agencies and social workers have had to depend upon interagency referrals and the cooperation of other agencies to get results.

Other assets and liabilities

Public assistance applicants and recipients have become more aware of their legal rights to public assistance and services.

The legal profession, through legal aid societies and the Legal Services Corporation, has become more active in poverty law.

Consumer involvement in decision making in public welfare policies and practices has not been widespread.

The efforts of consumer-action groups has not resulted in adequate assistance payment levels or adequate welfare services.

Public welfare recipients are not effectively organized to support their position on welfare improvements before law making bodies.

NOTES

1. Income Security for Americans: Recommendations of the Public Welfare Study, Report of the Subcommittee on Fiscal Policy of the Joint Economic Committee, U.S. Congress Joint Committee, December 5, 1974, p. 1–4. Print 93rd Congress 2nd Session, U.S. Government Printing Office, Washington, D.C.

2. Growth of Government Spending For Income Assistance—A Matter of Choice. Prepared by the Congressional Budget Office For the Committee On the Budget, U.S. Senate December 3, 1975, U.S. Government Printing Office, Washington, D.C.

3. Spindler, A. *On decision-making and the social and rehabilitation programs. Public Welfare,* 1971, 307–315. Also Spindler, A. *Management by crisis or management by plan. Public Welfare,* 1972, 44–47.

4. Ibid, Income Security for Americans: Recommendations of the Public Welfare Study, p. 87.

5. Ibid, The public policy issues discussion is excerpted from Chapters II, IX, and X in *Income Security for Americans: Recommendations of the Public Welfare Study.*

6. Papers No. 13 and 14, Studies in Public Welfare, Subcommittee on Fiscal Policy, Joint Economic Committee, U.S. Government Printing Office. Washington, D.C., 1974.

7. Presidential Message, August 6, 1977 and *New York Times,* August 7, 1977.

8. The Social Security Amendments of 1971, Report of the Committee on Ways and Means on H.R. 1, May 26, 1971. Union Calendar No. 86. House Report 91-231, 92nd Congress 1st Session. U.S. Government Printing Office, Washington, D.C. p. 3–5.

9. Social Security and Welfare Reform, Summary of the Principal Provision of H.R. 1 as Determined by the Committee on Finance, United States Senate, June 13, 1972, U.S. Government Printing Office, Washington, D.C., p. 63.

10. Income Security for Americans: Recommendations of the Public Welfare Study, p. 155.

11. *New York Times,* July 6–7, 1976. Also, National Welfare Reform: A Bicentennial Priority, Task Force Report, National Governors' Conference, June 2, 1976.

12. *Washington Post,* July 6, 1976.

13. *Having the power, we have the duty.* The Report of the Advisory Council on Public Welfare, June 1966, U.S. Government Printing Office, Washington, D.C.

14. *Public Welfare,* 1977, Vol. **35,** No. 2, 17.

15. Okner, B. A. The role of demogrants as an income maintenance alternative. *Studies in Public Welfare.* Paper No. 9, Part 1, Concepts in Welfare Program Design, Subcommittee on Fiscal Policy of the Joint Economic Committee, U.S. Congress, 93rd Congress 1st Session, August 20, 1973, U.S. Government Printing Office, Washington, D.C.

16. Ibid, Income Security for All Americans. Recommendations of the Public Welfare Study, pp. 136–139.

17. Barth, M.C., Carcague, G. J, Palmer, J. L., & Garfinckel, I. *The form of transfer benefits, From Toward an effective income support system: problems, prospects, and choices.* University of Wisconsin-Madison, Madison, Wis.: Institute for Research on Poverty, 1974, pp. 47–50.

18. Ibid, *Having the power, we have the duty,* p. 47–48. Also see: APWA Committee on Social Services: *Policy statement on personal social services. Public Welfare,* 1977, Vol. 35 No. 2. 32.

19. Malone, M. Summary of selected proposals related to child care. Education and Public Welfare Division, Library of Congress Congressional Research Service HV 741 USA 71-162 ED June 24, 1971.

20. APWA Committee on Health Policy. Policy statement on national health policy. *Public Welfare,* 1977, Vol. 35 No 2. 50.

21. Major proposals for national health insurance before the 93rd Congress are summarized in Health Security News, Vol. 2 No. 6, May, 1973, Committee for National Health Insurance, 806 15th Street, N.W., Washington, D.C.

SUPREME COURT DECISIONS AFFECTING PUBLIC WELFARE

AID TO FAMILIES WITH DEPENDENT CHILDREN PROGRAM

Wyman v. James 1971   *Home visits by public welfare officers*
400 U.S. 309, 91 S.Ct. 381,
27 L.Ed. 2d 408

Home visitation by welfare officers which state statutes and regulations prescribed as conditions for assistance under AFDC program was a reasonable and proper administrative purpose for dispensation of the program. It does not violate any right guaranteed by the Fourth and Fourteenth Amendments. Home visitation, which is not forced or compelled, is not a search in the traditional criminal law context of the Fourth Amendment.

Burns v. Alcala 1975   *Unborn children as dependents*
420 U.S. 575,   95 S.Ct. 1180,
43 L.Ed. 2d 469

Unborn children are not covered in the definition of "dependent" children in Section 406 (a) of the act, and pregnant women who will be eligible for program benefits with a child in care are not entitled until the birth. Dependent child within the Social Security Act establishing eligibility for benefits under the AFDC program, refers to an individual already born. States receiving federal financial aid under the AFDC program are not required to offer welfare benefits to pregnant women for their unborn children.

Philbrook v. Glodgett 1975   *Effect of eligibility for*
_____ U.S. _____, 95 S.Ct. 1893,   *unemployment*
44 L.Ed. 2d 525   *compensation*

A state regulation denying benefits to any household in which the father is eligible to receive unemployment compensation is inconsistent with Section 407 (b) (2) (c) (ii) of the act* which provides for denial of benefits to families for any week such compensation was actually received. The father can choose which form of assistance he wants to receive. State welfare regulations, as applied to exclude unemployed fathers who were merely eligible for unemployment compensation from receiving Vermont ANFC Aid (Aid To Needy Families With Children) impermissibly conflicted with federal statute permitting assistance to dependent children whose deprivation is caused by unemployment of a parent only if participating states deny aid with respect to any week for which child's father receives unemployment compensation.

Van Lare v. Hurley 1975   *Shelter allowance*
_____ U.S. _____, 95 S.Ct. 1741,   *deduction because*
_____ L.Ed. 2d _____.   *of lodgers*

New York regulations, reducing pro rata the shelter allowance provided AFDC recipients to the extent there are nonpaying lodgers living in the household, conflict with the Social Security Act and federal regulations, based on the assumption that the nonpaying lodger is contributing to the welfare of the

*Unless otherwise specified, "act" means the Social Security Act.

household, without inquiry into whether he in fact does so, conflicts with federal law and regulations. State is barred from assuming that nonlegally responsible persons will apply their resources to aid the welfare child.

Shea v. Vialpando 1973   *Deductability of work-*
416 U.S. 251,   94 S.Ct. 1746,   *related expenses*
40 L.Ed. 2d 120.

A state's maximum limitation on certain work-related expenses available to offset income in the computation used for determining need and amount of assistance payments violates Section 402 (a) (7) of the act, requiring mandatory consideration of any reasonable expense. Congress intended to provide for individual treatment of expenses despite the allocation of objective criteria in calculation of average family needs. Standardized expense allowance are not per se invalid. It is not the adoption of a standardized work-expense allowance per se that violates Section 402 (a) (7), but the fact that the standard is in effect a maximum or absolute limitation upon the recognition of such expenses.

Jefferson v. Hackney 1972   *Variance of standards of*
406 U.S. 535,   92 S.Ct. 1724,   *need among programs*
32 L.Ed. 2d 285
rehearing denied 409 U.S. 898,
93 S.Ct. 178,
34 L.Ed. 2d 156

A state's pooled welfare fund allocation scheme which applied different percentage reduction factors to arrive at standards of need for the various programs does not violate Section 402 (a) (23) of the act or the equal protection clause of the Fourteenth Amendment. The Texas system for allocating its fixed pool of welfare money, under which a percentage reduction factor which was lower for AFDC than for other categorical assistance programs was applied to arrive at a reduced standard of need, did not violate the Fourteenth Amendment. The Social Security

Act does not require equal percentages for each categorical assistance program.

Carleson v. Remillard 1972   *Absence of parent due to*
406 U.S. 598,   92 S.Ct. 1932,   *service in armed forces*
32 L.Ed. 2d 352

A state cannot deny eligibility for assistance because the continued absence of one of the parents is due to service in the U.S. Armed Forces. California regulation excluding absence because of military service from definition of "continued absence" of parent from home as condition of eligibility for benefits from programs for AFDC is invalid under the supremacy clause.

Townsend v. Swank 1971   *Student eligibility, ages 18*
404 U.S. 282,   92 S.Ct. 502,   *through 20*
30 L.Ed. 2d 448

A state providing eligibility to needy dependent children ages 18 through 20 and attending high school or vocational training school, but denying those attending college or a university violates Sections 402 (a) (10) and 406 (a) (2) (B) of the act. The 1965 amendment extended eligibility to the latter group in all states electing to entitle any member of the age group.

Engleman v. Amos 1971   *Availability of nonadopting*
404 U.S. 23,   92 S.Ct. 181,   *stepfather's income, and*
30 L.Ed. 2d 143   *direct payment to vendors*

A state regulation which included the income of a nonadopting stepfather in a calculation of available income subject to an excess adjusted income benefit offset without regarding its actual availability for current use by the child violates Section 402 (a) (8) of the act. Also, Section 406 (b) of the act does not restrict a state from making direct payment to vendors of goods and services to program beneficiaries out of nonfederally matched funds.

Dandridge v. Williams 1970   *Family maximum benefit*
397 U.S. 471,   90 S.Ct. 1153,   *limitation*
25 L.Ed. 2d 491
Rehearing denied 398 U.S. 914,
90 S.Ct. 1684,   26 L.Ed. 2d 80

A state's family benefit amount maximum does not effect a pre-emption of new beneficiaries from a portion of the assistance in violation of either Section 402 (a) (10) of the act, or the equal protection clause of the Fourteenth Amendment. Congress recognized the state's interests in the conservation of limited resources, and such a provision represents a valid exercise of the overriding necessity. Maryland maximum grant regulation, which places an absolute limit of $250 per month on amount of a grant under AFDC regardless of size of family and its actual need, is not in conflict with the federal statute governing AFDC.

Goldberg v. Kelly 1970   *Requirement of*
397 U.S. 254,   90 S.Ct. 1011, *pretermination hearing*
25 L.Ed. 2d 287

A state's practices of providing recipients with only one week's notice of a decision to terminate benefits, and their nonaccess to an evidentiary hearing until after the termination, deny them procedural due process guaranteed by the Fourteenth Amendment, because welfare benefits are a matter of statutory entitlement. Timely and adequate notice, and an impartial decision-maker must be provided. A pretermination adversary hearing is necessary upon request, and a litigant should be allowed representation by counsel. It need not be formal and does not require a comprehensive written opinion.

Lewis v. Martin 1970   *Availability of income of*
397 U.S. 552,   90 S.Ct. 1282, *nonadopting stepfather or*
25 L.Ed. 2d 561   *man assuming the role of a*
                                   spouse

A state cannot automatically include the income of a nonadopting stepfather or a man assuming the role of a spouse in its computation for standard of need and amount of assistance payment without regarding the actual availability of the funds for family support. "Parent" in Section 406 (a) of the act includes only real or adoptive parents in "consensual relationship to the family" attendant with it a legal obligation to contribute, and a "reasonably certain" social reality of compliance. Support can only be presumed to arise from other relationships where state law establishes a legal obligation consistent with that relied on by the federal statute.

Rosado v. Wyman 1970   *Exclusion of existing*
397 U.S. 397,   90 S.Ct. 1207,   *standard of need*
25 L.Ed. 2d 442, on remand   *elements*
322 F. Supp. 1173, affirmed 437 F. 2d 619,
affirmed 402 U.S. 991, 91 S.Ct. 2169,
29 L.Ed. 2d 157.

A state's modification of its standard of need formula by excluding certain previously included items from the need computation violates Section 402 (a) (23) of the act providing for recomputation of benefit rates and maximums only for implementing cost of living adjustments. Where benefits will be lowered for some recipients already in pay status, a state must demonstrate that the items it proposes to exclude no longer constitute a part of the reality of existence for a majority of benefit recipients.

King v. Smith 1968   *Substitute for an absent*
392 U.S. 309,   88 S.Ct. 2128,   *parent*
20 L.Ed. 2d 1118

A state regulation which classifies any able bodied man with whom an applicant mother cohabits in or outside of the home as a "substitute" for an absent parent thereby disqualifying the family for assistance, contradicts the meaning of "parent" within Section 406 (a) of the act. Congress determined that immorality and illegitimacy should be dealt with through rehabilitation rather than measures that punish dependent children and that protection of such children is the paramount goal of AFDC program.

Batterton, Secretary, Department
of Human Resources, Md. et. al.
v. Francis et. al.
No. 75-1181, 45 LW 4768, 1977

State standards defining
unemployment of fathers
under AFDC-UF

Section 407 (a) of the Social Security Act delegates to the Secretary of Health, Education and Welfare the power to prescribe standards for determining what constitutes unemployment for the purposes of eligibility for benefits under the AFDC-UF program. A regulation by the Secretary, in 1973, gave the states the option of excluding from the definition of unemployed fathers those who are on strike or whose unemployment would result in disqualification from the state's unemployment compensation law. In class actions on behalf of families denied AFDC-UF under a Maryland rule promulgated under the Secretary's regulation, the latter was upheld as a proper and reasonable exercise of the Secretary's statutory authority.

GENERAL ASSISTANCE PROGRAMS

Lavine v. Milne 1976
_____ U.S. _____, 96 S.Ct. 1010,
_____ L.Ed. 2d _____

Voluntary termination of
employment, eligibility
for home relief

The New York statute providing that a person who applies for home relief within 75 days after voluntary termination of employment will be deemed to have voluntarily terminated his employment, in the absence of evidence to the contrary supplied by the applicant, will be ineligible for home relief benefits, is constitutional.

New Jersey Welfare Rights
Organization v. Cahill 1973
411 U.S. 619,   93 S.Ct. 1700,
36 L.Ed. 2d 543

Excluding illegitimate
children from benefits

Provision of New Jersey's statutory "Assistance to Families of the Working Poor" program limiting benefits to legitimate children and denying benefits to illegitimate children violates the equal protection clause of the constitution. Benefits extended under the program were as indispensable to the health and well-being of illegitimate children as to those who were legitimate.

FOOD STAMP PROGRAM

U.S. Department of Agriculture   *Households including*
v. Moreno 1973   *unrelated individuals*
413 U.S. 528,   93 S.Ct. 2821,
37 L.Ed. 2d 782

Section 3(e) of the Food Stamp Act of 1964, as amended in 1971, which denied eligibility to household containing individuals not related to any other members violates the due process clause of the fifth amendment because the classification is irrelevant to the stated purpose of the act and unrelated to other legitimate government interests.

U.S. Department of Agriculture   *Tax dependents of other*
v. Murry 1973   *households*
413 U.S. 508,   93 S.Ct. 2832,
37 L.Ed. 2d 767

Section 5(b) of the Food Stamp Act of 1964 provided that any household including a member age 18 or older who had been claimed as a dependent child on a federal income tax return by a taxpayer who is not a member of an eligible household was not eligible for benefits during the tax year or the following year. Hearings which were only provided on the tax dependent status issue violated the due process clause of the Fifth Amendment. Taxpayer status was not a rational measure of need of household with whom a child of tax-deducting parent lived, rested on irrebuttable presumption often contrary to fact and was invalid for lacking critical ingredients of due process.

ADULT ASSISTANCE CATEGORY PROGRAMS

Edelman v. Jordan 1974
415 U.S. 651,   94 S.Ct. 1347,
39 L.Ed. 2d 662,
rehearing denied 416 U.S. 1000,
94 S.Ct. 2414,
40 L.Ed. 2d 777

State liability for wrongfully
withheld retroactive
benefits

A state which delayed the award of AABD benefits to recipients because of regulations which violated federal assistance and application processing standards is immune from liability for lost assistance benefits under the Eleventh Amendment, unless the state waives its protection. The act does not require states participating in the program to forfeit their privilege. Remedy is only available against a state retroactive of the date of a judgment in court.

Graham v. Richardson and
Sailer v. Leger 1971
403 U.S. 365,   91 S.Ct. 1848,
29 L.Ed. 2d 534

Duration of residence for
aliens

State laws requiring resident aliens to meet a duration of residence test of several years, or denying their assistance outright violates the equal protection clause of the Fourteen Amendment, and encroaches upon the federal power over entrance and residence of aliens.

MEDICAL ASSISTANCE PROGRAM

Association of American Physicians
and Surgeons v. Mathews 1975
____ U.S. ____,   96 S.Ct. 388,
____ L.Ed. 2d ____

Constitutionality of
professional standards
review

Professional standards review legislation establishing methods and procedures to assure that services provided under Medicare and Medicaid are necessary and of professional quality is constitutional and does not interfere with physicians' and surgeons' right to practice their professions. Legislation properly balances right of privacy with government interest in maintaining proper health care in an economical manner.

Memorial Hospital v.　　　　*Durational residence*
Maricopa County 1974　　*eligibility requirement*
415 U.S. 250,   94 S.Ct. 1076,　*for medical care to indigents*
39 L.Ed. 2d 306

Arizona durational residence requirement for providing medical care to indigents is unconstitutional. The right of interstate travel is a basic constitutional freedom. The conservation of the taxpayers' purse is not a sufficient state interest to sustain a durational residence requirement which, in effect, severely penalizes exercise of right to freely migrate and settle in another state guaranteed under the Fourteenth Amendment.

Beal, Secretary, Department of　*Nontherapeutic abortions*
Public Welfare of Pennsylvania et. al v.
Doe et. al.
No. 75-554, 45 LW 4781, 1977

Maher, Commissioner of Social Services of
Connecticut v. Roe et al.
No. 75-1440, 45 LW 4707, 1977

John H. Poelker, etc. et al. v.
Jane Doe, etc.
No. 75-442, 45 LW 4794, 1977

Title XIX of the Social Security Act which establishes a Medical Assistance Program under which participating states financially assist qualified individuals in five general categories of medical treatment does not require the funding of nontherapeutic abortions. A state, however, may provide such coverage, if it so desires (BEAL). The equal protection clause of the Fourteenth Amendment does not require a state participating in the Medicaid program to pay expenses incident to nontherapeutic abortions for indigent women simply because it has made a choice to pay expenses incident to childbirth (MAHER). The city of St. Louis is not violating the Constitution in electing to provide publicly financed hospitals for childbirth without providing corresponding services for nontherapeutic abortions (POELKER).

WORK INCENTIVE PROGRAM

New York State Department of Social Services v. Dublino 1973 413 U.S. 405,   93 S.Ct. 2507, 37 L.Ed. 2d 688

State's authority to continue pre-existing work incentive program

A preexisting state work incentive program is not preempted by the federal plan, insofar as it does not contravene the programs and provisions of WIN. Indicative of the federal/state nature of the program, they are to serve as guidelines designed for political subdivisions with sufficient resources, leaving the state to implement a more comprehensive program.

CHILD WELFARE PROGRAM

Gomez v. Perez 1973 409 U.S. 535,   93 S.Ct. 872, 35 L.Ed. 2d 56

Responsibility of natural father to support his legitimate children

The natural father has a continuing and primary duty to support his legitimate children, extending beyond dissolution of marriage, despite the fact that the father may not have custody of the child. The duty is enforceable by the state on the child's behalf in civil proceedings and is subject to criminal sanctions. A state may not invidiously discriminate against illegitimate children by denying them substantial benefits accorded children generally. Once a state posits a judicially enforceable right on behalf of children to need support from their natural fathers, there is no constitutionally sufficient justification for denying such essential right to a child simply because the natural father has not married the mother, and such denial is a denial of equal protection under the Fourteenth Amendment.

Application of Gault 1967
387 U.S. 1,   87 S.Ct. 1428,
18 L.Ed. 2d 527

Protected rights of a
juvenile committed as a
delinquent to a state
institution

A juvenile committed as a juvenile delinquent to a state institution has the right of notice of charges, to counsel, to confrontation and cross-examination of witnesses, and to privilege against self-incrimination in commitment proceedings by the state. The due process clause of the Fourteenth Amendment requires juvenile court delinquency hearings to measure up to essentials of due process and fair treatment.

Kent v. United States 1966
383 U.S. 541,   86 S.Ct. 1045,
16 L.Ed. 2d 84

Protected rights of a
juvenile in juvenile court
proceedings

Under the District of Columbia Juvenile Court Act allowing the Juvenile Court to waive jurisdiction over a juvenile after full investigation, as a condition to a valid waiver order, the juvenile was entitled to a hearing, including access by his counsel to the social records and probation or similar reports which presumably were considered by the court, and to a statement of reasons for the Juvenile Court's decision.

Stanley v. Illinois 1972
405 U.S. 645,   92 S.Ct. 1208,
31 L.Ed. 2d 551

Rights of unwed father in
dependency proceeding
involving his child

An unwed father is entitled under the due process clause of the Fourteenth Amendment to a hearing on his fitness as parent before his children could be taken from him in dependency proceeding instituted by the state after the death of the children's natural mother.

ALL PROGRAMS

Wyman v. Boddie 1971
402 U.S. 991,   91 S.Ct. 2169,
434 F.2d 1207

Area differentials in
state-wide standards of
assistance

A state may not enforce in 50 upstate counties of New York, schedules of grants and allowances in AFDC and AABD programs other than according to objectives, nondiscriminatory standards based upon cost of needs of such recipients; state statutory provisions for living allowances, exclusive of rent, fuel for heating and special grants, which are higher for public assistance recipients living in New York City conflicts with Social Security Act requirement for uniform application of standards; evidence presented to district court tends to establish absence of objective justification for differentials; hence, schedule for upstate counties identical to those used in New York City must be promulgated and used.

Shapiro v. Thompson 1969
394 U.S. 618,   89 S.Ct. 1322,
22 L.Ed. 2d 600

Duration of residence
requirement for
Federal/State welfare
assistance

A State's duration of residency requirement of any length for entitlement of welfare assistance violates the equal protection clause of the Fourteenth Amendment and the constitutional right to interstate movement, despite the implication of language in Sec. 402 (b) of the Act limiting HEW approval of State plans with provisions requiring residency of more than one year. Benefits cannot be apportioned on the basis of past tax contribution. All citizens must be free to travel throughout the United States uninhibited by statutes, rules or regulations which unreasonably burden or restrict this movement.

INDEX

ABLE (Allowance for Basic Living Expenses)
(proposed), 464–465
Abandoned children, 69, 146, 342
Ability to pay, 284, 326, 449
Absence of parent, 19, 66, 81, 89, 90, 95, 111, 147,
153, 373–374, 432–433
Abuse of adults, 130, 135, 383–384
Abused children, 25, 46, 69, 130, 135, 144, 146, 211,
317, 342, 360, 383, 415
Accountability for administration, 392–404
Accountability for results, 414
Accountability methods (public welfare), 338, 368–404
Accountability standards, 23–24
Accounting and fiscal functions, 215, 216, 217,
306–307, 369
Accounting period, 92–93, 123, 163, 175, 452–453
Activism in public welfare, 266–268
Administration for Handicapped Individuals
(D/HEW), 312, 427–428
Administration of justice, 416, 429–430
Administrative costs, 43, 130, 303, 308–324, 328, 393,
399, 453, 459
Admission practices, 376–379, 384, 387, 425
Adoption, 70, 145–146, 211
Adult Assistance Category Programs, Supreme Court
decisions, 501
Adult education, 417–419
Adult services, 215
Advice and consent of the Senate, 199, 256
Advice and referral centers, 230–232
Advisory committees, boards and councils, 33, 213,
215, 218, 389
Advisory Council on Public Welfare, 456, 472–474
Age of children, 89, 90, 97, 102, 132, 153, 154, 164,
188–189, 462, 469, 475
Age of family heads, 64
Age of welfare workers, 237
Aged, 28, 32, 40, 54, 60, 64, 67–68, 71–72, 80,
106–117, 133, 149, 152, 159, 164, 167, 170, 171,
175, 178, 188, 211, 228, 249, 253, 264, 288, 311,
318, 339, 347, 358, 362, 393, 412, 413, 416, 419,
421, 426, 428–429, 430, 433, 441, 456, 458, 460,
462, 465, 469, 474, 478
Agricultural programs, 412, 419
Aid to Families with Dependent Children (AFDC)
program, 25, 33, 35, 65–67, 131, 134, 136, 152,
153, 159, 178, 183, 188, 190, 237, 270, 417, 430,
458, 460–465, 468, 470
administering agencies, 82, 145, 203, 209, 215
caseload, 82, 88–89, 340
Characteristics Study, 65, 67, 399
eligibility requirements, 46, 89–97
financing, 278, 287, 308–310, 317, 322, 329–331,
439
methods, 102–104, 342, 347, 350–357, 369–374,
393–395
objectives, 81
program description, 75–105
services and benefits, 97–101
Supreme Court decisions, 493–499
Aid to the Blind (AB), 19, 33–35, 54, 65–68,
106–117, 283, 356, 370, 435, 441, 460, 462, 463
Aid to the Permanently and Totally Disabled (APTD),
34, 40, 54, 65, 67, 68, 106–117, 283, 356, 370,
435, 441, 460, 462, 463
Alcoholism, 114, 131, 133, 172, 177, 313, 351, 416
Aliens, 94, 113, 124, 163, 173, 193
Alimony, 137, 374, 451
Allotment accounts, 307
Allowances, 100, 190, 323, 419, 421
American Federation of Government Employees
(AFGE), 266
American Federation of Labor-Congress of Industrial
Organizations (AFL-CIO), 266, 477
American Federation of State, County and Municipal
Employees (AFSCME), 266
American Hospital Association (AHA), 477, 479
American Indians, 40, 66, 77, 138–139, 142, 175,
237, 367, 382, 418, 424, 425, 431, 475
American Medical Association (AMA), 477, 478
American Public Welfare Association (APWA), 17,
267, 382, 467–468, 477–478
Appalachian programs, 411
Appeal rights, 46
Applicants for public assistance, 25, 46, 54, 102–103,
336, 340, 342–348, 398

Application of funds, 307–329
Application of Gault, 504
Applications for assistance or services, 102–103,
115–117, 142, 168–169, 176, 254–255, 272–274,
337, 340, 344–349, 399
Apportionment of funds, 217, 306–307, 324, 325
Apprenticeships, 187, 203
Appropriateness of admissions, 375–379
Appropriation laws, 210, 289, 306–307
Armed Forces dependents, 424–425
Asset ownership, 93, 96–97, 102, 111, 113, 115,
123–124, 163, 165–166, 174–175, 339, 344–345,
354, 356, 451–452, 462
Assignment of property, 94, 124, 164, 358
Association of American Physicians and Surgeons v. Mathews,
501–502
Audit agencies, 211, 397
Audits, 44, 211, 215, 224, 368–369, 394, 397–398,
455
Authorization cards (food stamps), 172, 179
Automated data processing, 117, 219, 237, 273, 311,
354, 358, 373, 375, 389–380, 434, 455, 459
Automobile ownership, 93, 96, 111, 163, 165, 174,
356, 451
See also Asset ownership
Availability of services, 379, 380, 400, 448, 449

Bachelor's degree in social work, 236, 249–251, 255
See also Social work education
Bank accounts, 94, 137, 347
Batterton v. Francis, 499
Barriers to program coordination, 434–435
Beal v. Doe, 502–503
Behavioral patterns, 147, 429, 442
Behavioral problems, 142, 147, 359, 383
Benefit-loss rates, 447
Benefits, adequacy of, 443, 446
Benefit reduction rate, 161–163, 171
Blacks, 58–63, 65, 187, 237
Blind persons, 28, 33, 40–41, 54, 67–68, 80, 106–117,
133, 139, 149, 152, 159, 164, 203, 211, 213, 228,
271, 288, 311, 339, 343, 344, 347, 351, 358, 427,
430, 441, 456, 458, 460, 463, 465
Boarders, 139, 172, 174
Brotherhood of Railway and Airline Clerks (BRAC),
186
Budget authority, 212
Budget classification, 305
Budget deficit, 357
Budget estimates, 212, 395
Budget functions, 215
Budget method (for determining eligibility), 357
See also Need standards
Burial expenses, 108, 125, 344
Burns v. Alcala, 493–494
Buy-in agreements (Medicaid), 168, 318
See also Medicare

Caretakers, 147, 159, 188, 358, 361, 373, 381,
383–384, 411, 464
Carleson v. Remillard, 496
Case aides (see Eligibility determination workers)
Case and Administrative Services System (CASS), 390
Case control and management, 143, 147, 348–349,
389, 390
Casework, 265, 268, 336, 361, 412
Cash assistance, 18, 22, 33, 46, 50, 51, 53, 60, 63, 66,
67, 69, 77, 81–125, 136, 142, 194, 209, 226, 285,
308, 309, 311, 313, 324, 325, 340, 345, 352, 354,
356–358, 393, 423, 427, 442, 445–465, 471–473
See also Income maintenance
Cash-out of in-kind programs, 233, 470–472
Catastrophic Health Insurance Plan (proposed),
481–482
Catastrophic illness, 480–482
Categorically needy, 153, 159, 161, 163, 167
Certification by applicant, 344–347
Certification period, 175, 353, 354
Charitable institutions (see Voluntary agencies)
Check disbursements, 102, 117, 226, 285, 306, 308,
311, 358, 393, 395, 397, 398, 414, 426
Chief executives, 198, 201, 221
Child care, 92–94, 131–133, 139, 144, 147, 172, 183,
184, 187, 188, 211, 321–323, 330, 403, 416, 432,
458, 464, 468, 474–476
expenditures, 133, 183, 308, 314, 316, 317, 322,
323, 382, 444

facilities, 25, 46, 70, 89, 95, 146–147, 366, 380–382, 475
Child Care, Bureau of (proposed), 464
    See also Day care
Child Day Care Social Services Act, 132–133, 382
Child Development, Office of (D/HEW), 382
Child development programs, 474–476
Child health services, 167, 340–342, 363, 364, 426, 474, 479, 481
    See also Maternal and Child Health; Early and Periodic Screening, Diagnostic and Treatment (EPSDT) program
Child nutrition, 138, 201, 419, 474
Child placement agency, 111, 432
Child population, 50, 58–66, 69, 70, 144
Child support enforcement program, 95, 218, 373–374, 432–433
Child Welfare League of America (CWLA), 267
Child welfare services (CWS) program, 25, 33, 41, 46, 69–70, 75–77, 95, 128–129, 213, 232, 267, 429
    administering agencies, 27, 144, 145, 203, 209, 215–218, 232–233
    caseload, 146
    education grants, 327
    eligibility requirements, 146
    financing, 288, 316–317, 327, 330
    methods, 147, 342, 389, 394
    objectives, 144
    program description, 144–148
    services and benefits, 146–147, 360–361, 380–383, 423–424
    Supreme Court decisions, 503–504
    workers, 231, 267
Childless couples, 65, 69, 71, 72, 123, 425, 458, 467, 468
Children's Bureau (D/HEW), 144, 145, 201, 383
Children's earnings, 92, 111, 138, 173, 356
Children's institutions, 144, 225, 419, 429
Citizenship requirements, 94, 113, 124, 163, 177, 194
Civil service, 116, 211, 245–246, 256, 263, 267, 271
    See also Merit systems
Claims representative, 116, 117, 254, 272–275
Classroom training, 263, 326, 367
Client/community relationship, 359
Clinical services, 167, 193
Clothing needs, 25, 97, 100, 102, 118, 356, 446
    See also Need standards
Co-insurance (see Cost sharing)
Collective bargaining, 267
College education, 61–62, 66, 172, 236, 249–250, 255, 257, 326, 416
Colocation of offices, 230–231, 415
Committee on Economic Development, 466
Commodity Credit Corporation, 419
Communication services expenditures, 305, 328
Community action programs, 282, 342, 343, 380, 431
Community development and planning, 268, 359, 360, 419–422, 457, 476
Community health facilities, 364, 378
Community mental health centers, 364, 416, 426
Community organizations, 231, 265, 395
Community programs and resources, 28, 143, 218, 264, 360, 362, 390, 395, 412, 429, 474
    See also Voluntary agencies
Community service agencies (see Voluntary agencies)
Community Services Administration, SRS (see Public Services Administration)
Community Work and Training Program (Title IV, SSA), 183
Compensatory education, 366, 417
Comprehensive annual social services plan, 138, 395
Comprehensive Child Development Act of 1971 (proposed), 474–476
Comprehensive Employment and Training Act (CETA), 184, 201, 289, 401, 476
Comprehensive Program of Basic Social Guaranties (proposed), 467
Confidentiality of information, 47, 133, 143, 168, 216, 349–350, 398, 432, 453
Congressional Budget Office, 212, 439
Constitutional basis (public welfare), 35, 45, 338
Consumer groups, 253, 379, 439, 477
Consumer price index (CPI), 55, 57–58, 101, 107, 173–174, 339
Contracting out, 224, 237, 268, 412–413
Cooperative research and demonstration projects, 401–403
Coordination of services, 231, 415
Correctional institutions, 24, 28, 139, 429
Cost allocations, 217
Cost benefit analysis, 401, 403

Cost effectiveness, 23, 401
Cost sharing, 150, 161, 162, 168, 284, 286, 314, 445, 448–449, 474, 477–481
Counseling, 72, 129, 138–139, 143, 147, 188, 190, 193, 230, 231, 314, 359–362, 367, 383, 384, 420, 427, 429, 474
County welfare agencies (see Locally administered programs)
Coupon allotment (food stamps), 170–179
Court commitments, 368, 384
Court supervision, 46, 70, 146
Crime (see Administration of justice)
Crippled children, 28, 32, 364
    See also Handicapped children
Cuban refugee assistance, 25, 27, 33, 35, 50, 53, 70, 75–77, 128, 192–194, 203, 210, 233, 287, 304, 324–325, 353, 355, 367–368, 424, 438

Dandridge v. Williams, 497
Day care, 25–28, 72, 132–133, 139, 144, 147, 187–188, 218, 249, 253, 314, 362, 380–382, 404, 416, 445, 457, 461, 470, 474–476
    See also Child care
Death of a parent, 19, 54, 81, 89, 153
Decentralization of functions, 215, 228
Deafness, services for, 427
Delinquency prevention, 429
    See also Administration of justice
Delinquent children, 25, 46, 69, 144, 146, 456
    See also Child welfare services (CWS) program
Delivery mechanisms, 355–368, 402, 414–415
Demographic analysis, 339–342
Demographic characteristics, 20, Chapter II
Demogrants, 468–470
Demonstration projects, 33, 183, 186, 283, 401–404, 420
    See also Cooperative research and demonstration
Dental services, 72, 167, 169, 319, 364, 385, 478–481
Dependent care deductions, 174
Deprivation of parental support, 19, 81, 89, 90, 153, 159
Desertion by a parent, 82, 95, 137, 462
Detention center services, 138, 424
    See also Administration of justice
Detoxification 133
    See also Alcoholism; Drug abuse
Developmental disabilities (see Mental retardation institutions and Mentally retarded)
Diagnostic centers, 230–231
Diagnostic evaluation of children, 147
    See also Child welfare activities
Diet and dietary services, 170, 171, 385, 387, 418, 419, 446
Disabled persons, 28, 34, 35, 40, 54, 64, 67–69, 72, 106–117, 133, 143, 149, 152, 159, 164, 211, 228, 249, 253, 264, 271–275, 288, 311, 339, 343–347, 352, 358, 393, 416, 417, 430, 432, 441, 456, 460, 463, 465, 467, 472, 478
    See also Supplemental Security Income (SSI) Program
Disability, 19, 66, 69, 106, 139, 153, 176, 178, 188, 203, 339, 344–345, 351–352, 427–428, 468
Disability determinations, 116, 203, 303, 350–352
Disasters, 171, 178, 353
Discrimination barriers, 423, 442
Disincentives, 445–446
District offices, 225, 272–275
Dividend income, 60, 108, 136, 450–451
Domestic Council, 201
Donated services, 284, 285, 314
Drug abuse, 114, 131, 133, 172, 177, 313, 351, 424, 429
Drugs, 150, 167, 285, 362, 377, 386, 478, 481
Dual eligibility of benefits, 415, 424–426, 431
Duplication of services, 413–415

Early and periodic screening, diagnostic and treatment services (EPSDT) program, 167, 285, 340–342, 363–364, 403, 416, 425
Early childhood development, 474–476
Earmarked taxes, 284, 448–449
Earned income tax credits, 459
Earnings disregard, 81, 92, 123, 161, 162, 173, 339, 356, 403, 415, 451
Earnings income, 60, 63, 92, 108, 111, 116, 123, 135, 150, 161, 171, 173–174, 187, 356–357, 423, 450, 462, 468, 478
Economic Opportunity Act, 474
Economic Opportunity Act, Office of (OEO), 342, 380
Edelman v. Jordan, 501
Education programs, 24, 131, 138, 142, 192, 194, 236, 265, 278, 326, 360, 412, 417–419, 475

Educational attainment, 61–62, 65, 66, 187, 249–252, 344
Educational grants and loans, 173, 175, 257, 258, 324, 327, 418
Educational services, 363, 367, 380, 381, 457
Educationally deprived, 412, 417–419
Effectiveness of operations, 228, 231, 232, 235, 331, 360, 380, 395–397, 400–402, 416, 434, 435, 440–442, 454–456
Elective hospital admissions, 378–379
Elementary school education, 61–66, 66–68, 187, 380, 415, 417–419
Eligibility determination workers, 230, 235, 236, 254–255, 343, 344–350, 371, 418
Eligibility determinations, 22, 24, 26, 27, 35, 44, 47, 102–105, 115–117, 142–143, 168–169, 178–180, 215, 217, 225–231, 254–255, 268–270, 273, 304, 319, 335–336, 344–354, 369–373, 393, 399, 441, 449–454, 471
Emergency assistance, 19, 26, 28, 81, 89, 116, 118, 122, 146, 195–196, 228–229, 308–309, 325–326, 352–354, 367, 412, 459
Emergency food stamp assistance, 171, 178
Emergency relief (see General Assistance program)
Emergency shelter, 142, 362, 432
Employability plan, 190–191, 365–366
Employee organizations, 263, 266–267
Employer payroll tax, 478, 481
Employers, 132, 183–185, 374, 430, 432, 480, 481
Employment and Training Administration (D/Labor), 29, 184, 203, 236, 404
Employment and training research, 401, 404
Employment goal, 365–366, 427
Employment incentives, 358
Employment of recipients, 42, 46, 54, 66, 89, 93–94, 102, 132, 159, 174, 183, 189, 344, 347, 365–367, 382
Employment services, 22, 26, 80, 93, 102, 124, 148, 183–191, 194, 203, 319–323, 358, 460, 464, 467–468, 474
Employment training, 24, 46, 72, 89, 148, 183–191, 194, 211, 231, 321–323, 340, 355, 360, 365–367, 379–381, 404, 411, 416–417, 422–423, 427, 429, 431, 438, 443, 446, 456–457, 460–461, 464, 467, 468, 474
Engleman v. Amos, 496–497
Entitlement for welfare benefits, 232, 337, 344–354, 384
Errors in eligibility determinations (see Quality control)
Evidentiary documents, 345, 347
Excess foreign currencies, 284, 325, 326
Excess payments for services, 376–379
Expenditure classification, 305–306
Expenditure controls, 306–307, 477
Exploitation of adults, 130, 135, 384
Exploitation of children, 130, 135, 144, 146, 360, 383
Eye care, 150, 167, 351, 363, 479

Failure to report client changes, 371
See also Redetermination of eligibility
Fair hearings, 42, 46–47, 143, 179, 266, 345, 399
Fair Labor Standards Act, 366
Family Assistance, Office of (SSA), 82, 193, 195, 368
Family Assistance Plan (FAP) of 1971, 270, 460–463
Family day care homes, 133, 381, 382, 474–476
See also Day care
Family disintegration, 147, 360, 367, 403, 445, 473
Family Health Insurance Plan (FHIP) (proposed), 481
Family income, 132, 134–135, 143, 149, 162, 285, 339, 356–357, 374, 422
Family planning, 129, 131, 138, 147, 167, 188, 211, 285, 315, 362, 424, 426, 461
Family relationships, 54, 89, 102, 130, 143, 147, 336–337, 339–340, 347, 360, 394, 418, 442, 443, 453, 464
Family life, strengthening it, 25, 81, 128, 130, 144, 445–446
Farm income, 175, 354
Farm workers, 175, 418
Federal accounting and auditing standards, 310, 315, 320, 323–325, 328
Federal administration, 23, 40–41, 115–117, 232, 236, 269–275, 311, 319–325, 328–329, 447–448, 454–456, 462, 466, 477
Federal Department of Health (proposed), 479
Federal Financial participation (FFP), 34, 41, 130–131, 149–150, 161, 254, 257–258, 283, 314, 315, 318, 321, 329–331, 378, 380, 383, 389, 395, 426, 434, 447–449, 466
Federal government organization, 199–212, 271–275, 454–456

Federal personnel, 235, 236, 271–275
Federal Interagency Day Care Committee, 380
See also Day care
Federal judiciary, 198, 212
Federal Medical Assistance Percentage (FMAP), 287, 309, 317, 375
Federal oversight, 371, 394, 397, 468
Federal Reserve Banks, 180, 310, 321
Fees for service, 131, 132, 284, 285, 314, 448–449, 472, 476
See also Cost sharing
Female-headed families, 58–59, 62–64, 66
Field investigations, 370, 372, 453
Financial incentives, 443–444, 446
Financial management and control, 306–307
Financial need, 24, 146, 344, 474
See also Need standards
Financial plans, 307, 394–395
Fire protection, 384, 386, 387
"First dollar" concept, 416
Fiscal agents, 224, 237, 306, 318, 319
Fiscal records and reports, 216–217, 384
Fiscal relief of State and local governments, 459
Fixed price contracts (medical care), 403
Follow-up services, 143, 194, 230, 368, 416
Food and nutrition programs, 419, 424, 450, 470–472, 475
Food and Nutrition Service (D/Agriculture), 29, 43, 44, 171, 179, 201, 205, 236, 270, 289, 320–321, 354, 372, 399
Food needs, 26, 97, 100, 102, 118, 125, 170, 196, 325, 344, 353, 356, 419
See also Need standards
Food stamps, 19, 22, 26, 34, 41, 42, 44, 47, 50, 58, 67, 68, 71, 72, 75–76, 92, 107, 125, 148, 236, 255, 269, 270, 417, 419, 428, 438, 439, 456, 462–465, 468, 470, 471, 472
administering agencies, 171, 201, 210, 215, 217, 230, 233
eligibility, 171–177
financing, 178, 283, 286, 306, 313, 319–321, 330
methods, 178–180, 336, 340, 342, 345, 350, 353–355, 358–359, 364, 372–374, 393–395, 397–399, 404
objectives, 170
program description, 170–188
services and benefits, 178
Supreme Court decisions, 500
Formula grants, 144, 287–288, 313–317, 475–476
Foster care, 19, 46, 70, 81, 89, 111, 131, 138, 142, 144, 146, 308, 317, 362, 382–383
Foster homes, 25, 95, 138, 142, 144, 146–147, 159, 172, 308, 317, 382–383, 429, 432
Fragmentation of services, 414–415
Fraud and welfare abuses, 33, 47–48, 171–172, 179, 219, 348, 350, 375, 391–392, 439, 453
See also Audits; Quality control; Medicaid abuses
Freedom of choice, 169, 360–363, 470–472
"Front-end" funding, 283
Full employment, 422, 438, 456

Garnishment of wages, 374
General Accounting Office, 44, 211, 397
General Assistance (GA) programs, 25, 35, 50, 65, 69, 72, 75, 77, 136, 178, 428, 430, 431, 468, 478–481
administering agencies, 119
caseloads, 119–122
eligibility requirements, 122–125
financing, 286, 287, 313, 318, 330
methods, 339, 351–354, 364
objective, 118
program description, 118–125
services and benefits, 125
Supreme Court decisions, 499–500
General fund receipts, 284
Ghettos, 412, 421, 424
Gifts, 108, 138, 175
Goldberg v. Kelly, 497
Gomez v. Perez, 503–504
Graham v. Richardson, 501
Grants-in-aid, 21, 148, 233, 310, 314, 315, 338, 371, 394, 397, 448
Griffiths, Rep. Martha, 437–438, 464–465, 478
Gross National Product (GNP), 21, 476, 483
Group homes, 70, 146, 474
Group insurance (employees), 263, 271
Group meetings, 231, 343
Group social work, 265, 359, 361

Half-way houses, 138, 424
Hand processing of case information, 390, 434
Handicapped persons (see Disabled persons)

508

Heads of household, 26, 46, 54, 59–67, 172, 183, 432
Health care (see Medical services)
Health Care Financing Administration (D/HEW), 29, 151, 203, 289, 328, 391–392
Health Care Plan (proposed), 480–481
Health care prospective reimbursement experimental and demonstration projects, 401–404
Health Care Corporations (proposed), 479
Health Care Services Plan (proposed), 479
Health education, 424–425, 477
Health insurance, 166, 168, 224, 476–481
See also Medicare
Health Insurance Association of America, 477, 480–481
Health Insurance Board (proposed), 479
Health Maintenance Organizations (HMOs), 211, 318, 363, 480, 481
Health Security Board (proposed), 478
Health Security Plan (proposed), 478
Health Security Trust Fund (proposed), 478
Health status, 102, 339, 341, 400, 424–425
Hearing aids, 150, 285, 363
High risk health groups, 423–427, 445
High school education, 61–62, 66, 417–419
Higher education, 257, 265, 327, 417–419
Historical background (public welfare), 20–23, 29, 81–82, 106–107, 118, 130–131, 149–151, 170–171, 183–184, 192–195, 218
Hold-harmless provision, 311, 459
Home care, 130, 139, 147, 381
Home-delivered meals, 170, 178
Home health services, 150, 161, 167, 285, 388–389, 424, 481
Home management services, 188, 189, 359, 363, 420
Home ownership, 93, 96, 104–105, 111, 163, 165, 174, 356, 421, 451–452
Home Relief (see General Assistance program)
Home repairs, 19, 33, 101, 104–105, 308, 309, 420, 421
Home visits, 102, 370
Homemakers services, 139, 147, 188, 189, 249, 363, 381, 403
Homes for the aged, 386–388, 421
Hospitals, 138, 142, 152, 169, 319, 363, 375–379, 391, 403, 424–427, 476–481
Household allowances, 421
Household income, 173, 344
See also Family income
House of Representatives, committees affecting public welfare, 210–211, 460
Housing, 19, 53, 344, 360, 362, 419–422, 438, 457, 470–472
Housing and Community Development Act, 457
Housing improvement services, 189, 363
Housing loan guarantees, 421
Housing location services, 324
Housing supply, 421
Housing-welfare cooperation, 420
Human Development Services, Office of (D/HEW), 29, 133, 145, 184, 203, 289, 328, 382, 427

Illegitimate children, 95, 218
Illiterate applicants, 348
Incentive performance contracts (medical care), 403
Incentives for program improvement, 434–435
Income levels, 55–58, 102, 339, 469–470
Income maintenance programs, 21, 22, 25–28, 35, 41, 43, 46, 47, 54, 75–125, 213, 216–218, 224–226, 270–275, 278, 308–313, 342, 356–358, 399, 402–403, 439, 442–472
Income-producing property, 93, 96, 163, 165, 174, 451–452
Income redistribution, 219, 369, 443
Income security, 430–431, 438, 457, 482–483
Income taxes, 80, 173, 431–433, 459, 463–465, 468–470, 478–479
Income-tested programs, 77, 80
Incompetent persons, 143
Individual data file, 142–143
Ineligible recipients, 369–373, 441, 453
Inflation, 58, 282, 307, 392
Information and referral services, 135, 138, 209, 230–232, 249, 254–255, 314, 343, 361, 416
Information systems, 24, 237, 318, 330, 331, 398–400, 455
Inheritances, 108, 138, 175, 344, 451–452
In-kind services as benefits, 21, 50–51, 58, 149–191, 278, 317–324, 445–446, 470–472
Inpatient hospital services, 150, 152, 161, 167, 285, 476–481
Inspector General, Office of (D/Agriculture), 320

Institute for Social Research, University of Michigan, 53–54
Institutional care, 22, 28, 46, 130, 133, 142, 150–151, 164, 167, 360, 375–378, 403
Institutional standards, 217, 379–380, 385–388
Institutional status, 124, 151, 153, 164, 172, 177, 360, 393
Institutional training, 190, 191, 323, 367, 461
Intake processes, 230–232, 344–349, 367, 399, 459
Interagency service agreements, 131, 415–416, 433
Interest income, 60, 108, 136, 450–451
Intergovernment relations, 205, 209, 211, 232–233, 302
Intermediate care facilities, 34, 138, 142, 150, 152, 167, 318, 363, 375–379, 386–388, 403
Internal Revenue Service, 270, 374, 431–433, 455, 464, 479
See also Income taxes
Interprogram financing, 425–427
Interviews, 102, 116, 176, 179, 229, 341–348, 370, 372
Investigations, 369, 375, 397–398
Irregular income, 111, 173, 452

Jefferson v. Hackney, 495–496
Job Corps, 203
Job counseling, 183, 190, 194, 253, 323, 365, 429
Job opportunities, 186, 458
Job orientation, 139, 252–255, 365–366
Job placement, 139, 183, 190, 194, 322–323, 365–367, 416, 423, 427, 429, 454, 460
Job restructuring, 247
Job search, 190, 365, 458
Job slots (WIN), 191
Job vacancies, public welfare, 252
Joint action programs, 413, 415, 420–421
Joint agreements (see Interagency service agreements)
Joint Commission on Accreditation of Hospitals, 388
Joint Economic Committee, U.S. Congress, 53, 211, 404, 442, 464–465
Joint funding of programs, 416
Joint in-service training programs, 415, 425
Joint payees, 358
Judicial authority, 146, 212, 360, 361
Judicial reviews, 33, 44–45
Juvenile delinquency, 18, 28, 264, 289, 360, 412, 417, 429, 467, 473–474

Kent v. United States, 504
King v. Smith, 498–499

Labor market, 185–186, 190, 365–367, 422–423, 454, 460, 464, 472
Labor Statistics, Bureau of (D/Labor), 57, 339
Laboratory services, 150, 161, 167, 285, 385, 476–481
Landlord/tenant relations, 359, 361
Lavine v. Milne, 499
Law enforcement agencies, 95, 375, 391, 416, 429
Learning disability, 418, 475
"Least cost" principle, 444
Legal basis (public welfare), 29, 32–40, 338
Legal representative, 33, 46, 196, 344, 371, 383–384
Legal services, 363, 384, 429
Legal Services Corporation, 431
Letter of credit, 310, 315, 319, 320, 323, 326
Lewis v. Martin, 497–498
Licensing of facilities, 147, 369, 380–388
Lien on property, 94, 124, 153, 164, 451
Life insurance, 93–96, 108, 113, 163, 165, 173–175, 344, 451
Live-in attendants, 172–174
Living arrangements, recipient, 54, 66–68, 89, 97, 172
Local government, 199, 224–226
appropriations, 287
budgets, 304–307
treasuries, 310, 315, 319, 323, 327, 432
Locally administered programs, 22, 28, 82, 119, 133, 138, 144, 171, 184, 193–195, 199, 216, 224–226, 236, 237, 256, 269–271, 309, 310, 313, 315, 320, 322, 326, 331, 343, 356, 358, 368, 372, 415, 426
Longshoremen's benefits, 431
Lump sum payments, 173, 175

Maher v. Roe, 502–503
Mail surveys, 341, 343
Mailed applications, 102, 115, 168, 344
Male-headed family, 53, 57, 62–66, 72, 81
Management-by-objectives (MBO) (see Operational planning)
Management and Budget, Office of (U.S.), 201, 303, 307
Management of institutions, 385, 387

Mandatory services, 138, 146–147, 150, 167, 189–190, 285
Mandatory supplements (SSI), 108
Manpower development, 18, 28, 183, 422–423
Manpower Development and Training Act [*see* Comprehensive Employment and Training Act (CETA)]
Manpower utilization, 263
Manuals, program, 47, 336
Marketing and Consumer Services, Assistant Secretary (D/Agriculture), 203
Matching funds, 287, 308–310, 313–324
Maternal and Child Health, 32, 70, 90, 189, 193, 376, 377, 426, 475
Means test (*see* Need standards)
Median family income, 134–135, 285, 288, 472
Medicaid (Medical assistance program), 19, 23–26, 33, 35, 40, 41, 46–47, 50, 54, 58, 66–72, 75–76, 108, 116, 131, 139, 148, 162, 236, 237, 255, 269, 415–416, 423–428, 438, 439, 445, 460, 471, 476–481
  abuses, 150, 391, 392, 477
    See also Fraud and welfare abuses
  administering agencies, 151, 203, 205, 215, 216, 221–224, 230, 233
  caseloads, 152
  eligibility requirements, 153–166
  financing, 152, 278, 281, 285, 287, 304, 306, 309, 317–319
  management information system-general systems design (MMIS-GSD), 391
  methods, 168–169, 340, 342, 345, 347, 350, 351, 354, 360–364, 370–379, 384, 389, 394–400, 403, 404
  objectives, 149
  program description, 149–169
  services and benefits, 166–168
  Supreme Court decisions, 501–503
Medical assistance for the aged, 19, 149
  See also Medicare
Medical claims processing and payments function, 224, 237, 318–319, 391–392, 397, 399, 477
Medical examinations, 188, 196, 350, 352
Medical history and disability report, 116, 345
Medical necessity of care, 375–379
Medical rehabilitation services, 389, 478
  See also Vocational rehabilitation
Medical review team, 351, 376
Medical screening, 193, 341, 350–351, 363–364, 416
Medical services, 20, 24, 33, 40, 94, 125, 128, 139, 148, 151, 166, 167, 188, 192, 193, 211, 221, 224, 304, 351, 355, 360, 363–364, 367, 377, 380–389, 403–404, 411, 412, 424–428, 431, 443, 446–449, 456, 457, 475–481
Medical Services Administration (*see* Health Care Financing Administration)
Medical social services, 360, 361
Medical supervision, 387–389
Medical vendor payments, 119, 149, 152, 166, 318, 319
Medically indigent (*see* Medicaid)
Medicare, 29, 58, 116, 136, 139, 150, 151, 166, 168, 203, 318, 328, 375–378, 385–391, 403–404, 415, 424, 425, 460, 478–481
Medicredit (proposed), 478–479
Memorial Hospital v. Maricopa County, 502
Mental health institutions, 231, 368, 375, 377, 403, 423–427, 481
Mental health programs, 22, 28, 364, 403, 423–427, 475
Mental retardation institutions, 231, 377, 386–388
Mentally ill, 35, 50, 94, 164, 167, 188, 194–196, 325–326, 353, 368, 418, 426, 473
Mentally retarded, 28, 131, 144, 264
Merit systems, 42, 217, 245–246, 394
  See also Civil service
Migrants, 89, 125, 132, 211, 353, 380, 404, 417, 424, 475
Migration and Refugee Assistance Act of 1962, 192
Mine workers benefits, 80, 431
Minimum wage, 173, 176, 366, 458, 466
Minority groups, 55–68, 137, 220, 264–265, 418–419, 431, 473, 475
Mobile offices, 229, 424
Moderate income persons, 419
Monthly premium charges (*see* Cost sharing)
Monitoring client progress, 361–362

National Academy of Sciences, 339
National Association of Social Workers (NASW), 267
National Center for Health Statistics (D/HEW), 339

National Center for Social Statistics (D/HEW), 65–66, 339, 399
National Council of Local Public Welfare Administrators, 267
National Council of State Public Welfare Administrators, 267
National Council on Social Welfare (NCSW), 267
National Federation of Federal Employees (NFFE), 266
National Fire Protection Association, 386
National Governors Conference, 448, 465–466
National health insurance, 269–270, 438–443, 476–481
  See also Health insurance
National Health Insurance Partnership (proposed), 481
National Health Insurance Standards Act (proposed), 481
National origin discrimination, 370, 443
National school lunch program, 415, 419–420
Near-poor, 19, 35, 50–65, 480
Need determinations, 356–358
Need standards, 21, 91, 97, 100, 283, 340, 356–358, 392, 467, 468
Needs assessment, 341–342
Negative income tax, 270
Neglect of adults, 130, 135, 384
  See also Protective services
Neglected children, 25, 46, 70, 130, 135, 144, 146, 342, 360, 383, 402, 411, 417
  See also Protective services
Neighborhood health centers, 363, 424, 426
Neighborhood service centers, 138, 228–231, 343, 415
Neighborhood organizations, 20, 228–231
New Jersey Welfare Rights Organization v. Cahill, 499–500
New York State Department of Social Services v. Dublino, 503
Non-compliance of state plans, 44–45
Non-compliance with standards, 389
Non-English speaking persons, 342, 418
Nurse coordinators, PSRO, 378
Nursing home administrator, 387
Nursing homes, 108, 150, 167, 169, 229, 319, 478
  See also Skilled nursing homes
Nursing services, 167, 384–387, 388
Nutritional deficiency (*see* Diets and dietary services)

Occupational health and safety, 176
Occupational therapy, 389, 427
Old Age Assistance (OAA), 19, 27, 33, 65, 106, 107, 149, 159, 161, 167, 283, 356–358, 370, 435, 441, 460–463
Old Age, Survivors and Disability Insurance (OASDI), (*see* Social Security program)
Older Americans Community Service volunteers, 432
On-the-job-training (OJT), 184, 185, 190, 203, 249, 323, 366
Open-ended funding, 130–131, 287, 309, 317, 319
Operational planning, 395–397
Opportunities for Families Program (proposed), 460–463
Optional services, 135, 138–142, 150, 167, 285
Optional supplements (SSI), 108
Outpatient hospital services, 150, 161, 167, 285, 378, 479
Outreach, 230–231, 254, 342–343, 363
Overpayments (*see* Quality control)

Paperwork in public welfare, 335–336, 344–350
Paraprofessionals, 236
Parent locator service (*see* Child support enforcement program)
Parolee services, 429
Part-time employees, 247, 253, 423
Patient care practices, 375–377, 385–387
Patient records, 384–389
Payment levels, 21, 28, 35, 40, 82–83, 340, 356–358, 443–446, 454–455, 461–468
  See also Need standards
Peer reviews (*see* Utilization review; Professional Standards Review Organization (PSRO)
Pensions, 53, 67–68, 107, 116, 136, 263, 266, 271, 423, 430–431
Per capita income, 144, 288, 316, 468–469
Per capita premiums, 166, 168
Per capita taxes, 284, 432
Performance standards, 256, 369
Personnel administration, 42, 224, 235–275, 400
  benefits, 235, 258, 263, 267, 286, 308, 311, 312, 318–329
  caseload ratios, 237, 272–273

510

Testing (employability), 190
Thrift incentives, 443–444, 451–452
Townsend v. Swank, 496
Traineeships, 257, 327
Training allowances, 190, 461
　See also Work Incentive Program
Training and employment counselors, 231, 418
Training in child development, 475
Transfer agreements between institutions, 385, 387
Transfers of property, 94, 164, 177
Transients, 125
Transportation expenses, 92, 97, 125, 190, 323, 325, 329, 356–357
Transportation services, 167, 189, 194, 196, 230, 253, 360–363, 366, 418, 427
Tuberculosis, 94, 164, 167, 194, 253
Tuition, 111, 173
Turnover of staff, 252, 255, 256
　See also Public welfare employees

"Umbrella" agencies, 23, 219, 221, 233, 255, 403, 425, 434–435
Underpayments (see Quality control)
Unearned income, 60, 92, 108, 118, 136, 137, 175, 354, 450–452
Unemployable persons, 69, 118, 123, 188, 354, 423, 458, 460–463, 466
Unemployed fathers, 81, 83, 88, 93–94, 189, 365, 462–465
Unemployment, 55, 101, 184–186, 429
　insurance, 18, 24, 32, 77, 90, 137, 176, 203, 263, 416, 431, 438, 451
Unserved populations, 412, 481
Uniform national standards, 28, 106, 454–455, 462–468, 474
Uniform statewide standards, 356
Uninsurables (health insurance), 480
Union membership, 176
Universal comprehensive social services, 472–474
Universal eligibility for income maintenance, 468
Universal health insurance coverage, 477
University-based research, 400, 403
Unmarried mothers, 70, 144, 147
Unrelated individuals, 56, 64, 67, 68, 71, 161, 425, 458, 467, 468
Urban family budgets, 57, 339
Urban Institute, 404
U.S. Congress, 198, 209–212, 439
U.S. Department of Agriculture v. Moreno, 500
U.S. Department of Agriculture v. Murry, 500
U.S. savings bonds, 175
U.S. Supreme Court, 198, 199, 493–505
U.S. Treasury, 289, 310, 311, 315, 316
Utilization of services, 375–379, 449–450
Utilization review, 150, 304, 375–379, 385, 388, 389, 405

Van Lare v. Hurley, 494–495
Vendor payments, 69, 125, 149, 308, 309, 313, 318, 358, 399
Verification of applicant information, 102, 116, 168–169, 179, 254–255, 273–274, 345–348, 369–373, 453, 471
Veterans Administration, 77, 455
Veterans benefits, 77, 116, 137, 173, 424, 425, 430, 431
Veterans health agencies, 424, 425
Vocational education, 81, 139, 174, 419

Vocational rehabilitation, 18, 22, 24, 28, 115, 116, 188, 189, 203, 209, 289, 311, 312, 351, 352, 415, 427–428, 461, 472–474
Voluntary agencies, 129, 193, 314, 324, 328, 341, 359, 364, 367, 390, 395, 402–403, 412–417, 424, 433–435, 472–476
Volunteers, 42, 139, 184, 189, 218, 235, 236, 247, 253–254, 258, 326, 343, 365, 432
Volunteers in Service to America (VISTA), 431
Vouchers, 471–472

Wage earners, 430, 431
Wage levels, 21, 186, 366, 422, 447
Wage supplements, 463
"War on Poverty," 342, 417
Waste of funds and resources, 232, 413–416
Welfare checks (see Cash assistance)
Welfare investigators, 453
Welfare reform, 232–233, 270–271, 329–331, 392–394, 437–472, 481–483
Welfare research centers, 329
Welfare rolls (see Public welfare recipients)
White House Conference on Children and Youth, 144
Whites, 58–64, 67, 68, 187, 237
Women workers, 186–187, 237
Work Administration (proposed), 464
Work benefit and income support program (proposed), 458
Work bonus (proposed), 463
Work ethic, 20, 442–443
Work expenses, 86, 92, 323, 356
Work experience, 187, 190, 191, 323, 344, 365, 367
Work Experience and Training program (Title V, EOA), 183
"Workfare" program (proposed) 460, 464
Work Incentive Program (WIN), 26, 33, 46, 67, 148, 201, 203, 209, 422–423, 429, 432, 454, 476
　administering agencies, 184, 203, 209, 215,
　caseload, 184–187
　eligibility requirements, 93–94, 142, 176, 188–189
　financing, 302, 321–324, 330
　methods, 190–191, 340, 354, 360, 361, 365–368, 380, 399, 404
　objectives, 183
　program description, 183–192
　services and benefits, 187–190
　Supreme Court decisions, 503
Work status, 60–61, 64–71, 89–90, 93–94, 123, 153, 172–173, 179, 183, 340, 403, 423, 442, 454, 460–462, 466, 468
Work training, acceptance of, 94, 165
　See also Work Incentive Program (WIN)
Worker-client relationship, 143, 146, 359–360
Workers' compensation, 18, 108, 137, 423, 432
Working mothers, 62–64, 144, 475
Working poor, 60–61, 458
Workmen's compensation (see Workers' compensation)
Workshops, 257, 268
Work-study program, 173, 416
Wyman v. Boddie, 505
Wyman v. James 493

X-ray services, 150, 161, 167, 285, 385, 481

Youth, 183, 365, 380, 423, 429, 472, 475

513

DATE DUE

HIGHSMITH 45-220